Religion in India

Religion in India is an ideal first introduction to India's fascinating and varied religious history. Fred W. Clothey surveys the religions of India from prehistory through the modern period. Exploring the interactions between different religious movements over time, and engaging with some of the liveliest debates in religious studies, he examines the rituals, mythologies, arts, ethics, and social and cultural contexts of religion as lived in the past and present on the subcontinent.

Key topics discussed include:

- Hinduism, its origins, context and development over time
- Other religions (such as Christianity, Judaism, Islam, Sikhism, Zoroastrianism, Jainism, and Buddhism) and their interactions with Hinduism
- The influences of colonialism on Indian religion
- The spread of Indian religions in the rest of the world
- The practice of religion in everyday life, including case studies of pilgrimages, festivals, temples, and rituals, and the role of women

Written by an experienced teacher, this student-friendly textbook is full of clear, lively discussion and vivid examples. Complete with maps and illustrations, and useful pedagogical features, including timelines, a comprehensive glossary, and recommended further reading specific to each chapter, this is an invaluable resource for students beginning their studies of Indian religions.

Fred W. Clothey is Professor Emeritus of Religious Studies at the University of Pittsburgh. He is author and co-editor of numerous books and articles. He is the co-founder of the *Journal of Ritual Studies* and is also a documentary filmmaker.

Religion in India

A Historical Introduction

Fred W. Clothey

Routledge
Taylor & Francis Group
LONDON AND NEW YORK

First published in the USA and Canada 2006
by Routledge
270 Madison Avenue, New York, NY 100016

Simultaneously published in the UK
by Routledge
2 Park Square, Milton Park, Abingdon, Oxon. OX14 4RN

Reprinted 2008

Routledge is an imprint of the Taylor & Francis Group, an informa business

Typeset in New Baskerville by
Keystroke, 28 High Street, Tettenhall, Wolverhampton
Printed and bound in Great Britain by
TJ International, Padstow, Cornwall

British Library Cataloguing in Publication Data
A catalogue record for this book is available from the British Library

Library of Congress Cataloging in Publication Data
Clothey, Fred W.
Religion in India : an historical introduction / Fred Clothey.
p. cm.
ISBN-13: 978–0–415–94023–8 (hardback : alk. paper)
ISBN-10: 0–415–94023–0 (hardback : alk. paper)
ISBN-13: 978–0–415–94024–5 (pbk. : alk. paper)
ISBN-10: 0–415–94024–9 (pbk. : alk. paper)
1. India–Religion. I. Title.
BL2001.3.C56 2006
200.954–dc22
2006017656

ISBN10: 0–415–94023–0 (hbk)
ISBN10: 0–415–94024–9 (pbk)
ISBN10: 0–203–96783–6 (ebk)

ISBN13: 978–0–415–94023–8 (hbk)
ISBN13: 978–0–415–94024–5 (pbk)
ISBN13: 978–0–203–96783–6 (ebk)

Contents

Preface

"Fools rush in where angels fear to tread." Nowhere is this old adage more appropriate than in the development of this volume. The study of religion in India has become the work of a vast array of specialists who have carved the subcontinent into sub-regions or eras. Theories have come and gone as to how Indian religion should be studied. Indeed, to attempt to put into a single brief volume a "history" of Indian religion that will be accessible to the beginning student has proven to be an enterprise that cannot possibly do justice to the complex developments in South Asia or to the scholars who study them.

Nonetheless, this book has emerged out of years of teaching and listening – listening, on the one hand, to the concerns of undergraduates beginning the process of understanding Indian religions, but also, on the other hand, listening to scholars, Indian savants, and hundreds of regular folks in the villages and cities of the Indian subcontinent. My intention in these pages is to provide a skeletal panorama of the development of India's rich religious heritage, starting from its prehistory and working into the present.

Certain themes and concerns that have engaged me for some years spiral their way through these pages. I have become convinced, for example, that one of the most fundamental ways religious persons in India have expressed their identities, passed on their "traditions," and made manifest their religious orientations is through their ritual life. So, time and again, the reader will find reference to religion that is enacted and embodied, perhaps more than to the religion expressed in conceptual terms. Another concern has been to reflect the transnational character of India's religious landscape – to suggest how the subcontinent has been informed by currents, both indigenous and external, and, how in turn, the subcontinent has impacted the rest of the globe.

Yet another concern has been to depict something of the enormous diversity and plurality in India's religious experience, and especially how religious minorities have been transplanted to and grow in India, as well as spawned therein. The interactions between these communities teach us much about the way people do or can interact with those with alternative commitments. I have also tried on occasion to weave in the voices of those often overlooked in discussions of Indian religion for I am persuaded that those who have perpetuated "classical" forms of religion in India have been enriched in their interactions with and indebted to groups sometimes thought to have been marginal – that is, to "folk" and subaltern peoples.

These are heady ambitions indeed. Hence, the reader should beware, that, in a book of this size, not all aspects of India's rich religious landscape will be explored in depth, nor will all these very concerns be evident on every page. The task becomes even more daunting when one believes, as I do, that religion is best understood when seen in the social, cultural, and political contexts in which it occurs. Nonetheless, I have attempted in this volume to couch the history of India's religious expressions in the settings in which they plausibly originate or develop. This is a hazardous undertaking for a variety of reasons: just one of them is that the texts on which historians of Indian religion often rely are difficult to date, are almost always the product of an elite literate minority of the population, and are often the end result of a process which has included oral discourses, performances of various kinds, and political agendas. Nor are texts necessarily explicit as to the contexts, sources, or reasons why a certain expression occurs. As a result, I have tried to be sensitive to non-textual sources; indeed, on occasion I have made (hopefully cautious) inferences about these contexts as reflected in certain texts themselves. No doubt specialists will be uncomfortable with some of these suggestions; yet I hope the reader will, nonetheless, appreciate the dialectic between religion and the broad sweep of history in the Indian subcontinent.

Perhaps a word is appropriate as to how the term "India" is used in this volume. "India" is used in its broadest sense, much as it was used prior to the coming of independence in 1947, to refer to the South Asian subcontinent as a whole. While the term refers to a geographic setting, it also evokes many perceptions and images, so much so that Chapter 1 is devoted to summarizing some of the ways "India" and especially its religion have been perceived.

The religious landscape of "India" has taught me a great deal; not least of all, it has kept me humble insofar as I am constantly learning new things about it. It has forced me often to become self-conscious of my presuppositions and to regularly rethink my self-definitions. I shall feel rewarded if a single reader of this book is similarly invited on a voyage of discovery, not only of "India" but also of the self.

There are many people and agencies that have had a part in the preparation of this volume. The American Institute of Indian Studies and the Fulbright-Hays program have both provided grants (four times each) over the years that have enabled me to do research and consult with colleagues and numerous informants in India. Undergraduates at Boston University and, for the last thirty years, at the University of Pittsburgh, have taught me something about teaching. More specifically, I have received feedback on this volume from undergraduates on my courses on India over the last three years and active assistance from graduate students, especially from Jeff Brackett, who helped in the development of the text and with the glossary, and Rob Phillips who provided feedback on the text, helped with the glossary, and provided several of the photographs. Colleagues at the University of Hyderabad served as ad hoc consultants for different portions of the volume, especially historians Aloka Parasher Sen and R. L. Hangloo, and members of the Folk Studies Center, especially M. K. Murty, P. Nagaraj, and A. Anand. I am grateful to Dr. Richard Cohen and to a number of anonymous readers who offered helpful suggestions for revisions. Finally, several persons deserve my gratitude for typing and preparing the draft for publication, especially Cristina Lagnese who not only typed the final revisions but also offered substantive suggestions along the way. To all these people and many others who remain nameless, I am indebted. Of course, no one but I should be blamed for the deficiencies that are bound to be evident in a volume of this kind.

Certain of the maps and poetic excerpts have been reprinted in this volume with the express permission of publishers in whose books they previously appeared. I am pleased to acknowledge these permissions here:

The "Hymn to Puruṣa" and an excerpt from the *Milindapañha* are reprinted from *Sources of Indian Tradition*, Vol. I, edited by Ainslee T. Embree with the permission of Columbia University Press.

Excerpts from the *Chandogya Upaniṣad* VI and the *Mundaka Upaniṣad* III are reprinted from *Upaniṣads* translated by Patrick Olivelle (Oxford World's Classics, 1998) by permission of Oxford University Press.

Poems by Nammāḻvār and by Māṇikkavācakar are reprinted from *Hymns for the Drowning: Poems for Viṣnu by Nammāḻvār*, translated by A. K. Ramanujan, courtesy of the publishers, Penguin Books India Private Ltd.

Poems of Kabīr and Sūrdas are reprinted from *Songs of the Saints of India*, edited by John Stratton Hawley, translated by John Stratton Hawley and M. Juergensmeyer, copyright 1988 by Oxford University Press and used by permission of Oxford University Press.

Four maps – those of Aśoka's empire; the Gupta empire; India at the close of the ninth century; and the Mughal empire at the Death of Akbar are reprinted from *A Cultural History of India*, edited by A. L. Basham (London: Clarendon Press, 1975) with the permission of Oxford University Press.

The map "European Bases in India" is reprinted from "Lectures in Indian Civilization" edited by Joseph Elder (Dubuque, IA: Kendall/Hunt Publishing Co., 1970) with the permission of Joseph Elder.

List of illustrations and maps

Illustrations

Maps

1

On Wearing Good Lenses

Lenses used through the years
Pejorative putdown
Romanticism
"Noble savage"
Interpretation by imposition
"Benign neglect"
On understanding the "nature" of religion
Recommended reading

How clearly can you see? This is an apt question as one begins an attempt to understand the religious heritage of India. It is apt because metaphors of vision spiral their way throughout Indian religion and thought: the term, ***darśan***, for example, "seeing" (the deity) is the highpoint of Hindu ritual. *Darśan* is also the viewpoint from which one sees something of the truth. Another term, *vidyā* – "knowledge" – is derived from the Sanskrit term *vid* – "to perceive or know"; ***avidyā*** ("not seeing/knowing") is perceived to be the fundamental human problem. ***Buddhi*** (enlightenment or awaking) is a matter of understanding, of seeing correctly. Indian religions ask again and again: "How well do you see?"

This is also an apt question because it invites us to check our lenses before we start this enterprise. *What* one sees in the Indian setting is often a product of how one sees. We bring agendas, presuppositions, and images to our examination of Indian religion which may not be accurate or helpful. It is important in our viewing that we be self-conscious of the lenses we bring. As one studies Indian religion, one finds that there is wisdom in stepping into the optometrist's office to check one's focus and the adequacy of one's vision.

Lenses used through the years

Seeing clearly is especially important when one reflects on the various lenses that have been worn throughout the years by those purporting to interpret the religious landscape of the Indian subcontinent. All of us stand in a long line of "viewers" whose lenses have colored, shaped (often mis-shaped) that landscape. Those lenses have affected the kinds of books that have been written on India, for every book about India, even every translation, reflects the viewpoint of the writer or the translator.

It may be useful as we begin this journey toward understanding to make self-conscious a few of the lenses that have been employed in the interpretation of India. Five such points of view will illustrate the dynamic.

Pejorative putdown

One of the least desirable perspectives that have been used in the interpretation of India is that which has described her in such terms as "heathen," or "benighted." One of the early expressions of this point of view occurs in a book by **William Ward**, written around the turn of the nineteenth century. Ward was a member of the "Serampore Trio," the first English-speaking missionaries in India; Ward was seeking to gain England's support for the missionary enterprise. His strategy was to record all the negative things he could observe about the India of his time, taking little care to put things in perspective or engage in objective historical scholarship. His conclusions are expressed baldly in the preface of his book:

> There is scarcely anything in Hindooism, when truly known, in which a learned man can delight, or of which a benevolent man can approve; and I am fully persuaded, that there will soon be but one opinion on the subject, and that this opinion will be, that the Hindoo system is...the most PUERILE, IMPURE, AND BLOODY OF ANY SYSTEM OF IDOLATRY THAT WAS EVER ESTABLISHED ON EARTH. [sic][1]

Ward's relentlessly dark descriptions of infanticide, widow burning, and other excesses, accompanied by letters and reports from some other missionaries, informed the mind-set of some Christians in England and North America for generations. This perception was expressed by a verse in a nineteenth-century children's book, entitled "The Heathen Mother":

> See that heathen mother stand
> Where the sacred current flows;

With her own maternal hand
Mid the waves her babe she throws.

Hark! I hear the piteous scream;
Frightful monsters seize their prey,
Or the dark and bloody stream
Bears the struggling child away.

Fainter now, and fainter still,
Breaks the cry upon the ear;
But the mother's heart is steel
She unmoved that cry can hear.

Send, oh send the Bible there,
Let its precepts reach the heart;
She may then her children spare –
Act the tender mother's part.[2]

This attitude persisted in much of the literature on India into the twentieth century. **Katherine Mayo**, an American writer, published *Mother India* in 1927. Purporting to be a friend of India, after a six-month trip, she nonetheless described India as a chamber of horrors from child-marriage and the low status of widows to unsanitary conditions, untouchability, the arrogance of ***brahmans*** and a host of other presumed shortcomings.[3] Needless to say, Mayo's "friendly advice" generated a hailstorm of reactions.

While this pejorative attitude was often the handmaiden of colonialism, it has not been the possession of Westerners alone. Certain Indian expatriates or their descendants have entertained pejorative perceptions of the homeland of their ancestors. Nobel-prize winning V. S. Naipaul, for example, after his first visit to India, wrote *India: A Wounded Civilization*, a book in which he recorded his embarrassment and revulsion of anything which he did not appreciate. Naipaul's views of India have moderated and become more sympathetic with subsequent visits, but the first impressions as expressed in his first book on India clearly revealed an "expat" delighted to be away from the subcontinent.

Pejorative attitudes continue to be expressed even into the present day. They surface in some American responses to the increased visibility of Hindus and Hindu temples in the US from "dot-busters" who harass Indian women to those writers of letters to the local paper in Aurora, Illinois, who, worried about the building of a Hindu temple in their city, voiced concern that the city would now be overrun with rats! Vandalism on newly dedicated Hindu temples (such as at the Jain-Hindu temple near Pittsburgh) and declarations by church bodies (like the Southern Baptist convention in 1999) that Hindus in the US needed to be "evangelized" perpetuate this image of a less than civilized India. This is hardly a perspective that engenders understanding or serious scholarship.

Romanticism

The apparent opposite of the arrogance of pejorative attitudes is that of selective romanticism. The romantic view of India goes back to at least the Greek period when Herodotus, Horace, and others rhapsodized about India's fantastic wealth and extreme forms of religion. Basing his comments on reports from travelers and the presence of Buddhists and Jain ascetics in certain cities of the Mediterranean region, the Greek historian Herodotus, writing in the fifth century BCE, for example, wrote of enormous ants, gigantic eels, fabulous gold and jewelry, as well as religious extremities.[4]

This tendency toward romantic overstatement in both India and the West is found in a whole range of writers, travelers, and scholars. In American history, this attitude was expressed, for example, in **Walt Whitman**'s celebration of India's "primordial wisdom": India was the "soothing cradle of man," "the past lit up again," "the old, most populous, wealthiest of Earth's lands," the home of "wisdom's birth," "reason's early paradise," and source of "innocent intuitions."[5]

Romanticism has sometimes taken a dangerous turn as when it feeds into certain forms of nationalism. In nineteenth-century Germany, for example, many intellectuals discovering Indian thought through still imperfect translations, saw in the texts affirmation of their own beliefs. Schopenhauer wrote of the Upaniṣadic collection that it was an "incomparable book" that:

> stirs the spirit to the very depths of the soul. From every sentence deep, original, and sublime thoughts arise and the whole is pervaded by a high and holy and earnest spirit. Indian air surrounds us and original thoughts of kindred spirits. And oh, how thoroughly is the mind here washed clean of all early engrafted Jewish superstitions, and of all philosophy that cringes before these superstitions. In the whole world there is no study except that of the originals, so beneficial and so elevating as that of the *Oupnekhat.* It has been the solace of my life; it will be the solace of my death.[6]

In a similar vein, Nietzsche, in first reading a translation of the *Laws of Manu,* saw in its presumed attitudes toward untouchables (*caṇḍālas*) a verification of his own sense of the "superman" (*Ubermensch*) and the inferiority of those not considered "Āryan."[7]

There have also been those Indians who, in the face of coloniality, have come to view their own tradition romantically. One of the earliest Indian travelers to the West, **Abu Taleb**, a Muslim, first sounded the often repeated notion of India's spiritual superiority in the face of Western materialism. **Vivekananda**, upon his visit to the US in the late 1800s rhapsodized what a "beautiful sight it would be if Indian civilization should be the foundation on which European civilization is to be built."[8]

In more recent years, romanticism has stimulated forms of Hindu nationalism and the reimagining of India's gloried past. Partially in response to colonialism and the critiques of Westerners, there has been a resurgence of Hindu pride, not least of all in the Indian diaspora; this nationalistic romanticism has become yet another lens by which India has been viewed: India is sometimes presented as the "cradle" of civilization; the eternal abode of religion (i.e., ***sanātana dharma*** – eternal dharma); the source of "Indo-European" culture; and the spring of the world's spiritual resources. History has been reimagined by some so as to dismiss immigrants to the subcontinent (such as Christians and Muslims are said to be) as extraneous to the Hindu motherland and to claim antiquity for the particular form of religion one practices, be it the worship of Rāma or vegetarianism. A call for renewed virility, whether of one's own body or of the nation, often accompanies this perspective. Sorting out reality from perception becomes more difficult for the scholar in the context of this exuberant nationalism.

At its worst then, romanticism has fed into forms of nationalism and the excessive glorification of the past. At its best, it inhibits a measured and judicious study of culture and religion. Even serious scholars of Hinduism and Buddhism have been influenced adversely by excessive romanticism. The work of a good scholar like Edward Conze may serve as one illustration. Conze, a convert to Buddhism, presents a Buddhism that reflects his values – "his" Buddhism. This sometimes leads to a selective adaptation of Buddhist ideas, especially those he finds most palatable. One finds it in one of his introductory books, *Buddhism: Its Essence and Development*, in which Buddhism is presented as "rejecting this world"; when laity are virtually dismissed as not "Buddhist," when *all* Buddhists are said to deny selfhood or ***ātman***. Some Buddhists may reflect these assertions, but not all Buddhist schools will necessarily do so.[9]

The difficulty with romanticism as a scholarly lens, in short, is that it picks and chooses what it will study and celebrate. It tends to "commodify" Indian religion and thought as "things" which can be purchased as if from a bazaar as desired. It commonly glorifies a past without facing up to the realities either of history or of the present. More seriously, romanticism is often a form of self-love – it takes seriously, studies, and celebrates that which reflects one's own values, and it interprets the "other" in the image of the self. In contrast, serious historians are obliged, as much as possible, to see the whole picture and seek to understand the parts (even those that seem less than pleasant) in terms of the whole.

"Noble savage"

Yet another lens which has been used to view Indian religion is characterized by the term "noble savage" made famous by the philosopher **Rousseau**. It lies somewhere between romanticism and disdain, but tends to be more paternalistic. It characterizes a tradition in relatively positive terms as the reflection of a primal innocence or even nobility. But as with the romantics of the post-Enlightenment period, there is an assumption that things progress for the better. The assumption, often implied, is that this innate nobility will be capped or fulfilled by that which the West affords.

One is tempted to include in this mode of viewing the work of one of the early "Western" interpreters of India – **Al-Bīrūnī**. Far more sensitive to Indian religion than many of the European interpreters who succeeded him, this eleventh-century Muslim astronomer worked with brahman pundits, studied Sanskrit and certain texts, and found in them much that reminded him of his own religion – Islam. Al-Bīrūnī confessed to having a "great liking for the subject [of Indian culture and religion]" and claims that his intention is mostly to "simply relate without criticizing."[10] Where there were differences from his own belief system, he offers plausible excuses, implying the subcontinent had not had the opportunities for more enlightening revelations. He concludes his descriptions, nonetheless, with this reason for his study:

> We have here given an account of these things in order that the reader may learn by the comparative treatment of the subject how much superior the institutions of Islam are, and how much more plainly this contrast brings out all customs and usages, differing from those of Islam, in their essential foulness.[11]

Some later missionary scholars and translators similarly had a genuine appreciation for aspects of the Hindu tradition, though they often attributed these positive developments either to the influence of Christianity or saw them as intimations of Christianity. G. U. Pope, for example, in translating in the nineteenth century the devotional poetry of the ninth-century (dates uncertain) Tamil saint, Māṇikkavācakar, celebrated the notions of grace (***aruḷ***) and divine love (***aṉpu***), which he thought were reminiscent of Christian pietism. Some missionary scholars of the twentieth century thought of Hinduism as a "*preparatio evangelica*" with the same relationship to Christianity as the Hebrew Bible or Greek mythology had – fulfilled, that is, by Christian teachings. The title of one of J. N. Farquhar's books, *The Crown of Hinduism*, reflects this attitude, inasmuch as Farquhar saw Christianity as the fulfillment of Hinduism. R. Panikkar's *The Unknown Christ of Hinduism* conveys a similar theme: there are thought to be intimations of Christianity even where not consciously seen by non-Christian adherents.[12]

Another term for this viewpoint may be "religionism," which, however unintended, might be seen as the sibling of racism and sexism. Religionism is the propensity to understand and evaluate another's religion in terms derived from one's own religion. Almost invariably in these kinds of comparisons, the "other's" religion is viewed less favorably than one's own.

The story is probably apocryphal, but a quote ascribed to Marco Polo aptly summarizes the spirit of those who see in Asian religions the "noble savage": "If Buddha had only been baptized a Christian he would have been a great saint before God."

Interpretation by imposition

This lens consists in the tendency to see the history, culture, and religious life of India in terms of preconceived theories and assumptions. Any number of scholars in seeking to interpret Indian peoples have employed a variety of theoretical models, not all of which have been faithful to the data, and virtually none tell the whole story. Early scholars like Oldenberg, for example, following E. B. Tylor and the general assumptions of the late 1800s, assumed cultural evolution was a fact of life. Hence, for Oldenberg, the Vedas were a "primitive" form of religion which evolved and culminated in the flowering of Buddhism.[13] Similarly, Indian rituals have been variously interpreted by theories extant at the time of the interpretation: as a form of cosmogony or re-creation of the world (Eliade[14]), as the following of linguistic structures (Staal[15]) or "archetypal" rules (Humphrey and Laidlaw[16]), the exchange of honors (Appadurai, *et al.*[17]); and many others. At the same time, some social scientists have tended to read into Indian social and religious life patterns sometimes derived from Western sources. Max Weber, for example, after exploring the connections between Protestantism and capitalism, concluded that there was no similar apparatus which made capitalism plausible in India – hardly an accurate perception.[18] Peter Berger concluded (without doing primary research in Indian sources) that the notions of ***karma*** and ***dharma*** found in Indian religion were forms of religious masochism![19] Some interpreters of Indian religion like Weber (and Albert Schweitzer in his *Indian Thought and Its Development*) claimed that the basic Indian worldview was life and world negating, hence, "other-worldly," which only in modern time (thanks presumably to Western influence) has become more socially conscious. Persistent perceptions such as these are not only inaccurate; they have also colored much Western discourse about India.

There are certain basic assumptions which need to be challenged as one begins to study Indian religion. One of these is what might be called "tempocentrism." This is a view that understands the "modern" to be the optimal moment in history, the apex of human achievement; development, often understood in economic terms, is thought to be superior to something called "tradition." The "past" is presumed to be bad or primitive and "tradition" something that needs to be discarded. In fact, India's past has been rich indeed, and, as we shall note later, "tradition" and "modernity" are not opposites. Indeed, the modern moment in India is frequently characterized by selective appropriation from the past, and the construction of "tradition."

Another of these basic assumptions is the supremacy of a "logocentric" approach to knowledge – that is, the idea that the word or the text should have priority in one's study of people. Many in the West, especially those engaged in the study of religion, have assumed that texts embody the quintessence of religion. Of course, Indian religion includes a vast reservoir of texts; but of at least equal importance in the expression of religion on the subcontinent is the role played by ritual, iconography, temple architecture, and other manifestations of visible, even somatic, expressions. Further, we soon learn that one cannot entirely trust *any* book (including this one) which purports to interpret Indian religions, for every book has a point of view; even every text written in India reflects the milieu of its author.

Yet another perspective that inhibits the study of Indian religion is that which assumes that certain forms of practice derived *from* India are the same as the classical forms of religion found *in* India. Nowhere is this more clearly demonstrated than in the way ***yoga*** has been appropriated in the West. Yoga has become a form of bodily exercise, taught in churches and YMCAs, usually stripped of its cosmological and soteriological underpinnings. It has been adapted to the Western penchant for health and bodily fitness, but is not necessarily consistent with the way it was understood or practiced in classical India. Similarly, various techniques of meditation have been marketed in the West as "quick fixes" for whatever ails one and have been accommodated to various religious orientations. One cannot assume these Westernized practices are one and the same as classical practices of meditation in India.

In short, some of our perceptions of religion in India need to be unlearned or, at least, "put on hold," as one seeks to gain a balanced understanding of religion on the subcontinent. There is a need to re-examine the presuppositions, theories, and paradigms with which any author or student engages in the study of religion in India.

"Benign neglect"

Yet another lens commonly used in approaches to people of alternate religions or cultures is one that can be euphemistically called "benign neglect." This is an approach that assumes one can live in one's own world and let the "others" live in theirs. This may be the most common approach in the American and European attitudes toward India. After all, in American schools, a student is lucky in the course of twelve years of schooling to have had more than three to five hours of study on India. American history is presumed to have started in Greece and Rome, worked its way through Europe, and culminated in North America. Further, many religious persons and communities, whether in India or in the United States, tend to live, think, and interact socially within religious enclaves. Many undergraduates still receive baccalaureate degrees without ever having studied seriously a culture outside their own.

There are a number of reasons why "benign neglect" is no longer a viable option (if indeed it ever was). For one thing, Hindus, Muslims, and Buddhists are no longer exotic objects existing on the opposite side of the world; nor are Christians and Jews to be found only in "the West." All are neighbors living in cities of North America and Europe and on every populated continent. A globalized world makes it no longer possible to ignore people who may be different. Indeed, to paraphrase James Baldwin, "to ignore a person is to think of him/her as dead." In that sense, to avoid study of any culture or peoples becomes a form of psychic or academic genocide. Further, one does not understand oneself without the context of difference: self-understanding is enriched, perhaps even made possible, only in the context of understanding others. Moreover, people who do not make an effort to understand another's point of view are destined eternally to be "victims" – victims, that is, of any demagogue who wants to characterize, stereotype, or demonize the other.

Violence in the name of religion has become commonplace in today's world. Many factors go into these eruptions – economic disparity, political marginalization, the quest for ethnic territory or personal space; cynical exploitation by the powerful; and many other factors. But invariably in the mix is a basic ignorance – ignorance of the religious and cultural values of others as well as an ignorance of the finitude and limitations of one's own religious commitments.

The study of the religions of India is an invitation to a pilgrimage – a pilgrimage of understanding a rich, multifaceted, complex universe as well as a pilgrimage to self-understanding. For as we let "India" ask its questions of us, we find we are constantly in need of rethinking our answers and refocusing our lenses.

On understanding the "nature" of religion

The viewpoint of the observer/interpreter is reflected in the way very basic terms are defined. The term "religion" is no exception. In fact, it may be presumptuous to use the term "religious" to speak of the manifold expressions of "religion" in the Indian subcontinent, inasmuch as the term "religion" has Western origins and is not indigenous to India. Deriving as it has from the Latin *religare,* meaning "to be incumbent upon" or binding, and from *religio/nes* as an act directed to the Roman household deities, it has nonetheless come to mean a great many things in Western discourse. At the very least, theories and definitions of "religion" as much reflect the world and cultural/religious orientation of the theorist as they do that of the people they purport to describe. Two theories of religion will illustrate this difficulty.

Rudolph Otto, a Lutheran theologian, writing early in the twentieth century, became interested in comparing the "essence" of religion across cultures.[20] Starting with his own reading of the Hebrew Bible and Lutheran theology, he was intrigued when studying the *Bhagavadgītā* by what seemed to him to corroborate his view as to what was at the heart of religion. There was Arjuna, hesitant to go to battle, being instructed by Kṛṣṇa, his charioteer and a manifestation of the divine; Kṛṣṇa offered an epiphany to Arjuna, revealing himself in all his glory; Arjuna was overwhelmed, and with goose bumps prostrates himself.

In this, Otto perceived the essence of religion as the experience of the "numinous" – that which is "wholly other," "Holy," beyond words. Arjuna's experience seemed to match that of Isaiah, Ezekiel, and Luther. Ironically, the "numinous experience" is indeed not far removed from the experience of Arjuna and the idea of a "numen," a "wholly other" to which the mystic responds, is not inconsistent with the idea of ***brahman***, the cosmic essence of which the Upaniṣadic thinkers spoke. What then is the problem with Otto's view of "religion"? First, it is derived from his own tradition and applied *post facto* to another. Second, it may do justice to the Upaniṣadic mystic but it is not fair to the classical Buddhist, who denies the existence of *brahman* or anything numinous or "wholly other." Third, most religious persons on the Indian subcontinent have never had the intense mystical experience of which Otto wrote, but rather express their religious commitments in household rituals, temple visitations, or in a host of other relatively routine ways. Should one say of them they are not "religious"?

A very different understanding of religion is that expressed by the American anthropologist Clifford Geertz.[21] Geertz, after years of studying religion and culture in Southeast Asia and the Islamic world, suggested that religion is a symbol system that is created by human beings in such a way that it is modeled *from* the social reality and becomes a model *for* the social reality. This symbol system, he added, pervades human moods and motivations and becomes one of the ways by which human beings find meaning in times of crisis, such as when confronted by their own mortality or intellectual or moral bafflement. Human beings then clothe this "symbol system" with an aura of ultimacy to give it legitimation.

Suggestive as these ideas are, some religious people will have trouble conceding that the idea of ultimacy or of the divine is a human construction. Nonetheless, in both Otto's and Geertz' systems there is the insistence that there is much about religion that expresses the human situation. In Otto, for example, every perception or thought one has about the numinous is an "ideogram," a human perception or creation.[22] Hence, everything one says or thinks about the divine is a human thought or expression. There is something humbling and constructive about remembering that about our religions – at the very least, they are a creative and fascinating expression of the human spirit. Religious ideas, practices, phenomena etc. are not derived in a vacuum, but do reflect the social and cultural situation in which they arise. That is one reason it is necessary to view the development of various religious expressions in India in their historical and social, even political context. At the same time, we do well to remember that in all such study, there is apt to be a "more than" that transcends our interpretations.

In contrast to Western theorists, were one to ask a Hindu as to the nature of religion, an answer one is very likely to receive is that it is *dharma.* The term *dharma,* derived from the Sanskrit *dhṛ,* implies a sense of reciprocity between the cosmic process as a whole and each individual within the cosmos. *Dharma* is doing that which maintains cosmic "balance." As such, it is a "way of life," the fulfilling of social, legal, and ritual obligations in a way that does not disrupt that balance. *Dharma* is not so much a belief in a deity or the performance of weekly rituals so much as it is a total orientation, a way of being in the world.

One implication of this discussion is that the study of "religion" in India should cause us to rethink continually some of the basic paradigms and assumptions we make. We will need to adjust our understanding of what "religion" is, just as we will need to readjust our lenses – our images and presuppositions. That task alone is an exciting yet challenging opportunity.

Recommended reading

On the study or interpretation of India

Barrier, N. Gerald. *India and America: American Publishing on India, 1930–1985*. New Delhi: American Institute of Indian Studies, 1986.
Brown, W. N. *The United States and India and Pakistan*. Cambridge: Harvard University Press, 1963.
Brown, W. Norman. *India and Indology: Selected Articles*. ed. Rosane Rocher. Delhi: Motilal Banarsidass, 1978.
Halbfass, W. *India and Europe, an Essay in Understanding*. Albany: SUNY Press, 1988.
Inden, Ron. *Imagining India*. Oxford and Cambridge, MA: Blackwell, 1990.
Sachau, E. C. *Alberuni's India: An Account of the Religion, Philosophy, Literature, Geography, Chronology, Astronomy, Customs, Laws, and Astrology of India about AD 1030*. Two volumes. London: Trubner & Co., 1888.
Welbon, G. *The Buddhist Nirvana and its Western Interpreters*. Chicago: University of Chicago Press, 1968.

For a general history or overview of South Asia

Basham, A. L. *The Wonder that was India*. New York: Grove Press, 1959.
Basham, A. L. ed. *A Cultural History of India*. Oxford: Clarendon Press, 1975.
Bhattacharyya, H. ed. *The Cultural History of India*. Four volumes. Calcutta: Ramakrishna Mission, 1953–56.
Elder, J. W. ed. *Lectures in Indian Civilization*. Dubuque, IA: Kendall Hunt Publishing Co., 1970.
Keay, John. *India: A History*. New York: Harper Collins, 2002.
Schwartzberg, J. E. ed. *Historical Atlas of India*. Second edition. Chicago: University of Chicago Press, 1990.
Thapar, Romila. *A History of India*. Baltimore: Penguin Books, 1966.
Wolpert, J. Stanley. *A New History of India*. Sixth edition. New York: Oxford University Press, 2000.

General introductions to Indian religion

Basham, A. L. *The Origins and Development of Classical Hinduism*. New York: Oxford University Press, 1991.
Coward, H. and Goa, W. *Mantra*. Chambersburg, PA: Anima Books, 1991.
Eck, Diane. *Darśan: Seeing the Divine Image in India*. Third edition. New York: Columbia University Press, 1998.
Embree, A. ed. *Sources of Indian Tradition*. Volume one. New York: Columbia University Press, 1988.
Flood, G. *An Introduction to Hinduism*. New York: Cambridge University Press, 1996.
Kinsley, David. *Hinduism: A Cultural Perspective*. Englewood Cliffs, NJ: Prentice Hall, 1982.
Klostermaier, K. *A Survey of Hinduism*. Albany: SUNY Press, 1994.

Knipe, David. *Hinduism: Experiments with the Sacred.* San Fransisco: Harper, 1991.
Koller, John. *The Indian Way.* Upper Saddle River, NJ: Prentice Hall, 1982.
Oxtoby, W. ed. *World Religions: Eastern Traditions.* Second edition. Oxford: Oxford University Press, 2002.

2

Sources of Indian Religion

Hunting communities
Agricultural communities
The "Indo-European" influence
The Vedic period
The ritual system
Hymns and commentaries
Recommended reading

The question as to the "origins" of Indian religion and culture is still a hotly debated topic on the subcontinent, just as it was in Europe in the nineteenth century. If part of the European fascination with India had to do with Europe's search for its own origins, the "essence" of its own character, and a rationale for its own "superiority," so the concern for "origins" in India has to do with self-definition and the affirmation of a certain superiority based on antiquity. So Hindu nationalists speak of *sanātana dharma,* or "eternal dharma," an ideology that presumes its sources are rooted in a pristine past. The same ideology argues for the indigenous antiquity of the "Āryan," or "Vedic" culture, that period in Indian history from which all else is presumed to spring. Many non-brahman communities, on the other hand, claim their cultural roots precede those of brahmanic culture and are therefore more ancient and superior to those "later" developments. Many Europeans, for their part, at least until the archaeological work of the 1920s in the Indus Valley, had assumed that such culture as existed on the subcontinent was the product of external sources, generally characterized as the Indo-European migration.

We know, of course, that this search for "origins" is rather fruitless. Much archaeological work remains to be done as to the earliest nature of Indian civilization, and archaeologists are not agreed on the meanings of artifacts that have been unearthed. Nor is it the case that there is any single origin of culture on the subcontinent or that such an "origin," if it did exist, would have remained intact into later history.

What seems the more prudent way to discuss this issue is to recognize the existence of multiple sources of what became Indian religion and civilization. In this chapter we will identify some of those sources and reflect on some of their possible implications for the emergence of religion on the subcontinent.

Hunting communities

It is believed that human beings existed on the subcontinent from at least 100,000 BCE. That those people were the result of migrations out of Africa is plausible, though difficult to establish with certainty. The earliest stage of this culture is known as the Lower Paleolithic period; "lower" for the fact artifacts of those peoples are found at the lowest stratum of archaeological digs. The Middle Paleolithic period (25,000–5500 BCE) may have been supplemented by additional migrations possibly including hunter-gatherers spread across the north in the Gangetic plain along the east coast. The Upper Paleolithic period (*c.* 5000 BCE) represents a later stage of hunting culture. Many of these hunting communities lived in forested areas, lower hill slopes up to an elevation of 2,000 feet, and near riverbeds.

Of course, all Indian culture did not spring from these early communities, but it is important to note that hunting motifs persisted into later periods and did influence the lives of later peoples and even of certain forms of classical religion. It is possible, for example, that some (but by no means all) contemporary tribal peoples are distant relations of these early hunters. Further, hunting societies were described in some of the early literary sources dating in the early centuries CE. These societies did lend certain motifs to the mythology and symbology of later forms of religion. Several deities in the Hindu pantheon, for example, either passed through a hunting stage or assumed the role of hunter at certain points in their histories. These include such deities as Viṭhobā, one of the most popular deities of Maharashtra; Murukaṉ, a popular god in Tamil Nadu; Śāstā and Aiyan, popular in Kerala; and Bhairava, a fierce forested "manifestation" of Śiva. Further, forest animals were incorporated into mythologies of the later high gods, for example, the elephant (which became a part of the mythology of Ganeṣa); or the tiger often associated with powerful goddesses of later mythology. Even Narasiṃha (the manifestation of Viṣṇu which is half-human, half-lion), who apparently incorporated motifs of the lion now virtually extinct in India, but once found along the Eastern Ghats, has had hunter/tribal roots in Andhra Pradesh.[1]

Agricultural communities

By at least 3500 BCE cultivation was occurring in many parts of the subcontinent. Certain grains and fruit were being cultivated; some animals were domesticated, including cattle and fowl; pottery was an increasingly important part of the economy; and small settlements had become a part of the landscape.

There appear to have been at least three broad areas of neolithic culture – each somewhat autonomous.[2] In the northeast, in the lower Ganges and in other river valleys there were settlements skilled in the use of polished stone, but where no pottery was in use; in the south, esspecially in the Southern Deccan where such settlements as Utnur and Brahmagiri have been excavated, cattle had become an important part of the economy (and the religious use of cattle may have been developing).[3] Here too such grains as millet and wheat were being cultivated by 3500 BCE and pottery was being made by hand. In the northwest, one finds polished stone and a type of pottery made on wheels. The culmination of the northwestern culture was to be found in the Indus Valley.

These agricultural communities seem to have resulted from indigenous development and from further migrations. It is possible that the development of agriculture and cultivation skills owed something to its women who had been food-gatherers (the collecting of wild fruits, etc. which had not needed cultivation). (It is interesting to note that to this day most of the people who work on the land are women.) Some of the settlements may have been matrilineal suggesting women had a significant role in the social and economic life of agricultural peoples, and contributed something to the religious imagery associated with agricultural production.[4]

This period also witnessed several migrations. Peoples sometimes referred to as Australoids (*c.* 2000 BCE?) may have come in from Southeast Asia, perhaps first as hunters but eventually developing skills in cultivating such fruit as the banana. A migration of megalithic peoples reached the south by about 800 BCE.[5] This was a culture characterized by the construction of large stones over graves: these are known as menhirs (a single large rock, placed erect) or cairns (piles of large rock). These peoples also practiced urn burial, remnants of which are found in such disparate places as the Indus Valley and the Palni Hills of South India. Irrigation was another of the skills attributed to these peoples. Yet another complex of civilizations ranging from Iran to Baluchistan, sometimes called the "Turkmenistan Circle," may have formed something of a matrix of which the Indus Valley civilizations were a part.[6]

It is possible that this mélange of cultures emerged into what is sometimes known as the "Dravidian" culture. "Dravidian" is an umbrella term for those people who today speak some twenty-two languages, including the four major ones associated with the four southernmost states – Tamil (Tamil Nadu); Telugu (Andhra Pradesh); Kannada (Karnataka); and Malayalam (Kerala). While these languages have been strongly influenced by Sanskrit, in the early stages they may have been a congeries of oral languages used in the indigenous agricultural settlements and influenced in still unclear ways by the megalithic and Indus cultures.

Before summarizing the religious contributions of agricultural peoples, a brief word is appropriate about the Indus Valley civilizations. While this was a culture that may have had some affinities with agricultural communities to the west (that cultural complex sometimes referred to as the "Turkmenistan Circle"), it nonetheless developed into one of the most sophisticated societies of its time (*c.* 2500–1750 BCE).[7] The Indus culture was a diverse set of civilizations where trade occurred with Mesopotamia and the Persian Gulf and where such entities as coral, gold, and lead were exchanged. Its people were skilled in the use of copper and bronze and had domesticated a number of animals – bison, cats, dogs, sheep, and pigs are known to have been domesticated; indeed, it is apparently here that fowl were first domesticated. There is evidence of sophisticated systems for sewage and irrigation, granaries, and complex urban planning. Public baths have been excavated which may have been used ritually. No temples have been found to date but large public platforms were constructed, apparently for public rituals which seem to have been addressed to a goddess. The script is still undeciphered, but numerous seals have yielded a volume of interpretations. Some of the seals may have been used in domestic worship (others for commercial or artistic purposes). Seals and other artifacts suggest a variety of religious possibilities: a goddess (or goddesses) appears to have been the dominant deity and her creativity and control of nature and animals intimated. Several seals, for example, depict an inverted feminine figure, out of whose womb vegetation is growing. In other seals, a complex relationship between deity, humans, plants, and animals is suggested: the goddess appeared to control animals and nature; human and presumably human leaders emulated the goddess in controlling nature; and males sometimes seemed to be identified with animals and sometimes as controlling animals. It is possible that public sacrifices were practiced where animals were presumably substituted for humans and where both priest and priestess were thought to preside. Some kind of public pilgrimage has been hypothesized, partially because of patterns found earlier in other parts of the "Turkmenistan Circle."[8] Rituals associated with water seem probable. It is even possible (though little specific evidence surrounds it in the Indus Valley) that a practice found in Mesopotamia in the late third millennium BCE of royalty's libating an image of a deity filtered into the valley.[9] In any case, a common ritual in later Indian settings is very similar to the Mesopotamian libations and became known in India as ***abhiṣeka*** (libations). Disposal of the dead appears to have been done differently at various stages of the civilization's history or in different areas of the valley: these included inhumation in graves and burial in urns.[10] Finally, earlier speculation that one famous seal depicted a proto-Śiva in a yogic posture, suggesting that both Śaivism (worship of Śiva) and yoga had their roots in this culture, has been disputed by subsequent scholars, and remains, at the least, a highly controversial hypothesis.

What have been the religious contributions of agricultural societies? Because no documents exist to supplement our knowledge of the early agricultural context, it is difficult to state definitively what was practiced in those communities in the first few millennia BCE. But it is apparent that agricultural lifestyles and motifs have persisted through the history of Indian civilization and religion, even into the present day. It is also apparent that agricultural motifs have filtered their way into certain "classical" forms of Indian religion, especially those associated with Hinduism, in almost every period. It is worth speculating, in general terms, as to what some of the possible contributions of agricultural communities have been to the religious life of India. Here are some possibilities.

1) The land was generally understood to be feminine, the matrix and giver of life. The agricultural process may therefore have had sexual imageries (e.g., the furrow as female, the furrowing pick as male creative principle). In later sources, we have many intimations of this association between land and the female/goddess: terra-cotta female figurines that suggest fertility; an early icon was that of Lajjā Gauri, a goddess squatting naked on her haunches, apparently representing the land's creativity; there were associations in literature and mythology between landscape (especially land and rivers) and goddesses.[11]

2) Goddesses had at least one of their roots in agricultural settings. Goddesses, especially those in "folk" settings, even today, often represented the forces of nature, its creativity, and barrenness; its power and/or willfulness. This natural force of the goddess may have been enhanced by her social force, insofar as she would have represented the role of women in matrilineal settings.

3) Cyclicality in Indian speculation may have received impetus from agricultural settings, inasmuch as agriculture and its seasons were cyclical. Lunar chronometry (measuring time by the cycles of the moon, which appeared in classical chronometry around the fourth century BCE) may have its roots in agricultural settings as well, where the moon was often perceived as feminine. Cyclicality may also have been associated with the menstrual cycle. The term *karma* (the law of cause and effect) was apparently first

articulated as a form of transmigration in the lower Gangetic basin around the sixth century BCE by **Yājñavalkya** in the *Bṛhadāraṇyaka Upaniṣad.*[12] While there are intimations of cause and effect in the earlier Vedic ritual sequences, agricultural perceptions may have given further impetus to the idea.

4) Burial is still practiced by certain communities indigenous to India. It probably had its roots in agricultural imagery insofar as the body, like a seed, was placed in a grave, or eventually, in an urn, possibly to await rebirth.

5) Plants became analogous to human beings. In later Hindu ritual, fruits such as the banana or coconut, and grains such as rice, often came to be surrogates for human beings. The coconut, for example, in some later Hindu speculation, became a surrogate for the human or for the divine: the coconut became analogous to the human head – it had a hard shell that must be "broken" to get at the tender interior; there were two "false" eyes and a third eye for entry into the coconut just as with the human head; the three lines on the shell became symbols of the bonds that keep humans from being open to the divine, etc.

6) Duality may have intimations in agricultural settings. Unlike hunters whose world tended to be unitary and oriented by their hunting/living grounds, agricultural imagery tended to evoke a sense of sky that watered/fertilized the earth. Agricultural myths of cosmogony tended to be dualistic with a male sky impregnating female earth. The Vedic Pṛthvī (earth) and her consort Dyaus (sky) apparently reflected this agricultural imagery. This sort of setting may be one of the sources for later dualistic cosmological speculation. ***Sāṁkhya***, a product of the Gangetic basin, for example, posited a dualistic cosmogony: ***puruṣa*** was male, sky, spirit, the knower of the field; ***prakṛti*** was matter, female, earth, the field. Cosmological speculation in India often asked the question: is the world one (monistic) or two (dualistic)? Dualistic imageries may have an agricultural basis.

7) Sedentary pastoral images refer to domestication and the relationship between humans and herd. Themes of domestication abound in Hindu mythology: there are deities such as Kṛṣṇa as cowherd who is also known as Govinda (lord of cattle). In the south the term for temple (*kōyil*) is etymologically related to that of cattle-pen (*kō* is cattle); most Hindu deities have their vehicles (*vahanas*), many of them animals that have been domesticated. This pastoral imagery provides the metaphor for the role of deity over nature and the human spirit over passion.

In sum, what is sometimes called "folk" religion has some of its roots in the agricultural settings of India. The conclusion is difficult to resist: that these imageries of agriculture have influenced the way in which some forms of religion have developed on the subcontinent, not only in the later millennia BCE, but also throughout history even to the present. The "classical" and the "folk" have been engaged in a dialectic, each influencing the other.

The "Indo-European" influence

There has been considerable discussion in recent years as to the sources of the culture and religion that eventually comes to be known as "Vedic." There are basically two points of view: the traditional view is that there was a migration of "Indo-Europeans" that influenced the Indian subcontinent (as well as Iran and other cultures); the other is that much of that culture is, in fact, indigenous to India.

The traditional hypothesis, based on the comparisons of languages and religions, is that there were migrations of nomadic pastoral peoples that occurred, starting around 2000 BCE, which eventually affected the Indian subcontinent. These peoples, usually called "Indo-European" were thought to have been a widely spread and loosely connected confederation of tribes wandering the steppe lands of Eurasia. That some of those migrated west is suggested by their apparent influence on the culture and language of the Nordic, Germanic, Greek, and Slavic regions. Others, known as Indo-Iranian, were thought to have moved south and east across Afghanistan and to have influenced both Iranian and Indian cultures. These tribes are believed to have had several features in common; they had little sense of the sacrality or creativity of the earth; rather as pastoral nomads, the sky served as the model for the community's sense of direction. Their deities were gods of the sky, virtually all of them male inasmuch as the tribes were patrilineal. At night, the community centered around the fire that served as the focal point of ritual, and the agency, or messenger, by which peoples could have access to the gods. Fire could also transform and served as the center for sacrificial libations, most commonly of a sap known in ancient Iran as ***hoama*** and in India as ***soma***. The communities were believed to have practiced cremation of the dead.

In addition, Georges Dumezil, a French scholar, influenced by Durkheim, hypothesized that the Indo-Europeans were organized into a tripartite social order: those who did the teaching and priestly tasks were thought to be at one level; at another were those who filled positions associated with tribal leadership, warfare, and protection; at yet another level, were those who were the maintainers or "fecundators" of society who performed the necessary work of daily life.[13] These social roles, Dumezil further maintained, led these communities to infer a cosmic order which was similarly tripartite: a supra-atmospheric level of the cosmos in which "high gods," roughly homologous to the role of priestly/teaching functionaries, presided (e.g.,

Odin, Ouranos, Varuṇa); an atmospheric level wherein gods of storm and warfare presided (e.g., Indra and Thor); and a sub-atmospheric order in which one found those gods who maintained the everyday functions of the cosmic order. The socio-cosmic contract between the realm of the gods and that of humans was thought to be maintained through the sacrificial ritual system centered on the fire. It was thought that these tribal groups migrated into Northwestern India by about 1750 BCE, after the decline of the Indus civilization, and began to settle in rural areas.

Some Indian scholars insist this idea of a migration into India was a construction of colonialist European discourse and that the subsequent developments on the subcontinent were of purely indigenous origins. These indigenous origins, which might be called "proto-Vedic," are said to have been a part of the early civilizations of Northwestern India, possibly including the valleys of the Indus and Sarasvatī rivers. These claims are based on various fragments of evidence: archaeological finds that suggest there were settlements (for example, at Mehrgarh) datable several centuries prior to the Indus civilizations; references in the *Ṛg Veda* to astronomical events (for example, eclipses) that are said to have occurred some centuries earlier; references in the *Ṛg Veda* to the river Saraswatī, which is said to have dried up around the nineteenth century BCE; and others. These kinds of evidence have emboldened some scholars and Hindu nationalists to claim that the *Ṛg Veda* should be dated several centuries earlier than traditionally thought and that India was, in fact, the source of "Indo-European" culture. It is still too early to conclude that this view should supplant the traditional one relative to the origins of the "Indo-Europeans," but clearly a number of questions wait to be resolved.[14]

The Vedic period

Whatever its origins, a post-Indus culture developed in Northwest India which became the matrix for what comes to be known as the Vedic period. The social order of the Vedic period was primarily patrilineal, though women did have certain privileges. Women, for example, could own certain properties, did participate in certain rituals – in fact, wives were required to be present with their husbands at rituals and were involved in reciting certain chants.[15] There were several forms of marriage, both monogamous and polygamous.

While the social hierarchy may not yet have been characterized by the strictures on upward mobility found in the later caste system, three classes of "Āryan" society known as ***varṇas*** (color or characteristic) were identified; these were the ***brāhmaṇas*** associated with the priestly and teaching functions and the chief purveyors of the religious system; the ***kṣatriyas*** or ***rājanyas***, associated with protection and tribal leadership; and the ***vaiśyas*** who engaged in those chores that helped perpetuate the social and commercial order.[16] These classes came to be known as the "twice-born" inasmuch as they had access to the ritual life and other privileges.

In the early stages of this period, interaction with many of the indigenous people was discouraged. Indeed, the term *dāsa* ("servant") was used to refer to such people pejoratively.[17] Nonetheless, over a period of centuries, there was indeed intermingling of the "Āryans" with other peoples. By the tenth century, at least, a fourth class of workers, known as ***śūdras*** had been included at the lowest echelon of the social structure. The skills developed during this period were clearly those of a well-settled rural people: the cultivation of grains, domestication of cattle, the use of brick in constructing sacrificial areas, and many others.

By at least the twelfth century BCE, and possibly earlier, there had emerged a complex ritual system which represented the crux of Vedic religion. In sum this religion/worldview included at least the following features.

1) An elaborate ritual system which enacted the socio-cosmic "contract" and the reciprocities within society itself. These rituals were often pragmatic – designed to enhance prosperity, afford a good crop, assure immortality, etc. They employed a rich system of symbols including the construction of symbolic spaces and the use of symbolically rich libations. A burgeoning community of priests (*brāhmaṇas*, anglicized as brahmans or brahmins) were the chanters and officiants, while the patrons (*yajamānas*) were usually wealthy members of the other layers of the social structure.

2) The exercise of a lively mythological imagination. Myths were created which speculated on how the world came to be and how the sacrifice, therefore, reproduced the creative process. These myths were undoubtedly *post facto* to the ritual system, and served to legitimate it. By purporting to tell the story of the world's creation the mythmaker had a template as to how to act within the world. That is, the myth became both a model of the perceived reality of the world and social order and a model for that order.

3) There was a tendency to classify the social and cosmic order and to make connections and homologies.[18] By the use of puns and homophones, entities could be linked or equated to other entities. In this way virtually anything could be said to be consistent with Vedic images and hence "Vedic" themselves. This is the formula by which later developments in what we refer to as Hinduism could be termed "Vedic," so long as a brahmanic interpreter could make the connection that legitimated the later developments. One can see illustrations of this process throughout the history of Hinduism.

The ritual system

By the tenth to eighth centuries BCE, the ritual system had become especially complex. Its purpose was several fold: not least important, the sacrifice re-enacted the creative process and maintained the socio-cosmic contract – that is, as people did in the social order, the gods were invited to do in the cosmic order. Their rituals also enacted the reciprocities between brahmans and other communities; not coincidentally, this also enabled brahmans to retain considerable hegemony as only they knew the correct formulations for the rituals. In sum, the ritual enabled the community to affirm its place in the socio-cosmic order.

There were two main types of rituals. ***Śrauta*** or "corporate" rituals were public rituals ranging from those done twice a day to those done for specific seasons and those done for grand occasions. The *agnihotra*, for example, was a daily sacrifice but was also done at the new and full moon and every four months with seasonal change. The *agniṣṭoma* included the offering of *soma* (the sap derived from the pressing of *soma* plants, which was believed to have transformative power). By at least the eighth century BCE and beyond, large sacrificial rituals were used in connection with the royal trappings of kings or would-be kings. The ***rājasūya***, for example, was a coronation ritual that lasted some thirteen months and served to legitimate the role of the king. In the ***aśvamedha*** (horse sacrifice), a special horse was maintained for over a year only to be eventually sacrificed and dismembered; during this ritual, the queen engaged in verbal intercourse with the dead horse – the entire ritual was intended to valorize the status and authority of the king and to assure continuing prosperity.[19]

In these fire rituals, symbology was rich. The sacrificial hut, in which public rituals were performed, became a representation of the universe; the fire was homologized to the sun (and the *soma* libation to the moon). The sacrifice of animals was eventually replaced by the use of milk, itself symbolically suggestive – for example, a ritual to bring harm to someone would use the milk of a sick cow in libation. Numerical symbols were important. A three-layered sacrificial hut would represent the three layers of the cosmos and perhaps the three seasons (rain, heat, and harvest); a five-layered arena offered the three primal layers plus two mid-spaces, etc.;[20] the upper layer of the cosmos became known as *svarga loka* and eventually *brahma loka* – that is, bright or heavenly world nearly equal to the Milky Way. The sacrificial altars were oriented to the east apparently because this upper space was thought to be accessible by way of the North Star, seen in the east in Northern India during the winter[21] and also because the rising sun was thought to be an opening to those upper reaches.

Sound was extremely important in the exercise of these rituals. Sound was personified as ***vāc***, the female creative force. Pre-discursive sound was in the beginning; hence, the recitation of chants evoked the creative power operative at the beginning of creation. Often in later religious systems, the evocation of sound provided access to the power of creation or to the nature of the divine. In the Vedic setting, it was the brahman who had access to the appropriate sounds.

In addition to the *śrauta* or public rituals, there was the practice of some household (***gṛhya***) rituals. Though not systematized until later, there are indications that funerals and marriages at least were performed in the late Vedic period. The funeral, for example, served to offer the body of the deceased as a sacrifice through the fire and to permit the "subtle essence" of the self to escape and be temporarily housed in a surrogate body usually made of rice cakes, then to be eventually elevated to the first level of the cosmos. In four generations, this "subtle self" would attain the level of the ***pitṛloka***, the abode of the ancestors, from which there need be no return.[22]

This sacrificial system was legitimated by the cosmogonic myths which purported to describe the beginnings of the world. These myths were eventually recorded in the later texts emerging from the Vedic period, specifically in the *Ṛg Veda*, the tenth book. Two such myths illustrate the dynamic.

The myth of Prajāpati reported that in the beginning of time, the primal one, Prajāpati (the lord of beings) or Puruṣa immolated himself. From his parts, the social order was made – *brāhmaṇas* springing from his head, *kṣatriyas* (warriors) from his shoulders and chest, *vaiśyas* ("fecundators") from his loins, and *śūdras* (menial workers) from his feet. Also coming from his person was the natural order – from his hair, vegetation; from blood, the waters; etc. This myth, of course, had several levels of meaning: a) because all creatures came from a primordial sacrifice, performing sacrifice replicated the creative process; b) all things social and natural came from a single source – that is, the universe was monistic and society and nature were congruent; c) nonetheless, the social hierarchy was sanctioned as having been given in the beginning; not least important, brahmanic hegemony was also legitimated. The myth of Puruṣa, found in the tenth book of the *Ṛg Veda* (10.90) reads in translation as follows:

> Thousand-headed Puruṣa, thousand-eyed, thousand-footed – he, having pervaded the earth on all sides, still extends ten fingers beyond it.
>
> Puruṣa alone is all this – whatever has been and whatever is going to be. Further, he is the lord of immortality and also of what grows on account of food.

> Such is his greatness; greater indeed, than this is Puruṣa. All creatures constitute but one-quarter of him, his three-quarters are the immortal in the heaven.
>
> With his three-quarters did Puruṣa rise up; one-quarter of him again remains here. With it did he variously spread out all sides over what eats and what eats not.
>
> From him was Virāj born, from Virāj there evolved Puruṣa. He, being born projected himself behind the earth as also before it.
>
> When the gods performed the sacrifice with Puruṣa as the oblation, then the spring was its clarified butter, the summer the sacrificial fuel, and the autumn the oblation.
>
> The sacrificial victim, namely, Puruṣa, born at the very beginning, they sprinkled with sacred water upon the sacrificial grass. With him as oblation, the gods performed the sacrifice, and also the Sādhyas (a class of semidivine beings) and the *ṛṣis* (ancient seers).
>
> From the wholly offered sacrificial oblation were born the verses (ṛk) and the sacred chants; from it were born the meters (*chandas*); the sacrificial formula was born from it.
>
> From it horses were born and also those animals who have double rows (i.e., upper and lower) of teeth; cows were born from it, from it were born goats and sheep.
>
> When they divided Puruṣa, in how many different portions did they arrange him? What became of his mouth, what of his two arms? What were his two thighs and his two feet called?
>
> His mouth became the brahman; his two arms were made into the *rājanya*; his two thighs the *vaiśya*; from his two feet the *śūdra* was born.
>
> The moon was born from the mind, from the eye the sun was born; from the mouth Indra and Agni; from the breath (*prāṇa*) the wind (vāyu) was born.
>
> From the navel was the atmosphere created, from the head the heaven issued forth; from the two feet was born the earth and the quarters (the cardinal directions) from the ear. Thus did they fashion the worlds.
>
> Seven were the enclosing sticks in this sacrifice, thrice seven were the fire-sticks made when the gods, performing the sacrifice, bound down Puruṣa, the sacrificial victim.
>
> With this sacrificial oblation did the gods offer the sacrifice. These were the first norms (*dharma*) of sacrifice. These greatnesses reached to the sky wherein live the ancient Sādhyas and gods.[23]

The myth, in sum, affirmed that the entire universe came from a single source and the sacrificial act replicated the creative process.

A different myth – that of the ***hiraṇyagarbha*** (golden reed or germ) reflected the idea of the poet imagining creation to be like the sun rising out of the waters of a river at dawn. The myth suggested that in the beginning a golden seed was deposited in the primal waters. From the seed a reed began to emerge and became the universe. Here the golden seed/reed was likened to the rising sun and the rising of the fire from its pit. Once again, the sacrificial fire was said to replicate the creative act and any number of "risings" came to be seen as creative.

Both of these myths and others served as templates in later forms of religion in India, especially in that stream which became known as "Hinduism." Well after the heyday of the Vedic sacrificial system, the imagery of sacrifice was evoked as the model for religious living – in the city, the life of the householder was a sacrifice, the role of the wife was sacrifice, even the sexual act was understood to be sacrifice in the *Kāmasūtra* insofar as the female was the altar and the male was the spark. Similarly, the *hiraṇyagarbha* has been homologized to towers, pillars, and trees; the temple tower was eventually understood to be the *hiraṇyagarbha*, as was the ***yogin***'s spine or the *pīpal* tree which was thought to stand as the symbolic center of the world.

Hymns and commentaries

One of the legacies of the Vedic period has been remnants of hymns and eventually commentaries that were passed down orally for generations within priestly families. Some of the materials were eventually written, but, in some cases, perhaps not until as late as the fourth century BCE. Attempts to reconstruct something of the character of Vedic society and religion based on these written sources has therefore been subject to a great variety in interpretation and considerable uncertainty.

Nonetheless, it is generally agreed that the first generation of these hymns was retained by four different sets of priests and were known as *saṃhitās*. The oldest of these *saṃhitās* was the *Ṛg Veda*, believed by many historians to reflect a tribal culture to be dated around 1200 BCE.[24] Chanted and preserved by priests known as ***hotṛs***, some 1,028 hymns have been preserved and arranged in ten ***maṇḍalas*** or cycles, though the first and last cycle are thought to have been later additions. These are hymns which were used in sacrifice, addressed to such deities as Indra (over 250 hymns), the lord of war and storm, and celestial counterpart to the *kṣatriya*; and to Varuṇa (some twenty-five hymns) – counterpart to the *brāhmaṇa*, who presided at the highest reaches of heaven, holding the world together with his net of ***ṛta***: the hymns were also addressed to fire personified as Agni; to Soma, the favored drink of Indra; and to other deities.

The later *saṃhitās*, in their oral form, reflected rudimentary patterns of agriculture and made reference to the area between the Jumna and the Ganges (the *Ṛg Veda* made no reference to the Ganges) and are generally dated to the tenth–eighth centuries BCE. These *saṃhitās* include the *Sāma Veda*, verses preserved by priests known as ***udgatṛs*** (and possibly including women) whose chanting apparently represented the beginnings of Indian music insofar as their chants were "sung" and included several tones, perhaps representing levels of the cosmos.

Yet another *saṃhitā* was the *Yajur Veda*. These stanzas were preserved by ***adhvaryu*** priests more in the form of prose than poetry. These priests preserved the details and techniques of the ritual; hence, their prose was more explanatory in nature – for example, because these were the priests involved in dismembering animals for sacrifice, they retained information about anatomy. This collection of material may have been the latest to be preserved.

A fourth *saṃhitā* was the *Atharva Veda*. These were retained by those *brāhmaṇa* priests who presided over the rituals at large, but also retained the chants and incantations for specific private rituals. In this collection, for example, were intimations of "domestic" rituals and rites for marriage and funeral. The *Atharva Veda* was especially concerned with spells and rituals with "magical" intent; the exorcizing of spirits, cursing of enemies; and the ensuring of prosperity or success in love, battle, commerce, and other arenas. Many of the hymns and rituals are thought to reflect a more "popular" or "folk" form of religion.[25]

A second generation of oral materials, and, eventually, texts are those known as the *Brāhmaṇas* generally dated around the ninth–seventh centuries BCE. These were the "elaborations," provided by each school of priests, which served as commentaries. They were more likely to answer questions about why and how rituals were to be done. They embodied the sacred sound of the ritual and provided the rules (***vidhi***) for ritual. They included cosmological speculations from each school and expositions on the meanings and aims of ritual acts.

A third generation of reflections and texts, known as the *Āraṇyakas*, represented a transitional period when the complex ritual system was beginning to change. The *Āraṇyakas* (or "forest texts") emerged around the eighth–sixth centuries BCE. They represented an attempt to reflect on the inner significance of the elaborate rituals. Teachers (***gurus***) and their disciples (*śisyas*) were now thinking about rituals and internalizing their significance. The symbolism of the rituals became more critical than ritual performance itself and the attempt to make homologizations became a fundamental strategy to make "new" things seem consistent with the older "tradition."

The shift of emphasis intimated in the *Āraṇyakas* served as prelude to the next stage of Indian culture and religion, a stage when towns were beginning to emerge in the Gangetic basin. Those who inherited the Vedic symbol system, primarily brahmans, were beginning the process of adapting to a changing landscape. There was apparently more questioning than before of the efficacy of ancient rituals, which led to speculations about the how and why of sacrifice.

The religious expressions of the Vedic period are often called "brahmanism." For the brahmans steeped in these traditions the Vedas came to serve as the authenticating and definitive core of their religious landscape. They spoke of the hymnic tradition as ***śruti*** – heard or revealed "literature." Even though the practice of religion changed considerably in subsequent years, the orthodox legitimated most changes by referring them back to Vedic symbolism. Hence, all who sought to trace their lineage to those Vedic imageries were said to be ***vaidika***. Those who did not (such as Jains and Buddhists) were said to be ***avaidika***. Yet, it is worth recalling that even the Vedic symbols were themselves the product of a "dialectic" between pastoral and agricultural images, and between those who represented the brahmanic practice of ritual and the "folk" elements they had already begun to appropriate. This dialectic would recur often in the history of "vaidika" religion and is something of the "genius" of its preservation, adaptation, and change. This process is what some have called the "brahmanic synthesis."

Recommended reading

On Indian prehistory

Allchin, Bridgett and Raymond. *The Birth of Indian Civilization: India and Pakistan before 500 BC.* Cambridge: Cambridge University Press, 1982.

Bryant, Edwin. *The Quest for the Origins of Vedic Culture: The Indo-Aryan Migration Debate.* Oxford and New York: Oxford University Press, 2001.

Kennedy, K. A. R. and Possehl, G. L. eds. *Studies in Archeology and Paleoanthropology of South Asia.* New Delhi: American Institute of Indian Studies, 1984.

Lincoln, B. *Myth, Cosmos, and Society: Indo-European Themes of Creation and Destruction.* Cambridge: Harvard University Press, 1986.

Marshall, J. *Mohenjo-daro and the Indian Civilization.* Three volumes. London: Oxford University Press, 1931.

Parpola, A. *The Sky Garment: A Study of the Harappan Religion and the Relation to the Mesopotamian and Late Indian Religions.* Helsinki: Finnish Oriental Society, 1985.

Parpola, A. *Deciphering the Indus Script.* Cambridge: Cambridge University Press, 1994.

Piggott, Stuart. *Prehistoric India.* Baltimore: Penguin Books, 1961.

Possehl, G. ed. *Ancient Cities of the Indus.* Durham: Carolina Academic Press, 1979.

Possehl, G. ed. *Harappan Civilization: A Contemporary Perspective.* Warminster: Aris and Phillips, 1982.
Renfrew, C. *Archeology and Language: The Puzzle of Indo-European Origins.* London: Jonathan Cape, 1987.
Sankalia, H. D. *The Prehistory and Protohistory of India and Pakistan.* Poona: Deccan College, 1974.
Shengde, M. J. *The Civilized Demons: The Harappans in Rig Veda.* New Delhi: Abhinav, 1977.
Wheeler, M. *The Indus Civilization.* Cambridge: Cambridge University Press, 1953.

On Vedic culture and religion

Gonda, J. *Aspects of Early Vishnuism.* Delhi: Motilal Banarsidass, 1965.
Gonda, J. *Vedic Literature, History of Indian Literature.* Weisbaden: Otto Harrassowitz, 1975.
Gonda, J. *The Ritual Sūtras, History of Indian Literature.* Weisbaden: Otto Harrassowitz, 1977.
Gonda, J. *Vedic Ritual: The Non-Solemn Rites.* London: Brill, 1980.
Griffiths, R. T. H. *Texts of the White Yajur Veda.* Banares: Lazarus, 1957.
Heesterman, J. C. *The Inner Conflict of Tradition: An Essay in Indian Ritual, Kingship and Society.* Chicago: University of Chicago Press, 1985.
Heesterman, J. C. *The Broken World of Sacrifice: Essays in Ancient Indian Ritual.* Chicago: University of Chicago Press, 1993.
Jamison, Stephanie W. *Sacrificed Wife, Sacrificer's Wife: Women, Ritual, and Hospitality in Ancient India.* Oxford: Oxford University Press, 1996.
Knipe, D. *In the Image of Fire: Vedic Experience of Heat.* Delhi: Motilal Banarsidass, 1975.
O'Flaherty, W. D., Tr. *The Rig Veda: An Anthology.* New York: Penguin, 1981.
Renou, L. *Religions of Ancient India.* London: Athlone Press, 1953.
Renou, L. *Vedic India.* Calcutta: Sunil Gupta, 1957.
Smith, B. K. *Classifying the Universe, The Ancient Indian Varna System and the Origins of Caste.* Oxford: Oxford University Press, 1994.
Smith, Bryan K. *Reflections on Resemblance, Ritual, and Religion.* New York: Oxford, 1989.
Smith, Frederick M. *The Vedic Sacrifice in Transition; A Translation and Study of the Trihanandamandana of Bhaskara Misra.* Poona: Bhandarhar Oriental Research Institute, 1987.
Staal, Frits. *AGNI: The Vedic Ritual of the Fire Altar.* Two volumes. Berkeley: University of California Press, 1983.

3

The Early Urban Period

The *Upaniṣads*
The "heterodoxies"
Jainism
Early Buddhism
Recommended reading

The time from roughly the seventh century BCE through the fifth was a period when culture and the geographical center of Indian creativity was shifting. Sometimes known as the post-Vedic period, these were centuries when one finds the locus of culture shifting to the Gangetic basin. (The *Ṛg Veda* had made no mention of the Ganges, though the later Vedic corpus does refer to the area between the upper Jumna and the Ganges.) Agriculture had intensified; crafts were being produced; pottery of a black polished variety was common. People were organized, not tribally, or in rural settlements as in the earlier period, but territorially – that is, in units of land sometimes referred to as chiefdoms. Cities were emerging in the Ganges valley with diverse populations, with increasingly wealthy mercantile communities and would-be rulers carving out large roles and territories for themselves. At the same time, these cities were not yet stable economic or political centers; changing lifestyles, political infighting and disease reduced the viability of these urban centers.[1] Indeed, there is evidence of heavy taxation on the peasantry and exploitation of the people by those in power. As the *Śatapatha Brāhmaṇa*, an apparent textual product of this period, aptly put it: "The state authority (*rāṣṭra*) feeds on the people; the state is the eater and the people are the food."[2]

Whatever the factors, the seventh through the fifth centuries BCE were marked by a significant shift in the paradigms of religious life. There was a search for alternative lifestyles, given neither to the unpleasantries of proto-urban life nor to the grandiose expense of the sacrificial system. To be sure, some chieftains and would-be rulers called on *brāhmaṇa* priests for the conduct of elaborate sacrifices such as the *rājasūya* or the *aśvamedha.* But for increasing numbers, the "forest" became a place of refuge. Not only were there still heavy forests in the upper Ganges valley; but the "forest" also became a metaphor for the life of seeking and reflection, a haven from urban problems and a liminal space for finding the "truth"; the life of contemplation and asceticism was viewed favorably by the "trendsetters." If there was an ongoing dialectic in Indian culture and religion in subsequent centuries between city and forest, culture and nature, the favored metaphors in this period of transition appear to have been those of nature and forest.

The *Upaniṣads*

On the *vaidika* side, that is, amongst *brāhmaṇas* and others who sought to maintain legitimation from Vedic sources, the mood of the period is represented in the *Upaniṣads.* The term *Upaniṣad* seems to connote "connections," from the term *bandhu.*[3] The search for equivalences, classifications, or congruences is suggested by the term. This quest for "connections" often occurred in small groups as disciples (*śisya*) gathered around a teacher (*guru*). Both teacher and student were drawn largely from *brāhmaṇa* and *kṣatriya* communities and were both male and female. Indeed, at least two women – **Gārgī Vācaknavī** and **Maitreyī** – were mentioned as serious students cum teachers. The oldest of these *Upaniṣads* (no doubt reduced to writing some centuries later) represented oral exchanges occurring around the seventh century BCE. These included the *Bṛhadāraṇyaka Upaniṣad,* centered perhaps in the lower Gangetic basin and a product of the Yajurveda school of Vedic hymnists. The most commonly mentioned teacher in this school is Yājñavalkya. The other early set of dialogues is that of the *Chāndogya Upaniṣad,* centered perhaps northwest of the upper Ganges in an area brahmanic writers referred to as Āryāvarta. It was a product of the *Sāmaveda* singers. Other significant *Upaniṣads* representing reflections occurring by the sixth to fifth centuries BCE are the *Taittirīya, Aitareya,* and *Kauṣītaka Upaniṣads.* Such collections as the *Kena, Kaṭha, Īśā, Śvetāśvatara,* and *Muṇḍaka Upaniṣads* were probably products of the last few centuries BCE and, among other things, expressed a more theistic orientation.[4]

These circles of seekers were hardly unanimous in their speculations, and their discussions covered a wide range of topics. There was some interest in the efficacy of rituals (albeit in somewhat less elaborate form) and descriptions of rituals for specific occasions – from those to assure a woman's becoming pregnant to those intended to prevent pregnancy. Yet a common pattern through the discourses was an attempt to make congruences between the older Vedic ritual symbolism and other domains, especially the body or person of the individual. While in the earlier Vedic discourses, connections were sought between the ritual system and cosmic processes, now the connections sought were more commonly those between parts of the human being and cosmic processes. The use of the numbers three or five continued the symbolic power of the older numerology – hence, reflections on the five "breaths," for example – breaths which were thought to flow in various ways throughout the body.[5] Similarly, "heat" (***tapas***) could be internalized to connote the meditative techniques which were thought to bring about ultimate release. While there were indications of an urban landscape in the discourses – for example, references to certain crafts and the court[6] – there was greater emphasis on the value of ascetism in seeking freedom from urban malaise. Homologies were made between sacrificial space and bodily space. Punning and homophones were not uncommon. In the course of these discussions certain fundamental terms were used which became basic for much later speculation in India. In fact, many of the key questions which drive much of Indian religion and thought in subsequent centuries were raised by these Upaniṣadic seekers:

1) What is the nature of the world or cosmos? This was a question already intimated in the cosmogonic myths of the Vedic hymnists.
2) What is the nature of the self? That is, what does it mean to be a person? Is there a permanent entity that can be called a Self? The Upaniṣadic sages invariably answered this last question in the affirmative.
3) What is ultimate? The term *brahman* was used to describe the ultimate essence, though this was articulated in various ways by different scholars. Further, ***satya*** ("truth" derived from the verb *as* – to be), was perceived to be one and the same as being itself. Knowing that *brahman* was the essence of the universe was to know the "truth" that was ultimately liberating.
4) How does one attain ultimacy? The preferred path of the Upaniṣadic sages was the path of wisdom (***jñāna***), attained through stringent ascetism and contemplation, though ritual was not eschewed.

Many of these basic concerns were intimated in a passage that has become especially well known to Western students (*Chāndogya* 6); here a sage is teaching a younger man, Śvetaketu, the nature of the universe.

> "Bring a banyan fruit."
> "Here it is sir."

"Cut it up."
"I've cut it up, sir."
"What do you see there?"
"These quite tiny seeds, sir."
"Now, take one of them and cut it up."
"I've cut one up, sir."
"What do you see there?"
"Nothing, sir."
Then he told him: "The finest essence here, son, that you can't even see – look how on account of that finest essence this huge banyan tree stands here.

"Believe, my son: the finest essence here – that constitutes the self of this whole world; that is the truth; that is the self (*ātman*).

And that's how you are, Śvetaketu."

"Sir, teach me more."

"Very well, son."

"Put this chunk of salt in a container of water and come back tomorrow." The son did as he was told, and the father said to him: "The chunk of salt you put in the water last evening – bring it here." He groped for it but could not find it, as it had dissolved completely.

"Now, take a sip from this corner," said the father. "How does it taste?"

"Salty."

"Take a sip from the center – How does it taste?"

"Salty."

"Take a sip from that corner – How does it taste?"

"Salty."

"Throw it out and come back later." He did as he was told and found that the salt was always there. The father told him: "You, of course, did not see it there, son; yet it was always right there."

"The finest essence here – that constitutes the self of this whole world; that is the truth; that is the self (*ātman*). And that's how you are, Śvetaketu."

"Sir, teach me more."

"Very well, son."[7]

The term *brahman* was used to identify the fundamental essence of the cosmos – it was like the banyanness of the banyan tree, the saltiness of salt-water – it was unseen, had no name (***nāma***) or form (***rūpa***), but it was there in the beginning and pervaded all reality now. In earlier Vedic ritual, *brahman* had connoted the basic sound to which priests had access and with which they could "re-create" the world. Now it had become the "essence" or underlying reality of the universe. The individualized counterpart to *brahman* in the same passage was *ātman* – that manifestation of *brahman* in all beings. "You are that" (***tat tvam asi***) says the sage to the pupil to denote the oneness of the cosmic "self" and the individual "self." Such a vision became the basis for monistic thought in certain later Hindu schools including the thought of the eighth-century CE philosopher **Śaṅkara**.

The *Muṇḍaka Upaniṣad* appears to suggest a slightly different vision, however:

> Two birds, companions and friends,
> nestle on the very same tree.
> One of them eats a tasty fig;
> the other, not eating, looks on.
>
> Stuck on the very same tree,
> one person grieves, deluded
> by her who is not the Lord;
> But when he sees the other,
> the contented Lord – and his majesty –
> his grief disappears.
>
> When the seer sees that Person,
> The golden-coloured, the creator, the Lord,
> as the womb of *brahman*;
> Then, shaking off the good and the bad,
> the wise man becomes spotless,
> and attains the highest identity.[8]

Here *brahman* and *ātman* were like two birds in a tree, *brahman* on a higher branch and *ātman* lower; they shared the same quality but appeared to be two different entities. This vision informed those *vaidika* schools which tended to be more nearly dualistic, possibly including the thought of **Rāmānuja**, the great eleventh-century theologian.

Other ideas found their way into the discourses. There was, for example, a proto-psychology that emerged. Quite apart from reflections on breath, self, speech, etc. one finds analogized the relationship between senses, "mind," and wisdom. The senses were like horses that run after external stimuli. The mind (***manas***) – that with which one thinks and accumulates knowledge – was like the charioteer who controls the senses and prevents them from running amok. Yet wisdom (*buddhi, jñāna,* etc.) transcended mere knowledge. It was the understanding that comes from seeing the truth about existence – it was liberating, enlightening wisdom.

The fundamental human problem then, was *not* understanding, *not* seeing (*avidyā*). In the same *Chāndogya* passage cited above, the seeker was likened to a blindfolded person seeking the path to ultimacy.

> "Take, for example, son, a man who is brought here blindfolded from the land of Gandhāra and then left in a deserted region. As he was brought blindfolded and left there blindfolded, he would drift about there towards the east, or the north, or the south. Now, if someone were to free him from his blindfold and tell him, 'Go that way; the land of Gandhāra is in that direction', being a learned and wise man, he would go from village to village asking for directions and finally arrive in the land of Gandhāra. In exactly the same way in this world when a man has a teacher, he knows: 'There is a delay for me here only until I am freed; but then I will arrive!'
>
> The finest essence here – that constitutes the self of this whole world; that is the truth; that is the self (*ātman*). And that's how you are, Śvetaketu."
>
> "Sir, teach me more."
>
> "Very well, son."[9]

The unseeing person was to find a guru, who could lead him at least part of the way to a destiny where *brahman* and *ātman* were indeed conjoined. This state of liberation came to be known as ***mokṣa***, the ultimate awareness which frees one from all social constraints.

Other terms also became a part of the vocabulary of these speculations. ***Māyā*** referred to the measurable or changeable world. It was a value-neutral term nonetheless interpreted in different ways depending on one's world-view. Some schools saw *māyā* as a problem to be overcome, as a veil which hid the truth (*satya*) about the nature of the universe. Others insisted it was pervaded by *brahman*, that essence of the universe, hence had a certain "relative" reality. Still others, especially in the context of later theism, claimed *māyā* was the playground (***līlā***) of the gods, to be affirmed and celebrated.

Karma (or *karman*) was another crucial term. *Karma* represented the law of cause and effect, a fundamental logic to the universal process. Once again, *karma* could be value-neutral – one could "use" the law of *karma* to bring about desired results, including one's own enlightenment. *Karma*, as articulated by Yājñavalkya, could also connote the process of reincarnation. In time, *karma* came to be used in the hands of the powerful as a legitimation of status and power, as in *our* status is the result of past *karma*; while *their* low status is a result of their past *karma*. Yet the intention of the term in its early stages seemed to indicate that just as there is a logic of cause and effect to the universe, so in human affairs, favorable actions and/or causes could bring about favorable consequences. The term became an even more significant part of the path to ultimate liberation for Jains and Buddhists than it was for the Upaniṣadic thinkers.

The terms *mokṣa* and *dharma* could be found in Upaniṣadic discussions. Derived from the verb *dhṛ* (to hold up/bear/support), *dharma* appeared to represent a fundamental cosmic principle – the larger cosmos "supported" all beings within it, while all beings were obliged to "support" the cosmos. It epitomized the principle whereby one lived within the world. *Mokṣa* was release from all the world's processes. If the universe were imagined to be a gigantic gyroscope, *mokṣa* would represent the axis around which it spun where there was total quiescence. One inched toward that axis in search of *mokṣa* but in such a way that the reciprocity of *dharma* was maintained. *Dharma* was living with the "system," engaging in appropriate legal, ritual, and social behavior while working one's way toward the ultimate possibility of *mokṣa*. The practice of *dharma* assumed greater significance in subsequent centuries within *vaidika* circles.

Finally, ***samsāra*** was the cyclical process of death, life, devolution, and renewability – the logical consequence of the law of *karma*. The term *samsāra* represented the world of change and transience that came to be viewed in a variety of ways in subsequent schools. The Upaniṣadic sages tended to view this "sea of change" as the arena from which one sought liberation (*mokṣa*), on which one practiced *dharma* or ritual to chart an appropriate course. For the Buddhists, this domain was impermanent and fraught with a sense of the unsatisfactory. For later theists, *samsāra* was the realm in which the deity became manifest and offered "grace."

The "heterodoxies"

During this same period the Gangetic basin was alive with other kinds of seekers and schools of speculation, less oriented by *vaidika* imagery, though not necessarily ignorant of it. A certain mood or temper characterized much of this speculation. For example, just as in the *Upaniṣads* one hears of individual teachers by name, so it is that individuals in the valley became more dominant as shapers of public discourse: a king or chieftain could control an urban complex; an individual could be a teacher and even a paradigm or model to be followed. There was less interest in the class system perpetuated in the *vaidika* circles and more emphasis on classlessness or at least the accessibility of salvation to all irrespective of birth. In fact, these "heterodox" systems were often initiated by *rājanyas* (members of the royal communities) and other non-brahmans, though not a few brahmans also became involved. Followers of these movements were often drawn from the trades and other groups which were not accommodated by the sacrificial system. The movements that arose in the Gangetic plain often challenged "Vedic" authority – they were perceived, by some *brāhmaṇas*, as *avaidika* – people who did not adhere to the primacy of *vaidika* metaphors. They were also called ***nāstikas*** (that is, "unbelievers"). Further, most of the "heterodox" schools that emerged were not theistic – that is, interested in the idea of "god." (Even the early Upaniṣadic speculations did not articulate a notion of a theistic being, rather of a monistic/non-personal essence.) Those heterodoxies that were monistic, even chthonic (Cārvākas, Ājīvikas, Buddhists) referred to matter as the single reality; dualistic schools (Jainism, Sāṁkhya) spoke of two co-eternal but impersonal realities. These heterodox movements tended to stress action (*karma*) more than wisdom (*jñāna*) as a way to attain liberation, though both Jainism and Buddhism spoke of wisdom as prelude to attaining one's destiny.

Among the less well known "heterodoxies" were the schools known as Cārvākas (materialists) and Ājīvikas (those who deny the existence of eternal entities [***jīvas***]). As their names suggest, both were materialistic schools; only matter was believed to have existed and this perpetuated itself by the logic of *karma*. There was no eternal self or life after death, nor was there a "god" or a universal essence. Life was as it appeared and was to be accepted as it was if one chose to be free from the folly of thinking otherwise. Sāṁkhya, on the other hand, was a dualistic system. There were two co-eternal realities: *prakṛti* – matter, the feminine, the "field"; and *puruṣa* – spirit, the male, the "knower of the field." These two entities pervading the universe were expressed in three attributes or ***guṇas***: ***sattva*** – the propensity toward nobility, knowledge and goodness; ***rajas*** – the propensity toward action; and ***tamas*** – the propensity for torpor, lethargy, and inaction. Clearly the three had intimations of older Vedic numerology and spiraled their way through certain later expressions of Indian thought – not least importantly, in the later chapters of the *Bhagavadgītā*.

Jainism

The best-known of these "heterodoxies" are Jainism and Buddhism. It is worth looking with more care at the development of each.

By the sixth century BCE Jainism had become a recognizable option in the Gangetic basin. Its systematization is attributed to a teacher called **Mahāvīra** (literally, "great hero"). The Jain tradition claims he was the twenty-fourth in a long line of ***tīrthaṅkaras*** (literally, "forders of the stream") who epitomized Jain teachings. In fact, little historical evidence exists for any earlier figures and much that is ascribed to Mahāvīra has become clouded by myth and legend. The tradition claims that he was of noble birth, he renounced wealth, and set out in search of the truth, the same pattern as is found in the story of Buddhism's founder. Jains insist the truth was already there, the result of the previous *tīrthaṅkaras*, but that Mahāvīra systematized it and made it accessible. As a *tīrthaṅkara*, Mahāvīra was believed to have crossed over from this world to a purely "jīvic" state of liberation. Before doing so, however, he became a *guru*, gathered a group of disciples around him and began to articulate the principles of Jainism. His monks and the movement spread northwest as well as south into the Deccan and Southern India. They became advisers to kings, students of language and literature, and exemplars of the Jain ethic.

Tradition has it that during Mahāvīra's lifetime, he attracted a number of followers, including some brahmans, so many brahmans, in fact, that some ambiguity existed in the early centuries as to the appropriateness of the term "*avaidika*" or "heterodox."[10] Jain texts claim that the followers were clustered into four groups – monks, nuns, laymen, and laywomen, in each case more women than men.[11] It is evident that, despite the rigor of Jain discipline, it was attractive to some. Why? There may have been several reasons. There must have been some disenchantment with urban life and a sense of being excluded from the elaborate, expensive brahmin-dominated sacrificial system and even from the relatively esoteric Upaniṣadic cells. Perhaps more important, the Jain movement (and later the Buddhist one) was attractive to merchants and other tradesmen who welcomed the opportunity to work out their own liberation. Jainism seemed to have encouraged and rewarded those who in their daily lives pursued the ideal of the "perfected person" or "pure one" (*śreṣṭhin*).[12] Not least of all, persons from the lower echelons of society saw in such a movement an opportunity for social egalitarianism and religious enlightenment. But why more women than men? Women were no doubt even more restricted in their access to brahmanic rituals; many may have preferred this option to widowhood or even to the growing restraints on marriage. Probably most important, men may have had several wives and, when "converted" brought their wives with them.[13]

After the death of Mahāvīra, the community was led by persons known as Gaṇadharas. Around the third century BCE, one of these, **Bhadrabāhu**, led a group of monks into the Deccan to avoid a pending famine; upon his return, he found that those who had stayed had formed a more liberal group organized by **Sthūlabhadra**. A schism resulted: Bhadrabāhu's followers became known as Digambaras (sky-clad) for their unwillingness to wear clothing; Sthūlabhadra's followers became known as the ***Śvetāmbaras*** (white-clad).

The basic belief system of the Jains may have been in place as early as the sixth century BCE, though it was certainly elaborated over the ensuing centuries. As with most Indian schools of thought, one starts with a fundamental cosmology: for the Jains, the world was composed of an infinite number of *jīvas* ("life-monads") and ***ajīvas*** (entities that have no life-substance, and which are therefore heavy and "karmic"). These two sets of entities were thought to intermingle in the universe in a process known as ***bandha*** (connection, binding, etc.). The "life-monads" (*jīvas*), being lighter, tended to rise, while the *ajīvas* tended to sink. Hence, the universe was like a gigantic hierarchy with those organisms which were most jīvic being nearer the top and those which were ajīvic sinking to the bottom. The earth and human beings have remained somewhere in the middle – the *tīrthaṅkaras* have risen to the top as they have burned off karmic entities. Liberation from this intermingling was attainable by burning off *ajīvas* and thereby rising in the cosmic order. In addition, Jain mythology envisioned time as proceeding in a series of six cycles. The first was thought to be one of perfection, when human beings were giants and acted in accordance with *jīvas* and the truth. In subsequent cycles, the world became progressively bad, humans became smaller, and there was a diminution of life span, knowledge, and truthful activity. After the sixth cycle, it was believed, the progression would reverse, moving back to the primordial age of perfection.

One attained liberation from this spatial-temporal matrix by following five basic vows: These were: 1) Non-possession (***aparigraha***) – one was expected to gain and keep only the basic necessities of life and give the rest away. 2) Celibacy (***brahmacarya***) – monks were to remain completely celibate, while the laity was not to exploit anyone sexually. Not only was the loss of sexual fluids thought to represent the loss of power, but the sex act itself was also generally thought to be selfish and exploitative. 3) Non-stealing (***asteya***). Taking or coveting anything which was not one's own was the epitome of self-aggrandizement, which only nurtured the *ajīvas* in one's nature. 4) Truthfulness (*satya* from *as* – to be) had the implication of being true to the fundamental character of the universe. 5) Non-violence (***ahiṃsa***). The best-known of all the Jain vows was that of non-violence. Monks were to eschew the taking of any life altogether, while laymen were selective in the observance of this vow. Non-violence, for the monk and the layman, entailed the avoidance of: a) occupational violence – one should avoid occupations that cause one to take life (i.e., butcher, fisherman, hunter); in some cases, kings were exempted from this vow, insofar as war was understood to be a last resort; b) protective violence – one should refrain from taking a life even if attacked, again more carefully followed by monks than laymen; c) intentional violence – any intentional harm to a living being was considered detrimental to the pursuit of liberation; d) accidental violence – monks, in particular, have been known to use a whisk broom to sweep the path before they take a step or to wear gauze over the mouth lest an insect be inadvertently swallowed. It was partially to avoid the possibility of catching insects in the folds of one's garments that the Digambara monks chose to eschew garments of any kind.

The rationale behind these vows was self-discipline and the burning off of *ajīvas*. By non-exploitation of others and the purification of one's own lifestyle one was thought able to attain ultimate liberation (*kevaljñāna*). Obviously, this process could not occur all at once, so some fourteen stages on the path to liberation were envisioned.

As the Jain community took its place on the subcontinent in subsequent centuries, the community placed a high degree of emphasis on education – monks were the teachers and exemplars par excellence. Many lay Jains went into occupations consistent with their vows – commercial enterprises, craftsmanship, the study of language and literature, and the production of the arts especially of miniature portrayals. They were advisers to kings (for example, of the Kaṭamba, Ganga, and Pāṇṭiya dynasties); writers of lexicons and producers of artistic expressions.

One of the most significant contributions of the Jains to the Indian landscape was the principle of non-violence itself. Apparently they were the first people in the world to espouse such an ethic, and its practice was adapted by Buddhists and selectively appropriated by Jain and Buddhist dynasties alike. Eventually, it was adapted by *vaidika* communities so that, by the end of the seventh century CE, foreign travelers from China would report that vegetarianism was a common practice in India. The ethic has remained an option in some circles even into the present: **Mahatma Gandhi**, for example, was influenced as a young man by Jain neighbors in the state of Gujarat.

Another important contribution of Jain thought was the role their "logic" played in maintaining peaceful discourse on the subcontinent. Jains emphasized the principle of "epistemological relativity" or "many-sidedness" (*anekāntavāda*). That is, "truth" had not only two possibilities but several as expressed in the "doctrine of may be" (*syādvāda*). According to this logic, there were several ways of perceiving a thing:

1) We may affirm a proposition (*syādasti*) – that is, a room may *seem* warm.
2) We may negate the same proposition (*syānnāsti*) – for example, a room may seem cold, especially if we have just stepped from a warmer room.
3) One may affirm and negate the proposition at the same time (*syādastināsti*) – that is, a room may seem both warm and not warm.
4) One may say a thing is indescribable (*syādavaktavya*) – a room may seem warm/not warm; both/and; neither/nor; that is, the true nature of the room may be elusive. Some three other more pedantic points follow from these principles and were developed by later schools.

Similarly, there was the Jain doctrine of relative viewpoints (*nayavāda*). These included seven propositions: 1) An object may be considered in several connotations at once (*naigana-naya*). For example, a man may be both an individual and a representative of the species *homo sapiens.* 2) An object may be considered as representing only a generic character (*saṃgraha-naya*) – a man may represent *homo sapiens.* 3) An object may embody all idiosyncrasies of its term (*vyavahāra-naya*) – that is, a man may represent all the connotations people have of him as a person. 4) An object may represent only a specific moment and place, quite apart from its past or future (*ṛjusūtra-naya*). 5) An object may embody synonyms or implications (*śabda-naya*); 6) An object may be understood only in its conventional meanings, without regard to its etymology (*samabhirūḍha-naya*). 7) An object may be understood in terms of its etymology (*evambhūta-naya*).[14]

It is fair to say that these principles contributed to a climate of tolerance amongst disputants in the Indian subcontinent in later centuries. While Jain philosophers were not reluctant to argue that their own position was the most nearly true, they insisted on the relativity of viewpoints and hence the necessity to see truth in various positions. Contemporary students of symbols, engaged in the subdiscipline known as semiotics, could do much worse than reflect on those Jain principles of interpretation.

Jains were starting to produce their thought in textual form by the third and second centuries BCE. These early sources included such texts as the *Ācārāṅga, Sūtrakṛtaṅga,* and *Uttarādhyana Sūtras.* The canon was edited and finalized by one **Devardnigaṇi** in 526 CE. Much of Jain thought is in place by the sixth century CE.

Early Buddhism

Around the sixth century BCE, yet another "heterodox" movement developed that proved to be highly significant in a number of ways. Founded by a person variously called **Siddhārtha** (literally, "he who has achieved his goal") or **Gautama** (from the name of the warrior clan [Śākyas] into which he was born), the movement came to have the name Buddhism.

Little is known of the historical figure who came to be called "the Buddha" save as later texts multiply stories about him. He was apparently born around 560 BCE (though some scholars suggest a later date) as the crown prince of a clan chief in the city republic of Kapilavastu in the foothills of the Himalayas, in an area near Nepal. Siddhārtha was being groomed to the life of royalty and governance, when, legends tell us, he was curious about his kingdom and prevailed upon his charioteer to ride him about the city. On subsequent days, the legend maintains, he saw an old man, a sick person, and a corpse being borne in a funeral procession. After each sighting he was reminded by his charioteer that illness, old age, and death were very much a part of life. On yet another "field trip" he saw an ascetic, with arms upraised, staring into the sun and was told here was one seeking answers to life's mysteries. Whatever the historicity of this story, it was intended to demonstrate the young prince's increasingly troubled mind at the tragedies of existence. His restlessness became known to his father, the story goes on, who decided to throw a gala party intending to relieve the prince's brooding mind. Yet, as the evening of the party wore on and dancing girls became increasingly tired and disheveled, and the music faded, the transitoriness of pleasure and wealth was dramatized. Gautama determined to leave the palace and seek for answers in the forests. According to some early texts, this occurred while the young man was in his teens; later texts indicate it was after he had married and had a child.

Gautama spent a number of years in quest of the answer to life's traumas. Much of that time was spent with Jain mendicants, when fastidious fasting and other extremities were practiced. Whether or not these events occurred as later legends have it, they do nonetheless reflect a prevailing mood of this transition period – a disenchantment with city life, and the allure of the forest and the life of the ascetic, known as ***śramana*** in the non-Vedic movements.

Gautama's quest ended with his attainment of enlightenment. It is said to have occurred under a "bo" tree at the mythological center of the world along the Ganges. "Enlightenment" encompassed several levels of experience: there was a dawning of intuition that allowed him to transcend everyday knowledge (*manas*) and attain wisdom (*buddhi*). The experience may have had physiological overtones as well, insofar as the nervous system is sometimes triggered by such stimuli as fasting and discipline into energetic or quiescent responses. Ultimately, a certain cognition occurred that offered Gautama a basic framework with which to comprehend existence. Known as the four noble truths, this became the foundation of Buddhism. His enlightenment and the insights it afforded became the central paradigms of Buddhism.

Tempted to stay where enlightenment occurred, the Buddha rather chose to offer his ideas to fellow seekers and to spend the rest of his life as a teacher. His first sermon, said to have occurred in a deer park near Banāras, summarized the "four noble truths," shared by all Buddhists even today though interpreted differently.

The first formulation of this framework, as is so common in Indian speculations, was a statement about the nature of the world. The world was ***duḥkha*** (unsatisfactory). This concept had several implications. For one thing, the entire universe was understood to be chthonic, that is, comprised only of matter. All things were impermanent (***anitya***) though there was a certain logic to the succession of these things based on the principle of *karma.* The river that flows past one now is not the same river that flowed a minute ago insofar as the molecules of water are quite different ones from those that flowed earlier. This also implied there was no permanent self (Pali: *anattā* or Sanskrit *anātman*). Unlike the Upaniṣadic sages, there was a denial that there was a permanent cosmic essence (*brahman*) or an individual manifestation of it (*ātman*). What then constitutes a person? A person was comprised entirely of matter, made of five aggregates known as ***skandhas.*** These *skandhas* were commonly illustrated by the phenomenon of a toothache: 1) in the tooth, there may be a cavity. This is a product of matter. 2) From the cavity arises pain or sensation – this is again derivative of the matter and is not the product of some non-material entity that might be called a spirit, soul or even mind (for the mind also is comprised of matter). 3) From the sensation of pain arises the perception that pain is occurring. 4) From the perception arises mental formations and ideations – an awareness that one has a toothache. 5) From this ideation arises consciousness – an awareness that one is a person feeling the pain of a toothache.

Why was this materialistic monism said to be unsatisfactory, even painful? Of course, there is happiness but it is evanescent; ultimately, everything is impermanent; the more time, money, energy invested in that which is impermanent, the larger the disappointment when it is gone. Nothing lasts; hence, the "bottom line" in Buddhist cosmology was that death was inevitable – that's painful!

How did things get to be this way? The second formulation in the Buddha's framework was the idea of the "chain of dependent causation" (*pratītya-samutpāda*). A chain of twelve attributes were co-dependent and endlessly successive, each leading to the next. In that chain were two links which were particularly important as they marked points at which the chain could be broken. One of these links was "thirst" (*tṛṣṇā*; Pali: *taṇhā*) – one's thirst, particularly for impermanent things, led to greater investment of energy in such things and merely perpetuated the process. Such thirst could not bring ultimate happiness and so was a basic problem of sentient beings. The other important link (the twelfth in the chain) was ignorance (*avidyā*); not knowing the true nature of existence, its impermanence and hence its unsatisfactory character, merely served to keep the cycle going. If one could address the problem of thirst and of ignorance, one might find liberation and peace.

This was the third truth in the framework. There was indeed the possibility of deliverance from the chain – it was known as ***nirvāṇa*** (Pāli: ***nibbāna***). *Nirvāṇa* has been variously understood, especially in the history of Western interpretations; but early Buddhist texts were quite clear in indicating that *nirvāṇa* was a "blowing out" (as of a candle); a "cessation of thirst"; no longer putting logs on the fire. That is, *nirvāṇa* was not a place (such as "heaven") nor immortality – it was, at most, a change of consciousness which enabled one to live without attachments and with equanimity of mind. It was putting an end to one's thirst.

How was this done? The fourth truth, known as the eightfold path outlined a pattern which combined appropriate action with appropriate mindfulness. It was a discipline designed to make the path a foretaste of the goal. Succinctly summarized, these eight principles were right insight, understanding, or vision; right intention or thoughts; right speech; right action; right livelihood; right effort; right mindfulness and memory; and right concentration.

This path to enlightenment represented a coalescence of several factors. It represented the interplay between performing acts of merit (*puñña*) and eschewing acts of demerit (*papa*). It embodied an ethic intended to encourage charitable acts, humane social relationships, sexual control, and non-violence. The incorporation of non-violence was clearly a reaction to the perceived excesses of Vedic sacrifices and to the coerciveness of the chiefly power brokers; it may also have reflected the shift from pastoral to agricultural economies. Renunciation, as the early Buddhists understood it, was not so much the life of an ascetic – the loner who eschewed all attachments to social ties; rather, it was to assert a certain moral authority and to join with a group of fellow-renouncers who, by engaging with laypersons on the fringes of the towns, were offering an alternative way of life.[15]

Enacting this fourth principle was not easy. But it was thought to be available to anyone irrespective of birth or gender. It was not a path of extreme asceticism and certainly not one of hedonism or pleasure, hence, it was called the middle way. Seekers had to learn the way to enlightenment on their own, albeit with the help of instruction. That is, there was no god to offer salvation, but there were teachers and exemplars. One story suggested something of this ethic. A woman, having just lost her only child, came to the Buddha for help. "Sir, do you have medicine for me?" The answer was: "No; but eat some mustard seeds, but make sure you get the seeds from a family that has never experienced death." Some time later she returned and Buddha asked her if she had found the seeds. "No," she replied, "but you have healed me." She had learned that there was no family which had not experienced death, and the perspective of that realization proved liberating. In fact, the story continued, the woman joined the community of nuns.[16]

The question often asked of the early Buddhists was on the issue of "permanence" versus "impermanence." Can a candle be the same if it is burned to the end or if another candle is lit from its flame? Not really, was the common answer; there was a logic of continuity as one entity of matter succeeded another by the logic of *karma*, but even every human organism changed over the years, as cells died and were replaced. Nor is the name one gave something the same as the thing itself; nor was any name permanent. One called a chariot a chariot, but no single part of the chariot was the chariot; nor was the name one gave the chariot the same as the chariot, and certainly no chariot was permanent, even though another chariot may be built from the image of a chariot the craftsman bore in his mind. A passage from the *Milindapañha* illustrated this idea:

> "Reverend Nāgasena," said the King, "is it true that nothing transmigrates, and yet there is rebirth?"
>
> "Yes, your Majesty."
>
> "How can this be? . . . Give me an illustration."
>
> "Suppose, your Majesty, a man lights one lamp from another – does the one lamp transmigrate to the other?"
>
> "No, your Reverence."
>
> "So there is rebirth without anything transmigrating!"[17]

During the life of the Buddha, a community of followers was gathered that grew rather quickly. Both men and women could enter monasteries or be recognized as laypersons. A cadre of sixty enlightened monks was commissioned to proclaim the Buddhist message to one and all. Merchants and royalty were attracted to the message as it offered them the opportunity to shape their own destinies. People, including some brahmans, were converted, not only as individuals, but also as clans, clusters of friends, or sectarian groups. A monastic order for women was initiated, including the Buddha's own foster mother and her attendants, despite considerable ambivalence about the role of women in the movement.

At first, monks wandered homeless depending on the donations of laity for their livelihood. Soon, however, they were clustering in donated dwellings and by at least 200 BCE, they began to live in rock-cut residences (***vihāras***) donated by wealthy patrons. Monks and nuns had separate quarters, on the fringes of the cities, from which they could interact with laypersons – preaching the ***dhamma*** to them and receiving donations from them. People from the lower echelons of society were also attracted to the message because it was accessible and offered them the opportunity for enlightenment. The monastic communities maintained a strict discipline (known as ***vinaya***). This discipline involved instructions as to lifestyle, moral behavior, daily activities, and principles for addressing offenses. These guidelines were designed (among other things) to help refine entrants drawn from the lower strata of society and to make all monks and nuns worthy of emulation.[18]

Meanwhile, laypersons were expected to observe those aspects of the Buddhist ethic appropriate for the householder – for example, generosity to the monks and refraining from killing, stealing, and sexual misconduct; but laypeople were not expected to practice meditation. In turn, they were promised happy rebirths and improvement in their religious and mundane lives. As with Jainism, the Buddhist movement was attractive to merchants who were economically powerful but didn't necessarily receive social status in the *vaidika* system. Those from lower echelons of society also saw the movement as offering them opportunities, both religious and social.[19]

Within a century of the Buddha's death, questions were already arising as to the nature of the *dhamma* – the teaching of the Buddha. A meeting at Rājagṛha along the Ganges led to a split in the community of monks. Those who were more "conservative" in their understanding came to be known as Sthaviras (literally, "heroic elders"); and the more "progressive" group became known as the Mahāsāṅghikas (those of the large assembly). The questions that divided them included the rules for monastic living – the *vinaya*. Some of the questions were significant: should a monk possess anything? Some questions were trivial: should a monk refrain from eating until sundown or only until the sun was three fingers from the horizon? A more important issue was how the life of the Buddha should be understood and consequently what was the role of the monks. The Sthaviras maintained that Buddha was an ideal man, a perfected *arhat* (that is, one who had "killed" the passions); hence, all monks were *arhats* seeking to attain Buddhahood. The Mahāsāṅghikas doubted that the notion of perfection was available to mere mortals – Buddha must have been one who transcended the five *skandhas*; further, they thought *arhats* were flawed and subject to retrogression. Within centuries, in this school, there was a sense that the ideal for monks was the role of a ***bodhisattva*** – one who was characterized by the virtue of wisdom, who postponed attainment of ultimate *nirvāṇa* until all creation had been enlightened. By the first century, this group was maintaining that the Buddha nature was innate in all sentient beings (not the attainment of the few) and that those who had become Buddhas were supra-mundane. This stream of Buddhism came to be known as *Mahāyāna* (the "great vehicle") as opposed to the Theravāda schools which sprang from the tradition of the Sthaviras.

Several schools emerged in the first few centuries of Buddhism. Two of these are worth mentioning here. The Sarvāstivādins argued that the past and the future did not exist. More important was their articulation of the paths of virtue thought to be appropriate for the monks, known as the six perfections: generosity, morality, patience, vigor, meditation, and wisdom. This appears to be the school that most influenced **King Aśoka**'s interpretation of Buddhism, though Aśoka (third century BCE) eschewed the last two perfections in favor of an ethic for laypersons. These perfections also became the basis for eventual iconic representations in Buddhism, when attributes were expressed iconically, often in the female form.

Another school which started some two to three centuries after the death of the Buddha is the one known as the Vātsiputrīyas. This school also held there was no past or future, only a present. Founded by a converted brahman, named **Vatsīpūtra**, the school became especially important for its articulation of a notion of personal "continuity." This group was known as the "*pudgala-vādins*" for their belief in a "person" (***pudgala***) (not in contradistinction to the *skandhas*, yet not the same as the *skandhas*) which continued after death by the logic of *karma*. This school provided a basis for later schools of Buddhism in Tibet and East Asia which espoused the doctrine of reincarnation. We are told that by the fifth century CE some one-quarter of all the monks in India were members of this school.[20]

Buddhism was to have a major impact on the history of Asia. On the Indian subcontinent alone, nearly thirty schools of Buddhism flourished. Thanks to the patronage of such kings as Ásoka and **Kaniṣka**, its monks and laity contributed to the art and architecture, literature, drama, philosophy, and education of India. What we now call Hinduism is scarcely intelligible without recognizing the impact of Buddhism and the dialectic between the communities. Buddhist *stūpas* (funerary structures) influenced the character of the Hindu temple; its iconography and perceptions of the Buddha informed Hindu art and theism. Its philosophers were to shape the intellectual life of the literate. Monastic communities later supported medical centers, as at Nāgārjunakonda; institutions of higher learning as at Nālandā; and repositories of art as at Ajanta and Ellorā. And even though Buddhism had virtually disappeared from India by the thirteenth century, it experienced a revival in the late twentieth century when hundreds of thousands of "untouchable" persons converted, following their leader, **Dr. B. R. Ambedkar**.

But, if anything, the impact of Buddhism outside of South Asia proved to be even greater. Its Theravādin schools made their way to Sri Lanka and into much of Southeast Asia where Pāli texts were written, Buddhist kingdoms flourished; and Buddhist-Hindu forms of art proliferated. Mahāyāna schools made their way into Central Asia and beyond, into East Asia where Buddhism took on a flavor given by the cultures in which it grew. There is even evidence of a Buddhist presence in the Mediterranean world. Something of these stories will be explored in subsequent chapters.

Clearly the centuries we have referred to as the "early urban period" were a creative time, spawning heterodox movements in the Gangetic valley and changing paradigms in the *vaidika* communities. Reflecting an urban environment, yet somewhat contra-urban in its mood, the religious creativity of the period tended to stress asceticism and the life of seekers who combined understanding with disciplined action. It was a period during which theism played little role and where the two most common ways for the serious seeker to attain ultimate destiny were through wisdom (*jñāna*) and appropriate action (*karma*). The sacrificial system of the Vedic period was less visible, though it was no doubt retained in certain royal circles with the help of priests. Clearly, non-brahmanic communities had left their mark on the Indian landscape, though it is more difficult to discern to what extent the developments represented contributions from "folk" or non-elite sources. It had been, in many ways, a transitional period which led to an explosion of religious developments in the later urban period. It is to that period in Indian religious history that we now turn.

Recommended reading

On the *Upaniṣads, et al.*

Deussen, P. *The Philosophy of the Upaniṣads.* NY: Dover, 1966 (reprint)

Keith, A. B. *The Religion and Philosophy of the Vedas and Upaniṣads.* Cambridge: Harvard University Press, 1925.

O'Flaherty, W. D. ed. *Karma and Rebirth, Classical Indian Tradition.* Berkeley: University of California Press, 1980.

Olivelle, P. tr. *The Aśrama System: The History and Hermeneutics of a Religious Tradition.* New York: Oxford University Press, 1953.

Olivelle, P. tr. *Renunciation in Hinduism: A Medieval Debate.* Two volumes. Vienna: Institute of Indology, University of Vienna, 1986–87.

Olivelle, P. tr. *Saṃnyāsa Upaniṣads. Hindu Scriptures in Asceticism and Renunciation.* Oxford: Oxford University Press, 1992.

Olivelle, P. tr. *The Upaniṣads.* Oxford: Oxford University Press, 1996.

On Jainism

Babb, Alan. *Absent Lord.* Berkeley: University of California Press, 1996.

Bhattacharya, Narendra Nath. *Jain Philosophy in Historical Outline.* Delhi: Manshiram Manoharlal, 1976.

Caillat, C. and Kumar, R. *The Jain Cosmology.* New York: Navin Kumar, Inc., 1981.

Cort, John. ed. *Open Boundaries, Jain Communities and Culture in Indian History.* Albany: SUNY Press, 1998.

Dundas, Paul. *The Jains.* London: Routledge & Kegan Paul, 1992.

Fischer, E. and Jain, J. *Art and Rituals: 2500 Years of Jainism in India.* New Delhi: Sterling Publishers, 1977.

Folkert, Kendall W. *Scripture and Community: Collected Essays on the Jains.* ed. John Cort. Atlanta: Scholastic Press, 1993.

Granoff, P. ed. *No Clever Adulteress, A Treasury of Jain Literature.* Oakville: Mosaic Press, 1990.

Humphrey, C. and Laidlaw, J. *The Archetypal Actions of Ritual.* Oxford: Clarendon Press, 1994.
Jaini, Padmanabha. *The Jaina Path of Purification.* Berkeley: University of California Press, 1979.
Jaini, P. S. *Gender and Salvation: Jaina Debates on the Spiritual Liberation of Women.* Berkeley: University of California Press, 1991.
Satyaprakash. ed. *Jainism: A Select Bibliography.* Gurgaon: Indian Document Service, 1984.
Sharma, J. P. *Jaina Yakṣas.* Meerat: Kusamanjali Prakashan, 1989.
Tatia, N. *Studies in Jaina Philosophy.* Benares: Jain Cultural Research Society, 1951.

On Buddhism

Conze, E. *Buddhist Scriptures.* Baltimore: Penguin Books, 1959.
Conze, E. *Buddhist Texts Through the Ages.* New York: Harper & Row, 1964.
Conze, E. *Buddhist Thought in India.* Ann Arbor: University of Michigan Press, 1967.
Conze, E. *Thirty Years of Buddhist Studies.* Oxford: Cassirer, 1967 (reprint).
Du Bary, Theodore. ed. *The Buddhist Tradition in India, China, and Japan.* New York: The Modern Library, 1969.
Dutt, Nalinahsha. *Aspects of Mahāyāna Buddhism and its Relation to Hinayāna.* London: Lazac, 1932.
Dutt, Nalinahsha. *Early Monastic Buddhism.* Calcutta: Calcutta Oriental Book Agency, 1960.
Dutt, Sukumar. *Buddhist Monks and Monasteries of India.* London: George Allen & Unwin, 1962.
Gombrich, R. F. *Theravāda Buddhism: A Social History from Ancient Benares to Modern Columbo.* London: Routledge & Kegan Paul, 1988.
Mitchell, D. W. *Buddhism: Introducing the Buddhist Experience.* New York: Oxford, 2002.
Murti, T. R. V. *The Central Philosophy of Buddhism.* London: Allen & Unwin, 1955.
Narada, Thera. *The Buddha and his Teachings.* Colombo: Vajinarama, 1964.
Paul, Diana. *Women in Buddhism: Images of the Feminine in the Mahayana Tradition.* Berkeley: University of California Press, 1985.
Prebish, Charles S. *Buddhist Monastic Discipline.* University Park, PA: Penn State University Press, 1975.
Rahula, Walpola. *What the Buddha Taught.* New York: Grove Press, 1959.
Robinson, R. H. and Johnson, W. L. *The Buddhist Religion: A Historical Introduction.* Belmont, CA: Wordsworth Publishing Co., 1996.
Streng, F. J. *Emptiness: A Study in Religious Meaning.* Nashville, TN: Abingdon Press, 1967.
Thomas, E. J. *The Life of the Buddha in Legend and History.* London: Routledge & Kegan Paul, 1927.
Thomas, E. J. *The History of Buddhist Thought.* London: Routledge & Kegan Paul, 1933.
Thomas, E. J. *Early Buddhist Scripture.* London: Routledge & Kegan Paul, 1935.

Timeline of Chapters 2 and 3

Cultural/political events		**Religious events**	
6000	"Turkmenistan Circle" of cultures		
3500?	Emergence of Neolithic culture in India	c. 3500	Agricultural motifs in religious expression and some proto-Vedic developments?
2500–1750	Indus Valley civilization		
1850–1700	"Indo-European" settlements in NW India?		
		c. 1500	Elaborate ritual system taking shape
		c. 1200	Oral composition of *Ṛg Veda*?
1100–900	Shifting of "Āryanized" culture into area between Jumna and Ganges?	1000–800	Oral composition of *Sāma*, *Atharva*, and *Yajur Vedas*; the *Brāhmaṇas*
800–700	"Āryan" culture found in NE India: use of forest for seeking and meditation		Composition of the *Āraṇyakas*
c. 800–600	Emergence of urban settlements and kingdoms in Gangetic valley	7th–5th	Early stages of *Mahābhārata* "ethos"?
		7th–6th	Upaniṣadic cells of teachers and seekers; oral compositions of *Chāndogya* and *Bṛhadāranyaka Upaniṣads*; development of doctrine of transmigration
		563–483?	Gautama Buddha
		c. 550–460	Mahāvīra and systematization of Jainism
		c. 480	First Buddhist council at Rājagṛha
		c. 5th–4th	Early composition of Buddhist *Tripiṭaka*

Note: All dates are BCE unless otherwise stated.

4

The Urban Period

Sometimes referred to as the Epic period or the "golden age" of classical India, the urban period was indeed a rich age for the explosion of religion, the arts, and culture generally. What occurred during this period was fundamental to the shaping of religion, and especially Hinduism and Buddhism for centuries to come. From about the fourth century BCE until about the sixth century CE, kingship was becoming a more stable and definitive aspect of the North Indian landscape, and the urban centers were becoming increasingly autonomous city-states. Brahmans served as ministers in the courts of "*vaidika*" kings. Among the results of this urban landscape were the emphasizing of an ethic suitable for urban life and the patronage of arts and literature. Not least important was the emergence of a new theism complete with "high gods," an elaborate mythology, and a ritual life focused on the deity, often embodied iconographically in temples. Similarly, Buddhism underwent change reflective of the era inasmuch as the Buddha came to be regarded as a "cosmic king," depicted anthropomorphically. Buddhist art flourished in the form of *stūpas* (elaborate "memorials"). In short, it was a period important for the development of both "*vaidika*" and Buddhist life in a way that informed much of the rest of Indian history.

The context

The rise in the significance of the city was generally associated with the rise of the Mauryan empire in the late fourth century BCE. The famed Greek emperor Alexander the Great had come to the banks of the Indus in 326 BCE preparing his troops for entry into Northwest India. Because of Alexander's death, the invasion never occurred; yet among those princes preparing to battle Alexander was one **Candragupta Maurya**. Candragupta before long had amassed the largest army on the subcontinent with hundreds of elephants and tens of thousands of infantrymen. By either conquering or making alliances with the princes of other city-states, he established an empire that stretched across much of North India. Candragupta's grandson, Aśoka, enlarged the area of Mauryan hegemony, until after a particularly brutal battle with the Kaliṅgas on the east coast he was moved to convert to Buddhism, or, at least, to selectively appropriate the teachings of his Buddhist mentors. Under Aśoka's selective application of Buddhist *dhamma,* the rudiments of a compassionate judicial system were implemented, non-violence and vegetarianism were encouraged and various religious sects were honored, though monasteries were patronized and Buddhist principles favored. Aśoka came to be known by later Buddhist kings as the model Buddhist king – he was both *bodhisattva* and ***cakravartin*** (literally, "turner of the wheel" – the Buddhist term for the emperor who maintained stability in the state and presided over *dhamma*). Aśoka sent emissaries into Persia, Afghanistan, and Sri Lanka. In fact, the emperor **Tissa** in Sri Lanka was converted to Buddhism by a relative of Aśoka's, and Sri Lanka eventually became a center of Theravāda Buddhist culture.

With the decline of the Mauryas in 181 BCE the sense of nationhood dissipated and the subcontinent reverted to city-states and regional satrapies

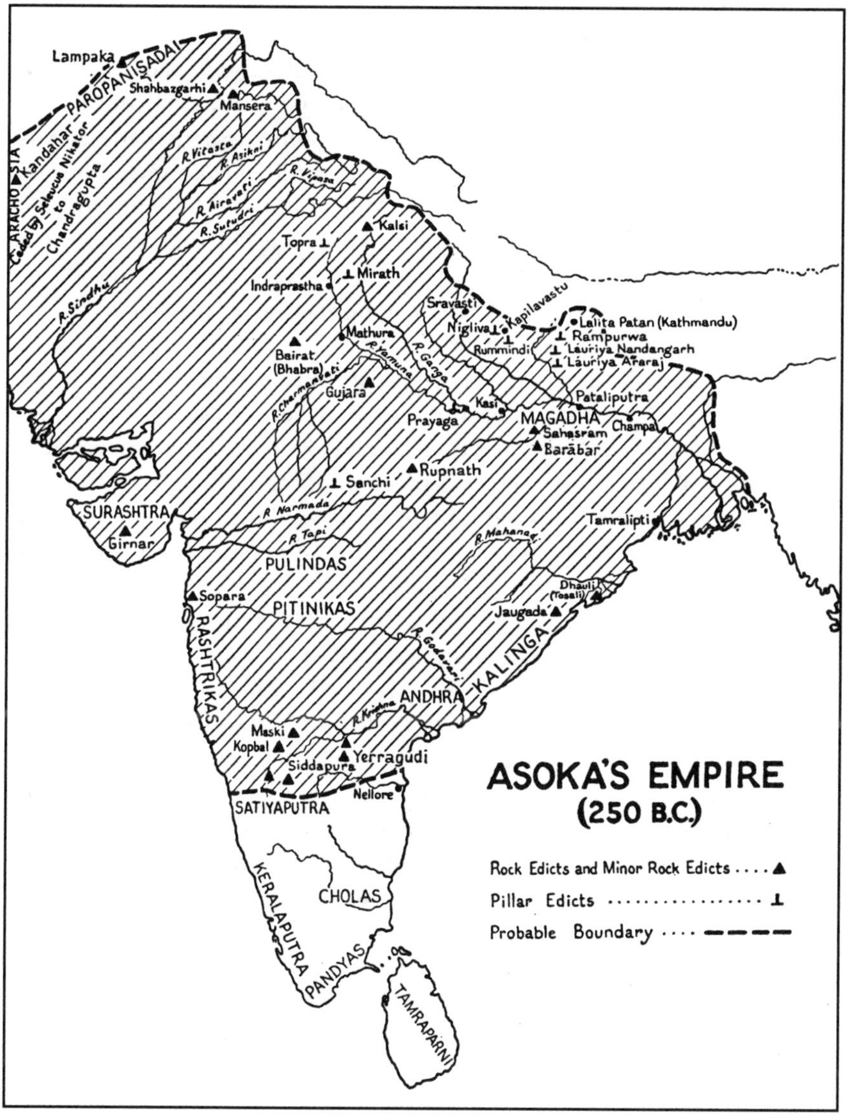

Map 1 Aśoka's Empire

Reprinted from *A Cultural History of India*, ed. by A. L. Basham (Clarendon Press, 1975), p. 587, by permission of Oxford University Press.

for several centuries. The immediate successor to the Mauryas in the Gangetic basin was a brahman clan known as the Śuṅgas. Its founder **Puṣyamitra** sought to repress Buddhism and restore brahmanism in his realm. He is known to have performed at least two horse sacrifices (*aśvamedha*).[1] Upon Puṣyamitra's death, Śuṅga hegemony weakened and several foreign dynasties entered the scene. Among these foreign dynasties was one known as the Bactrian Greeks, who governed in the northwest and who mediated Indian and Greek culture. The Pahlavas (of Persian ancestry) began to govern in the northwest toward the end of the first century BCE and were responsible for the infiltration of certain Zoroastrian and Persian motifs into the subcontinent.[2] These included the Persian term for king, ***tratāra*** (he who presides over all kings), which informed Indian notions of kingship; and the imagery of light/sun (from the Zoroastrian high god Ahura Mazda) which influenced Buddhist perceptions of Buddha in Northern India. One of these kings, **Gondophernes**, according to certain Greek texts, hosted the apostle Thomas.[3]

Another dynasty known as the Yüeh-chis or Kuṣāṇas established hegemony in parts of Northern India from the first into the third century CE. It was during this period that commerce with China increased; the migration of Mahāyāna Buddhist monks to Central Asia and by the Silk Route into China increased; and certain Chinese influences filtered into India – these may have included the use of paper and the Chinese notion of the emperor as the son of heaven.

The Kuṣāṇas played a major role in the early centuries CE with their patronage of eclectic forms of religion and art. Under them we find the earliest forms of the Buddha figure expressed anthropomorphically and intimations of a Buddhist pantheon. Further to the south, the Śakas had gained hegemony and became patrons of *vaidika* art forms and mythologies of a newly emergent brahmanized pantheon. This urban period came to a climax when **Chandra Gupta I** founded the Gupta dynasty in the Gangetic basin, in the area known as Magadha. Under the two centuries of the Guptas, Sanskritic literature and the arts flourished, temples were built, science was encouraged, and popular devotionalism mushroomed.

These dynasties in the north were quite eclectic and cosmopolitan. Even by Aśoka's time Magadha included influences from Persia and the Middle East. The cities included peoples who had come in from rural areas, who spoke various dialects (known as Prākrits) and brought their deities and religious practices with them. The task of incorporating these various strands under the hegemony of the court became the responsibility of brahmans who now were serving as court rhetoricians, advisers to the kings, and public relations agents to the people. This combination of factors – the increased political power of kings; the rhetorical power of brahmans, and the pluralism of urban settings – had several consequences. The city was perceived not only as stable, but also as the appropriate center and venue for living out one's obligations. Kings were to govern, not head for the forests. Indeed, there emerged a form of religion and lifestyle that could perhaps be termed "urban." We sketch in some of those developments.

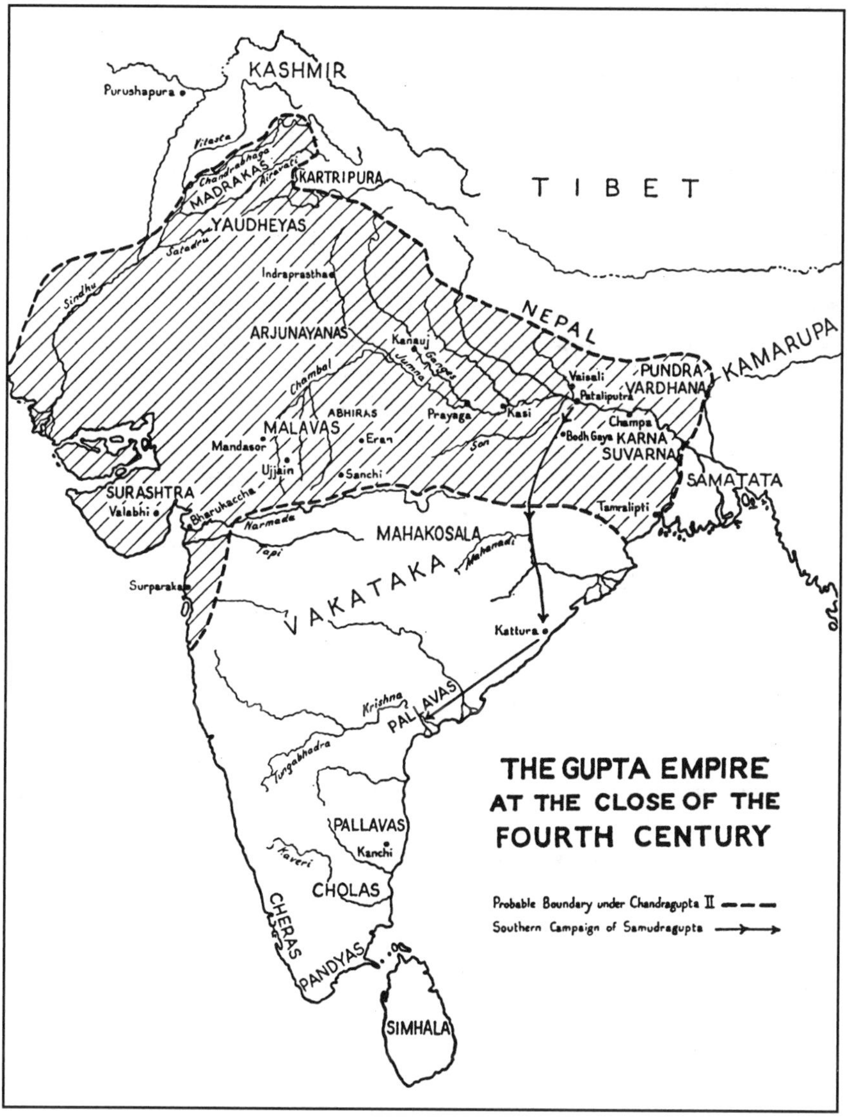

Map 2 The Gupta Empire

Reprinted from *A Cultural History of India*, ed. by A. L. Basham (Clarendon Press, 1975), p. 588, by permission of Oxford University Press.

Kingship and *artha*

One major development of this period was the sacralization of kingship and the legitimation of statecraft (***artha***). Perhaps as early as Candragupta Maurya's time there appeared a text known as the *Arthāśāstra*, which articulates principles by which the king was to govern. **Kauṭilya**, traditionally thought to be a brahman minister in Candragupta's court, is said to be author of this treatise, but in fact, the text is no doubt a compilation occurring over several centuries. The text included the doctrine of ***mātsya nyāya*** (literally, "the law of the fishes"). The idea presented here was that bigger fish eat smaller fish – that is, that as city-states were threatened, a king was forced to have strategies that would preserve the stability of his own domain. These strategies could include ***daṇḍa*** ("club") – the Indian equivalent of just war; force could be used when necessary, though, presumably, as a last resort. Short of force, one could use ***sāman*** – "conciliation" or "appeasement"; ***dāna*** – "gift" or the fine art of bribing or rewarding a neighboring king with booty; and ***bheda*** ("divide") – the art of becoming an ally with your enemy's enemy. Of course, one cannot assume that these strategies were followed by all kings.

In addition to the strategies of statecraft articulated in such texts, kings throughout this period became increasingly extolled and sacralized, thanks in part to the vocabulary provided from Iran and China and the rhetorical role of their brahman ministers; the king became known as ***mahārāja*** (great king); ***rājarāja*** (king of kings); and not least important, ***devaputra*** (son of the gods). The effect of this rhetorical support was to make the king (at least in *vaidika* settings) the preserver of *dharma*, he who preserved order and rendered the city-state the very microcosm of the universe itself. The king's palace was similarly a microcosm. He was perceived as the personification of wisdom, the epitome of culture, and patron of the arts. Despite this rhetorical enhancement of the role of the king, his power could nonetheless be restrained by brahmans and other ministers in his court and even by pressure of the populace.[4]

Theism: Buddhist and *vaidika*

Concurrent with this rhetorical increase in the role of the king was the emergence of a new form of theism. Before discussing the form this takes in brahmanical discourse, it would be fruitful to trace the development of Buddhist ideology in this regard. By Aśoka's time we find the construction of *stūpas* – simple gravesites where ashes or relics of the Buddha or Buddhist monks are said to have been placed. These *stūpas* became more complex by the second century BCE, in some cases patronized by the increasingly affluent classes of artisans themselves, many of whom were Jains or Buddhists. These later *stūpas* would have the form of a rotunda or "egg" (***aṇḍa***) with a walkway around it, up to four entryways with lintels carved with animals and symbols depicting Buddhist themes. The carvings on these entryways included motifs borrowed from the "folk" landscape: *yakṣis* (voluptuous young maidens), for example, were depicted on the lintels entwined with vegetation – these figures were undoubtedly borrowed from agrarian representatives of goddesses associated with vegetation. Elephants were another such symbol – by now, representative of royalty, insofar as emperor/warriors rode elephants into battle, but also emblematic of the wild world of nature "domesticated" by the spirit of Buddhism.

On top of these *stūpas* one would find a ***caitya*** (a three-layered pillar) representative of the Buddha who was said to be resting in *nirvāṇa*. It is important to note that at this stage, the Buddha was not depicted anthropomorphically. Rather, he was represented by symbols: the bodhi tree (where he is thought to have been enlightened); footprints (intimations of his path); a wheel (the wheel of *dhamma* and of life, emblematic of his first sermon); a turban (indicative of what had been renounced); a lotus (that which was "self-created" out of the "defilements" of existence); or a *caitya*, etc. It was under the aegis of the Kuṣāṇas, and especially Kaniṣka (*c.* first or second century CE), a convert to Buddhism, that we find the Buddha represented anthropomorphically. Artisans were brought in from the Greco-Roman world who began to portray the Buddha first in very Mediterranean forms, but eventually in more indigenous ways. Buddha had come to be "divinized" as the epitome of light (as in the figure of Amitābha) perhaps under the influence of Zoroastrianism's Ahura Mazda. A Buddhist pantheon had begun to emerge and at the top of the cosmos, much like a king, sat the Buddha. The Buddha gave warrant or privilege ("*varan*"), like the king, to his ministers – in this case to the bodhisattvas.

The bodhisattvas indirectly helped people by serving as exemplars and providing common people with the opportunity to gain merit by venerating them. The emergent Buddhist "pantheon" now included various representations of buddhas and bodhisattvas depicted iconographically. In the meanwhile, by the third century CE, the thought of the great Buddhist philosopher **Nāgārjuna** had provided in the doctrine of *śūnyatā* a rationale for the veneration of icons and bodhisattvas. *Śūnyatā* was the notion that nothing had its own being (***svabhāva***); that is, nothing existed independently; *samsāra* – the realm of the tangible world – did not have *svabhāva* (its independent existence); nor did *nirvāṇa*. It followed then that *samsāra* was congruent to *nirvāṇa*. *Nirvāna* was evident in *samsāra*; all apparent opposites were collapsed; buddhahood was innate in all things. Concrete objects and symbols such as icons and representations of Buddha could symbolize the state of Buddhahood insofar as the phenomenal world was potentially a reflection of "ultimacy," that is, Buddha. Buddhism had been more or less turned on its head – from an atheistic movement for the highly disciplined to a movement in which Buddhahood could be seen and venerated virtually anywhere.

We return now to the brahmanical response to this process. Theistic brahmanism became increasingly visible by the third century BCE. A number of elements stimulated this phenomenon; kings were powerful figures in their own right and became the patrons of specific deities who were represented as the celestial counterparts to the kings. Tribal folk groups and clans who were now part of the city and who had brought their indigenous deities with them were incorporated under the hegemony of the king by virtue of having their deities co-opted into the mythology of the emerging "high gods." The brahmans were the mythmakers who told the stories of these gods' emergence to power and of their exploits. They linked newer deities to the older gods of the Vedic period by equating them, by making them their genealogical heirs, or by ascribing them the weaponry of the older deities. As a result of this process, certain deities emerged to the status of a high god with full patronage of dynasties. Incidentally, a very similar process occurs today in cities on the subcontinent to which rural folk have brought their deities, which are, in turn, classicized by the brahmanized interpreters of the tradition.

It is worth sketching in these stories of the deities briefly: Śiva was one of these gods. The mythmakers linked the "Epic" Śiva to the "Vedic" Rudra (both were red and strong), even though Śiva apparently had a number of non-brahmanic roots. The Vedic Rudra was a relatively minor deity of storm and terror. By the late urban period we find Rudra-Śiva to be a warrior par excellence, celestial counterpart to the warrior king. But because he was red Rudra-Śiva was also linked mythically to the brahmanical sacrificial tradition of Agni, the personified fire. Moreover, some scholars claimed Śiva to have been part of the Indus Valley (a somewhat dubious claim, to be sure), yet he was the god of outsiders, associated with cemeteries, forests, and non-urban places. In other depictions he was the yogin par excellence, the cosmic counterpart for the ideal person described in the literature of this period. In short, Śiva was the god of warrior king, brahmin sacrificer, forest dweller, yogin, etc. – a god for all people.

In a similar way, Skanda emerged as a high god in the courts of the Śakas, Kuṣāṇas, and Guptas. The mythmakers linked him to Vedic images of youthfulness (*kumāra*) and wisdom, and described him as the son of Rudra and Agni; yet, he apparently also embodied some six folk hero deities who were co-opted into his six heads. He also reflected the heroism of the post-

Alexandrian age (Alexander was known as Iskander in India) and in multiple ways reflected the character of the times. Skanda became the coalescence of all relevant forms of divinity.[5]

Viṣṇu also became a high god during this period. Viṣṇu was mentioned as a relatively minor deity in late Vedic literature, and is plausibly the most *vaidika* of these "rising" urban deities. However, it appears that other deities, presumably of clans or tribal communities, became associated with Viṣṇu – names such as Bhāgavan or Vāsudeva, for example, may have such origins. By way of illustration, some scholars have suggested that Vāsudeva, depicted iconographically by the Kuṣāṇa period, represented the coalescence of two streams – one heroic, one brahmanic. In the city of Mathurā, a heroic clan known as the Vṛṣṇis practiced a form of ancestor worship. Their cultic practice and deity are thought to have been linked to the brahmanic practice of memorializing the dead in the rituals know as ***śrāddha***.[6] In addition, it is also possible that the teriomorphic beings eventually depicted as incarnations or ***avatāras*** (anglicized as avatars) of Viṣṇu have their origins in tribal or folk culture – the tortoise, the boar, etc. may have had their origins as totemic deities, though this is clearly speculative.

What is more apparent is that the two major figures, eventually thought to be avatars of Viṣṇu – namely, Kṛṣṇa and Rāma – had significant roles in this period. By the time Rāma's story was told in the *Rāmāyaṇa,* he was at the least a folk hero and paradigmatic son, husband, warrior, etc., as well as a sacral king, at least as sacralized as other kings of the period. As for Kṛṣṇa, some scholars have suggested that his worship was connected to Mathurā, a center of Buddhist art and culture, where he was cowherd and warrior.[7] He was teacher par excellence in the *Bhagavadgītā* where he was also the embodiment of the cosmos and the epitome of all attributes, cultural and geographic, in short, the personification of totality. In short, Kṛṣṇa came to be seen as a *vaidika* alternative to the figure of the Buddha.

All these deities were seen as personifications of *brahman,* and, in the later *Upaniṣads, brahman* was indeed depicted as personal deity. All of them were ascribed links to *vaidika* imagery, provided a model for different strata of society, served to link king to his people and to incorporate various communities of people into the urban complex. Not least important, they provided an alternative to Buddhist imagery, as they not only incorporated Buddhist ideology (teacher, virtuous attributes, etc.) but also went beyond the Buddha in accessibility, for, after all, Buddha did not come directly to people's aid, whereas, Śiva, Skanda, or Viṣṇu would.

Goddesses were also a part of this theistic pantheon, but the goddesses of which we read in the classical texts of the period have not yet reached the status of high deity. For the most part, the goddesses of this period were of three types: 1) They were consorts to male deities, often benign, and only relatively powerful but always subservient to male deities. 2) They were mothers; however, divine mothers were usually mothers by adoption – the male gods remained the primary progenitors. 3) They were attendants, at the beck and call of such deities as Skanda, to attack or bring the forces of nature to play on particular situations.[8] These goddesses were often the bearers of diseases or held the power of healing etc. It is probable the appropriation of goddesses into classical settings in this period represented the integration of agricultural village peoples into the purview of the city-state, but they may also have epitomized something of the role ascribed to women during this period – an issue to which we shall return later.

Devotionalism

Thanks in part to the emergence of "high gods" in the late urban period, devotionalism became a third way by which one could attain one's ultimate destiny (after wisdom [*jñāna*] and action [*karma*]). The term given to this religious practice was ***bhakti***; the term *bhakti* was derived from the Sanskrit verb *bhaj* ("divide, distribute, share with or in, grant, partake with, enjoy, experience, possess, honor, love revere, worship"[9]). *Bhakti*, that is, was partaking of the deity; it was relishing, honoring, sharing the deity. *Bhakti* entailed wisdom inasmuch as one understood the deity to be *brahman*, the ultimate, the fullness of the cosmos. It was *karma* (action) insofar as it entailed acts which reflected this orientation. These acts usually took the form of ritual addressed to the deity, now housed in a temple (itself a microcosm) and represented iconographically. The icon/deity was treated as though it were a king. Whereas ritual acts and libations were addressed to the fire in the Vedic period and to the king in such rituals as the coronation ceremony (*rājasūya*), by the Gupta period, at least, such libations were addressed to the deity in the form of an icon. The use of iconography in worship was consistent with the understanding that *brahman* pervaded the entire universe and hence any material object could embody *brahman*. Further, an icon, beautifully carved, and sacralized by priests who ritually invoked the deity's presence in it, was deemed an appropriate expression of divine accessibility.

The directing of ritual toward an icon was called ***devapūjā*** (the worship of god). The term ***pūjā*** may have had indigenous origins, meaning literally "the doing of flowers". In any case, this form of worship became the most popular way of expressing one's religious orientations in circles with *vaidika* orientations. While few temples remain extant from this period, it is clear they have already combined several symbolic roles. They were congruent to the palace; its inner sanctum was homologous to the "egg" or dome of the Buddhist *stūpa*;[10] its "hallway" (***maṇḍapa***) was analogous to the Buddhist *vihāra* (where monks lived). In addition, the inner sanctum (***garbhagṛha***) may have incorporated the imagery of a cave which served as early shrines in non-classical settings and as dwelling places for Jain and Buddhist mendicants.[11] Like the palace, the temple was deemed homologous to the cosmos itself and, at least by the late Gupta period, its tower was deemed congruent to Mt. Meru, the mythical center of the universe, to the *hiraṇyagarbha,* the primal "golden reed," and to the human torso, itself thought to be congruent to the "body" of the divinity. It is probable that, during this period, the ritual known as *abhiṣeka* was being used (though more evidence for the full-blown practice of this ritual came considerably later). *Abhiṣeka* (libations or bathing) was constituted of the pouring of certain materials on the icon, such as may have been earlier offered to the fire or to the king.

Devotionalism, in sum, seemed to be the coalescence of several strands that merged in the urban context: the sacralization of the king and the mythological elevation of the deity as his celestial counterpart; the bringing together of various cultural elements – *vaidika,* Buddhist, folk – designed to appeal to various communities; the use of artistic forms to express religious reality (on which more later); the possibility of participating in the "ultimate" in more accessible form, and thereby combining the paths of both wisdom and action.

Articulation of an "urban" ethic

It appears there was a shifting of basic paradigms in the urban period as to what constituted appropriate lifestyle and ethical behavior. In the *vaidika* system, there was an effort to adjust "continuities," such as the notions of "sacrifice," monism, *varṇa,* and the ethic of renunciation to urban-based society. Asceticism, while still practiced in some quarters, was no longer the highest priority – householding was. Insofar as the city-state had been sacralized, new options and compromises occurred. We have already observed how *artha* (statecraft) had come to epitomize the ethic of kingship and the king's role in maintaining public *dharma.* In some contexts, *dharma* had come to take precedence over *mokṣa. Dharma* now connoted the law of the city-state, social interactions, and ritual activities. Indeed several bodies of texts evolved, summarizing these duties. These are the *Dharmasūtras* – concise verses and aphorisms summarizing ritual and legal obligations appearing in textual form between the fourth and first centuries BCE; the *Dharmaśāstras,* a more elaborate articulation of these matters, appearing a few centuries later; and the *Gṛhyasūtras* which provided a systematization of household rituals, including the forty or so rites of passage done at critical stages of the lifecycle.

The texts that developed in this period in *vaidika* circles were understood to be *smṛti* ("remembered" or derivative) rather than *śruti* (heard or revealed) such as the earlier Vedic materials were termed by the orthoprax. It is important to remember that these texts were the products of the elites – almost always brahman males – and that therefore what they articulated were brahmanic attempts to adapt to the vicissitudes of the period. They do not necessarily reflect the reality of religion as practiced by the general public nor, for that matter, of all the "elites" themselves. We refer to them with some caution as they are, at best, some authors' attempts to posit an "ideal" by which the orthoprax should live.

One such text, the *Manusmṛti* (*Laws of Manu*) edited sometime after the first centuries BCE, portrayed the "ideal" lifestyle for the brahman. It articulated an ethic for brahmans who no longer have access to physical ritual centers (such as Vedic fire huts), yet could continue the principles of sacrifice and ritual purity. In the *Manusmṛti*, one finds connections made between the sacrificial system and a legal-ritual code with a mix of continuities and reinterpretations. These continuities included the importance of *vaidika* learning; the imagery of sacrifice, and the superiority of the priest and brahman. Here laws and everyday practice were presented as appropriate extensions of the older Vedic system. It sought to demonstrate how one could maintain ritual purity and identity, and fulfill religious obligations while living in the city.

Some of the principles of this reinterpreted ethic can be sketched by way of illustration. Not the least important such shift was that of renunciation. No longer need one renounce deeds and actions; rather it was the *fruit* of one's actions that one renounced. The *Bhagavadgītā*, for example, referred to "fruitless" actions and non-attachment to the fruits of one's deeds. It was okay, in effect, insofar as it was one's *dharma*, to kill one's enemy so long as one took no pleasure in it. This shift was also implicit in the system known as the ***varṇāśrama dharma*** system – the four stages of life formulated for the brahman male. The first stage was that of the celibate-student (*brahmacarya*) who sought a *guru* and lived as a celibate. The second stage now seemed to be the most important, just as it may have been in the Vedic period – that of the householder (*gṛhastya*); the home and marriage were seen as a cosmogony, a creation of the universe. It was usually only when children were grown that one entered the third stage and became the "seeker" or hermit (***vānaprastha***) – a stage of further seeking for the truth. This could be done within one's home. (Note that those Buddhist texts written in this period recounting the life of the Buddha insist that Gautama's stage of seeking [*vānaprastha*] occurs only after he had been married and had a child.) Finally, the stage of the ***saṃnyāsi*** or ascetic remained an option near the end of one's life, though it is not clear that many chose to implement it. We do know, however, that there were various ascetic sects competing for adherents by the late Gupta period.

The household

Despite the continued opportunity for asceticism, there was considerable emphasis during this period on the importance of marriage and the family. The orthoprax family was invariably patrilineal and included sons (and their wives and families) of the patriarch. While monogamy was considered the most desirable form of marriage in the legal literature, polygamy was not uncommon especially amongst the wealthy and royalty. Even polyandry was known to exist as in the case of Draupadī, depicted in the *Mahābhārata* as the wife of five brothers.

Family solidarity, at least among the orthoprax, was often expressed in its ritual life – not only in its daily rituals, but also in its rites of passage. Starting with pre-natal rites, designed, for example, to promote conception and assure a safe pregnancy and childbirth, they continued into a series of post-natal rites enabling the neonate to be accepted fully as a social person. The latter rites included the naming of the child, the offering of its first solid food (*annaprāśana*), and the first tonsure. These rites of passage (***saṁskāra***), intended primarily for sons of the "twice-born," continued into the rites of initiation (*upanayana*) or second birth when the child entered the stage of a student. Initiation (***dīkṣā***) for the brahman male included donning of a sacred thread, to be worn continuously from that time on, and having the sacred prayer known as the *gāyatrī* whispered in his ear, a prayer to the solar deity Savitṛ found in the *Ṛg Veda.*[12]

The education of the young orthoprax brahman male was to consist of studying under a guru where the proper performance of rites and the memorization of Vedic stanzas would occur. In addition, certain other sciences would be taught such as etymology, astronomy, or grammar. The sons of the court, however, would be trained in the principles of statecraft while those in the lower echelons of society would learn their craft from their fathers.

The role of women

It is also apparent that women were expected to fill certain roles in orthoprax *vaidika* settings. It may not be too simplistic to suggest that there were thought to be at least three "types" of woman.[13] The first was that of wife and mother. The role of wife and mother was auspicious. She was creatrix and perpetuator of the "traditions." She was ***satī*** (from *as* – to be) – that is, she fulfilled the role of ideal woman – chaste, competent in the household, making of her home a microcosm of *dharma.* She was to worship her husband (the *Manusmṛti* tells us) irrespective of a husband's worthiness. Just as her husband fulfilled the imagery of "sacrifice" in his role as husband, so she too was to perform "sacrifice" in her role as wife/mother. The wife who fulfilled her dharmic obligations was afforded respect and was thought to have considerable power even after death. She came to be known as a *sumaṅgalī*, an ideal woman through whom children could be born and wealth and religious merit could be accumulated.[14] Hence, the role of wife and mother was viewed with some ambiguity by the orthodox male. While honored, on the one hand, for the capacity to give love, comfort, and happiness, she was, nonetheless, expected to be obedient and subservient to her husband. And at least by the late centuries BCE, her freedom of movement outside the home was increasingly restricted and her ability to participate in public *vaidika* ceremonies curtailed. Yet by the eighth century CE, there were women poets, patrons of temple rituals and commentators on scriptures.[15]

Girls generally were prepared from childhood for marriage, the purposes of which were thought to include the promotion of religious traditions, assuring progeny, and enjoying sexual pleasure. Boys were supposed to marry after their years of studentship, while, in the early years of this period, brides were to be fully adult. However, in due course, girls were often married right after, or even before, puberty.[16] Girls came to be thought of as an economic liability, particularly if remaining at home unmarried. In addition, the assumption that women were naturally sexually driven had become widespread, hence, the perceived need to marry them as early as feasible.[17] Marriages were arranged by the parents of the couple and were solemnized by a complex series of rituals, usually funded by the bride's parents. The ceremony would be climaxed by the couple's walking together around a sacred fire and the taking of seven steps, the bride stepping on a small pile of rice at each step.

A second type of woman was the widow. Such texts as the *Manusmṛti* tell us she was "auspicious" only insofar as she remained faithful to her dead husband. In fact, however, her life was deemed to be inauspicious indeed. Especially by the early centuries of the common era, she was expected to live a life of simplicity in the home of her in-laws and not remarry. Her regimen, at least in orthoprax homes, was that of an ascetic: eating simply, dressing without ornaments or colored garments, sleeping on the ground. She was expected to spend her time engaged in performing religious rites on behalf of her deceased husband awaiting the possibility of rejoining him.

It is in the context of those circumstances that the practice of a widow's being immolated on the funeral pyre of her dead husband – the practice which came to be known as *satī* – is to be viewed. Precisely when this practice started is not clear – it was apparently rare during the early years of this period, as occasional reference to it is made in the epic literature.[18] Interestingly, however, even in the conservative *Laws of Manu* where the widow's lot is described, there is no suggestion that she should cast herself on her husband's funeral pyre. Around the start of the common era, one does find "hero stones" erected for fallen warriors or hunters and one could occasionally find a stone for the dead wife there.[19] The first identifiable inscription of a *satī* having occurred is on a memorial stone dated 510 CE.[20] In any case, in certain orthoprax and royal families in the medieval period – most notably the Rājputs who sought to maintain a "heroic" image – widows were, in some cases, expected to immolate themselves on the funeral pyres of their dead husbands.

A third "model" of the woman in this urban period was that of the courtesan. The courtesan was an auspicious figure (as described in the *Kāmasūtra*) not only because of her sexual power, but also because she had access to the highest circles of the court. She could appear and dispute in public settings; she had access to many of the "arts," and not only those which might be considered "feminine." Rather, she could be a mathematician, engineer, and virtually any other of the occupations and avocations of her time. Frescoes of the Gupta period depict courtesans favorably, accompanied by attendants. It is conceivable that the role of courtesan coupled with that of wife/mother provided some impetus for the depiction of goddesses who are described in the classical literature of the period.

A variation of the court mistress was that of temple courtesan. The earliest inscriptional reference to "religious prostitution" was in Ramgarh, Central India, in the second century BCE.[21] Insofar as the deity in a temple was perceived to have all the accouterments of royalty, by the fourth century in many parts of India, a harem was considered an appropriate part of the deity's entourage.[22] Known as *devadāsīs* (female servant of god) in the south, and usually the daughter of a woman who had served in a similar capacity, she would have been given for a lifetime of service to a temple, where she could be available to serve those whom the deity "favored." Often she became proficient in the arts, not least the sacred dances associated with worship. By the eleventh century, large temples were known to have significant "staffs" of *devadāsīs* – some 500 in the temple of Sōmnath in Gujarat, for example,[23] and 400 in the Cōḻa temple to Bṛhadiśvara in Tanjore, Tamil Nadu.[24] These women have been known by various terms over the centuries by Indian or colonialist interpreters: sacred artists who emulated the dancing of the heavenly dancers (*apsaras*); dancing "virgins" and/or sexual slaves.[25]

A fourth "model" may be evident in this period as well. Illustrated by the women who joined the Buddhist monastic settings or entered forested circles of seekers: she was the woman who eschewed the expected social conventions and opted to have direct access to the way of truth or to a life of mysticism. This model became even more visible in the post-classical period when we learn of poetesses (e.g., **Mahādevyakka**, **Mīrābaī**, Āṇṭāl) and others who avoided marriage or normal social interaction in order to "be at the feet of the lord".

Jāti or "caste"

Another aspect of lifestyle during this period was the brahmanic attempt to account for social and cultural diversity. As we have noted, there was a significant increase in the number of non-*vaidika* peoples in cities of the Gangetic basin, some of them of rural or tribal background. There was a concomitant increase in the kinds of jobs and occupations held by this diverse population. Guilds were increasingly representative of these diverse occupational groups. Further, many of these occupations were passed on from father to son. Occupation, that is, had become increasingly a matter of birth (*jāti*). Brahmanical attempts to classify these new occupational groups and communities tried to link them to the older *varṇa* system, in which there had been four categories. In the *Manusmṛti* we find these "new" communities were to be classified in one of three ways: they resulted from a mythological intermarriage between two (or more) of the original four categories; or they "fell" from the level of the twice-born groups because they had neglected their *vaidika* rites, and hence, they could theoretically be reinitiated; or they were simply beyond the pale and not included in the system – this could be the case with ***mleccha*** (barbarians or "outsiders") and *caṇḍāla* (outcasted). In this third grouping, we find the legitimation of untouchability in the name of maintaining brahmanical ritual purity (see *Manusmṛti*, Chapter 10).

These groups or *jātis* classified in the brahmanic literature, are what eventually came to be known as "caste." The term "caste," a relatively recent one, is derived from the Portuguese term "*casta*" and refers to the multiple strata of Indian society wherein occupation (and relative status) was largely hereditary. Viewed in its most positive light, "caste" did generally provide a sense of kinship within a given caste, training for an occupation, and some degree of reciprocity between "castes" as skills and products were exchanged. But as an endogamous system, it became increasingly rigid, and social mobility and intermarriage were discouraged if not forbidden. Those in the higher circles of society sometimes sought to legitimate their status by arguing that it was the result of *karma* from past actions as well as a way to preserve ritual purity and social position in the face of urban pluralism and the presence of people who engaged in "polluting" occupations. For those in the lower brackets of society and "outcastes," however, it meant increasingly not being allowed access to opportunities, social and religious, available to the "*vaidika*" elites. For "untouchables" it would mean living outside the area of the cities where the "twice-born" lived and refraining from letting their very shadows fall on the person or path of the upper classes.

The symbolism of food

One of the ways in which social distinctions and reciprocities were upheld in "*vaidika*" society was in the practices associated with the consumption of food. Some early texts had used food as a metaphor for social status wherein the consumption was likened to the control or destruction of those one hated or over whom one claimed superiority. As an author of the *Śatapatha Brāhmaṇa* put it: "The sacrificer [makes] food of whoever hates him, of whomever he hates, and puts them into [the sacrificial fire]."[26] Now, on the other hand, many of the texts of the urban period offered extended discussions on which foods were appropriate to eat and which were not. The *Dharmasūtras* – treatises on proper behavior designed primarily for brahman males – offer scores of stanzas declaring what foods should be eaten or avoided, how they should be prepared, and how and when they should be offered to the gods or other persons.

In a certain sense, one was what one ate – or, at least, one's identity and relative ritual purity were enacted in the ways food was cooked, eaten, and served. Foods were thought to reflect the basic character of the universe (cf. *Bhagavadgītā* 17: 7–10) – "sattvic" foods, such as most vegetables, milk, or dairy products, were believed to enhance spiritual awareness and ritual purity, so were favored by orthoprax brahmans; foods which had the character of *rajas* (such as meat, garlic, or onions) were thought to generate passion and action and were, for the most part, appropriate for the warrior but not for the brahman; "tamasic" foods such as liquor or stale food were thought to instill inertia and slothfulness and hence were appropriate only for the lower strata of society. The qualities of various castes were thought to have been consistent with the nature of the food they ate.[27]

Many rules developed as to when one should fast or feast, to whom and when one should offer food, and, not least important, when and how to offer food to the gods. By the medieval period, for example, many of the offerings made to the deities in temples were of foods. These offerings, once "consumed" by the deity, would be redistributed to devotees in the form of ***prasāda*** (literally, "favor"). Such *prasāda*, incidentally, was the only form of "leftovers" believed to be auspicious for the orthoprax to consume. To this day, rituals associated with food embody much as to the ways in which various Indian communities express themselves and their relationship to others and to the deities.

Yoga

In addition to the disciplines of the householder and the correct preparation and eating of foods, room was left open for more stringent disciplines, especially those in which the male might engage after his sons had grown. Even in one's lifetime, household rituals came to be perceived as a form of "sacrifice" continuing the Vedic metaphor, albeit without a massive sacrificial complex. The technique known as *yoga* served as the sacrifice par excellence.

Derived from the term *yuj* (yoke), *yoga* had been used in the later *Upaniṣads* as a generic term for the techniques to attain *mokṣa* (liberation). Sometime around the middle of the second century BCE, the *Yogasūtras*, ascribed to a sage called **Patañjali**, were written. Herein we find the spelling out of the ways in which the body could be homologized to the cosmos and became "sacred space." It was a form of ritual; indeed it was sacrifice; in fact the *Bhagavadgītā*'s discussion of yogic techniques began with a reference to the myth of the primal sacrifice. Meditation was *tapas*, inner heat – the sacrificial system was internalized: the yogin's backbone was the *hiraṇyagarbha*; ***cakras*** (circles) rendered the body congruent to the universe.

Some forms of *yoga* were clearly borrowed from Jainism and Buddhism. Such was the case with the system known as *laya yoga* (ethical yoga) and here two forms of ethical behavior were prescribed: ***yama*** (restraint) was the path of refraining from activities believed to be injurious (hence, the practice of celibacy, non-stealing, and others); on the other hand, ***niyama*** was an ethic of commission – taking appropriate action that prepared the person for further exercises. *Haṭha yoga* was the term given for the use of the body ritually. This included, most particularly, hundreds of ***āsanas*** – postures designed to enhance the body–cosmos equation. The lotus posture, for example, was intended to place the seeker at the "beginning of the universe" where the lotus was first thought to have arisen. ***Prāṇayama*** or breath control included techniques thought to purify the mythical channels which permit the flow of the five breaths of which Upaniṣadic sages had spoken. Finally, there were developed stages of *yoga* which were focused in the mind and known as ***rāja yoga*** (the "king" of *yogas*). These stages and techniques included ***pratyāhāra*** (control of the senses); ***dhāraṇa*** (focusing on a symbolic object – for example, an icon, the navel); ***dhyāna*** (the term from which Chan, Zen, and Thien came, names for schools of Buddhism in China, Japan, and Vietnam respectively) was the capacity to meditate or approach insight in a way that transcended any object or word. It was "wordless contemplation" and the penultimate stage to the attainment of transcendent consciousness (***samādhi***), the final stage the seeker would attain.[28]

No doubt this system had its roots in the Upaniṣadic setting where asceticism and the forest life took high priority. Yet *yoga* continued as a viable way to maintain the renunciate life even within one's household or in an urban setting. It was a technique preserved for the disciplined few.

Summary

Certain consistent themes recurred throughout the various attempts by bṛahmanical pandits and writers to reinterpret the *vaidika* tradition and accommodate it to the pluralism of the urban complex. These themes included sacrifice, *dharma*, and ritual. Worshiping the deity in the temple was ritual; it was also *dharma* and sacrifice. Following certain prescribed laws and behaviors was *dharma*; it was also sacrifice and ritual. Living the life of the householder and maintaining the sacrality of the home was *dharma* and sacrifice and was perpetuated by ritual. It was in enactment, gesture, and performance that *vaidika* tradition was purveyed and one's identity was expressed. Texts, for the most part, described these enactments and were *post facto* to them. It is difficult to overstate the significance in this period of ritual enactment as perhaps the quintessential way of being religious and of expressing who one was. This appears to be true as well for much of the rest of Hinduism's religious history.

The epics

We have referred to many of the texts that were produced during this era and suggested that many may have been descriptions (probably more than prescriptions) of ritual enactments of various kinds. The two most famous "texts" to emerge in this period were the major epics, the *Rāmāyaṇa* and the *Mahābhārata*. When one speaks of them as "texts," however, one cannot forget the oral and performative dimensions of both. The *Rāmāyaṇa* was, to be sure, produced in written form, some of its earliest snippets perhaps as early as the fifth to fourth century BCE.[29] This written material is said to have been edited in its Sanskrit form by **Vālmīki**. Yet the morality tale is based largely on oral stories and poems and, more importantly, was reproduced in oral and dramatic form in villages all over South Asia. The story, in short, was fluid; in each telling or dramatization different nuances would be highlighted, depending on context and dramatic troupe. As a result, there were many variations to the *Rāmāyaṇa*, and it is enacted to this day even in Thailand and Indonesia where the story has changed. Each retelling had its own "local flavor"; so, in some Jain enactments, for example, Rāvaṇa was the hero insofar as he represented the non-*vaidika* protagonist.[30] The *Rāmāyaṇa* was a morality tale based on the story of Rāma, a folk hero and his wife Sītā. Among other things, the enacted stories stressed the importance of the role (*svadharma*) of the good warrior/king who is faithful to his word (*ṛta*) and to his duty; it portrayed the ideal of wifely fidelity in Sītā. The narration reconciled the imagery of kingship and urban duty with that of asceticism and forest life. Among other things, it legitimated warfare insofar as Rāvaṇa was the paradigmatic enemy.

The basic "plot" of the epic followed Rāma's heroic exploits. He was the eldest son and heir to his father Daśaratha, king of Ayodhyā. His stepmother, however, demanded her own son be made heir and crown prince (cashing in on a boon made available long before). Rāma voluntarily withdrew to the forest with Sītā (literally, "furrow").[31] In the forest, sages sought Rāma's help against harassing demons. Rāma agreed to join the conflict against the demons, whose king, Rāvaṇa, abducted Sītā, keeping her captive. Rāma was aided by the monkeys of the forest, led by the general Hanuman, and eventually Rāvaṇa was overcome and Sītā was rescued. Rāma was restored to the throne of Ayodhyā. In a later addition to the text the chastity and fidelity of Sītā were questioned and she proved herself by surviving fire. Eventually, she returned to the earth and resumed her rightful place as a goddess.

Many of the themes discussed earlier were reflected in this epic – the importance of kingship, the dialectic between city and forest (note now that it was important to have Rāma return to his throne); and the sacred duty of husband and wife. Many of the stories told to Rāma to inspire him and provide an example of how he should behave were stories of gods (like Skanda) who were heroes in their celestial roles. Over the years, the main characters in the epic have been understood in various ways depending on local retelling. Rāma, for example, has been seen, not only as a "sacred king" and incarnation of Viṣṇu, but also as a major deity in his own right, especially amongst Hindi-speaking people after the seventeenth century when his story appeared in a Hindi dialect. Hanuman, his monkey general, was eventually divinized and was perceived by some as the model of fidelity, virility, and patron-hero of warriors and wrestlers. Sītā herself was not merely the dutiful wife, but by some women has been seen as a model of independence and strength, willing to stand up to her husband when asked to defend herself.

The other epic is the *Mahābhārata*. Its origins appear to be in songs sung by bards in praise (*stotra*) of their noble patrons. The verse form is generally known as ***mahākāvya***, wherein well-known themes are put into verse form.[32] Songs sung for kings or patrons became songs sung for deities. Between the fourth century BCE and the fourth century CE, many additions, stories, and anecdotes were added by various reciters until some 100,000 ***ślokas*** comprised the final text organized into eighteen books – the longest single volume ever reduced to writing. Whether the epic reflected the affairs of actual historical figures has been hotly debated, and, if so, when they may have lived is unclear. It is plausible that the *Mahābhārata* reflected some of the infighting that was occurring earlier in the Gangetic basin. In any case, there is a thread of a "plot" that holds the various strands of the epic together.

A basic feud arose over succession to the kingdom of Kurukṣetra. The rivals were two sets of cousins, descended from a legendary King Bharata; five sons of Pāṇḍu, known as the Pāṇḍava brothers; and 100 sons of Dhṛtarāṣṭra (who was blind and hence ineligible for the throne). Pāṇḍu retired to the forest, still without offspring, then fathered five sons, the Pāṇḍava brothers. These five brothers were educated in the court of Dhṛtarāṣṭra, who had become regent in Pāṇḍu's absence. Their teachers included their great uncle Bhīṣma (spiritual power) and the priest Drona (master of archery). These brothers exceeded their cousins in all virtues, including martial skill, incurring the jealousy of Duryodhana, Dhṛtarāṣṭra's eldest son. Duryodhana plotted to get the throne; Yudiṣṭhara, eldest son of Pāṇḍu, and rightful heir to the throne, lost his kingdom in a dice game, said to be "crooked." Duryodhana refused to step aside when the Pāṇḍavas returned after their thirteen year exile. War became inevitable and lasted for eighteen days.

Numerous sub-plots and subsidiary stories flesh out the didactic value of the account. These were often told by raconteurs or enacted dramatically. Tucked into the *Mahābhārata* is one of those literary pieces that has become so well known in the Western world – the *Bhagavadgītā* (literally, the "Song of God"). The *Bhagavadgītā* was set on the battlefield of Kurukṣetra. Dhṛtarāṣṭra heard of the war through the narration of *Sanjaya.* Implied also was an inner battle as Arjuna, a Pāṇḍava brother, is instructed by Kṛṣṇa.

The structure of the *Gītā* includes some four sections: the first, chapter one, set the stage by recounting Arjuna's dilemma: he did not want to go to battle against his own cousins. In the second stage, chapters two to seven, Kṛṣṇa summarized some options for living. There was a dialectic presented between sacrifice and action (chapters three and four) and between renunciation and action (chapters five and six). The third section (chapters eight to twelve) appears to represent the "core" of the text; this part, at least, if not the entire text, was clearly written by a devotee of Kṛṣṇa, as this section provided an epiphany of Kṛṣṇa, who was presented as the fulfillment of all cosmologies and devotion (*bhakti*) to him as the culmination of all paths. The final section, chapters thirteen to eighteen, apparently using the dualistic Sāṁkhya system as a base, presented homologies to two polarities – *puruṣa* and *prakṛtī* – and to the three characteristics (*guṇas*).

The *Bhagavadgītā* did many things at once. Clearly, it presented *bhakti* and Kṛṣṇa as the epitome of all previous options. As indicated earlier, some scholars believe the cult of Kṛṣṇa to have had connections to the city of Mathurā, a city where Buddhism was also strong, and that Kṛṣṇa, at the least, thus offered a *vaidika* alternative to Buddhism. But other themes and issues were addressed – these include: an articulation of the appropriate forms that *dharma* should take; a reconciliation of dualistic (*sāṁkhya*) cosmologies and monistic ones; reconciliation of the ways of wisdom (*jñāna*); action (*karma*) and devotion (*bhakti*); and integration of various soteriological paths (sacrifice, asceticism, *yoga*). Not least of all, it highlighted theism and devotion to Kṛṣṇa as the *summum bonum* of religious practice, especially as an alternative to Buddhism. In the process it taught disciplined action (*karmayoga*) and lack of attachment to the fruit of one's action (*karma-phalasaṅga*).

Aesthetics and the arts

In the later urban age, and especially by the time of the Guptas, the arts were flourishing and fundamental principles which informed artistic expression were in place. Clearly art was not an afterthought or an appendage to the creativity of the period; rather it was a consistent part of the total landscape, if not a driving force in the shaping of that landscape. Whether in Mahāyāna Buddhist or brahmanical hands, human expression, like much of nature itself, assumed a sacral character. Especially in the hands of brahmanical synthesizers the expression of art was a form of ritual; further, it represented the incorporation of themes and motifs from the pluralistic landscape including borrowings from Buddhist and "folk" sources which were in turn linked to *vaidika* motifs. It is as if all of culture was sacralized.

Aesthetic expression made several statements about the nature of the universe and the human being's place in it. For one thing, the arts were a celebration of the material world and of life itself. The world was increasingly seen as *līlā* – the playground of the gods. Matter and society had become an arena in which the sacred (whether *brahman* or buddhahood) was present. Further, the body, for example, in dance or icon, was affirmed. The body was used as the medium through which the sacred was depicted; the body and its gestures and pose replicated the reciprocity between body and cosmos insofar as in the body, cosmic rhythms and sacred moods could be re-enacted. Moreover, sound and speech as used in drama, music, or ritual chant were intended to have resonance with the creative process of the universe itself. At the same time, the stories told in drama ennobled the stories found in "folk" culture and enacted emerging mythologies. Creativity itself became a form of "*yoga*" – a means of bringing both artist and audience closer to the realm of the sacred. That is, the artist became an embodiment or conduit of *brahman* and sought to evoke an enlightening experience on the part of the "audience." In that sense, the audience was to become the "actor" and the artist the "prompter" in such a way as to enable all participants to experience the "flavor" (***rasa***) of *brahman.*

These principles are at work in the very use of the Sanskrit language itself. By the time of Aśoka, Magadha was already a multilingual area. Indigenous dialects known as the Prākrits abounded – some of these died out; some were eventually systematized into distinct languages in their own right; most were incorporated in various ways into the Sanskrit language. By the fourth century BCE, what was once the exclusive language of the priests had been systematized by the brilliant grammarian **Pāṇini**, who wrote a definitive, scientific grammar for Sanskrit called the *Astadhyayi* (book of eight chapters). Therein we find the articulation of six types of grammar (might these be in response to the six perfections of the Sarvāstivādins?) One of the "types" of grammar was ritual.

The use of Sanskrit often had a religious character. Not only had earlier forms of oral Vedic Sanskrit been used liturgically; even in its written form it assumed a sacred aura. *Saṃskṛta* means "well-formed, polished or perfected"; it was written in the ***devanāgirī*** script – literally, the writing of the "city of the gods." Rendering something in Sanskrit, whether orally or in written form, became a way of linking "new" expressions to a sacred past. J. A. B. van Buitenen once noted that, among other things, the Sanskrit language "carried with it associations of a sacral character" and served to refine or correct "one's nature and conduct by ritual means." That which was "Sanskritic" therefore was perceived to be that which was "most ancient," "most pure," and "hierarchically the most elevated," assuring "correct descent" "by relating oneself to an ancient lineage or myth and safeguarding the purity of future offspring."[33]

In sum, to chant or write in Sanskrit was to engage in ritual; it became the instrument by which all elements of a changing landscape could be linked to the *vaidika* tradition. If Pāli was the language of the court in Aśoka's time and continued to be the language used in Theravāda Buddhism, Sanskrit was the lingua franca in the Gupta courts and the basic language of Mahāyāna Buddhism.

Much of the Sanskritic literature then was perceived to be sacred. More specifically, this literature took many forms: poetry, for example, included the early form known as *mahākāvya,* which used various principles of aesthetics – different meters, similes, tropes, and ornamentation. The work of the great dramatist **Kālidāsa** reflected this genre well. Folk tales also found their way into classical dress. The *Pañcatantra,* for example, was the Sanskritic compilation of oral fables and folk tales that may date back to several centuries BCE and which eventually influenced folk tales told in Europe by way of Arabia and the Islamic world. Similarly, the *Jātaka Tales* were folk tales and fables purporting to tell anecdotes from Buddha's life, and served a didactic purpose. Myth was ascribed an aura of historicity (*itihāsa*); it embodied anecdotes and motifs derived from folk and other sources and found its way into the epics and eventually into the *Purāṇas* – collections which began around the fourth century CE and continued to be written and collected even into the seventeenth century. The *Purāṇas* drew upon the social landscape and became a means for anonymous authors to address major themes and describe the exploits of the deities.

The aesthetic principles informing not only literature but all the other arts were recorded eventually in the *Nāṭyaśāstra*, the core of which was written around the second to sixth centuries CE and enhanced in subsequent years. Based on oral principles handed down by theatrical troupes, the *Nāṭyaśāstra* offered considerable detail about the role of the artist. Central to this role is *bhāva* – that which conveyed the meaning intended through words, physical gestures, and facial expressions.[34] The art was "successful" insofar as its audience shared in the fundamental moods intended. Art enacted mythologies; speech, sound, and bodily gestures became expressions of the sacred. The expression of art, in short, was ritual.

There were three basic principles informing artistic expressions by the Gupta period. The first was *rasa* – literally, flavor, essence, taste, sentiment, orientation. *Rasa* was the flavor of *brahman*. Eventually, *rasas* became the eight major "moods" which both body and cosmos embodied: love, heroism, disgust, wrath, mirth, pleasure, pity, and wonder.[35] By the eleventh century (and the work of **Abhinavagupta**), gentleness and quiescence were added to these moods. *Rasa* was acted out in art, drama, music, and literature – the artist was the "conduit" who sought to enable the listener to be a participant, to experience the "flavor" of the universe.

Another fundamental aesthetic principle was ***alaṃkāra*** – ornamentation or embellishment – it entailed the use of metaphors, puns, and other appropriate means to enhance the beauty and power of an artistic expression. "Ornamentation" could take many forms. In literature, it was the use of tropes, similes, and images which embellish meaning.[36] A woman's eyes, for example, were likened to "darting fish." In acting, *alaṃkāra* included the use of costuming, makeup, headwear, and especially the use of such primary colors as white, blue, red, and yellow (colors which also evoked certain *rasas*). Similarly, when priests are dressing an icon in the typical Hindu temple even today they are performing *alaṃkāra* – an aesthetic as well as religious enterprise.

A third aesthetic principle was ***śilpa*** – the "art of appearance." *Śilpa* included the guidelines for crafts and architecture from indigenous clay art to sculpting, iconography, temple and city building. These arts were practiced by *śilpis* who handed down their traditions from father to son. Architectural texts, which were not written until much later, often started by reciting a myth of creation as if to remind the builder that building a city or a temple was like the re-creating of a world.

These principles were expressed not only in literature, iconography, and architecture but in dance, drama and music. Dance, for example, embodied the story of the gods and fundamental moods, both human and cosmic. It was intended to "carry" *rasa* to the audience. In fact, the term ***abhinaya***, the "performing" of *rasa*, meant literally "carrying to" an audience. Later, dance was combined with music to create its own art form. Dance included the use of stylized "hand gestures" (***mudrās***). By the fourth century CE some thirty-seven *mudrās* were listed, as well as many other poses.[37] *Abhinaya* or "carrying to an audience" could include verbal expressions – for example, the use of sound, rhythm or plot; bodily gestures from head to feet; ornamentation – for example, painting the face, costuming, or makeup; and the re-creation of emotions (*Nāṭyaśāstra* Chapters VII ff.).

Music, for its part, encompassed at least three components. First was meter or beat (***tālā***) – some twenty-two were enumerated in the *Nāṭyaśāstra* with many more added later (Chapter XXXI). Meter was sustained by a drone and the beat of a drum in such a way as to replicate the rhythm of the cosmos. The second element of music was the "tune" (***rāga***) – the *rāga* consisted of

Figure 1 Yashoda scolds her mischievious son Kṛṣṇa as expressed in the Kuchipudi dance form. Dancer: Suvarchala Somayajalu. Photograph by Dr. Raman Venkataraman.

at least five notes; each *rāga* evoked a particular *rasa*, each suitable for a particular time of day. The *rāga* Bhairava (Śiva in his fierce form), for example, was the *rāga* for dawn, the *rāga* of rage, awe, or fear. In this period of musical production there were said to be six basic *rāgas*;[38] now there are many. A final component in music was the scale, *grāma* (*Nāṭyaśāstra* Chapter XXVIII). The scale is probably traceable to the old *Sāmaveda* singers who were multi-tonal in their chanting. Over twenty-two microtones were developed, each part of a scale that was thought to comprehend the universe. It is useful to recall that sound was thought to be primordial and cosmogonic in the Vedic period; hence, the scale was congruent to the totality of the universe and to *satya* (being itself). Music, like dance, had ritual overtones, evoking cosmic rhythm, embodying *rasa*, the flavor of *brahman*, and inviting the hearer to participate in the human–cosmic ambience.

Drama became an increasingly popular art form in the classical settings in the first century CE, though classical performance no doubt grew out of the enactments of myths, folk tales, epics, and village dramas.[39] Though **Aśvaghoṣa**, a Buddhist, was the first to mention drama, it is Kālidāsa who became known as the most popular dramatist of the period. Most early plays included elements from one or more of the epic tales, material often familiar to the audience, and used both prose and verse. Sanskrit was used for the lead male roles, representing authority figures, while Prākrits were used for lesser roles. Drama was intended not merely for the amusement of audiences, but also to instill or evoke one or more of the fundamental *rasas*. Drama was instructive, whether in re-enacting the themes of folk heroes and mythological figures, or in presenting the spectrum of human emotion. Invariably, plays of this period presented a conflict and its eventual resolution.

The *Nāṭyaśāstra* made explicit the ritual character of early drama. The playhouse was likened to a temple or the old sacrificial hut of the Vedic period. The drama was an oblation, a sacrifice, acted out at a miniature cosmos (Chapter III). Its characters were often depicted as representations of the ideas of *dharma*. Usually performed at a festival or other ceremonious occasion, the costumes, stage props, masks, colors – all eventually stylized – were intended to enhance the mood or *rasa* portrayed in the drama itself. Clearly drama as it was made part of the classical Sanskritized tradition like the other arts was closely aligned to ritual.

Religious life at the popular level

Clearly many of the people of the "urban" period were affected very little or not at all by the "classical" forms of religion articulated in the texts. There were, for example, people living in villages oriented by the agricultural cycle, and tribal peoples only marginally being assimilated into urban life. It is most difficult to reconstruct the religious life of such communities for several reasons. For example, while certain practices found today in "folk" settings may have "ancient" roots, it is difficult to ascertain precisely how far back these go. Further, certain practices cited in the texts of the period may have had their roots in folk settings, but are already in the process of being assimilated into Hinduism. Nonetheless, some scholars – for example, A. L. Basham and P. V. Kane – do speculate as to some of the forms that "popular religion" was taking in this period.

Religious practices at the popular or folk level may well have included the following features. Worship of goddesses in local villages seems highly likely. Each such goddess would have been seen as protectoress of land and village and the one who controlled the forces of nature, including diseases. These village goddesses were probably pacified in a special way (as they are today) at the coming of the rainy seasons in order to avert diseases and assure fertility of the land.[40]

Goddesses would have been worshiped with flowers, peacock feathers, and wine but also by the sacrifice of animals, especially buffaloes, goats, sheep, and chickens.[41] The spilling of blood would satisfy and empower the goddess, invoke her protection, and keep the land fertile. Rituals associated with buffalo sacrifice were intimated in this period: a buffalo demon identified as a fierce ***asura*** known as Mahiṣa was mentioned in the *Mahābhārata* and by the name Dundubhai in the *Ramāyāṇa.*[42] That this buffalo demon was slain by a goddess who came to be associated with Durgā, is suggested by terra-cotta representatives of a four-armed goddess riding a lion and slaying a buffalo.[43] In addition, both A. L. Basham and P. V. Kane believed that the sacrifice of human beings was probable in some settings.[44] Goddesses were probably represented by a stone or simple clay effigy set up under a tree thought to be sacred.[45] Such trees as the *pīpal*, banyan, or *aśoka* were ascribed special sacrality and/or the power to help women bear children.

Ritual life in villages was no doubt oriented by the seasons, especially the monsoons and the agricultural cycle. Ritual bathing in rivers in spate is attested in some sources datable to this period as are the collective dances of young women in praise of the deity.[46] Snakes were apparently venerated as symbols of both death and fertility and may have been given offerings at the start of the rainy season.[47] Anthills may have been respected as the houses of snakes.[48]

As suggested by the references to the buffalo demon, a belief in demonic beings was probable – these demons would have been thought to control certain distinctive forces or to have appeared at inauspicious times. In addition, any number of gods would have been understood to offer protection or preside over particular areas or functions. The names of some of these gods appeared in the epic literature – one such example was Viśakha who was eventually assimilated into the person of Skanda.[49] Goddesses, gods, and demons alike were considered able to possess people.[50]

There are also indications that a number of stories appearing in the epic literature had folk variants, suggesting either that the classical stories had folk antecedents or were given nuances reflecting later "folk" settings. This was the case, for example, with accounts of Arjuna found in Rājasthānī, Garhwadī, and Tamil traditions wherein Arjuna was said to have married a princess of the underworld and where, in the course of providing a funeral for his father, Pāṇdu, he had to fetch back the hide of a rhinoceros.[51] Similarly, Draupadī, heroine and wife of the five Paṇḍāva brothers, was described in various ways in later folk variants. Among other things, in these variations, she was depicted as a destructive virgin goddess, born of fire, taking on a gypsy disguise; she was associated with fire walking and was given temple guardians, such as Potturāja, the buffalo king.[52]

In addition, we have already alluded to some of the probable influences that "folk" culture had on "classical" forms of religious practice of this period. This would have included the role of village dramas in disseminating various tellings of the *Rāmāyaṇa* stories and in the classicization of drama itself. "Folk" deities were co-opted into the "high gods" of the period, including, no doubt, most of the teriomorphic forms of Viṣṇu's avatars. Images and stories drawn from popular life found their way into both Hindu and Buddhist iconography and hagiography from the *yakṣīs* found in *stūpa* lintels to the episodes ascribed to the life of the Buddha in the *Jātaka Tales.* Stories ascribed to the Hindu gods as recorded eventually in the *Purāṇas* similarly made use of motifs found at the popular level. Even the emerging ritual life associated with temple and icon probably reflected in some way practices present in the "folk" landscape.

These practices and others illustrate the ways in which common folk acted out their religious orientations at a level relatively unaffected by the elite. Some of these practices can still be found in rural settings even as some of them were "domesticated" and made part of the purview of "classical" Hinduism and Buddhism.

Developments in Buddhism

We have sketched some of the developments in the *vaidika* response to urban culture. Before leaving this time period, it is appropriate to return to Buddhism and sketch some of the developments therein. First, it may be helpful, by way of summary, to outline a comparative frame which indicates how Buddhist communities and brahmanic communities were reflecting the period.

Kingship

In the brahmanic or *vaidika* view, kingship was sacralized as in *mahārāja*, *devaputra* (son of the gods), and other terms. The king was to practice *artha* (statecraft) and was rhetorically legitimated for the people by brahmans.

In the Buddhist context, the emperor, especially Aśoka, was *cakravartin* (wheel-turner); he exemplified the lay *bodhisattva*, and maintained stability in the social order, legitimated and advised by monks.

Ethics

In *vaidika* settings, there was emphasis on *artha* (statecraft), *dharma* (responsible living in the world), and *varṇaśrāmas* (stages of life, now emphasizing the role of householder). Ethics was a form of sacrifice and ritual.

In Buddhism, the emphasis of laypersons was on *karma* (appropriate action), including donations and morality. For monks, rules (*vinaya*) for the monastic setting were articulated and the doctrine of the six perfections developed by the third century after Buddha.

Attitude toward city-state

In brahmanic discourse, the city-state was where *dharma* was to be enacted; the world was increasingly seen as the playground (*līlā*) of the gods; renunciation was to be of "fruits" not of action.

In Buddhist contexts, the city-state had become the arena for working out enlightenment; dialectic interaction existed between monk and laity; the role of the *bodhisattva* (the wise one who had "dispassionate compassion" for all sentient beings) took precedence in *Mahāyāna* schools. By the third century CE, the distinction between *nirvāṇa* and *samsāra* was collapsed in Nāgārjuna's doctrine of emptiness (*śūnyatā*).

Pantheon

In *vaidika* settings, there was the mythologization of "high deities" (e.g., Śiva, Viṣṇu, Skanda) as well as personification of the once impersonal *brahman*; deities incorporated Buddhist, "folk," and *vaidika* motifs.

In Buddhism, by the second century CE, under the Kuṣāṇas, the Buddha had become like a king atop the cosmos, enhanced by Iranian notions of light and Greco-Roman artistic forms. Buddha gave warrant (*varan*) to his "ministers," the bodhisattvas.

Iconography

In *vaidika* settings, early forms were probably in wood and other non-permanent materials, but became permanent by the late Gupta period. The icon was the embodiment of the divine, equated to king and cosmos, and the center of worship. Iconic representations of the deities often emulated Buddhist and Jain poses, gestures, etc.

In the Buddhist case, until the first century CE, Buddha was depicted aniconically (e.g., as the "bo" tree, lotus, throne, *caitya*), then anthropomorphically by the first century CE. By the third century CE, one finds depictions of the "life" of the Buddha reflecting folk tales adapted for his "life." Iconic representations were viewed as embodying buddhahood now non-distinct from the realm of matter and *samsāra.*

Sacred spaces

Vaidika religion was now usually housed in a temple (though none have survived from before the fifth century CE). The temple was congruent to the palace, cosmos, and human torso. Its tower (***śikhara***) may have been intimated in the form of the *stūpa,* and its assembly hall (*maṇḍapa*), may have been congruent to the Buddhist *vihāra* (living quarters); the inner sanctum (*garbhagṛha,* "womb house"), housing the icon like an embryo, emulated early cave sanctuaries and the caves where Buddhists and Jains dwelt.

Buddhist structures included the *stūpa* to be used as memorial housings for ashes or relics. The *stūpas* included an "egg" (*aṇḍa*) representing the cosmos, topped by a *caitya* or representation of Buddha atop the cosmos; walkways and doorways around the *stūpa* by the second century BCE included carvings reflecting the landscape – e.g., totemic animals, *yakṣīs* (buxom female attendants equated to vegetation, etc.); the *vihāra* was the living quarters for monks and could include sculpting drawn from the Buddha's life, *caityas,* etc.

Even though brahmanically informed expressions of religion were prolific and often responded to Buddhism, the latter flourished as well. Given patronage by Aśoka, the Kuṣāṇas, and such other dynasties as the Sātavāhanas in the Southern Deccan, Buddhist settlements were numerous and their influence in certain settings considerable. In some Buddhist centers, for example, Nāgārjunakonda and Amarāvatī in the Southern Deccan, monastic communities were established and schools or colleges supported. In

Nāgārjunakonda, for example, one of the earliest medical schools on the subcontinent flourished in the third and fourth centuries CE.

By the first century CE, there had arisen within Buddhism a movement which called itself Mahāyāna (the "great vehicle") in contrast to what was called Hinayāna (lesser vehicle), also known as Theravāda. Mahāyāna emerged from the Mahāsāṅghika schools, which from the early days had disparaged the *arhats* and espoused such views as that the Buddha was transmundane, and that the historical Buddha was a mere manifestation of him. The Mahāyāna schools claimed that buddhahood was innate to all, that the path of the bodhisattva could be followed by any, and that a pantheon of superhuman bodhisattvas and Buddhas existed to help devotees in various ways. Buddhist literature flourished in Pāli for the Hinayāna schools and Sanskrit for the Mahāyāna ones, the latter often offered with the claim that the represented doctrine was preserved from the mouth of the Buddha himself.

The Mahāsāṅghikas, together with the Sarvāstivādins, were especially influential in the Kuṣāṇa period (first–third century CE). The Sarvāstivādins were particularly strong in Mathurā and Kashmīr and, like the Mahāsāṅghikas, were influenced by Greek and Persian ideas.[53] These groups provided the rationale for the explosion of Buddhist art when Buddhas and bodhisattvas were iconographically depicted. Under the Kuṣāṇas one found the concrete personifications of Amitābha, the Buddha embodying light, enlightenment, and wisdom, and of the bodhisattvas: Maitreya (the compassionate one, personifying light), Mañjuśrī (the "crown prince" of dharma), and Avalokiteśvara (rich in love and compassion and Buddha's chief attendant).

Nearly thirty schools of Buddhist thought and practice grew in India, many of them during this period. It will suffice by way of illustration to mention but two of these. From the school once known as the Mahāsāṅghikas (those of the larger congregation) emerged the Mādhyamika school by the late second century CE. Indebted to Nāgārjuna's doctrine of "emptiness" (*śūnyatā*) this school collapsed all dualities. Simply put, the argument goes as follows: existence was characterized by *svabhāva* (having its own independent existence). But, in fact, nothing had *svabhāva* as all were interdependent – neither *nirvāṇa* nor *samsāra* had *svabhāva*. It follows then that *samsāra* (the phenomenal world) was homologous to *nirvāṇa*. Hence, buddhahood itself was found in this world; all dualities were collapsed – those between self and other, wisdom and action included. Hence, tangible symbols could be used to depict buddhahood.

Nāgārjuna's doctrine of *śūnyatā* and the concomitant idea that buddhahood could be found in all material objects provided an added rationale for the forms of worship that occurred at a popular level. Buddhist piety was often expressed by the laity in ways not unlike those of their "*vaidika*" counterparts, in that it incorporated elements from the local "folk" landscape, and could include offerings of food, incense, flowers, or water. Cultic centers developed at places where the Buddha was believed to have been present or where the relics of saints were buried. Devotion could be focused toward tree spirits, fertility goddesses, reliquary mounds, and eventually toward representations of the Buddha himself. The use of prayer flags, prayer wheels, and other symbolic objects became commonplace. Important events in the Buddha's life were grafted onto the seasonal calendar and became occasions for celebration – most notably, his birth and enlightenment, said to have occurred at the full moon of the month of April–May.[54]

Another school emerging by the third and fourth centuries CE was that known as *yogācāra.* As the name suggests, this school was characterized by the adoption of *yoga* to Buddhism: the cosmos was homologized to the body and enlightenment could occur in and through the body. In this school, the six perfections became ten and were personified concretely. Hence, for example, the attribute of wisdom (***prajñā***) could be expressed in concrete iconic form, not so much to be worshiped but as a focus for meditation and a model for emulation. Some of these attributes were expressed in feminine form, a foretaste of the later Vajrayāna school also known as tantric Buddhism. (We will return to Vajrayāna in a later context.) The Yogācāra school was also known for its doctrine of ***ālaya-vijñāna***, which might be translated as "storehouse of consciousness." The *ālaya-vijñāna* was located within the body, yet seemed to store seeds of consciousness that, because of the logic of *karma*, could be passed along to subsequent generations. Intimated here was the possibility of reincarnation, which became so common a part of Buddhism in Tibet, China, and Japan. Indeed, Yogācāra was one of these schools that migrated to China.

Another conviction of the Yogācāra school was the doctrine of ***tathāgata-garbha*** ("essence of the thus-gone-one"). That is, the Buddha existed in embryonic form as in a womb that existed within all human beings. That "womb" was equatable to the "storehouse of consciousness."[55] All human beings therefore had the innate nature of buddhahood and need only be enlightened to that truth. As one made one's way toward buddhahood one could become a *bodhisattva* who vows to postpone ultimate enlightenment until all beings can be enlightened as well. In the meanwhile, *bodhisattvas* could share their merit with laypersons (thereby helping both petitioner and *bodhisattva* to accrue additional merit); all persons were thereby helped along the path.

It was during this age of empire that Buddhism spread out of India. Aśoka, for example, sent Buddhist emissaries into the Greek world (more on this in a later context). During the Kuṣāṇa period, monks of the Mahāyāna schools started making their way via the Silk Route into Central Asia and eventually to China. Not least important, Emperor Aśoka is said to have sent his own relative as an emissary to the court in Sri Lanka. Emperor Tissa is said to have been converted and Sri Lanka ever since remained a center of Theravāda Buddhist culture, literature, and thought. Indeed, it was from Sri Lanka that Theravāda Buddhism flowed into Southeast Asia – to Myanmar, Thailand, Cambodia, and Indonesia.

By the fifth century CE, many of the Buddhist texts were systematized. Some portions of the earliest, *Vinayapiṭaka* (discourses or literally "baskets" on the monastic discipline) and *Suttapiṭaka* (dialogues to elucidate points of *dhamma*), may even have been pre-Mauryan. During the fourth to third centuries BCE, such texts as the *Dīgha*, *Majjhima*, *Saṃyukta*, and *Aṅguttara Nikāya* ("collections" of discourses) were being recorded. The *Pāli sūttas* followed around the second to first centuries BCE. The *Abhidammapiṭaka* (literally, "basket of scholasticism") is to be dated about the first century BCE to the first century CE, and the *Dīpavaṃsa* (fourth to fifth centuries CE) and the *Mahāvaṃsa* (both historical chronicles in Pāli, fifth to sixth centuries CE) followed.[56]

Without doubt, the religious developments that occurred in this urban period, from the Mauryas to the Guptas, permanently changed the religious landscape of the subcontinent and had an impact, especially through Buddhism, in Southeast Asia, East Asia, and the Middle East. What eventually becomes known as "Hinduism" with its theism and devotional complexity is scarcely intelligible without seeing its roots in this period. The ways in which the Sanskritizing process works throughout the rest of Indian history is aptly illustrated in these Gangetic urban complexes. The dialectic between the "new" and the legitimating "old" is evident here as is the central metaphor of ritual. Enactment of "sacrifice," of "doing the truth," became a fundamental way of affirming lineage and identity and of passing along a perceived heritage to later generations. The profound changes taking place in urban India, from the fourth century BCE to the fifth century CE, were integrated and assimilated so smoothly by the brahmanic synthesizers, one scarcely notices that there has been change at all. That has been something of the genius of this religious stream – accommodating tributaries into it and spawning additional rivulets out. Of course, the religious practice of the cities was innovative and different, but they were still *vaidika* or non-*vaidika* insofar as there was a normative community who could make "connections" and link each community's perceptions to an authenticating past. It is a process that continues to this day.

Recommended reading

On history, culture, ethics

Eliade, M. *Yoga: Immortality and Freedom.* Princeton: Princeton University Press, 1973.
Gonda, J. *Ancient Indian Kingship from the Religious Point of View.* London: Brill, 1966.
Heesterman, J. C. *The Ancient Indian Royal Consecration.* The Hague: Mouton, 1957.
Majumdar, R. C. ed. *History and Culture of the Indian People. Vol. 2. The Age of Imperial Unity.* Bombay: Bharatiya Vidya Bhavan, 1951.
O'Flaherty, W. ed. *Karma and Rebirth in Classical Indian Traditions.* Berkeley: University of California Press, 1980.
Pandey, R. *Hindu Saṁskāras: A Socio-Religious Study of The Hindu Sacraments.* Second edition. Banares: Motilal Banarsidass, 1969.
Sharma, R. S. *History of Pañcala to c.AD 550.* New Delhi: Munshiram Manoharlal, 1983.
Srinivasan, D. M. ed. *Mathura: the Cultural Heritage.* New Delhi: American Institute of Indian Studies, 1989.
Thapar, Romila. *Aśoka and the Decline of the Mauryas.* London: Oxford University Press, 1961.

Some important textual translations and commentaries

Derrett, J. D. *Dharmasūtras and Juridical Literature: History of Indian Literature.* Weisbaden: Otto Harrassowitz, 1973.
Doniger, W. and Smith, B. K. trs. *The Laws of Manu.* Harmondsworth: Penguin, 1991.
Goldman, R. P. general ed. *The Rāmāyaṇa of Valmiki: An Epic of Ancient India.* Princeton: Princeton University Press, 1984–91.
Hiltebeitel, A. *The Ritual of Battle: Kṛṣṇa in the Mahābhārata.* Ithaca: Cornwell Press, 1976.
Mahābhārata, Critical Edition. With Pratika Index. 28 volumes. Poona: Bhandarkar Oriental Research Institute, 1933–72.
Miller, Barbara Stoller. tr. *Bhagavad-Gītā.* New York: Bantam Books, 1986.
Minor, R. *Bhagavad-Gītā, An Exigetical Commentary.* Columbia, MO: South Asia Books, 1982.
Olivelle, P. tr. *The Pañcatantra: the Book of India's Folk Wisdom.* New York: Oxford, 1997.
Olivelle, P. tr. *Dharmasūtras.* Delhi: Motilal Banarsidass, 2000.
Ramāyāṇa, Critical Essays. Seven volumes. Baroda: Oriental Institute, 1960–75.
Rangacharya, Adya. tr. *Nāṭya-Śāstra.* Bangalore: Ibh Prakashana, 1943.
Rangarajan, L. N. *The Arthaśāstra: Edited, Translated, and Introduced.* Delhi: Penguin, 1992.
Richman, Paula. ed. *Many Ramāyāṇas: The Diversity of a Narrative Tradition in South Asia.* Berkeley: University of California Press, 1991.
Van Buitenen, J. A. B. *et al.*, tr. *Mahābhārata.* Chicago: University of Chicago Press, 1973.

Aesthetics and the arts of India

Bhavani, E. *The Dance in India.* Bombay: Taraporavela & Sons, 1965.
Blurton, Richard T. *Hindu Art.* London: British Museum Press, 1992.
Bosch, F. D. K. *The Golden Germ: An Introduction to Indian Symbolism.* Delhi: Munshiram Manaharlal, 1994.
Brown, P. *Indian Architecture, Buddhist and Hindu.* Third edition. Bombay: D. B. Taraporevala, 1956.
Goetz, H. *India: Five Thousand Years of Indian Art.* New York: Crown Publishers, 1964.
Kliger, George. ed. *Bharata Nātyam in Cultural Perspective.* New Delhi: Manohar (American Institute of Indian Studies), 1993.
Kramrisch, S. *The Art of India: Traditions of Indian Sculpture, Painting, and Architecture.* London: Phaidon, 1954.
Popley, H. A. *The Music of India.* Calcutta: YMCA Publishing House, 1950.
Rowland, B. *The Art and Architecture of India.* Revised edition. London: Penguin, 1976.
Zimmer, H. *The Art of Indian Asia.* Two volumes. New York: Bollingen Foundation, 1955.

Timeline of Chapter 4

Cultural/political events			Religious events	
BCE				
400	c. 350	Pāṇini and systematization of Sanskrit	Late 4th	Early portions of *Arthāśāstras*
	327–325	Alexander nears Indus river	4th–1st	Composition of *Dharmasūtras*
	321	Candragupta founds Maurya dynasty		
300	c. 272/3–232	Reign of Aśoka	3rd	Buddhism "patronized" by state; early form of *stūpa* at Sarnath
	c. 183–173	Śuṅga dynasty	3rd–1st	Sacralization of kings; development of *bhakti*: theism, temple, iconography, cult of Kṛṣṇa
	c. 181	End of Maurya dynasty		
	c. 150	Bactrian Greeks in NW		
			2nd	Patañjali's *Yogasūtras*?
100	c. 100	Pahlavas in NW	1st	Final composition of *Rāmāyaṇa*? Rise of Śiva-Rudra and Viṣṇu to eminence?
CE				
	c. 78	Founding of Śaka era in NW	1st	Rise of Skanda as a high god Division of Jains into Digambara and Śvetāmbara
100	1st–3rd	Kuṣāṇas in NW		
			2nd	Gandhāra/Mathurā art: anthropomorphic representations of Buddha Fourth Buddhist Council: split between Mahāyāna and Theravāda schools Nāgārjuna and rise of Mādhyamika school of Buddhism Final systematization of *Laws of Manu*?
200				
300	c. 313–540	Gupta dynasty Flowering of Sanskritic literature, drama, poetry	4th–5th	Beginnings of *Purāṇas*; *Pañcatantra*? *Vaidika* art: temples in stone Early portions of the *Nāṭyaśāstra*

5

The Post-classical Period

South India

Up until now, the accounts of historical developments in religion have been focused on the northern part of the subcontinent, and especially in the Gangetic basin. We turn our attention now to South India which provides us many windows into the development of religion in the post-classical period. For one thing, we have, in the south, documentation and resources that help us understand the nature of religion and culture prior to the "brahmanical synthesis." The processes of brahmanization can be traced with some clarity. Not least important, the deep South became, arguably, the major center of "Hindu" civilization from the eighth through the fifteenth centuries. We shall use the term "Hindu" regularly from now on in our discussion even though the term is not indigenous. It was adapted from Islamic and Persian sources who by the sixteenth and seventeenth centuries spoke of "Hinduism" as the religion practiced by people on the "other side" of the Indus. Indeed, the "Hinduism" we see emerging in the deep south remains very similar in many ways to the "Hinduism" one finds in the southern part of the subcontinent even today and is a significant source for later developments in India.

The southern story begins in the third or fourth century BCE. A literature appeared in the Tamil language by at least the first century CE, much of it associated with an "academy" (*caṅkam*) of poets headquartered near the capital of the Pāṇṭiya chieftains in Maturai. In this literature one finds descriptions of a culture and landscape that largely pre-dated the coming of northern influences. This culture, generally called Dravidian, had its roots in several sources including neolithic settlements of the south and a megalithic culture that had penetrated South India by at least the eighth century BCE – this culture was characterized by its use of urns for burial and the erection of huge stones over their buried dead. In ways still not clear, some aspects of the script of the Indus Valley may have influenced the development of the Tamil language. Indeed a Tamil script was in place by the fourth or third century BCE and a Tamil grammar (*Tolkāppiyam*) by the second century BCE. After Sanskrit, Tamil has been the oldest continuous language on the subcontinent. The poetic *caṅkam* literature tended to be of two types: external (***puṟam***) – that which described the social order, warfare, and public affairs – and internal (***akam***) – that which described the world of home and spirit, the different types of love, and the world of the woman.[1]

The culture described in this *caṅkam* literature was relatively "democratic" inasmuch as hierarchialization appears not yet to have taken place. The poets divided their space into five landscapes (*tiṇais*): agricultural tracts, pastoral areas, hilly spaces, coastal zones, and barren tracts. Each landscape had its own character and ethos reflected in its lifestyle and deities. Certain flowers, for example, were associated with the "moods" of the people, and the differing kinds of love relationships in each area.[2] Each tract had its own deity. Murukaṉ, for example, was the god of the hills who was thought to be a hunter present in nature and the foliage of the hills. He could dispel negative power (*anaṅku*) from both nature and person and could possess the devotee. He was represented by his lance and the shaman who carried a lance (*vēlaṉ*). Similarly, the goddess Koṟṟavai roamed in the barren spaces embodying the hostility of this landscape. These deities were terrestrial in nature, and, in some cases, were seen as mythical ancestors to the peoples of that tract.

The worldview of this early poetry was chthonic – rooted in the earth. Little, if any, metaphysical speculation occurred. Elephants, peacocks, and flowers were symbols of the richness and fertility of life. While the land was seen as feminine, it could be dangerous if left uncontrolled. Individuality and the festivity of the auspicious landscapes were celebrated. Worship often occurred in cleared spaces where a pillar (*kantu*) was erected and smeared with peacock feathers, blood, etc. It was thought that the deity could possess people, especially the shaman and young warrior, though the poets showed considerable skepticism about claims of "possession." By the third century CE Maturai, the seat of the Pāṇṭiyaṉs, had become a center of culture; the god Murukaṉ had become the god of the city, his hunter-attributes replaced by those of the warrior and his role the counterpart of the chieftain/king. The poetry makes many references to commerce that had developed between South India and West Asia. The trade winds had been discovered by the first century BCE; there is evidence of visits by Greek and Roman merchants (they were referred to as *yavaṉār* – foreigners); many Greek or Roman coins were left behind and several Greek terms for spices were derived from the Tamil language (for example, terms for cinnamon, ginger).

As early as the third century BCE, at least three groups from the north had begun to migrate into the south: Jain monks had settled in caves outside the cities and along the coast; Buddhists, some of whom may have come from Sri Lanka, had begun to settle; and brahmans and their practices were mentioned in the *caṅkam* poems. By the third century CE a certain degree of "Prākritization" had occurred. Buddhists and Jains were writing texts in Tamil and had gained influence in certain of the courts (for example, some of the Pāṇṭiyaṉs had Jains as advisers in their courts, and the Ikṣvākas patronized Buddhists in what is now southern Andhra Pradesh). By the fourth or fifth century CE, Buddhism and Jainism enjoyed a certain hegemony in the south. Lifestyles, literature, and ethics took on a Jain or Buddhist cast.

It was in the seventh century that an explicitly "Hindu" culture developed. One of the purveyors of this culture was the Pallava dynasty, a royal family who established a capital at Kāñcīpuram and a seaport at Mahābalipuram. The Pallavas brought architectural styles and other influences from the Gupta era by way of the Cālukyas. The Pallavas formed an alliance with local landowners (*vēḷāḷas*) and imported brahmans to whom they donated land for villages, known as ***brahmadeyas***, centers from which brahmanic culture radiated outward. Brahmans became the "kingmakers" and together with *vēḷāḷas* legitimated kingship and participated in the construction and conduct of temples.[3]

Bhakti

Two distinct but related phenomena demonstrated the "Hinduization" that occurred from the sixth to the ninth centuries CE. The first was the explosion of devotional (*bhakti*) literature in the Tamil vernacular; the other was the construction of temples and incorporation of an elaborate symbolic and ritual life therein. We focus first on the experience of *bhakti*. Singers from various walks of life (brahman, royalty, common folk) sang the praises of the high gods. Myths from northern epic sources were selectively appropriated; epic "high gods" were grafted onto the indigenous deities; the local landscape was celebrated and extolled as the abode of the gods. An anti-Buddhist and anti-Jain polemic was replaced within a generation by a co-opting of Jain and Buddhist motifs. "Hinduism" was presented as the religion of Tamil country.

There were two sets of singers: *Āḻvārs*, literally "those who drown" (in the grace of the god), were those who extolled the virtues of Viṣṇu. Over a period of several generations, the *āḻvārs* composed thousands of stanzas singing of the bliss of surrender (***prapatti***) to god and exploits of their beloved deity. Among these poets were two known as **Periyāḻvār** (big *āḻvār*) and **Nammāḻvār** (our *āḻvār*). Another, Āṇṭāl, was perhaps the first woman poet in India, certainly the first devotional singer, who likened the relationship with god to that of husband and wife and lover to lover. On the Śaivite side, the *Nāyanmārs* extolled the virtues of Śiva, both his terror (as exemplified in his burning of the three cities) and his grace (*aruḷ*). While there were said to be sixty-three *Nāyaṉmārs*, perhaps in response to the notion of sixty-three Jain teachers, there were, in fact, some six to nine historical figures, some of whom were poets, including those known as **Cundarar**, **Appar**, and **Ñāṉacampantan**. The songs of those poets, Vaiṣṇava and Śaiva, were fluid and retained orally; but, both sets of materials were collected and edited in the eleventh century, the Vaiṣṇava corpus into the *Nālāyira-Divyaprabandham* and the Śaiva corpus into the *Tevāram.*

The work of two of these poets can illustrate the character of their devotion. Nammāḻvār, for example, evoked the creative powers of Viṣṇu in a manner appropriate for a period of transition and "creation" of a more nearly "Hindu" order.

> First, the discus
> rose to view,
>
> then the conch,
>   the long bow,
>   the mace,
> and the sword;

with blessings
from the eight quarters,

he broke through
the egg-shell of heaven,
making the waters bubble;

giant head and giant feet
growing away from each other,
time itself rose to view:
how the lord
paced and measured

all three worlds![4]

Similarly, Nammāḻvār voiced the poet's sense of oneness with his god:

Promising me heaven,
making a pact with me,

today he entered this nest,
this thing of flesh,

himself cleared away
all obstacles
to himself,
all contrary acts . . .[5]

The poet expressed his pleasure at being god's spokesperson:

My lord
who swept me away forever
into joy that day,

made me over into himself
and sang in Tamil
his own songs through me:
what shall I say
to the first of things,
flame
standing there,
what shall I say
to stop?[6]

Māṇikkavācakar, a Śaiva poet, only later accepted as one of the classical *Nayaṉmar* poets and variously dated between the sixth and ninth centuries, co-opted imageries of love and sexuality to describe the relationship with the divine. The natural landscape was sensually described but was thought to fade into insignificance in the presence of the divine. To be "possessed" by the god was like a form of madness – it transcended all other experiences. Relationships with women similarly faded in comparison with the relationship to Śiva. Indeed, the poet was like the beloved who was offered love (*aṉpu*) by the god and united with God as if in sexual union. Māṇikkavācakar described the bliss of being "possessed" by Śiva:

He grabbed me
  lest I go astray.

Wax before an unspent fire,
  mind melted,
  body trembled.

I bowed, I wept,
  danced, cried aloud,
  I sang, and I praised him.

Unyielding, as they say,
  as an elephant's jaw
  or a woman's grasp,
  was love's unrelenting
  seizure.

Love pierced me
  like a nail
    driven into a green tree.

Overflowing, I tossed
  like a sea,

heart growing tender,
  body shivering,

while the world called me Demon!
and laughed at me,

I left shame behind,
took as an ornament,
  the mockery of the local folk.
Unswerving, I lost my cleverness
  in the bewilderment of ecstasy.[7]

The *bhakti* experience as articulated by these singers reflected several patterns at once: first, they used the images of early Tamil poetry to localize the deities. The foliage and landscape of Tamil land was the god's – the god was "here," he had made his home here, learned the language, and established pilgrimage sites here. Similarly, imageries of love mirrored those used by the *caṅkam* poets. "Possession" and "intoxication" reflected the images by which the god made himself known in the "pre-Hindu" context. The poetry and the devotional experience were quintessentially Tamil. Second, the poets selectively appropriated myths from the northern epic setting thereby giving the local variations of the deities "sanskritic" or *vaidika* sanction. Śiva's destruction of the three cities was localized; Viṣṇu was grafted onto Māyōṉ, god of the pastoral tract. Skanda was grafted onto Murukaṉ. Third, the songs were responding to a Jain and Buddhist context, at first with some virulence (especially in the Śaiva case) then by selectively appropriating elements of Jain and Buddhist ethics and ideology. There was evidence in the early generations of poets (especially in the writings of the Śaiva N̄āṉacampantan) of attacks on Jain or Buddhist attitudes, reflecting the attacks of certain Śaivite kings on Buddhist or Jain establishments (such as that at Nāgārjunakonda). Yet, in time, one finds the co-opting of Buddhist or Jain themes – hospitality, a sense of community, etc. At least one deity, Śāstā, emerged in this period as an apparent alternative to the figure of Buddha – Śāstā was teacher; his poses emulated those in earlier Buddhist and Jain iconography; but Śāstā was also a son of Śiva and accessible to help the devotee. Pilgrimage centers made the deities accessible, unlike the reclusive Jain mendicants. Not least important, Buddhist sacred places (*paḷḷis*) became sites for "Hindu" temples.

The *bhakti* poets, in short, expressed a form of Tamil identity that claimed Tamil country for "Hinduism" and placed itself in contradistinction to its religious rivals. These patterns recurred wherever *bhakti* was popular; the vernacular language became the medium of religious expression, albeit enhanced by forms of Sanskritic culture and there was selective appropriation of and distancing from the ideology of "others."

The emergence of temples

A second major illustration of "Hindu" culture in the south was the emergence of the temple as a cultic and social center. Under the Pallavas (seventh to ninth centuries CE) temple construction received a significant impetus, first in the form of monolithic structures carved from rocks – such was the form of the shrines carved at Mahābalipuram, the Pallava seaport, in honor of the Pāṇḍava brothers, those heroes of the *Mahābhārata.*

Figure 2 The Shore Temple at Mahābalipuram, port city of the Pallavas. Photograph by Rob F. Phillips.

These were followed by temples constructed "from scratch," such as the carved shore temple at Mahābalipuram or those at Kāñcīpuram, the Pallava capital. These later temples had come to reflect much of the imagery of brahmanically "orthodox" temples – the tower (***vimāṉa***) was Mt. Meru or the *hiraṇyagarbha* and its parts were named as though it were a human torso. One entered an "omphalos" to reach the inner sanctum or "womb house" (*garbhagṛha*). At the same time, the temple served as a center of a town (*ūr*) and reflected the social and political reciprocities of its elites. For example, in the royal temples, kings, *vēḷāḷas* (landowners), and brahmans expressed their political-social reciprocities in the ritual life of the temple. Donations were made by landowners and royalty, both male and female; honors were afforded these patrons and the gifts and/or land were redistributed. In effect, the temple became an economic as well as a social and cultural space.[8]

By the time the Cōḻas had gained hegemony in the South (ninth to thirteenth centuries CE), with their capital in the Kāvēri basin, the temple had become a major institution. Architecturally, by the twelfth century the ***kōpuram*** (Skt: ***gopura*** – entrance way) came to be the dominant tower on the temple precincts, thanks to the donations of nobility and wealthy patrons, though, in some temples, such as at Citamparam, the central tower (*vimāṉa*) was gilded in gold. The Cōḻas were patrons of Śiva, but in an effort to incorporate rural areas under their hegemony, local village goddesses were made part of the royal cultus, the goddess thus serving as the consort of Śiva. Under the Cōḻas, iconography, especially bronze castings, became both an art form and a focus of ritual. Among the representations of the divine that became noted during the Cōḻa period was a bronze casting of Pārvatī, Śiva's consort, cast in the image of a Cōḻa queen. Even more enduring was the representation of Nāṭārajaṉ, the dancing Śiva, the presiding deity at Citamparam. Nāṭārajaṉ's symbology was complex: he had four arms, signifying omnipotence; in one hand he held a drum, promulgating the rhythm of the universe; his two dancing legs suggested both the standing and the moving of the cosmos. He danced within a circle of flames, representing the tradition of sacrifice, but also the circle of the universe, life, and *dharma* to which Śiva was thought to give coherence. He stood on a dwarf, emblematic of malevolence, evil, "chaos." Around him a snake was entwined, suggesting creativity, fertility, and primordiality were controlled by the dancer.

The temple structure itself was made congruent to the human body, not only vertically but also horizontally. Built by *śilpis* who practiced the rules of temple construction, the temple's ritual space became a microcosm, known as the ***vāstupuruṣamaṇḍala*** (a space which is congruent to human and cosmic form). Temples had become the arenas for the enacting of a complex festival and ritual life. Ritual sequences followed a complex chronometry, combining solar, lunar, and constellational markings. The solar year, for example, had its light half (from winter to summer solstice) and its dark half, with the light half thought to be most auspicious. The lunar cycle, similarly, was thought to be most auspicious in its waxing half. The sun was believed to pass through twelve constellations in a year and the moon through twenty-seven constellations (***nakṣatras***) each month. Similarly, the day was congruent to the solar year and had "sacred hours," three before dawn, equated to the period before the winter solstice; six sacred hours occurred between dawn and noon and were homologized to the six months of the sun's "light half." After noon, there was a period of inauspiciousness and ritual abstinence, just as in the three months after the summer solstice, temple festivals were rare. Finally, three hours occurred after dusk and were equated to the period immediately after the fall equinox. Not least important, the career of the deity was "grafted" onto the solar and daily calendar. Each year festivals enacted events in the life of the deity but also occurred at the appropriate juncture of the solar calendar, the full moon, and the lunar constellation (*nakṣatra*). Each temple kept its own festival calendar. In the Citamparam Temple, for example, at least by the eleventh century, two festivals had assumed major significance: an anointing festival in December–January (*mārkaḻi*) and a festival immediately after the summer solstice in June to July (*aṉi*).[9] By the fourteenth century in that temple a full annual festival cycle was in place.[10]

Similarly, each day, in fully brahmanized temples, the deity embodied in its icon would be awakened, brought to full empowerment, whence it would give out its energies to devotees, then would be retired at night. The rituals addressed to the icon in a given day could include:

1) anointing (*abhiṣeka*) with water, milk, fragrances, etc;
2) dressing (***vastra***) the icon;
3) adornment (*alaṅkāram*; Skt: *alaṃkāra*) with jewelry, garlands, etc. At this point in the ritual, the icon was thought to be fully sacralized. The rituals that followed may include praising with the deity's 1,000 names (***lakṣārcana***); offerings and gift-giving (*arccaṉai*; Skt: ***arcana***); and the showing of lights in adoration of the deity (*arātaṉai*).

The Cōḻas

The Cōḻa period was one of intensive Sanskritization in the south. Brahmans who lived in *brahmadeyas* and radiated their culture outward were the primary bearers of the Sanskritic stream of culture and religion. Many geographic places were given Sanskrit names and considerable Sanskritic literature appeared during this period. This literature included the continuation of the Purāṇic corpus, started during the Gupta period. During the eighth to tenth centuries stories were collected in the south and made part of the other *Purāṇas* even up to the seventeenth century. Another product of the southern priesthood was the collecting and writing of the ***āgamas*** (ritual handbooks). These "texts" started as material passed on orally from father to son, which was then written *post facto*, first in the vernacular, then finally in Sanskrit, usually under the aegis of a king or patron who preferred the ritual system of one temple over that of another. This process of collecting and writing such handbooks continued from the eighth to the seventeenth centuries. They were generally collected into three sets: the *Śaivāgamas*, some twenty-eight in number, represented the ritual possibilities used in temples to Śiva. Rituals in temples to Viṣṇu were represented in two separate ritual traditions: the *Pāñcarātrāgamas* (literally, "five nights") and the *Vaikānasāgamas*, a more conservative set of ritual formulations.

Another collection of materials making their way into written form, more commonly in Tamil, were the ***tālapurāṇas***, the story of sacred places. Starting as oral accounts of the history and mythology of a temple or pilgrimage site, these narrations purported to tell the exploits of a deity at a particular spot and of wondrous deeds done by worshipers and pilgrims to that place. These stories were eventually recorded at least until the fifteenth century.[11]

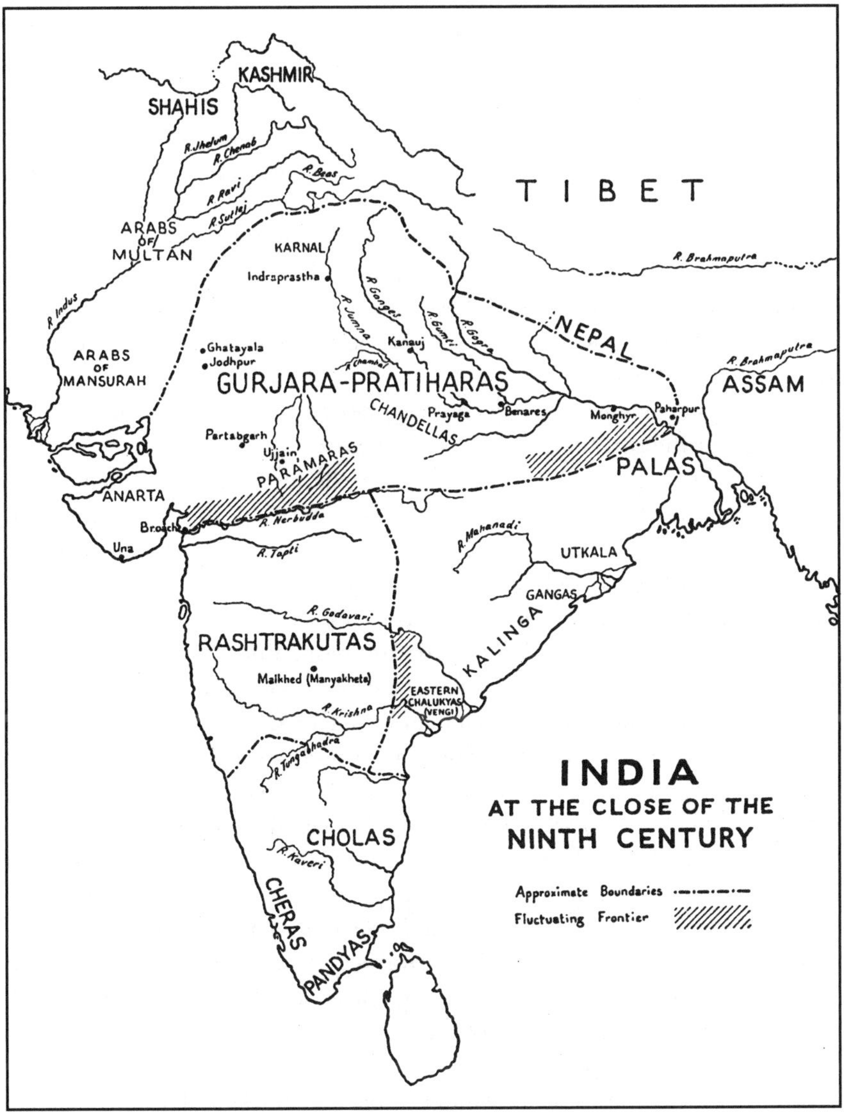

Map 3 India at the Close of the Ninth Century

Reprinted from *A Cultural History of India*, ed. by A. L. Basham (Clarendon Press, 1975), p. 589, by permission of Oxford University Press.

It is worth noting that the written records, whether they were ritual manuals or stories of temple sites, owed not a little to "folk" or non-classical sources. The *āgamas*, for example, while they described what brahman priests did (or should have done) in temple rituals, made allusions to rituals that must have had agricultural or non-Vedic antecedents. These included, among others, descriptions of water libations, the use of earthen vessels, and the use of various natural phenomena in worship like fruits, leaves, and sacred stones. Such practices must have had their roots in the Dravidian context, but in the hands of brahman priests were given a *vaidika* imprimatur. This process has moved at least one scholar to suggest these temple rituals were a compromise between Vedic and "folk" practice.[12] Similarly, *tālapurāṇas* which purported to tell the story of specific temples and their sites incorporated many elements that reflected long-standing Tamil perceptions of landscapes. These included the sacrality of land and its creativity and/or malevolence; the goddess as personification of land and her/its need to be pacified; and sacrifice as an element in the practice of religion; and others.[13]

The Cōḻa period also marked certain other developments in the religious landscape of the south. Monastic cells (***maṭams***; Skt: ***maṭha***) became established as schools or centers for study and meditation, often in alliance with certain temples. These *maṭams* were not unanimous in their teachings and often were in competition with each other for enrollees. Another significant development in the period was the way Śaivite culture was spread particularly into Southeast Asia. As Theravāda Buddhist culture emanated out of Sri Lanka, into Burma, Thailand, and Cambodia, Buddhist kings would set up capitals, palaces, and temples in such cities as Polonnaravu (Sri Lanka), Pagan (Burma), and Ayuthya (Thailand). These kings often turned to the brahmanic advisers of the Pallava or Cōḻa households for advice in building such structures. Those advisers who were Śaiva took with them the principles found eventually in the *Śaivāgamas*, while Vaiṣṇava forms often emulated the styles of the Pallavas. The result was a Hindu-Buddhist architecture and iconography in much of Southeast Asia.

It would be a mistake to assume that the religious landscape of South India was monolithic. Not only were there rivalries between *maṭams* and between Śaivas and Vaiṣṇavas. There were also pockets of Buddhists that remained, especially further north in such centers as Amarāvatī, now in Andhra Pradesh. Islamic settlements had also appeared by the eighth century, especially on the southwest coast and had become pockets of Islamic culture. Small Jewish and Christian settlements were also to be found in the area now known as Kerala (we will explore more of these minority groups later). Even within "Hindu" circles there were movements of protest and reinterpretation. One of these movements was known as the *ciṭṭars* (Skt: *siddhas*) – a group of mendicant ascetics who claimed to worship Śiva, yet eschewed visits to temples. Rather, they lived in isolated areas (such as where Jain monks had once lived) practiced forms of indigenous medicine and mysticism. The body, though considered defiled, nonetheless could be the medium through which the divine could be accessed. Another group of

Figure 3 Gopura at Bhramarambha Mallikarjuna Temple in Srisailam, Andhra Pradesh – Srisailam is the primary pilgrimage center of the Vīraśaivas. Photograph by Rob. F. Phillips.

Figure 4 Gopura at Srisailam: closer view. Photograph by Rob F. Phillips.

"rebels" were the Vīraśaivas, found in the hills of Karnataka and Andhra Pradesh. While probably rooted in forms of "folk" religion and trading communities, they were apparently tutored by *smārta* brahmans, so that by the tenth century they had become a discernible movement. The movement was led by poets – singers who critiqued temples as the domain of the rich, and brahmans for their hypocrisy and corruption. For the Vīraśaivas, Śiva was found in natural settings and could be embodied in small *liṅgas* (aniconic representations of Śiva) worn around the neck.[14]

Deities as reflections of cultural history

The religious-cultural history of South India (and for that matter, other parts of India) were often reflected in myths about the deities. In fact, a number of deities were coming into being or rising in popularity in various parts of India during this period. One who attained popularity throughout India (and not only in the south) was Ganeṣa, the elephant-headed "elder" son of Śiva. Ganeṣa came to represent the embodiment of "wisdom" and was worshiped as one who blessed "new beginnings," but his roots were probably to be found in a variety of pre-Hindu sources. These probably included the ways the elephant was honored in different settings, for example, as a totemic object in tribal or forested areas and as a symbol of royalty (for it was used as a mount for kings in battle or in royal displays). Whatever the origins, Ganeṣa was depicted iconographically by at least the sixth century CE[15] and became thereafter a permanent part of the pantheon, especially as a member of Śiva's family.

Another deity which arose to some significance after the sixth century and became especially popular in the area now known as Kerala is the deity known variously as Aiyaṉ or Śāstā. His story illustrates the way the symbolism of a deity can reflect its cultural history. Prior to the sixth century, the honorific term *ai* referred to heroic hunter figures or to honored Jain or Buddhist monks. Once divinized as Śāstā he was presented as a son of Śiva and a teacher par excellence making him a Hindu alternative to the Buddha and, in Kerala, as Aiyaṉ, a hunter par excellence, a deity of tribal peoples and protector on the fringes of villages. By the early medieval period, myths depict him as the son of Śiva and Viṣṇu (the latter in the form of the feminine Mohinī) and ascribe to him the name Hariharaputra (the son of Śiva and Viṣṇu). How does the birth of Hariharaputra reflect the cultural history of Kerala? One finds a rapprochement occurring there in this period between Śaiva and Vaiṣṇava communities perhaps in the face of Islamic and Christian settlements. Indeed most temples in Kerala by the twelfth century had combined Śaiva and Vaiṣṇava motifs and shared a common ritual tradition. Another factor may be reflected in the myth: apparently, during this period, the Nayars, a major landowning group in Kerala, were becoming matrilineal while the menfolk were off fighting. The Nayar women who were primarily Vaiṣṇava developed relationships with Nambūdiri (Śaiva brahman) men. The sons of these alliances alone were deemed fit to serve as kings in Kerala.[16] Yet another factor may have given the myth a political significance. Certain royal houses in Kerala may have found legitimation by linking their regime to that of the Hoysalas, a dynasty headquartered in Karnataka, where they had patronized Harihara (Śiva-Viṣṇu in combined form). Hence, the "son" of Harihara extended the power and authority of the earlier dynasty into the "newer" dynasty which patronized him. In a similar way, many variations on the birth, incarnation, and exploits of the deity reflected the self-perceptions of many communities: of tribals, for example, who claim the deity impregnated an ancestor or the toddy tappers who maintained the god once drank toddy to "save the world," hence was "one of us." Stories about the gods, like those about sacred places, often reflected the perceptions and social history of those who perpetuated the myths.[17]

Philosophical developments

South India was the arena in which significant philosophical and theological reflection occurred. These speculations often took the form of discourses, even arguments, between various communities, including Buddhists, Vaiṣṇavas, and Śaivas. The "primal insight" (***mūlamantra***) was usually given by a particular *guru* on the basis of experience. This insight would result in aphorisms and cryptic couplets (***sūtras***) often in poetic language. Then, on the basis of discussion and dialectic, elaborations and explanations would occur (***śāstras***). Finally, arguments and/or polemics (***tīkā***) would develop in which one viewpoint was defended over against another.

The reflection of two schools of thought rooted in the south will illustrate these "philosophical" developments. One tradition is associated with Śaivism and the other with Śrī Vaiṣṇavism, the primarily brahmanical sect in which Viṣṇu and his consort Śrī are worshipped. First, the Śaiva alternative.

Śaiva Siddhānta

Around the eleventh century CE one **Meykaṇṭar Tēvar**, a Tamil *vēḷāḷa* (a landowning community), articulated a theological system that came to be known as Śaiva Siddhānta.[18] His thought was rooted in the belief system of the earlier Śaiva ***bhaktas*** but was expressed in terse Tamil couplets, known as the *Śivajñānapōtam.* The devotional experience formed the basis for the intellectual system which then gave further legitimation to devotionalism. Here, as in many Indian schools, it was experience – that is, understanding with proper insight – that constituted the most effective way into comprehending what the universe was about.

In Śaiva Siddhānta – there were three fundamental concepts. The first concept was the divine (***pati***). The divine could take an abstract, aniconic, or non-anthropomorphic form (***civam***) such as may be expressed in the *liṅgam* (the creative principle embodied in a pillar). The divine could also take concrete form (***civaṉ***) such as in a particular manifestation of the deity as in Nāṭarajaṉ (the dancing Śiva). This form of the deity was considered active and expressed itself in five ways: creation, preservation, destruction, concealment, revelation or discernment.

The second basic concept was ***pacu*** ("soul," but literally, "cow"). The "soul" took on the character or form of that to which it was attached. The "souls" of all human beings were "attached" to the bonds of existence, hence unable by nature to relate to and become like the deity.

The third concept was ***pāca*** (the bonds of existence). These bonds constituted the fundamental problem of human being. These bonds were three in number: egocentricity (***āṇava***) – this was the orientation of one's life by selfishness and the will to have one's own way; *māyā* – this was the tendency to overvalue the "tangible world"; and *karmaṉ* – the principle of causation which, because it was ill-trained, tended to keep one attached to the bonds.

The goal of existence was to become attached to the lord (*pati*) through the grace (*aruḷ*) of god. The *summum bonum* of the religious experience was for the soul and the lord to become inseparable as in a new compound. Several analogies were used for this experience: it was like iron filings on the magnet; or like the fragrance of the flower – different from it but inseparable from it. One could attain this experience in a variety of ways, but most commonly, it occurred through *darśan* (viewing the deity) after the temple ritual sequences. The experience was illustrated in the context of worship in a temple when the foot of the deity (in the form of a crown) was placed on the head of the devotee.

Vedānta

The other major school rooted in the south is known as Vedānta (that is, the "end" or culmination of the *Vedas*) or Advaita (non-dualism) and its variants. This school was rooted in the *Upaniṣads* and was associated with the brahmans of the Śrī Vaiṣṇava sect. It was influenced by several sources, including the *Viṣṇu Purāṇa*, the *Bhagavadgītā*, and, not least important, the songs of the Tamil *Āḻvārs*. While the term ***advaita*** literally means monism or non-dualism, there are, in fact, several variations within the tradition.

The start of this school is ascribed to one **Bādarāyana** (apparently not a South Indian), who is said to have compiled the *Vedānta Sūtras* around the second century CE as a form of commentary on selected *Upaniṣads*. The tradition was maintained and refined in the south primarily by a succession of ***ācāryās***, that is, priests who were also preceptors or tutors affiliated with Śrīvaiṣṇava temples. One of the early *ācāryās* was **Yāmuna** (ninth century?), who was followed in succession by others, including the famed theologian Rāmānuja, who was associated with the temple at Śrīraṅgam, and **Madhva**, a dualist who became especially popular in Karnataka. An important figure in this intellectual climate was Śaṅkara (or *Śaṁkara*), an eighth-century brahman from Kerala, who eschewed the life of a householder and of a priest-preceptor in order to become a *saṃnyāsin*, a celibate-seeker cum teacher. Eventually, Śaṅkara is claimed by Śaivites and especially by *smārta* brahmans as the teacher par excellence and an "incarnation" of Śiva.

Most of the advaitin thinkers shared certain common principles.[19] The universe had as its fundamental essence *brahman*. *Brahman*, once the formless, nameless reality of the early *Upaniṣads*, is now understood to be either aniconic and formless or iconic – that is, manifested in specific forms. Hence, most agreed that specific deities were manifestations of *brahman*. Similarly, there was the individualized form of *brahman*, that is, *ātman*, which in its natural state was one with *brahman*, but for most human beings existed in "bondage" within organisms. The *ātman* was involved in the world because of *avidyā*, the inability to discern the reality about existence. The world was an expression of *brahman*, it was derived from *brahman*, and/or was pervaded by *brahman*. However, for some, such as Śaṅkara, the world was less "pure," even only relatively "real" insofar as it was considerably removed from its source.

How does one know the truth? In two ways – through "experience," that is, through intuitive wisdom or enlightenment, but also through the sacred texts especially those that are *śruti* (heard or revealed). More specifically, the *Upaniṣads* were revealed and were thus self-validating but also were validated by experience. Other *smṛti* literature was cited by some as authoritative (e.g., the *Bhagavadgītā* or the *Ālvārs*).

The ultimate destiny to which one should aspire was *moksa* (union with *brahman*). **Bhāskaran** insisted only brahmans could attain *mokṣa*, but Rāmānuja maintained any and all could approach the deity. Most of the proponents of the school, however, tended to exclude *śūdras* from those eligible for *mokṣa*.

Most believed there was logic to the cycle of life. *Samsāra*, the continual cycle of life, death, and rebirth could be sorrowful inasmuch as it could lead to a "second death." The logic of *karma* could affect one's birth and rebirth, a matter that critics point out becomes self-serving for brahmans to maintain. Most of them accepted the Purāṇic imagery of massive cosmic cycles of evolution and devolution known as ***yugas***; replicated in smaller cycles of time, down to moments within the day. There is a desirability of breaking through to *mokṣa* at moments which serve as the junctions of these cycles.

There was also a hierarchy of space – there was a center to the world, that is, "Mt. Meru" – where the gods reside. There were then mythical concentric circles of the universe (land, ocean, land, ocean, etc.) – the further one was from the center the further into chaos and away from the sacred center. The implication of the cosmology was that cities and temples were to reflect this pattern: temples were at the center of a city; brahmans lived near that center; while outcastes were to live on the fringes.

Enlightenment was generally thought to occur in stages. As one gained insight one saw the earlier stages as less helpful; hence one's perceptions of the world and social reality change as one neared fuller consciousness. These stages of consciousness were likened to stages of wakefulness (when one is caught up in the affairs of the world); to that of sleep when one dreams and hence retains perceptions and memories of the world; to deep sleep wherein such perceptions have been left behind. The ultimate state of consciousness or bliss was known as ***turiya***.

Individual members of the Vedānta school obviously made their own contributions and diverged to varying degrees from the above consensus. It is worth looking briefly at two of the most creative of South India's thinkers – Śaṅkara and Rāmānuja.

Śaṅkara was born a Nambudiri brahman around 788 CE in Kerala. Clearly a prodigy, tradition claims he was initiated into Vedic learning at the age of seven and within two years had mastered much of the tradition. Early in his youth, the tradition continues, he persuaded his mother to let him become a *samṇyasi* without having to become a householder first. He is said to have had teachers who were influenced by a Buddhist heritage. **Gaudapāda**, for example, one of his gurus, had been influenced by **Bhāvāvineka**, a Buddhist philosopher.[20] In short, Śaṅkara may have been indirectly influenced by a line of such Buddhist thinkers as Aśvaghoṣa, **Vasubandhu**, and especially Nāgārjuna. Indeed, his contemporary and rival, Bhāskaran, called him a crypto-Buddhist. In fact, Śaṅkara wrote commentaries on certain of the *Upaniṣads* and sought to base his reflections on those texts while appropriating some quasi-Buddhist ideas. The end result of his lifetime was his ability to outthink the alternative discussants of his day, including Buddhist ones and thereby, in effect, pulling the intellectual rug out from under Buddhist speculation and linking brahmanic speculation more persuasively to the Upaniṣadic sages. It could be argued that Śaṅkara was the brightest mind of his century in the world.

It is impossible to do justice to Śaṅkara's system in a brief space. Among other things, he argued that the world, and the self as well, were derived from *brahman*. The world was created at the act of *brahman*, but the result was less nearly "real" or "pure" than the source just as curds, though derived from milk, are less "pure" than the source. Hence, there were two forms of reality: ***vyavahāra*** – the manifold or phenomenal world; the many (a concept stressed by Rāmānuja); and ***paramātman*** – the one supreme *ātman* – that "reality" stressed by Śaṅkara. *Māyā* described our misunderstanding of the world, our propensity to think a rope is a snake, to assume what we see is ultimate. *Avidyā* (ignorance) caused one to think the world was ultimate, when, in fact, as one's consciousness was raised, one saw the world as having been derived from *brahman*. Śaṅkara's sense of the ultimate was ***nirguṇa*** – that which was without attributes. His followers, however, especially *smārta* brahmans insisted he believed that several specific deities (***saguṇa***), representing the various sectarian options of the time, were personifications of the absolute (*nirguṇa*), and that these deities were thought to reside within one.

For Śaṅkara, perceptions (*pratyāhāra*) were of different kinds: ***śabda***, for example, was perception through inner understanding (i.e., *jñāna* or *buddhi*). *Anusaṃdhāna* was "reflective consciousness," while ***anumāna*** was inference. *Anubhava* was to know the oneness of all things, an awareness that came at the highest stage of consciousness (*turīya*). Śaṅkara was a strict monist – everything was of one nature, though that which was derived was inferior to its source.

Śaṅkara is said to have traveled throughout India and to have established at least four monasteries (*maṭham*) including in Kāśī (Banāras), Śriṅgeri in Southwestern India, and at Kāñcīpuram near what is now Chennai (Madras). He is said to have died by the age of thirty-two but left behind a legacy still being interpreted by commentators and scholars alike.

Rāmānuja was of very different background. He was an *ācāryā* (priest-preceptor) in the famed Vaiṣṇava temple in Śrīraṅkam, son of an *ācāryā* and a disciple of Yāmuna. Rāmānuja sought to give the worship of a personal god a "philosophical" basis.[21] That is, he was perhaps India's greatest "theologian." He based his ideas on the songs of *Āḻvārs*, on the later theistic *Upaniṣads*, and especially the *Īśā* and *Śvetāśvatara Upaniṣads*, on the *Bhagavadgītā* and those *Purāṇas* relating to the exploits and worship of Viṣṇu.

For Rāmānuja, *brahman* was both formless (*puruṣa*) and accessible in various forms (*prakṛti*). The world was the form, the extension of god, like a paintbrush in the hand of an artist and the painting once completed. Hence, creation was the rhythm and energy of god and the phenomenal world was relatively good because it was a manifestation of the divine. The divine had its own forms (***svarūpa***) and those forms were many. Moreover, the divine had at least six functions in relation to the world: providence – that is, god was constantly interacting with the world; heroism (***vīrya***); majesty or prestige (***tejas***); power (*bala*); creativity (*śakti*); and omniscience (*jñāna*).

Rāmānuja is famed for his articulation of the two forms of grace operative in *bhakti*. Using analogies already known, he suggested, on the one hand, there was "cat grace" – the grace of "faith." The kitten surrenders itself to its mother, who picks it up by the scruff of its neck. So too was the grace of god – it is freely given, the divine does the work while the devotee surrenders in an act known as *prapatti*. He suggested this is most appropriate for followers of Viṣṇu.

The other kind of grace was "monkey grace" – the grace of "works." In this case the young monkey clings to its mother's fur. So too does the devotee work to experience divine grace. By doing certain deeds one could attain the deity's grace. *Prasāda* was a way of mediating grace – it is exemplified in the priest's sharing of the offerings with gathered devotees after the completion of a temple ritual.

Rāmānuja was responsible for the spread of Vaiṣṇavism in the south. Several temples were converted. It was also after Rāmānuja's time that virtually all deities, represented iconographically in the south, were given *two* consorts: one, according to the tradition, representing the devotee who merited the deity's favor, that is, the "grace of works"; the other representing the devotee whose faith was such that the deity bestows his grace freely. Further, while many other of the Śrīvaiṣṇava *ācāryās* believed that spiritual knowledge was available only to brahmans, Rāmānuja is said to have shared his ideas even with dalits, some of whom to this day claim Rāmānuja influenced their ancestors.

North India

We return to the northern part of the subcontinent to sketch some of the important developments after the decline of the Gupta dynasty. The reign of **Harṣa** in the Gangetic basin during the seventh century – a reign noted for its stability and patronage of various religious institutions – was perhaps the last relatively stable period in the north for some centuries. A Chinese pilgrim, **Hsüan Tsang**, reported that Buddhist institutions continued to flourish under Harṣa, not least important Nālandā "university," which had been founded in the Gupta period and had come to attract scholars from other parts of Asia.[22] With the decline of Harṣa's line, however, the north reverted to the rise of regional satrapis, vying for hegemony and expansion. The eighth through the twelfth centuries were marked by intermittent warfare and relative instability. Three clans, in particular, waxed and waned in importance: the Pratihāras, the Pālas, and Rāṣṭrakūṭas. Moreover, by the tenth century at least, hill kingdoms and small city-states had developed in such border areas as Assam, Nepal, and Kashmīr. There was in many respects a return to the classical style of the city-state of the urban period. Regionalism had taken precedence over empire, though in many instances local languages had not yet crystallized.

One of the "new" players on the scene of Northwest India were the Rājputs. The Rājputs were apparently of foreign origin – some scholars have even suggested they were descendants of the "Huns"[23] – but in their concern for acceptance and hegemony, they created "pockets" of "Hindu" culture, in some cases outdoing their rivals in orthopraxy. Brahmans were invited to become ministers in their courts to serve as rhetoricians and public relations agents. The brahmans were given land and the right to become kingmakers and to rhetorically claim *kṣatriya* status for Rājput rulers. There were several consequences of this alliance: Sanskrit became the lingua franca of the courts and there were attempts to copy earlier forms of literature and "dharmic culture." In the early years of the Rājputs these cultural expressions were more neo-classical than innovative and until the twelfth century the vernaculars remained underdeveloped under their aegis. There was a proliferation of sub-castes with a division of labor and a hierarchy that tended to become increasingly rigidified wherein upward mobility was rare.[24] The Rājputs viewed themselves not only as *kṣatriyas* but also as heroic (*vīrya*) warriors. As part of their attempt to maintain that image and to demonstrate Hindu orthopraxy, the widows in certain of the families by the fourteenth century were often expected to immolate themselves on the funeral pyres of their dead husbands in the practice known as *satī*.

The Hindu chieftains and would-be kings of the north practiced a strategy for retaining hegemony not unlike that of the Cōḻas in the south. Most particularly, there were three principal activities: 1) Brahmans were given land grants and invited to be the court advisers and public relations agents. This would assure that *vaidika* culture was preserved and provide a "religious umbrella" for all the peoples in the domain. 2) In some instances, large temples were built to institutionalize the royal cult and serve as a centralizing monument for the monarch. 3) Local deities, and especially goddesses, were incorporated into the royal cult. In Orissa, for example, even as early as the sixth century royal donations were made at the shrines of Maninageśvarī ("Goddess of the jewel serpent") and of Stambheśvarī ("Goddess of the pillar").[25] These acts of patronage served to give royal sanction to important pilgrimage sites and incorporate into the kingdom those folk and village communities for whom these goddesses were important. We will explore these developments further.

Temple construction

There were at least five areas in which temple construction and/or art proliferated in North India, especially between the ninth and twelfth centuries. These were often in the domains governed by rulers who sought to leave their stamp on the landscape. In Orissa, the Kaliṅgas patronized the building of impressive temples from 750 to 1250 CE in Puri, Bhubaneśwara, and Konārak. Both Bhubaneśwara and Konārak had been centers of Buddhism, so it is not coincidental that these sites became the centers of Hindu *dharma*. Local kings, in fact, sought to outdo each other and mandated that *śilpis* spend their entire lives on a single temple. The Rājputs patronized the construction of temples near Jodhpur, Rajasthan, between the eighth and ninth centuries, but most of these monuments were destroyed by various invaders. Khajurāho became another important center for temple architecture from 950–1050, thanks to the patronage of the Candellas, a Rājput clan. The Rāṣṭrakūṭas oversaw the construction of temples, including that of Kailāsanātha, near Ellora, in the late eighth century.[26] In the meanwhile, Ellorā, near Ajantā in Maharashtra, where Buddhist monks had lived in caves and had overseen an explosion of Buddhist art, became a center, not so much for the construction of temples, but where Hindu sculpting and paintings appeared between the seventh and ninth centuries.

Traditional patterns informed the architecture and ritual life of these temples. Aesthetically, the temple embodied *rasa* – the "flavor" of *brahman* – and was intended to invite the devotee to experience the flavor of the divine. Many temples, especially those at Khajurāho and Bhubaneśwara, presented a multiplicity of symmetry and sacral spaces. The temple was a microcosm both horizontally and vertically: the tower in the north was called a *śikhara* and was often curvilinear, though like those of the south, was congruent to the human torso, and its parts were even assigned names usually associated with the body. The temples also reflected the socio-political reciprocities of the domains of the patron-king. There were reciprocities and exchange of gifts and honors between royalty, sectarian leaders, and landowners and various concessions or additions made to alternate groups or patrons. The temple, that is, was also a socio-cultural space which mirrored the identities of its users. A full ritual life was possible within the temple environs. There was dramatization of āgamic rules, for example, the notions of circumambulation and concentricity. That is, space was increasingly sacralized the more one approached the center. The devotee moved inward and upward by virtue of the architecture; the energy and grace of the deity flow outward and "downward."

The architecture of such temples as that of Konārak and Khajurāho is replete with erotic sculpting on the outer face. These external sculptures were intended to demonstrate the wide variety of practices being incorporated into the ambiance of the temple. On some temple exteriors (for example, the Rāmappa Temple in northern Andhra Pradesh), one finds ascetics, probably Jain, side by side with copulating couples. The erotic imagery was probably the result of incorporating tantric motifs into the architecture of the temple. Tantrism was being "domesticated" and made part of the classical tradition throughout India but especially by the ninth to tenth centuries in the north. Tantrism was a significant variation of religious expression and is worth some consideration.

Tantrism

The origins of tantrism are probably beyond reconstruction. Suffice it to say that it appeared to combine "folk" and *vaidika* features and that it was undoubtedly practiced for centuries by groups who were outside the orthoprax mainstream. Its "folk" roots may be linked in an agricultural respect for soil and furrow but manifest themselves in veneration of the female genitalia. The famed "squatting goddess," Lajjā Gauri, for example, apparently represented this early relation between furrow and vagina. She was the goddess seated on her haunches, naked, her genitalia clearly visible – the earliest forms of this figure found to date in the upper Deccan plateau are first century CE.[27] Also part of this "folk" background was the belief that one could be "possessed" by the deity, or, more accurately perhaps, become one with the goddess. Tantrics further affirmed the senses (long eschewed by the orthoprax as "distracting") and celebrated all of matter, including things the orthoprax thought defiled, such as meat and liquor. Tantrics assumed the divine was present in all such things and hence they could be used ritually.

Mixed with these "folk" elements are aspects which have their roots in *vaidika* practice. This included the ritual use of sounds. Sound had cosmogonic power; hence, chants or ***mantras*** were thought to link one to the cosmos at large. *Vidyā* ("magical speech") was used in tantric ritual. This included meditation on a cryptic sentence and directing chants to the deity, almost always a goddess. Further, the body could be used symbolically in ways that resonate with the yogic tradition – winds were thought able to move from various *cakras* (centers on the body) through mythical veins. Gestures (*mudrās*) were used ritually as were postures (*āsanas*) of various kinds. *Prāṇayama* (breath control) was similarly borrowed from *haṭha yoga.* The body, in short, was congruent to the universe and to the alphabet of sounds and to the deities.

In tantra, a man usually worked with a *guru*, often female, who was believed to be able to lead the devotee to liberation and the use of occult powers. The culmination of the tantric experience was the reattainment of primordial androgyny, the collapsing of distinctions between separate selves, between males and females, and between deity and devotee. This was ritually expressed by sexual union in which no bodily fluids were ejected. Rather the couple became one.

Hindu tantrics understood their discipline to have seven steps. The first three were common to most Hindu devotees and included basic devotion to Viṣṇu and meditation on Śiva. The fourth stage, sometimes referred to as right handed worship (*dakṣinācāra*) entailed worship of the supreme goddess in ways consistent with orthoprax patterns. It is in the next stage, "left handed" worship (*vāmācāra*) when ritual use of the five "m's" assumed a significant role: *maṁsa* (meat); *matsya* (fish); *mudrā* (fried rice); *mada* (intoxicants); *maithuna* (intercourse). These practices were developed with the careful guidance of a guru and were accompanied by a complex system of symbols, including the use of geometric designs (***yantra***) and special points on the body (*cakra*). While these practices were mastered in secrecy, at the next stage one would "go public" inasmuch as the initiant had come to understand there was no distinction between the pure and the impure. Finally, one could reach the final stage (*kulācāra*) when all distinctions were believed to have been transcended.[28]

Tantrism became a part of Jain and Buddhist practice as well. In Buddhism, in fact, a new school emerged around the sixth century CE known as *Vajrayāna*. It is the school that made its way into Tibet where it was grafted onto the indigenous religion known as Bon. Like "Hindu" forms of tantrism, Buddhist tantra used body imagery and sounds and understood all of matter, including alleged defilements, to be sacred. The rationale in Buddhism, however, differed. It was rooted in the doctrine of *śūnyatā* wherein matter (*samsāra*) and *nirvāṇa* were rendered homologous since neither had its own existence (*svabhāva*). Further, the female principle was not perceived to be a goddess (except later in Tibetan forms of Vajrayāna). Rather, feminine forms were used to personify certain Buddhist perfections, such as wisdom or compassion. One did not worship these feminine forms so much as seek to emulate them or subsume their attributes. Further, the feminine forms were sometimes juxtaposed with masculine ones as in *prajñā/puruṣa* (wisdom/spirit). Hence, in ritual coitus, the distinctions between male and female and of all opposites were collapsed. One became the other; one assumed the attributes of those perfections rendered in male or female form.

It seems likely that tantrism flourished especially in border regions – such as Assam, Northern Bengal, and Northwest India – which were not systematically Hinduized prior to the tenth century. By the ninth and tenth centuries, as such areas were brahmanized, there was assimilation of foreign and/or "offbeat" expressions; families and clans who were previously obscure and outside the circles of power were now being given land grants or in other ways being incorporated into the body politic.[29] Now increasingly, tantric imageries made their way into temple sculptures and architectural symbolism; for example, the icon, at least in Śaiva temples, was the *liṅga* or male principle; the pedestal in which it was set was the *yonī* or female principle. Tantrism had to some extent been "domesticated" and made part of the brahmanic synthesis.

The rise of the goddesses to "high deity" status

One of the significant developments in the religious life of the subcontinent during the period under discussion was the emergence of goddesses to the status of "high deity." Up until about the sixth century CE, goddesses had appeared in classical contexts but in relatively subsidiary roles – for example, as consorts, wives, adoptive mothers, and attendants in urban complexes of the Gangetic basin. There was, of course, evidence of goddess worship in agricultural settings from early times – from the Atharvavedic hymn of praise to Pṛthvī, and terra-cotta representations of fertility goddesses in the first two millennia BCE to the iconography of the naked "squatting goddess" in the Deccan by the first century CE. Now these disparate streams were merging to propel the goddess into a place of supremacy she had not theretofore achieved. There appear to be several reasons for this development: 1) The increased visibility of "folk" and tribal communities in areas that had thereto not been fully integrated. Many of these communities were worshiping goddesses of particular places, of natural powers (e.g., diseases) or of particular families. 2) The propensity of kings and other would-be patrons to incorporate such people into their domain by "co-opting" their deities into the official cultus. Such was the case, for example, in Orissa and in the Cōḻa courts of South India, where the royal cult of Śiva was given a bride derived from the rural landscape. 3) The employment of brahmans in the courts and in public contexts who were prepared to make "connections" (*bandhu*) – that is, to link the "new" deities to the legitimating older ones. 4) The likelihood that goddesses became one strategy by which Hinduism came to replace Buddhism in several settings. There is evidence, for example, that shrines to the goddess were established occasionally on the site of Buddhist *paḷḷis* (sacred places) – Bhāgavatī shrines in Kerala are a case in point. These "replacements" were not necessarily arbitrary. Goddesses could personify those attributes (prosperity, creativity, etc.) deemed auspicious to *vaidika* adherents just as female icons had come to embody perfections and attributes within Buddhism. Further, the Buddhist understanding of the world with its ambiguities and dis-ease could be personified in the person of a goddess who represented the forces of nature and the ambiguous, even hostile, powers of the world. Such may have been the case with Durgā, emerging by the tenth century in Bengal, possibly representing a Hindu personification of *duḥkha,* the Buddhist term for the unsatisfactoriness of the world.[30] 5) The increased visibility of tantrism, especially in such places as Bengal, with its worship of the female form, almost certainly lent impetus to the classicalization of a powerful goddess figure. 6) Finally, one can identify a dialect of "self" and "other," when communities or kingdoms sought to differentiate or identify themselves over against other communities or kingdoms. In such dialectics, a mythology of militancy was often evoked – the "*asuras*" were the representations of the "other guys"; in the mythological rhetoric of warfare, "our deity" was more powerful than theirs. The great goddess was presented mythologically as more powerful than those deities who preceded her. Among the "others" being addressed may have been Buddhist, and eventually, Islamic communities.

Whatever the factors, there appeared during this period a Sanskrit text known as the *Devīmāhātmya.* The "text" was a series of myths, first recited, no doubt, in oral form, but reduced to writing somewhat later. The first two cycles of myths, at least – the "birth" of the goddess from the navel of the sleeping Viṣṇu and her battles with troublesome *asuras* such as the buffalo Mahiṣa – were probably datable between the sixth and tenth centuries and represented many of the factors mentioned above: 1) The patronage of a royal house – perhaps the Cālukyas of the Southwestern Deccan where one finds the oldest extant Durgā temple in Aihole and images of Durgā slaying the buffalo and of the squatting goddess (Lajjā Gauri) by the seventh century (though Bengal is another possible venue for such patronage). 2) Mythmakers who used the repertoire of legitimating strategies to announce the exploits of a powerful deity (that is, she was "born" of an authenticating deity, given the weapons of older deities, etc.). 3) Evidence of folk elements being incorporated into the myth. For example, the slaying of the buffalo demon Mahiṣa had a long history in folk culture and was also seen earlier as the protagonist in battles with Skanda. 4) There are even hints of a Buddhist presence in the way the goddess personified such attributes as wealth and prosperity (*lakṣmī*) etc. In any case the *Devīmāhātmya* announced the arrival of the goddess as the most powerful deity on the landscape, and once in place, her persona could be applied to any and all goddesses. Part three of the *Devīmāhātmya,* in fact, does precisely that, indicating how the goddess was indeed an expression of Durgā and Kālī, goddesses which were perceived to have destroyed "demons" associated with Northern India, more than likely Bengal where the third myth of the *Devīmāhātmya* may have been composed.[31]

After the tenth century, temples to goddesses proliferated as did their worship in classical contexts. Local goddesses were linked to those already known in the Sanskritic traditions (seven sisters, Pārvatī, etc.) and assumed a role not theirs hitherto. Such goddesses as Durgā and Kālī had by now entered the "national stage," while another figure – that of Rādhā – had become part of classical culture by the twelfth century. In fact, the story of Rādhā can illustrate something of the way goddesses became increasingly important. For the first six centuries CE she was mentioned only in certain Prākrit sources (that is, in any of several indigenous dialects) and in Jain writings, so she may have been a part of lower class Śaivism and folk culture.[32] She "entered" textualized classical religion in **Jayadeva**'s *Gītagovinda* (twelfth century CE) where she is transfigured from a human cowgirl into a deity. As such, she may represent the opportunity/model for women (such as earlier poets like Āṇṭāl had done) to transcend normal social conventions. In any case, Rādhā came to embody *prakṛti* (matter, earth), the co-eternal essence of the universe; she was also *māyā* (the tangible world and its force), and ***śakti*** – the power of the divine. Not least important, she was lover of Kṛṣṇa, whose dalliances with the divine flautist were enacted in music and dance throughout India. As Kṛṣṇa's consort, she mediated his grace to all and became the embodiment of compassion and the paradigm of the ideal devotee. There are intimations in her story of both tantric and Buddhist themes and, it is generally agreed, that it was in Bengal where her worship, like that of Kālī, was most popular at least until the eighteenth century. It is no coincidence that in Bengal both Buddhism and tantrism had been strong.[33]

Rādhā's assumption of supreme status was not unique to her. Each emergent goddess had her own origins, but once adapted into the classical tradition, she came to embody the power (*śakti*) of the divine, as well as the character of the world's force. Both Kālī and Durgā tend to embody this power in ways that are often seen as potentially malevolent. Kālī, for example, was portrayed as black, tongue extended as in combat, a necklace of skulls. She was the fierce destroyer of her enemies and powerful protector of those who worshiped her. At the same time, for those on good terms with her (as with the world itself), she was mother and sustainer of life.[34]

Buddhism and Jainism

By the fourteenth century, Buddhism had virtually disappeared from the Indian landscape, save for occasional pockets of Buddhist culture. This decline of Buddhism on the subcontinent may be attributed to four factors.

First, there was a migration of monks out of the subcontinent. Many Theravāda monks had begun to migrate as early as the first centuries BCE to Sri Lanka, which had become a stronghold of Theravāda culture and from there that school of Buddhism had spread throughout much of Southeast Asia and especially to Burma, Thailand, and Cambodia. In the meanwhile, Mahāyāna monks, especially of the Mādhyamika and Yogācāra schools, had made their way, starting as early as the first centuries CE, by way of Central Asia to China. By the ninth century, Vajrayāna Buddhism had spread into Tibet. Second, from the time of Śaṅkara, Buddhist intellectual life declined on the subcontinent. "Philosophy" based on the *Upaniṣads* attracted more inquirers; in the meanwhile, Buddhist speculations in China and Southeast Asia were on the rise.

Third, the devotional movement with its appeal to accessible deities concretely available in local places made Hinduism increasingly attractive at the popular level. In fact, in many respects, Buddhism was "absorbed" into popular forms of Hinduism. There is evidence of Hindu temples being built upon the site of Buddhist *paḷḷis*; of Hindu iconography and/or deities appropriating Buddhist motifs; and of Hindu popular literature assimilating Buddhist elements. In some cases, the conversions of Buddhist centers were gradual though probably quite self-conscious. Such was apparently the case with shrines at Bodhgayā, Sārnath, Nāgākoil, Kāñcīpuram, and Nāgārjunakonda. A shrine outside of Mangalore in Karnataka, for example, once devoted to the *bodhisattva* **Avalokiteśvara** became a shrine to "Mañjunātha," a manifestation of the Śiva *liṅga*.[35] Similarly, in a cave outside Nāgārjunakonda, once the home of Buddhist monks, one finds an icon to Viṣṇu as Adiṣesa (the sleeping Viṣṇu), perhaps depicted as a Hindu alternative to the quiescence sought by monks; Viṣṇu, however, unlike the Buddha, would awaken from his quiescence and was accessible to devotees. Similarly, deities such as Śāstā (the teacher), appeared to have been a Hindu alternative to the Buddha and was depicted iconographically in ways that emulated the pose of earlier Buddhist icons. Indeed Buddha came to be seen as an avatar of Viṣṇu. That Buddhist monks may have acquiesced in this process is suggested by Professor Padmanabha Jaini, who reports that only one text was written by Buddhist monks (and that only as late as the eleventh century) offering advice on conduct appropriate for the layperson.[36] Local kings and rulers, for their part, were increasingly inclined to patronize Hinduism at least partially because it had been able to assimilate or accommodate forms of folk and popular religion.

Finally, there were concerted efforts at times to destroy Buddhist institutions. It occurred in South India by the fourth century when Nāgārjunakonda was destroyed by Śaivite warriors. In Kashmīr, such kings as **Nara** and **Mihirakula** destroyed Buddhist establishments. Such destruction of Buddhist institutions was virtually completed by the armies of **Mahmūd of Ghaznī** in the eleventh century and **Timur of Samarkand** in the fourteenth. Even though some of the havoc may have been wrought for political rather than religious reasons, the outcome was the same: Buddhism was virtually gone from the subcontinent by the fourteenth century.

In the meanwhile, Jainism was also threatened by the wave of devotionalism with its accessible deities and colorful ritual life. Jainism, nonetheless, survived for a variety of reasons. Jain monks offered self-conscious alternatives to Hindu popular religion and literature. Unlike the Buddhists, they produced some fifty texts on conduct proper to a Jain layperson.[37] They produced alternative versions of the *Mahābhārata* and *Rāmāyana*, wherein Rāma and Kṛṣṇa were portrayed as Jaina heroes subject to the principles of Jaina ethics and Rāvaṇa was killed, not by Rāma, but by Lakṣmana, so that Rāma could be reborn in heaven for his observance of *ahiṃsa*.[38] Similarly, Hindu deities were to be found in some Jaina temples as "attendants" and/or *tīrthaṅkaras*-in-process. Not least important, in some schools of Jainism, rituals were sanctioned which emulated Hindu *pūjā* in many ways albeit given a Jain legitimation. **Jinasena**'s *Ādipurāna* (ninth century) seems to have been the earliest text mentioning such rituals for the Jain laity.[39] In this ritual tradition, the *tīrthaṅkaras* were depicted in anthropomorphic form and *pūjā* (worship) could be directed to them, not to obtain intercession from them on one's own behalf, but to honor the *tīrthaṅkara*, attain merit in doing so, and to find in him a model for one's own life. Jainism in this form has survived into the present and has remained particularly strong in portions of Rajasthan and Gujarat.

Recommended reading

History, culture, literature of the post-classical period

South India

Balasundaram, T. S. *The Golden Anthology of Ancient Tamil Literature.* Three volumes. Madras: South India Saiva Siddhantha Bombay Publishing Society, 1959–60.
Hart, George L. III. *The Poems of Ancient Tamil.* Berkeley: University of California Press, 1975.
Pillar, K. K. *A Social History of the Tamils.* Second edition. Madras: University of Madras, 1973.
Ramanujan, A. K. tr. *The Interior Landscape.* Bloomington, IN: Indiana University Press, 1969.
Sastri, K. A. N. *History of South India.* Madras: Oxford University Press, 1955.
Shulman, D. D. *Tamil Temple Myths: Sacrifice and Divine Marriage in the South Indian Śaiva Tradition.* Princeton: Princeton University Press, 1980.
Stein, Burton. *Peasant State and Society in Medieval South India.* Delhi: Oxford University Press, 1980.
Zvelebil, K. *The Smile of Murugan.* London: Brill, 1973.

North India

Kulke, Herman. *Kings and Cults: State Formations and Legitimation in India and Southeast Asia.* New Delhi: Manohar, 1993.
Thapar, Romila. *Ancient Indian Social History: Some Interpretations.* New Delhi: Orient Longman, 1978.

Philosophical developments

Banerjee, N. V. *The Spirit of Indian Philosophy.* New Delhi: Munshiram Manoharlal, 1958.

Carman, J. B. *The Theology of Ramānuja, An Essay in Inter-religious Understanding.* New Haven, CT: Yale University Press, 1974.

Cenkner, W. A. *A Tradition of Teachers: Śaṅkara and the Jagadgurus Today.* Delhi: Motilal Banarsidass, 1983.

Das Gupta, S. N. *History of Indian Philosophy, 5 vols.* Third edition. Cambridge: Cambridge University Press, 1961–62.

Devasenapati, V. A. *Śaiva Siddhānta as Expounded in the Sivajñāna Siddhiyar and its Six Commentaries.* Madras: University of Madras, 1960.

Devasenapati, V. A. *Of Human Bondage and Divine Grace.* Annamalai: Annamalai University Press, 1963.

Feurstein, G. *The Philosophy of Classical Yoga.* Manchester: University of Manchester Press, 1982.

Halbfass, W. *Tradition and Reflection: Explorations in Indian Thought.* Albany: SUNY Press, 1991.

Hiriyanna, M. *Outlines of Indian Philosophy.* London: George Allen & Unwin, 1958.

Mahadevan, T. M. P. *Hymns of Śaṅkara.* Madras: University of Madras Press, 1970.

Neeval, W. G. Jr. *Yamuna's Vedānta and Pāñcarātra: Integrating the Classical and the Popular.* Chico, CA: Scholars Press, 1977.

Potter, K. *Bibliography of India's Philosophies.* Delhi: Motilal Banarsidass, 1970.

Potter, Karl. *The Encyclopedia of Indian Philosophies.* Banares: Motilal Banarsidass, 1970.

Rādhākrishnan, S. and Moore, C. A. *A Sourcebook in Indian Philosophy.* Princeton: Princeton University Press, 1957.

Srinivasacari, P. *The Philosophy of Viṣiṣṭadvaita.* Adyar: Theosophical Society, 1946.

On temple and iconography

Banerjee, J. N. *The Development of Hindu Iconography.* Second edition. Calcutta: University of Calcutta Press, 1956.

Chandra, Pramod. *Studies in Indian Temple Architecture.* Delhi: American Institute of Indian Studies, 1975.

Gopinath, Rao T. A. *Elements of Hindu Iconography.* Second edition. Delhi: Motilal Banarsidass, 1985.

Kramrisch, S. *The Hindu Temple.* Two volumes. Delhi: MLBD, 1946, reprint 1977.

Kramrisch, S. *The Presence of Śiva.* Princeton: Princeton University Press, 1981.

Meister, M.W. ed. *Discourses on Śiva.* Philadelphia: University of Pennsylvania Press, 1984.

Michell, G. *The Hindu Temple.* Chicago: University of Chicago Press, 1988.

Michell, G. *The Penguin Guide to the Monuments of India.* Volume one. London: Penguin, 1989.

Sivaramamurti, C. *South Indian Bronzes.* New Delhi: Lalitkala Akademi, 1963.

Younger, P. *The Home of Dancing Śiva.* New York: Oxford, 1995.

On tantrism

Bharati, Agehananda. *The Tantric Tradition.* London: Rider & Co., 1965.

Bhattacharya, N. N. *History of the Tantric Religion.* Delhi: Manohar, 1982.

Brooks, D. R. *The Secret of the Three Cities: An Introduction to Śākta Hinduism.* Chicago: University of Chicago Press, 1990.
Chattophadyaya, S. *Reflections on the Tantras.* Delhi: Motilal Banarsidass, 1978.
Kinsley, D. *Tantric Visions of the Divine Feminine: The Ten Mahāvidyas.* Berkeley: University of California Press, 1997.
Padoux, A. *Vac: The Concept of the Word in Selected Hindu Tantras.* Albany: SUNY Press, 1990.
White, David G. *The Alchemical Body: Siddha Traditions in Medieval India.* Chicago: University of Chicago Press, 1996.
White, D. G. ed. *Tantra in Practice.* Princeton: Princeton University Press, 2000.

On deities, ritual, and devotionalism

Beane, W. C. *Myth, Cult, and Symbols in Śākta Hinduism: A Study of the Indian Mother Goddess.* London: Brill, 1977.
Bhattacharji, S. *The Indian Theogony: A Comparative Study of Indian Mythology from the Vedas to the Purāṇas.* Cambridge: Cambridge University Press, 1970.
Brown, C. M. *God as Mother: A Feminine Theology in India; an Historical and Theological Study of the Brahmavaivarta Purāṇa.* Hartford, CT: Claude Stark, 1974.
Brown, C. M. *The Triumph of the Goddess: The Canonical Models and Theological Visions of the Devī Bhāgavata Purāṇa.* Albany: SUNY Press, 1990.
Carman, J. B. and Narayana, V. *The Tamil Veda.* Chicago: University of Chicago Press, 1989.
Clothey, F. W. *The Many Faces of Murukan.* Leiden: Mouton & Co., 1978.
Coburn, T. B. *Devīmāhātmya: the Crystallization of the Goddess Tradition.* Delhi: Motilal Banarsidass, 1984.
Courtright, P. B. *Ganeśa: Lord of Obstacles, Lord of Beginnings.* New York: Oxford University Press, 1985.
Cutler, Norman. *Songs of Experiences: The Poetics of Tamil Devotion.* Bloomington, IN: Indiana University Press, 1987.
Dehejia, V. *Slaves of the Lord.* Delhi: Munisharam Manoharlal, 1988.
Dehejia, V. *Āntāl and Her Path of Love.* Albany: SUNY Press, 1990.
Feldhaus, A. tr. *The Deeds of God in Ṛiddhipur.* New York: Oxford University Press, 1984.
Gatwood, L. E. *Devī and the Spouse Goddess: Women, Sexuality, and Marriage in India.* Delhi: Manohar, 1985.
Hardy, F. *Viraha Bhakti.* Delhi: Oxford University Press, 1983.
Hawley, J. and Wulff, D. eds. *The Divine Consort: Rādhā and the Goddesses of India.* Berkeley: University of California Press, 1982.
Hawley, J. and Wulff, D. eds. *Devī: Goddesses of India.* Berkeley: University of California Press, 1997.
Hiltebeitel, A. *The Cult of Draupadī.* Volume one: *Mythologies from Ginsee to Kurukṣetra.* Volume two: *On Hindu Ritual and the Goddess.* Chicago: University of Chicago Press, 1988, 1991.
Kane, P. V. *History of Dharmaśāstra.* Five volumes. Poona: Bhandarkar Oriental Research Institute, 1930–62.
Kinsley, D. *The Sword and the Flute: Kālī and Kṛṣṇa, Dark Visions of the Terrible and the Sublime in Hindu Mythology.* Berkeley: University of California Press, 1975.
Kinsley, D. *Hindu Goddesses: Visions of the Feminine in the Hindu Religious Tradition.* Berkeley: University of California Press, 1986.

Lopez, Donald S. Jr. ed. *Religions of India in Practice.* Princeton: Princeton University Press, 1995.

McDaniel, J. *The Madness of the Saints: Ecstatic Religion in Bengal.* Chicago: University of Chicago Press, 1989.

Marglin, F. A. *Wives of the God-King: The Rituals of the Devadāsis of Puri.* Delhi: Oxford University Press, 1985.

O'Flaherty, W. D. *Śiva: The Erotic Ascetic.* New York: Oxford University Press, 1980.

Orr, Leslie C. *Donors, Devotees, and Daughters of God: Temple Women in Medieval Tamil Nadu.* New York: Oxford University Press, 2000.

Pandey, R. B. *Hindu Saṁskāras: Socio-Religious Study of the Hindu Sacraments.* Second edition. Banares: Motilal Banarsidass, 1969.

Peterson, I. *Poems to Śiva, the Hymns of the Tamil Sūtras.* Princeton: Princeton University Press, 1989.

Pintchman, T. *The Rise of the Goddess in the Hindu Traditions.* Albany: SUNY Press, 1994.

Raghavan, V. *The Great Integrators: The Saint Singers of India.* Delhi: Ministry of Information, nd.

Ramanujan, A. K. *Speaking of Śiva.* Baltimore: Penguin, 1973.

Ramanujan, A. K. *Hymns for the Drowning.* New York: Penguin, 1993.

Rocher, L. *The Purāṇas, History of Indian Literature.* Wiesbaden: Otto Harrassowitz, 1986.

Sontheimer, G. D. *Pastoral Deities in Western India.* Delhi: Oxford University Press, 1993.

Yocum, G. *Hymns to the Dancing Śiva: a Study of Māṇikkavācakar's Tiruvācakam.* Columbia, MO: South Asian Books, 1982.

Timeline of Chapter 5

South

		Cultural/political events		Religious events
BCE				
100	1st	Early Tamil inscriptions/ script		Buddhists/Jains in Sri Lanka
	1st BCE–1st CE	Trade with Greeks and Romans in south		
CE				
200				Pre-Hindu religious orientation
300	2nd–3rd	Tamil *Caṅkam* (poetic "academy")	1st–3rd	Jains, Buddhists, brahmans filtering into the south
	c. 300	Early Pāṇṭiyaṉs in Maturai		
400	4th	Kaṭampa era founded		
500	c. 550	First Cālukya dynasty founded		
600	7th–9th	Heyday of Pallava dynasty	7th–9th	Tamil *bhakti* movement
700			7th	First permanent stone temples in Tamil land (Pallava)
800	850–1267	Cōḻa era (Kāvēri basin)	8th	Śaṅkara
900				
	c. 973	Second Cālukya dynasty		
1000			11th	Śaiva Siddhānta articulated Cōḻa influence in SE Asia
			11th–13th	Cōḻa bronzes and temples
1100				
			1137	Death of Rāmānuja
1200	c. 1216	Return of Pāṇṭiyaṉs (Maturai)		
			12th–14th	Continued compilation of *Purāṇas, Āgamas, Tālapurāṇas*

North

Cultural/political events			Religious events	
CE				
500			6th	Late Ajantā paintings
600				
700	c. 757	Rise of Rāṣṭrakūṭa dynasty	c. 775	Kailāsanātha temple, Ellora
800	8th–11th	Regional kingdoms in Kashmīr and other border areas	6th–10th	Emergence of goddess to supreme status; *Devīmāhātmya* written?
900		Early Rājput clans in India	950–1050	Building of Khajurāho temples
			8th–13th	Temple construction in Orissa

6

The Coming of Islam

The origins of Islam
Sunnīs and Shī'īs
Islam in India
The political context
Diversity of Islam in India
Sunnīs
Shī'īs
Sūfīsm
Recommended reading

Some historians begin their discussion of "modern India" with the Islamic period because in many ways the presence of Islam on the subcontinent was a watershed in the self-perception and practice of Indian religion and culture, especially in Northern India. Much has been claimed and counter-claimed about Islam's presence in India, especially by Hindu militants. There are those Hindu nationalists who insist Islam was a brutal foreign intrusion whose rulers enforced conversions, demolished temples, and in other ways sought to wipe out "infidels." On the other hand, many historians, in seeking to refute these claims, may soft pedal the more unpleasant aspects of the Islamic presence. We shall attempt in this chapter and the next to sketch in the nature of Islam's presence and the subcontinent's response to it. What is obvious is that Islam in India has been no monolith – there have been many various strands that constituted its contribution to the subcontinent. Similarly, responses to it were diverse and cannot be simply characterized.

The origins of Islam

Islam is a product of **Muhammad**'s teachings in the seventh century on the Arabian peninsula. It is best understood in light of the pre-Islamic landscape. Arabia was a divided peninsula. A number of polytheistic tribes made up much of the population. There was infighting and fragmentation. Some 360 deities were honored at the ***ka'ba*** stone in Mecca (Ar: Makkah); many of these deities were deities of the sky (*el* – lifted up, lofty, high). One of the strongest tribes was the Quraysh, of which Muḥammad was a member.[1]

Also part of the pre-Islamic landscape were two monotheistic religious communities. Jews, especially in Yemen and along the coasts, were a largely mercantile community. Many were members of the Quraysh tribe. Christians were of varying sectarian traditions (Monophysite, Eastern Orthodox, Nestorian) and were often known on the peninsula serving as mercenaries fighting for either Byzantine or Persian rulers. Nonetheless there were Christian (especially Monophysite) monasteries in parts of the peninsula. Some scholars believe Muḥammad's ideas were influenced by these monotheistic communities, though orthodox Muslims are insistent that all his teachings were revealed.

Muḥammad was born around 570 CE in Mecca. He became a camel herder and married his employer. The tradition maintains that he was illiterate. By the age of twenty-five he was to have strange experiences and "visions." Troubled by these, he consulted with his wife and friend **Zayd** (a monotheist who was disgruntled with both Jewish and Christian communities). Muhammad decided he was in fact receiving revelations through the angel Gabriel. He came to be understood as a prophet (*nabī*) and a messenger sent by god (*rasūl*).

At first, however, his message was ill-received in Mecca, though a handful of converts joined him. One of the first of these was **Abū Bakr**, a friend and relative who eventually succeeded him as the first caliph (Ar: *khalīfa* – political leader). Vested commercial interests and doubters forced Muḥammad to leave Mecca in 622 CE. This became known as the *hijra* (flight) and the start of the Islamic calendar. Muḥammad had been invited to Medina (Ar: al-Madinah) by pilgrims who had visited Mecca and heard him preach. Medina was ready for a monotheistic message. Tired of Arabic infighting, many were impressed with Muḥammad's message and converted. Within a few years, he returned to Mecca, and made the *ka'ba* an Islamic center, eliminating the representations of tribal deities previously honored there. Within a decade, much of the peninsula was attracted to the message: God (Allah or Ar: Allāh – the lofty one) was presented to the Arabs in Arabic; unity on the peninsula had become possible. A way of life that provided a civil code and just treatment of others was made available across the peninsula. The Arab people were galvanized. By the time of Muḥammad's death much of the tradition was in place, to be interpreted and reinterpreted for centuries to come.

The basic tenets of Islam are not so much beliefs, as rituals. Known as the five pillars, they include: 1) A statement of faith (*shahāda*) consisted in affirming there was no god but Allāh, and Muḥammad was his prophet. Indeed, Muḥammad is perceived to have provided the final revelation, as the last of a prophetic tradition that included Abraham, Moses, Jesus, and others. 2) Prayer (*ṣalāt*) was to be done five times a day, facing Mecca as the center of the Islamic world. 3) Alms (a portion of one's income) were to be given in support of the poor (*zakāt*). Indeed, Muslims were to avoid usury (cheating in the lending of money) and were to share wealth that may accumulate. 4) Fasting (*ṣaum*) was to be done during the month of Ramaḍān when the faithful Muslim was to remember the hardships of Muḥammad in his period of exile from Mecca and enact the solidarity of the Islamic community by refraining from eating or drinking any thing from sunrise to sunset. 5) Pilgrimage (the ***ḥajj***) was enjoined as the duty of all faithful Muslims who were to go to Mecca at least once in their lives; to be sure, individual Muslims have followed these requirements to varying degrees throughout the centuries, but the orthoprax try faithfully to follow them.

Sunnīs and Shī'īs

Within a few years after Muḥammad's death, disputes began to rise over his succession. These disagreements led eventually to the division between Shī'īs (anglicized as Shīites) and Sunnīs. The division had both a political and a religious or legal character. Politically, the dispute centered on whether Abū Bakr (that early convert) or **'Alī**, the son-in-law of Muḥammad, should be the prophet's successor. Abū Bakr became the first successor and 'Alī the fourth, but followers of Abū Bakr (so it is believed) assassinated the son of 'Alī, **Ḥusain**, thereby disrupting that line of succession. Shīites were the followers of 'Ali, bitter to this day at the treatment of Ḥusain.[2]

The other division between Shīites and Sunnīs rested on matters of interpretation of the tradition. All Muslims claim two sources of authority. The first is the Qu'rān, believed to be the verbatim revelation given to Muḥammad from Allāh himself through the angel Gabriel. Muḥammad passed on these revelations orally whence followers wrote them down within decades of Muḥammad's life. The second source of authority is the ***ḥadīth***. These are commentaries (or traditions) on the ***sunna*** (the way of Muḥammad), that is, the record of his words and actions done in addition to the Qurānic messages.

It is at this point that Sunnī and Shīite interpretations diverge. Sunnīs, adherents of Abū Bakr, also follow the teachings of the ***'ulamā'***, a community of interpreters; these are "councils" which form a consensus as to how one of the first two authorities is to be interpreted. The Shīites, followers of 'Alī, came to believe that it was ***imāms*** – successors to the line of 'Alī – who were the authorized interpreters. For the Sunnī, in short, the caliph had political authority and the '*ulamā*' interpretive authority, and political power was often a negotiation between the two. For the Shīites, the *imām* was both political and spiritual authority.

Arabic hegemony spread rapidly within the first century of Islam's existence – across North Africa and throughout the Fertile Crescent. The first two caliphates were particularly strong: the Ummāyyads, headquartered in Damascus, and the 'Abbāsids, headquartered in Baghdad. By the mid-ninth century, Baghdad had become the Western world's center of civilization – the sciences, philosophy, the arts thrived as influences were welcomed from India, the Greek tradition, and from throughout West Asia and North Africa. Meanwhile, the Shīites, still uncomfortable with Sunnī caliphate rule, gravitated into Persia.

Islam in India

Islam came to the Indian subcontinent within decades of its birth. Arab merchants had been trading along the west coast of India even before the advent of Islam. Now, the Arab traders were Muslims. Increasingly, some of them settled along the southern and western coast, married locally, and formed pockets of Islamic culture interacting peacefully with their neighbors. These settlements were entirely pacific and interactions with neighbors remained virtually without conflict even into the recent past. There were also constant interactions with Muslim traders and craftsmen from Turkey and Central Asia in such areas as Northeast Panjāb, Kashmīr, and Eastern Bengal from the eighth century on. Many of these "foreign" artisans had settled permanently by the thirteenth century. There was also at least one military incursion, however – that in the area of Sind: **Muhammed Ibn Qasim**, pursuing pirates who had plundered an Arab ship, led an army of 6,000 against **Qahar**, king of Sind in 711. Within three years he had established hegemony in the Indus Valley region (much of the area that is now Pakistan).

It was the military incursions of Afghans that in hindsight have haunted Hindu–Muslim relations in recent years. The first of these invasions was that of the armies of Mahmūd of Ghaznī in the eleventh century. There are many varied interpretations of Mahmūd's activities in India. It appears he first entered to rescue some Turkish soldiers and craftsmen who had been "enslaved" and to retrieve payments for elephants and equipment, which had been promised by **Raja Jaipal**. It is also apparent that, in India, his armies plundered and razed temples and decimated Buddhist institutions. His motives appear to have been for profit, personal glory, and filling the coffers of his capital.[3] Yet sources in Persia and Central Asia, by the thirteenth century, were rhetorically praising him as a "great sultan" whose conquests were consistent with the earlier caliphs and were done in the name of ***jihād***. Originally, *jihād* had connoted the act of carrying out the will of Allāh and preparing oneself and the world for submission to Allāh. However, under the caliphs *jihād* became an excuse for "just war" against those who resisted conquest and it was eventually included in the legal codes as such.[4] Hence, for some Persian rhetoricians, Ghaznī was engaged in *jihād* for the conquest of infidels in the name of Allāh. On the other hand, even al-Bīrūnī, the Muslim astronomer who had been brought into India by Ghaznī and wrote descriptions of the Indian religious and scientific landscape, spoke of the sultan as having engaged in insensitive excess, of having "utterly ruined the prosperity of the country," and breeding an "inveterate aversion towards all Muslims."[5] At the least, Ghaznī's (or subsequent rhetoricians') use of Islam to justify his raids was a classic case of "civil religion," the use of religious rhetoric in support of political action.

While Mahmūd of Ghaznī had no long-term plans to establish hegemony in India, another Afghan raider did. A century later **Muhammed of Ghor**, perhaps less controversial than Mahmūd, nonetheless began to combine military engagements with alliances to extend his political control southward. Because a political and religious vacuum existed, especially in the border regions of the north, a result, in part, of centuries of infighting and regional skirmishes, Ghor was able to establish hegemony in Northwest India. His successor appointed as regents in Delhi members of his court who had been taken as "slaves" and trained for administration. These "slave kings" were to establish the first of four Delhi sultanates.[6] While this sultanate lasted only from 1206–90, it was powerful enough to fend off the brunt of Mongol expansion in the thirteenth century. Though the Mongols came to the fringes of Northern India, they marched rather into the Middle East burning cities and turning mosques into horse stables. Baghdad was sacked as blood literally flowed in the streets. One of the results of the Mongol thrust westward was the migration of Muslims from the Middle East to a "safe haven," namely, to a place with a sultanate where they could feel safe. The Islamic era had become a fixture in much of North India.

The political context

Three separate sultanates followed the slave kings: the Khaljīs (1290–1316) only ruled for twenty-six years, but in that period fended off the Mongols twice.[7] Their hegemony was largely on the boundaries – for example, Bengal, Kashmīr, and Panjāb. The Tughluqs followed (1320–88). It was they who established the tax (***jizyah***) on those who were not Muslims (***d̲h̲immīs***). This had been a policy in the early Islamic caliphates – the hierarchy usually had put Arabs at the top (and usually members of the Quraysh tribe at that); non-Arab Muslims next, and *d̲h̲immīs* last (a term then applied to non-Muslims who were "followers of the book" – that is, Jews and Christians). This group was generally permitted autonomy in Islamic polities, so long as *jizyah* was paid as an indication of one's recognition of the hegemony of the political ruler. The Tughluqs proved to be weakened rulers. **Muḥammed bin Tughluq**, for example, was a relatively free thinker, influenced by the logician **Ubaid**, who was for that reason opposed by ideologues of the '*ulamā*' who feared loss of power. A severe famine from 1355–42 also weakened Muḥammed's hand.[8] Among the results of these measures was that the sultanate came to be divided. Mongol armies were able to enter the domain during the Tughluq period and plundered Sind and Gujarat. Later yet (1398) **Tamerlane** of Central Asia invaded Delhi and pillaged and plundered in his wake.[9] The Tughluqs were eventually followed by the Lodīs (1451–1526). By this time more Hindus were learning Persian, the language of the courts, and were moving up in the power hierarchy. Some of the Lodīs continued to make alliances with Hindu princes in the outlying regions, following a strategy of governance the Tughluqs had initiated – that of establishing regencies to govern on their behalf on the fringes of the sultanate. The Lodīs also patronized Hindu arts and culture and combined Islamic and Hindu notions of kingship to bolster their legitimation. The Persian word ***huzūr*** – "sacred presence" – that is, Allāh's sanction in the court, was used to give divine sanction to the sultan.[10] The political leader thus also was a sacred leader. In the meanwhile, on the outskirts of the sultanate, outlying ministers were paid to maintain order and allegiance, while officials were appointed by the sultans to administer the land and see that taxes were paid by landowners. (These officials came to be known as *zamindārs* after the Mughal period and represented a practice continued by the British.) In fact, at least one new caste group was established at this time: the *kāyasthas*, a non-Muslim caste which was skilled at writing, knew Persian, and did the bookkeeping in the courts.

The Mughal dynasty which followed brought Indo-Islamic culture to its apex.[11] Established by **Bābur** in 1526, the Mughals increased the exchanges between Persia and India and made Delhi one of the most important centers of culture in Asia. By the mid-sixteenth century at least, Delhi was a major center for libraries and learning. Medicine flourished thanks to the combining of Arabic and Indian forms of medicine. Delhi housed at least five observatories.[12] Indo-Islamic forms of architecture, music, and dance flourished, practiced by Muslim and Hindu alike. **Akbar** (1556–1605), Bābur's grandson, was, by most measures, a ruler of great skill and sensitivity. As a boy, he was open to Shīite teachings and the mysticism of Persian poets. Early in his reign, however, his advisers were Sunnīs, some of whom persecuted Shīites, thereby incurring the emperor's wrath. This led to his sacking the Sunnī advisers and replacing them with Sūfīs.

In 1562 Akbar married a Rājput princess and the tenor of his reign was set. He was a charismatic leader concerned more with efficient organization than with Islamic orthodoxy. The result was an efficient central authority; the appointment of various local leaders, including many Hindus to be "governors" in outlying areas; and a minimum of corruption. Akbar's authority was enhanced by several other developments, including the increased manufacture of paper, which increased administrative efficiency; enhanced travel and income from European merchants; and the death of Iran's Shāh in 1522, encouraging Akbar to declare his sovereignty over a wider area. His religious perspective was eclectic, trying the patience of the Sunnī '*ulamā*'. He permitted Hindu practices within his court, including certain festivals, patronized Hindu arts and culture, and encouraged translations of such texts as the *Artharva Veda*, *Rāmāyana*, and *Mahābhārata*. With mixed success, he sought to abolish certain "excesses": child-marriage; large dowries; and the immolation of widows (*satī*). He was known to have presided over inter-religious discussions in his court, in which Hindu pandits, Jains, Zoroastrians, even Catholic priests from Goa participated. He finally created his own sect in 1585: Dīn-ilāhī ("Divine Faith"), known for its eclectic character and for making him the center of the sect and thereby further legitimating his status as emperor.

His son **Jahāngīr** (1605–27) decentralized the administration he inherited and increased the influx of Persians and Persian art and culture during his reign. His bureaucracy grew rapidly, expenditures increased, as did corruption. He was far less tolerant than his father of other religions as he patronized Islamic institutions more and restored the conservative '*ulamā*' to the role of court advisers. He was known to have persecuted Jains and to have had the Sikh guru **Arjun** executed in 1606. Jahāngīr, who had bestowed honors on certain Muslim dignitaries, nonetheless distrusted Sikhs (who had supported an uprising against him), and Sikhs indeed became increasingly alienated from the Mughal court. (A more systematic discussion of the Sikh movement will follow in the next chapter.)

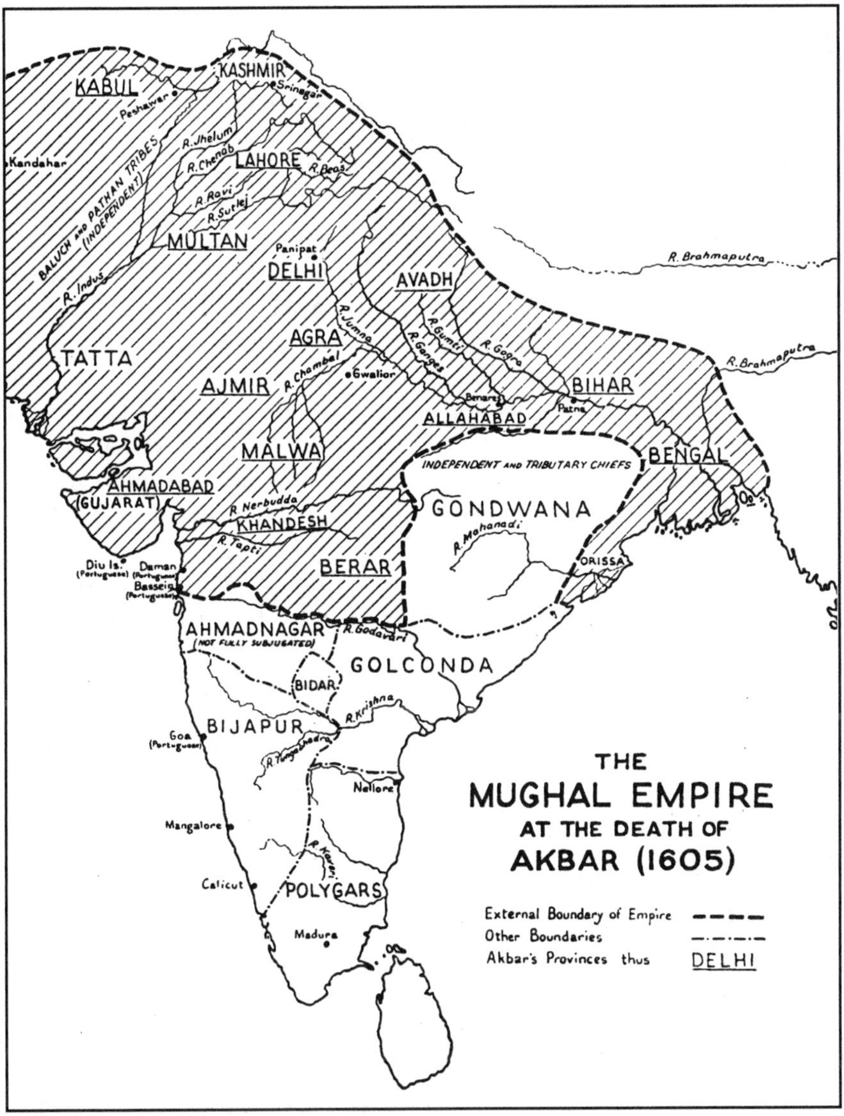

Map 4 The Mughal Empire

Reprinted from *A Cultural History of India*, ed. by A. L. Basham (Clarendon Press, 1975), p. 591, by permission of Oxford University Press.

Shāh Jahān (1628–58), a good administrator, became the patron of Indo-Islamic art and architecture at its peak. He built the Tāj Mahal as a memorial to his wife and the adjacent gardens as a replica of paradise. He was responsible for other tombs and forts. The architects for these projects were generally Muslim and the craftsmen Hindu. Some of the alliances with

Hindu princes were restored and the empire extending into Kashmīr and into the Deccan was maintained; yet his military power began to wane and the treasures of the court were increasingly depleted.

His son **Aurangzeb** (1658–1707) marks the last of the significant Mughal rulers. Putting his own father under house arrest and usurping the throne, Aurangzeb proved to be less flexible as a ruler. Most historians are not kind to Aurangzeb as it seems he was more interested in Sunnī orthodoxy than in administrative flexibility. He turned to the '*ulamā*' for legitimation and sought to make the state more nearly "Islamic." He was known to have assassinated yet another Sikh guru, to have broken alliances with Hindu leaders, and to have banned Hindu customs and music in the courts. He also found himself trying to retain Mughal power against several forces at once: Marāthās, Sikhs, and Afghans, for example. This continuous fighting in the Deccan managed to drain the treasury; he even moved his capital to the Deccan – to the town now known as Aurangabad in an attempt to control the Marāthās. He abolished any taxes which were not explicitly required by Islamic law (***sharī'a***) and reimposed the *jizyah* tax in 1679. The result of his policies was fragmentation in the empire, disenchantment by formally aligned sub-rulers, and the permanent weakening of the Mughal line. After Aurangzeb's death in 1707, the Mughals were effectively powerless even though they retained modest hegemony in Delhi itself into the nineteenth

Figure 5 Jama Masjid, Delhi, the oldest and largest mosque in India. Photograph by Rob F. Phillips.

century. In fact, in 1739, the Persian Shāh sacked Delhi and the era of Islamic power in India was at an end.

This brief sketch of the political landscape under Islamic rulers suggests several realities of the period. Islamic polity took many forms – there was no single policy toward subjects. Further, almost invariably, the hegemony was really only strong at the center; the further one went from the center, the less the control. Considerable autonomy and flexibility existed within certain of the sultanates and during much of the Mughal period. Certainly, there were military skirmishes, but these were almost invariably political in nature – Muslim princes against Muslim princes; Hindu princes against Hindu princes; Hindu mercenaries fighting in an army on behalf of a Muslim prince and vice versa. While the chief advisers in the courts were often Muslim, Hindus were increasingly employed and even the Muslim advisers varied from different schools of Sunnī to Sūfī character, from orthodox to eclectic.

Diversity of Islam in India

It is clear that Islam in the subcontinent was not monolithic. We turn now to something of the diversity and character of Muslim communities in India. To begin, there were clearly several cultures and languages that migrated into India. Arab merchants brought Arabic language, but Arabic patterns of governance were also applied, particularly in the early sultanates. More importantly, Arabic was the language of the Qur'ān, hence the language of orthodoxy, and the language taught in the *madrasas* (schools) when individuals and communities sought a sense of rootedness and identity, particularly in the period of the first several generations of migrants. Turkish and Afghan "culture" tended to the language of warfare. Turkish warriors were less cultured, yet Turkish soldiers were being employed even by Hindu princes as early as the ninth century. These soldiers of Turkish background continued to live on the subcontinent and tended to mingle with the "common" folk and effect exchanges of vocabulary and customs. The Persian cultural stream was the most significant influence in the courts especially by the fifteenth century when language, music, architecture, and other arts experienced the influence of Persian motifs. There was also some "exporting" of cultural forms into Persia.

Sunnīs

But Indian Muslim communities have showed great diversity in their religious orientations as well. The Sunnīs, for whom interpretation of Islamic law (*sharī'a*) depends on the councils (*'ulamā'*), are one of the forms of Islam in India. But there were at least four different schools of Sunnī interpretation of which the two most liberal are to be found in India: the Ḥanafīs and the Shāfi'īs.

The Ḥanafīs were traditionally the most "rationalistic" of the interpretive schools. Influenced by Aristotelian philosophy, they argued that revelation was to be tested and verified by reason. Somewhat pragmatic, their *'ulamā's* tended to be less strict in interpreting the *ḥadīth*. The Ḥanafīs were the school of choice in the heyday of the 'Abbāsid caliphate in Baghdad in the mid-ninth century. It was the Sunnī school most commonly associated with the Mughal court. Further, many South Indian Muslims today identify themselves as Ḥanafī Sunnīs without knowing the nuances of what that entails. In fact, each *'ulamā'* offered its own particular consensus (***ijmā'***) in interpreting the tradition, building on rulings from the past. Each region in India could have several *'ulamā's* and hence several possible interpretations of the tradition. It should be noted that, at least by the seventeenth century, lay Indian Sunnī Muslims were less likely to look to Mecca or Persia or the Middle East for their interpretations of Islamic practice – they looked rather to their regional *'ulamā's*, that is, to councils in Tamil or Bengālī areas, for example.

The other major Sunnī school on the subcontinent was the Shāfi'īs. The Shāfi'īs were more conservative than the Ḥanafīs. Originating in Egypt, the Shāfi'īs tended to mediate between the Ḥanafīs and the more conservative Sunnī schools known as the Mālikas and the Ḥanbalis. The Shāfi'īs emphasized the *ḥadīth* (the works and actions of the Prophet) as the basis for Islamic practice, yet argued that critical reasoning was appropriate in specific circumstances when "reasonable" rulings were needed. Relatively pacific in their understandings of the *sharī'a*, they tended to be more scholastic or neo-classical in their interpretations. More specifically, the Shāfi'īs had contributed several principles to Islamic jurisprudence, most importantly *fiqh* ("intelligence"), which indicates the importance of linking reason to the intimations of the Qur'ān and *ḥadīth*, and *ijmā'* ("consensus"), which indicates the importance of making decisions through the consensus of the *'ulamā'* – the specialists in legal interpretation.[13]

Shī'īs

Shīism is a second major form of Islam on the subcontinent. Shīites, of course, were those who considered the *imām* the appropriate interpreter of the Qur'ān and *ḥadīth* in both religious and political matters. Two schools of Shīites, in particular, influenced the subcontinent. The Ithnā 'Asharīs, also known as the "twelvers," started in Persia but were found in Mughal India and in such centers as Lucknow. The Ithnā 'Asharīs believed that in

878 CE the twelfth *imām* withdrew from the world, but would return in order to purify the world at the end of history.[14] The Shīites in India were not averse to following forms of Islam not considered appropriate in classical Islam. These Shīites, for example, believed in the efficacy of ***pīrs*** who could have been folk heroes or spiritual masters, even after death. The tombs of *pīrs*, known as *dargahs*, became centers of worship, and pilgrimage focused on such sites on festive occasions. The most significant commemorative event for Indian Shīites has been Muḥarram, the anniversary of Ḥusain's assassination, when mourning and family gatherings mark the occasion. Shīites also tended to observe more sacred days than the Sunnīs, including special events in the life of Muḥammad. But both Sunnīs and Shīites in India have made a feast (*'īd*) of Muḥammad's birthday and have incorporated a number of Indian customs into their rites of passage and ritual life. It is also not uncommon to find Muslims, and especially Shīites, sharing a pilgrim site with Hindus on the grounds that some Muslim saint had performed a significant act at that place. New sects of Shīism, indigenous to the subcontinent also appeared. One such movement was that known as the Ahmadīyah movement.[15] Its founder declared himself to be the Mahdī who had returned and the prophet (*rasūl*) for a new time. The Ahmadīyahs claimed that Jesus had survived persecution, and had fled to Northwest India where he eventually died. In short, the Shīites and their *imāms* in India tended to incorporate folk and indigenous elements into their religious orientation.

The other major branch of Shīism has been the Ismā'īlīs, also known as the "seveners." They claimed that the eldest son of the sixth *imām* was the appropriate successor of the interpretive tradition (the 'Asharīs had claimed that the younger son of that *imām* was the correct one).[16] Once strong in Egypt and anti-'Abbasid, even militantly "nationalistic" in their approach, they spread into Gujarat in Northwestern India, where they indigenized and took on various forms of the Indian cultural landscape. The Ismā'īlīs split into several groups, each group following a different *imām*. In recent decades, many Ismā'īlīs have come to be very progressive and highly educated, taking leadership roles in a number of Indian cities.[17]

Sūfīsm

The third major form of Islam impacting the subcontinent was Sūfīsm, perhaps the most generally liberal and most influential of all these movements. Sūfīsm had its start in the deserts of Arabia where it grew as a parallel movement to the rise of Islam. In the early stages of the movement, Sūfīs often thought the Caliphs to be corrupt and/or unresponsive to the best intentions of Islam and often differed with the '*ulamā's* as to the appropriate interpretations of Islam. Given to a mystical lifestyle, Sūfīs insisted that Allāh could be found within one – that he was accessible and to be enjoyed. Sūfī mystics practiced a quiescent asceticism characterized by experiential wisdom and ecstasy. The mystical experience was often expressed in terms of the metaphor of love and the dawning of an inner illumination, both deemed to be gifts of the divine. Both women and men had been attracted to the movement. Among the most notable were **Rabi'ah**, a woman born of poor parents in Basra, Iraq; the Persian **al-Ḥallaj**, who was executed in Baghdad in 922 for declaring himself to be one with Allāh; **al-Gazzali** (1058–1111), scholar and theologian who made the mystical experience an acceptable part of Islamic practice; and **al-Rumi** (1207–73), the great Persian poet and mystic.[18]

By the tenth century, some Sūfī orders were emerging in Iran that were influenced by Buddhism,[19] just as prior to that Sūfīs had incorporated Christian and Jewish practices. A Sūfī order would develop as seekers gathered around saintly leaders known as sheikhs and spent some three years receiving instruction. Several such orders entered India, the most widely spread of which was the Chistī order. Some came to flee the Mongols; others came at the invitation of Islamic sultans on the subcontinent and came to serve a role similar to that played by brahmans under "Hindu" kings. That is, Islamic rulers sometimes "imported" Sūfī leadership to help integrate the prince's central administration. They were, for the most part, eclectic and non-confrontational. The construction of tombs to *pīrs* served a purpose similar to the construction of earlier temples by Hindu rulers. It localized religious fervor and gave a sanction to the ruler involved. As a result, in many settings, Sūfī leaders enjoyed patronage of Islamic rulers: they were the educators, often teaching Persian as the *lingua franca* in the Islamic courts of Islamic rulers, but they also learned the local languages; they made connections with the common people and served to legitimate the state.[20]

Not all Sūfī sheikhs were politically engaged. Those who "dabbled" in politics were known as *'ulamā'-al-dunya*. When Akbar, for example, got rid of his Sunnī *'ulamā'*, he installed *'ulamā'-al-dunya* as his ministers. Such Sūfīs also served in the courts of Deccan rulers. Those who sought purely spiritual roles were *'ulamā'-al-ākhara*. Such were the Chistīs at first, who eschewed political roles. A third group was the *'ulamā'-al-sin*, who were informally consulted by rulers on occasion.[21]

Quite apart from their political role, Sūfī sheikhs had a significant religious role in the shaping of Islam on the subcontinent. Religiously, Sūfīs followed some ten principles. 1) Repentance was to be done in several stages and included an emptying of self-orientation. 2) Abstinence from materialism implied refraining from unnecessary accumulations of possessions, as well as living simple lives. 3) Piety entailed focusing on the sovereignty and accessibility of God. 4) Once one is ready, one takes a vow of poverty – to possess nothing other than what is needed as daily necessities. 5) Patience was a requisite part of self-discipline. 6) Gratitude for the mercies of God was accompanied by: 7) The fear of God. 8) Hope is the expectation of filling by the Divine nature. 9) Contentment with one's spiritual stature is followed by 10) submission to the Divine will. At this stage it was believed God had now filled one's person with the Divine presence. In a sense, one had become Allāh and Allāh had become one.[22]

Such an affirmation was not always popular with the orthodox Sunnī '*ulamā*' and, on occasion, Sūfī interactions with the '*ulamā*' were prickly. While some Sūfīs remained on good terms with orthodox Islamic '*ulamā*'s, others were more eclectic. Indeed, many Sūfīs borrowed freely from certain forms of Hindu devotionalism (especially from the Nāṭha sect of Śaivism and from Vaiṣṇavism).[23] They appropriated indigenous musical forms, even came to create their own indigenous forms of music, known as the ***g̱hazal***. In fact, insofar as Sūfī sheikhs lived in areas where Buddhism had been decimated and Hinduism underdeveloped, the sheikhs were found to be attractive spiritual leaders and teachers by common folk, who scarcely cared as to the religious label they or their *guru* had. Needless to say, this eclectic form of Sūfīsm attracted followers in such areas as Kashmīr, Bengal, and Panjāb and was also instrumental in carrying the message of Islam into Southeast Asia.

It is clear from this sketch that Islam took many forms on the Indian subcontinent and a Muslim in India could assume many identities at once. A Muslim could be a Ḥanafī Sunnī Muslim, but she may celebrate festivals of the Shiites and rites of passage that reverberate with the customs of her Hindu counterparts. She may have visited the local *dargaẖ* and Hindu women may have done so too; she may have visited a pilgrimage site where Hindus also went. Not only that, Muslim families usually continued to speak the vernacular language – for example, Tamil or Bengālī; and may have identified themselves by occupations that virtually assumed the character of a caste – for example, *rowthers* (growers) or *panjaṅkūṭis* (cotton-spinners). In fact, many converts to Islam retained their caste identities. These Muslims may even have come to affiliate themselves with a Sūfī order or *pīr* or Sunnī council ('*ulamā*') that represented the place of their birth and upbringing. Those local and regional identities often took precedence in Muslim families over any "global" or transnational religion called Islam. It is impossible, as a result, to speak of any single form or strategy that characterizes Islam in India. But by at least the sixteenth century and, in many cases, much earlier, Islam was a fully "Indian" phenomenon.

Recommended reading

Islam in India

Agrawal, C. M. *Akbar and His Hindu Officers.* Jalandar: ABS Publishers, 1986.
Alam, Muzaffar. *The Crisis of Empire in Mughal North India, 1707–1748.* Oxford and Delhi: Oxford University Press, 1986.
Asher, Catherine. *Architecture of Mughal India.* Cambridge: Cambridge University Press, 1992.
Eaton, Richard. *Sufis of Bijapur, 1300–1700: Social Roles of Sufis in Medieval India.* Princeton: Princeton University Press, 1977.
Eaton, Richard. *The Rise of Islam and the Bengal Frontier, 1204–1760.* Berkeley: University of California Press, 1993.
Esposito, John. *Islam: The Straight Path.* New York: Oxford University Press, 1991.
Israeli, R. and Johns, A. H. eds. *Islam in Asia.* Volume one. *South Asia.* Boulder, CO: Westview, 1984.
Nanji, Azim. *The Nizari Isma'ili Tradition in the Indo-Pakistan Subcontinent.* Delmar, NY: Caravan Books, 1978.
Qureshi, I. H. *The Muslim Community of the Indo-Pakistan Subcontinent, 610–1947: A Brief Historical Analysis.* The Hague: Mouton, 1962.
Rahman, Fazlur. *Islam.* Second edition. Chicago: University of Chicago Press, 1979.
Richards, John F. *The Mughal Empire.* Cambridge: Cambridge University Press, 1993.
Rizvi, S. A. A. *A History of Sufism in India.* Two volumes, reprinted. New Delhi: Munshiram Manoharlal, 1986.
Russell, Ralph and Islam, Khurshidul. *Three Mughal Poets: Mir, Sanda, Mir Hasan.* Cambridge: Cambridge University Press, 1968.
Schimmel, Annemarie. *Mystical Dimensions of Islam.* Chapel Hill: University of North Carolina Press, 1975.
Schimmel, A. *Islam in the Indian Subcontinent.* Leiden: Brill, 1980.
Sharma, S. R. *The Religious Policy of the Mughal Emperors.* Bombay: Asian Publishing House, 1972.
Subham, John A. *Sufism, Its Saints and Shrines: An Introduction to the Study of Sufism with Special Reference to India.* New York: Weiser, 1970.
Titus, M. T. *The Religious Quest of India; Indian Islam.* Oxford: Oxford University Press, 1930.
Yasin, M. *A Social History of Islam in India 1605–1748.* Lucknow: The Upper India Publishing House, 1958.

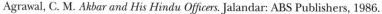

7

Developments in the Late Medieval Period

Orthopraxy
Hindu polities
Devotionalism
Marāthī
Bengālī
Hindī
Accommodation and appropriation
Conversion
Syncretism
Sikhism
Recommended reading

The centuries following the first appearance of Islam in the subcontinent were among the most creative in the history of religion in India. In some cases, these developments show little or no explicit relation to the role of Muslims. In other cases, the changes and continuities that occurred were the direct result of Islam's presence and/or were in response to it. These responses were as varied as the nature of Islam itself and differed from region to region and community to community. In this chapter, we broadly outline these developments in terms of five thematic rubrics which illustrate the diversity and scope of the period. These themes are: a) orthopraxy, b) devotionalism, c) accommodation and synthesis, d) conversion, and e) syncretism.

Orthopraxy

We begin with orthopraxy. Simply put, orthopraxy is the propensity to find one's "roots" in order to ascertain what is the "correct" way to act. In the context of pluralism of various kinds, orthopraxy is the propensity to retreat into enclaves or to reassert one's own sense of self in contradistinction to others. This had occurred at various times in India's religious history as Saivites, for example, sought to distinguish themselves from Vaiṣṇavas or Tantrics or Buddhists. Yet even in these movements toward reaffirmation one may borrow from "others" and/or be in proximity to "others." Such was the case in this period when Islamization has become a part of the subcontinent.

One form this took was in maintenance of polities, where Hindu *dharma* was upheld. By the twelfth century, in a number of courts, Sanskrit texts were appearing describing domains in which *dharma* was to be maintained in contradistinction to alternative cultural spaces.[1] In these settings, a particular prince engaged in reciprocities with landowners and invited brahmans to be the court's advisers in a manner similar to that found in earlier settings. Temple construction acted out these reciprocities between elites and also served to integrate folk or tribal people under the state's umbrella. Sectarian leaders could be patronized. *Maṭhas* or monasteries served as centers for the propagation of sectarian learning (just as the *madrasa* served such a role in Islamic polities). Brahmanical hegemony increased in the state structure and the ritual life became more varied. Festivals, often patronized by the king, became more visible – they demonstrated the king's status while incorporating commoners into the life of the realm. Mythologies of the deities were elaborated; pamphlets on various temple sites and on proper ritual behavior were produced. Folk traditions were accommodated into the religious life and were increasingly evident in the temples. Vegetarianism, though borrowed from Jainism and Buddhism, could be seen as an ideal in certain circles (though not in such places as Bengal or Kashmīr). In short, the tenor of the Hindu state was neo-classical.

Hindu polities

There were at least three such major polities in this period: the Vijayanagara dynasty, the Marāthās, and the Rājputs. The pattern can be illustrated aptly by sketching in the Vijayanagara context. The Vijayanagara dynasty was founded on the banks of the Tungabhadra river in 1336 by two brothers who had been fugitives from Wārangal when that seat of Kākatiya power was captured by a Tughluq sultan. The brothers were taken captive, Islamicized, and commissioned to consolidate rule in Kampīla; but the brothers renounced Islam and established a "Hindu" polity, which became a counterpart to the sultanate established at Bādāmi in the Western Deccan.[2]

The Vijayanagara kings patronized the arts, philosophy, temple building, and other forms of "Hindu" expression (even though they also hired

Muslims in their armies and courts and fought with other Hindu princes). In the area of philosophy three rival systems of Vedānta flourished with the writings of new works in the fourteenth century: by **Vidyaranya** (Advaita – Śaṅkara's tradition); **Nārāyana** (***Dvaita*** – the tradition associated with Madhva), and by **Venkatanatha** (Viśiṣṭādvaita – Rāmānujan's tradition). New epics were written – for example, the same Venkatanatha wrote a long narrative on the birth and rise of Kṛṣṇa and the princess **Gaṅga** wrote an epic celebrating her husband's victory over the "Turks."[3] Poets were patronized in the courts, not least of all the Ḍiṇḍima family (fifteenth century), including one who wrote a highly Sanskritized Tamil verse in praise of Murukaṉ, the Tamil deity. Temples were constructed that were larger than those built before – these temples were now mini-cities accommodating various forms of folk ritual, providing halls for marriages and entertainment and space for bazaars in ritual paraphernalia. The writing of *āgamas* was sponsored starting from handbooks purporting to describe the way certain rituals were to be done. Not least important, an elaborate festival known as the Navarātiri or Mahānavamī was sponsored in September–October. This festival of nine nights was in honor of the goddess and culminated in celebrating Vijaya Dasami, the conquest of Rāma over Rāvaṇa. While the Vijayanagara kings were patrons of Viṣṇu, the festival for the goddess, nonetheless, served many purposes: it legitimated their reign, became an occasion to demonstrate to all the kingdom and to foreign dignitaries the status of the king, and to evoke the goddess's patronage on the operations of the state. The festival was an enormous pageant complete with the performance of acrobatic women and parades of elephants and soldiers. Some scholars have suggested that the Navarātiri incorporated some of the features of the older *aśvamedha* (horse sacrifice) thereby evoking "*vaidika*" sanction on the king's regime.[4] Even after the decline of the Vijayanagara dynasty in the sixteenth century, similar kinds of activities (e.g., festivals to the goddess, construction of large temples, the patronage of "Hindu" acts) were carried on in the courts of the *nāyakkas* – those regional satraps who had paid homage to the Vijayanagara kings, but now maintained mini-kingdoms into the seventeenth century.

The Vijayanagara kings were not creating a kingdom from "scratch." They followed many of the precedents of the Cōḻas and other dynasties before them. They do represent, nonetheless, a pocket in the south where Hindu *dharma* was preserved and where neo-classical expressions prevailed.

The Marāthās followed a century after the fall of Vijayanagara. Founded by **Śivājī** in 1667, the Marāthā "empire" stretched across much of western Central India.[5] Śivājī took power by assassinating a Muslim general after having escaped captivity at the hands of the Mughals. Śivājī reorganized the territory in what is now Maharashtra and administered the realm according to Vijayanagara principles, organizing the army along principles borrowed from the Portuguese. He was noted for the sacking of Surat (by then a small enclave of the British East India Company) and for fighting and plundering the lands of Deccan kings (many of them Hindu) and of the Mughals. It is interesting that by the late nineteenth century, thanks to the rhetoric of another native of Maharashtra, **B. G. Tilak**, Śivājī is extolled as a brave Hindu hero and vanquisher of Muslims. The historical record is not so clear; he was known to have a number of Muslims in top positions in his administration and in his army. His battles were against Hindu as well as Muslim political figures and seemed to have been more political than religious in nature. In any case, Marāthā "country" came to be seen as a place where Hindu *dharma* was preserved.

The same was true under the Rājputs for a number of centuries. As described earlier, the Rājputs employed brahman ministers and patronized a particular form of orthodox "Hindu" culture. It is believed that *satī* (the immolation of widows), for example, was performed under Rājput aegis for the first time in 1382, and that it was especially continued under such ruling families as the Sisodiyas wherein, on at least one occasion, an entire harem of up to twenty women was immolated on the funeral pyre of their dead husband.[6] Yet by the time of the Mughals, the Rājputs were closely allied to them, thanks to intermarriage even in Akbar's time, and it became increasingly difficult to distinguish Rājput "culture" from that of the Mughals.

Hindu orthopraxy, in short, was the practice of "retaining" what was perceived to be proper "Hindu" practice. Whether these polities were created in explicit contradistinction to Islamic forms of orthopraxy has been debated. What is evident, nonetheless, is that in some Islamic courts, forms of Islamic orthodoxy prevailed. In these courts, the emperor was *huzūr* (omnipotent representative of Allāh),[7] and the *'ulamā'* or Sūfīs were usually the court advisers. The building of mosques and other monuments served both religious and political purposes. *Madrasas* – schools of Islamic (and especially *sunnī*) learning – were the counterpart of the *maṭhas*. In these *madrasas* Arabic was taught, and the Qu'rān was memorized and recited; in addition, pilgrimages to the tombs of *pīrs* increased, and women were encouraged to live in ***purdah*** (seclusion), increasingly used as a symbol of purity and Islamic identity.

Does orthopraxy sometimes give way to fundamentalism, even xenophobia and militancy? There is little doubt that it did, but it is difficult to sort out the historical reality from *post-facto* rhetoric and chauvinism. For example, by at least the thirteenth century, there was clearly a rhetoric of xenophobia in some Sanskrit sources addressed against Afghans. In these sources,

Afghans were described as ugly, white persons with broad foreheads on which their various atrocities could be inscribed. They were described as "horrible of speech," "impure of complexion," and the slaughterers of cows.[8] By at least the seventeenth century, there was a rhetoric accusing Muslim rulers of destroying temples and pillaging the countryside. To be sure, there were instances of sacking of mosques as well as of Buddhist and Hindu shrines. Sanjay Subrahmanyan reports, for example, on the destruction of a mosque in Khambayat, Gujarat, in the 1220s and of another instance some 500 years later in Ahmadabad, Gujarat.[9] Similarly, there was pillaging at temples, especially during "foreign" incursions (e.g., Afghans, the Mongols, Timur of Samarkand). Yet, as Subrahmanyan and others remind us, there were instances of inter-sectarian violence well before the coming of Islam.[10] The destruction of Buddhist institutions was occasionally done by "Hindu" rulers as at Nāgārjunakonda; even the looting of Hindu temples occurred in such places as Kashmīr by "Hindu" rulers seeking to avenge brahmans who were perceived to be too wealthy, corrupt, and powerful.[11] Conversely, there were Hindu temples constructed or renovated during periods of Islamic governance[12] or by individual Muslims who believed themselves to have been cured by a resident deity.

Devotionalism

A major wave of devotionalism (*bhakti*) occurred during this period when Islam was increasingly visible. Was it a coincidence? Possibly but probably not always. Certainly, *bhakti* had thrived in the Tamil vernacular marking the Tamilization of Śaivism and Vaiṣṇavism in the seventh to ninth centuries. And tantrism and worship of the goddess were occurring in the eighth to tenth centuries, in a number of regions of India. Yet these movements seemed to have occurred at times and in places of transition. There was reaffirmation of regional and vernacular idioms, and a dialectic of "self" and "other." The "other" had sometimes been other sects or communities. It had also included response to Buddhism and Jainism. Islam may well have been one of the catalysts of a resurgence of devotionalism in this period, whether directly or indirectly.[13] The connections were sometimes explicit in those *bhakti* poets who were singing after the thirteenth century, though there were clearly other factors as well. These factors included an emerging consciousness of regional and vernacular identities, the appropriation of indigenous and "folk" forms of religious expression, and the borrowing of (and distancing from) brahmanic forms of orthopraxy.

Three vernaculars in particular were beginning to reflect a rich devotional surge: Marāthī, Bengālī, and Hindī. We look briefly at each context.

Marāthī

Among the earliest of the Marāthī *bhaktas* was **Jnāneśvara** (1271–96). He was influenced by the popular Vārkarī sect which worshiped Viṭhobā, the god of Pandharpur. Also informed by the Nāṭha sect, Jnāneśvara wrote a commentary on the *Bhagavadgītā* in Marāthī known as the *Jnāneśvarī*.[14] Several features of the *bhakti* movement were evident in his work: the use of the regional vernacular, the appropriation of indigenous, even "folk," forms of religious practice, and the selective appropriation of Sanskritic sources. The result was the Vaiṣṇavization of Marāthī country, the equating of Viṭhobā to Kṛṣṇa, and the sanctioning of Marāthī as a literate form.

Nāmdev (1270–1350) was a low-caste tailor and devotee of Viṭhobā, by now a full-fledged form of Viṣṇu.[15] His songs were passionate and generally transcended caste and became very popular in the Vārkarī movement. He is generally credited with incorporating the *kīrtaṇ* (group singing) into the poetic repertoire, encouraging group chanting such as was used in semi-annual pilgrimage to Pandharpur.[16]

Eknāth (1553–99) was a brahman, but believed that religion could be practiced in every home. He was also something of a scholar as he provided a Marāthī commentary on the eleventh book of the *Bhagavata Purāṇa* and offered a new version of the *Rāmāyana*, known as *Bhāvārtha Rāmāyan*, thereby giving the story of Rāma a Marāthī cast.[17] Eknāth explicitly sought some accommodation between Muslims and Hindus as in one of his poems he offers a dialogue between a "turk" and a brahman in which each finds faults with the other, until in the end, accommodations are found and the discovery of "true" religion is offered.[18]

Tukārām (1598–1650) was born into a rural family of grain traders. His *bhakti* was born of tragedy – the death of his wife and son. Tukārām composed songs that became favorites of *vārkarī* pilgrims. His songs and his devotion were intensely personal; ecstasy was the *summum bonum* of religion. Though a mystic, his poetry reflected the language and life of the common people.[19]

The final figure in the devotional heritage of Maharashtra was **Rāmdās** (1608–81). He was the author of *Daśobhada*, a compilation of his writings and poems and of *Manace Śloka*, a compilation of "verses to the mind." Not part of the Vārkarī movement, he was a devotee of Rāma to whom he built a temple. He also managed to politicize *bhakti* in Marāthī country. He is said to have been concerned with the "degeneration" of brahmanic society and the perceived threat of Islam's spread. Rāmdās was believed by his followers to be an *avatāra* of Hanuman, Rāma's "monkey general," and was responsible for emphasizing the tradition of *bālapāsana* (worship of strength) in which gyms and Hanuman temples were established. Śivājī, the founder of the

Figure 6 Statue of Hanuman, monkey general of Rāma's army. Photograph by Rob F. Phillips.

Marāthī kingdom, was a disciple of Rāmdās who presented Rāma as the militant prototype of a dharmic Hindu king. A tradition had been started in Maharashtra wherein Rāma was politicized and "others" deemed to be undesirable were homologized to Rāvaṇa.[20]

These Marāthī poets were both reflecting and catalyzing the popular forms that religion was taking in Western India. Pilgrimage, especially to Pandharpur where the god Viṭhobā was enshrined, was one form of this devotionalism. Yet another was the way Hanuman became a popular deity, especially after the time of Rāmdās. (Rāmdās had equated Viṭhobā with Rāma and installed a Hanuman shrine at Pandharpur as Rāma's protector.) Known as Maruti in Marāthī-speaking country, Hanuman was the monkey general in Rāma's mythical army. Today he is portrayed as the protector-deity and warrior par excellence, the epitome of fidelity, virility, and fitness, an apt model for devout males to follow.[21]

Bengālī

We have observed how in Bengal there were several religious currents at work by the ninth and tenth centuries. There had been a significant Buddhist presence until the eleventh century and a sizable Muslim presence, especially in East Bengal, by the thirteenth century. Tantrism had been a strong movement into the tenth century and a number of goddesses emerged to the status of high deity by at least the twelfth century, especially Durgā, Kālī, and Rādhā. Rādhā's popularity, in particular, was catalyzed by the appearance of Jayadeva's *Gīta Govinda* in the twelfth century. Jayadeva's Sanskrit text was influenced by a variety of sources: the *Bhāgavata Purāṇa*; the songs of the Tamil *Āḻvārs* (probably brought to Bengal by pilgrims during the Cōḻa period); and tantrism. No doubt folk traditions were a part of the mix especially those associated with the herding communities. The *Gīta Govinda* rhapsodized about Kṛṣṇa as a lovable, approachable local "cowherd" god whose love for the *gopīs*, and especially Rādhā, was celebrated. The erotic imagery and allegories associated with this relationship came to be sung, danced, and enacted throughout India. The text served to classicize stories and traditions that earlier may have been found only amongst peoples living on the "margins" of society, and which in their earlier form may have had anti-establishment, even anti-brahman intimations.[22]

Chandīdās, a fourteenth-century poet, sang extensively to the mother goddess and to Kṛṣṇa and Rādhā. The *Kṛṣṇa Kīrtaṇ* (songs for Kṛṣṇa) became a favored form of expressing devotion in groups. Chandīdās also was not averse to acting out his love for god by embodying it in a relationship with a particular earthly person, a "recycling" of the tantric ritual tradition.[23] **Vidyāpati** (fourteenth to fifteenth century) composed in Maithilī nearly

1,000 love ballads, which have now been collected. His favorite subject was the relationship between Kṛṣṇa and Rādhā and the use of erotic imagery to speak of the *bhakta*'s relationship with the divine.[24]

One other significant contributor to the *bhakti* movement in Bengal was **Viśvambhar Miśra**, better known as **Caitanya** (1485–1533), who started a new movement within Bengālī Vaiṣṇavism. Appealing especially to a newly emergent "middle class" in Bengal – for example, merchants, farmers, artisans – Caitanya offered an egalitarian form of Vaiṣṇavism which borrowed brahmanical ideas while critiquing brahmanic hegemony. He sent six followers (*gosvāmins*) to Vrindāvan, pilgrimage center par excellence of the Kṛṣṇa cultus. There they were asked to work out a theology based on sacred texts, not least importantly, the *Bhāgavata Purāṇa* and the *Bhavadgītā*. In Caitanya's system, Kṛṣṇa was the highest form of the divine, its true essence, who was united with Śaktī, manifest in Rādhā. A devotee could ascend the ladder of *bhakti* until reaching the supreme state, known as *mādhurya* or sweetness. When one was identified with Rādhā, devotion was expressed in ***sankīrtaṇa*** – ecstatic dancing to the sound of tambourines. Sound in the form of chant and recitation of the deity's name was thought to enable the devotee to draw near to the divine.[25] Sound was cosmogonic, a *vaidika* assertion, but it also incorporated the Sūfī notion of becoming one with the divine. Kṛṣṇa was presented as consistent with the Qurānic imagery of Allāh, but more pervasive. The school Caitanya founded has survived into the present and is widely known as Gaudiā Vaiṣṇavism or the International Society for Krishna Consciousness.

Hindī

Though Hindī was only standardized by the early nineteenth century, the language was evolving in dialects by the fourteenth century. In fact, it evolved alongside Urdū, in the Indo-Islamic matrix with which it shared a grammar and a vocabulary.[26] Like the language itself, the *bhakti* singers were a product of their time, sometimes explicitly showing the connections between the Hindu and Muslim experience; sometimes those relationships were, at best, implicit.

The lineage of the "Hindī" *bhaktas* began perhaps as much as anywhere with **Rāmānanda** (1400–1470). Apparently from South India and a follower of Rāmānujan, he became an important catalyst for the forms of devotionalism that followed. For him Rāma was the supreme god who was to be worshiped with Śaktī, yet he was rather eclectic in lifestyle. Possibly influenced by Sūfīsm,[27] he was opposed to caste and other distinctions of "religion" and class. His own disciples are said to have included a Muslim, an outcaste, and several women. One of those he apparently influenced was **Kabīr**.

Kabīr (1440–1512) was apparently born of a low-caste Muslim weaver who, nonetheless, had contact with both Muslim and Hindu saints. His poetry, composed in the Bhojpurī dialect, had a rustic, simple flavor. His songs and religious vision incorporated aspects of Vaiṣṇavism, Haṭha Yoga, Sūfīsm, and Vedāntic monism: God was one but he had many names. The one way to god was through *bhakti,* devotion. The enlightening vision of god (*darśan*) was a gift of his grace. The self was purified by humility, renunciation, and the praise of god in *kīrtaṇ* (song) and meditation. Kabīr was something of an iconoclast as he attacked the "externals" of religion – for example, the scriptures, whether the *Purāṇas* or Qu'rān, were less important than the experience of the divine itself. Rituals, icons, caste, pilgrimages to various sites were extraneous. In a famous verse he made fun of the unnecessary strategies for attaining release: if celibacy were the way to enlightenment, then eunuchs would be at the head of the line; if going around naked were the way, shorn sheep would enter paradise immediately:

Go naked if you want,
Put on animal skins.
  What does it matter till you see the inward Ram?

If the union yogis seek
Came from roaming about in the buff,
  every deer in the forest would be saved.

If shaving your head
Spelled spiritual success,
  heaven would be filled with sheep.

And brother, if holding back your seed
Earned you a place in paradise,
  eunuchs would be the first to arrive.

Kabir says: Listen brother,
Without the name of Ram
  who has ever won the spirit's prize?

* * *

Pundit, how can you be so dumb?
You're going to drown, along with all your kin,
unless you start speaking of Ram.

Vedas, Puranas – why read them?
It's like loading an ass with sandalwood!
Unless you catch on and learn how Ram's name goes,
how will you reach the end of the road?

You slaughter living beings and call it religion:
hey brother, what would irreligion be?
"Great Saint" – that's how you love to greet each other:
Who then would you call a murderer?

Your mind is blind. You've no knowledge of yourselves.
Tell me, brother, how can you teach anyone else?
Wisdom is a thing you sell for worldly gain,
so there goes your human birth – in vain.

You say: "It's Narad's command."
"It's what Vyas says to do."
"Go and ask Sukdev, the sage."
Kabir says: you'd better go and lose yourself in Ram
for without him, brother, you drown.[28]

The legacy of Kabīr was several groups (*panths*) of seekers, most notably the Kabīrpanth. **Nānak**, the founder of the Sikh movement, may have been influenced by his teachings or at least by the spirit represented in Kabīr's poetry.[29]

Sūrdās (1483–1563) was a brahman reciting in the Braj-bhāsha dialect. A blind disciple of Vallabha, he was inspired by the *Bhāgavata Purāṇa* and declared that love of Kṛṣṇa was central to enlightenment. His stories were often poignant reminders of the true nature of sight – it was seeing within that was important.

Until you wake up to what you really are
You'll be like the man who searches the whole jungle
for a jewel that hangs at his throat.
Oil, wick, and fire: until they mingle in a cruse
they scarcely produce any light,
So how can you expect to dissipate the darkness
simply by talking about lamps?
You're the sort of fool who sees your face
in a mirror, befouled by inky filth,
And proceeds to try to erase the blackness
by cleaning the reflection to a shine.

Surdas says, it's only now the mind can see –
now that so countless many days are lost and gone –
For who has ever recognized the brilliance of the sun
but by seeing it through eyes gone blind?[30]

Yet another poet of the fifteenth or sixteenth century was **Ravidās**, an outcaste leather worker, born in Banāras. While Ravidās tended to be "anti-establishment" in his orientation, he was not interested in social reform. Rather, he valued his "low state" so he could attest to how far the divine would stoop to meet a devotee. His *bhakti* was that for the divine which transcended all forms (*nirguṇa*).[31] The form of the deity preferred by the *bhakta* may itself be a reflection of the times. The *nirguṇa* (formless) divine is consistent not only with classical Hindu devotion but with Sūfī and Islamic perceptions as well, whereas *saguṇa bhakti* (that directed to a specific form of the divine, such as Rāma) attests to the god's accessibility and concreteness perhaps in contradistinction to more remote perceptions of God.

Tulsīdās (1532–1623), writing in the Avadhī dialect, was an important contributor to the Hindī religious landscape. He was the author of the *Rāmcharitmānas* (the lake of the story of Rāma), a Hindī version of the *Rāmāyaṇa*, as well as of several other works. It was Tulsīdās who was largely responsible for popularizing the cult of Rāma in "Hindī" idiom, and it was after his time that pilgrimage sites for Rāma became more abundant in upper Central India. Tulsīdās' devotion was that of a servant for his master.[32]

Mīrābaī (sixteenth century) has become an especially popular poetess amongst women. She was apparently a Rājput princess who refused to consummate her marriage to her royal husband because of her devotion to Kṛṣṇa. She is also said to have defied the wishes of her in-laws in not worshiping Durgā in favor of Kṛṣṇa. Tradition also claims she refused to immolate herself on the funeral pyre of her husband when he was cremated.[33] In short, she was depicted as the prototypical woman who transcended social conventions in order to become the bride of Kṛṣṇa. The dialect of her compositions was Rājasthānī.

There were *bhakti* singers in other parts of the subcontinent as well. For example, **Dadu of Rajasthan** (1544–1603) was a mystic who espoused the perception of the divine as *nirguṇa*, yet benevolent and gracious in a manner consistent with both a *vaidika* vision and a Sūfī one. He was a contemporary of Akbar and the Sūfī eclectic mystic scholar **Dārā Shikoh** who may have influenced Dadu. In the south, a new wave of *bhakti* was beginning in Tamil, thanks in large measure to the musical poetry of **Aruṇakiri** (early fifteenth century?). Aruṇakiri was a master of poetic medium – alliteration, meter, assonance, etc. His deity, Murukaṉ, was extolled for his "military prowess" as if to suggest political instability needed the ministrations of a strong leader and to convey the need for internal victory over the passions. His poetry celebrated the Tamil language and landscape in ways that made him a forerunner of an eventual Tamil renaissance.[34]

While early waves of devotionalism in specific regions reflected local factors, certain general features might be highlighted. First, there was the use of vernacular idiom and the landscape of the particular region, suggesting an increased awareness of regional and linguistic particularities. Second, there was a selective "brahmanizing" of elements that were part of folk society. Even when the poets were not brahmans, there was borrowing of themes from classical myth or symbol, or, conversely, the classicizing of folk and regional idioms. Finally, there was an implicit dialectic of self and other, whether Kabīr's "othering" of the "externals" of both Hindu and Muslim traditions or Rāmdās' more explicit "othering" of non-brahmanic "threats" including that perceived to reside in Islam. At least implicit from the thirteenth century on was a sense that Islam was part of the landscape and response was explicit in the case of several (Eknāth, Caitanya, etc.). With some exceptions (e.g., Rāmdās and some Sūfīs), the poets were relatively apolitical and egalitarian.

Parallel and almost indistinguishable at times to this blossoming of vernacular devotionalism within "Hinduisim" was the presence, spread, and interaction of Sūfī pietism. Along with the Chistī order which influenced Uttar Pradesh and Panjāb, there was the Suhrwardī order which was common in Sind, and the Firdausī order in Bihar and Bengal. New orders also emerged in India such as the Qādirīs and the Shattārīs, both of which were pantheistic in character. Sūfīs interacted with "Hindu" streams of devotion. While they at first sang in Persian, by the fourteenth century their songs were in some form of Urdū: **Amīr Khusrau**, who died in 1325; **Valli** (1677–1741), who actually composed in the Deccanī language; **Ghālib** (1789–1876), *et al.* Their *ghazals* became a uniquely Indian poetic form expressed in Urdū or a dialect thereof, using a rich vocabulary of metaphors for the religious experience: a rose was like god; the nightingale or hummingbird was the poet; the garden was where the poet met god; wine was like a means by which a new state of being was attained. Often impatient with the political order, the Sūfī saints rhapsodized about the possibility of ecstatic union with the divine and of the desirability of being emptied of the orientations of the self and filled with the fullness of the divine, thereby becoming the vessel of the divine presence.

Accommodation and appropriation

Perhaps the most visible result of the Islamic presence in India was the way in which mutual borrowings and appropriations occurred leading to new creativity in the arts, architecture, languages, lifestyle, and, of course, religion. The patterns of these borrowings would vary from region to region, community to community, even family to family. As persons of varying cultural-religious backgrounds interacted there would be borrowings at the person to person or family to family levels. On the other end of the spectrum, in the courts, especially those of the Mughals and the Rājputs, there was the patronizing of an increasingly eclectic culture. Here it should be enough to summarize and/or illustrate some of these developments.

The emergence of new languages is one illustration of this phenomenon. By the thirteenth and fourteenth centuries, a variety of Indo-Āryan or Indo-Persian dialects was emerging. These included Braj-bhāsha, the vehicle of medieval Vaiṣṇava literature and of classical Hindūstānī music[35] and Avadhī in which both Hindu and Muslim *bhakti* poetry was written.[36] Dakhinī (or Deccanī), a language used primarily by Muslims in Central India by the fifteenth century, was part of the mix.[37] Such dialects as these evolved into Hindī and Urdū, first as spoken, then written languages. Urdū used an Arabic script but borrowed its vocabulary from Arabic, Persian, Turkish, and Sanskritic sources; its grammar reflects Sanskritic roots as well as others. Hindī, on the other hand, used a Devanāgarī (Sanskritic) script and borrowed words from Arabic, Persian, and Turkish sources and grammar from Prākritic as well as other sources. As we have observed, poetry and various forms of literature were rich, particularly by the sixteenth century. Similarly, the libraries to be found in Delhi were among the best in Asia as, under royal patronage, manuscripts were collected and vernacular materials were brought together from the Hindu and Islamic worlds.

Science flourished under Mughal and/or Rājput patronage. There was a combination of Sanskritic and Arabic medical traditions as medical texts from both traditions were translated and made available. It may not be an exaggeration to suggest that by the seventeenth century, Delhi was one of the finest medical centers in the world. Astronomy also flourished. Some five observatories were to be found in the Delhi area by the seventeenth century and Sanskritic and Arabic traditions of astronomy were in contact in ways seldom seen since the scientific heyday of ninth-century Baghdad.[38]

Accommodation and mutual influence were especially apparent in the arts. Musical forms were synthesized, for example, creating a "new" mode of "classical" music sometimes known as Hindūstānī or Indo-Islamic, in contrast to the southern Carnatic musical tradition. Sūfīs used the Indian musical scale while offering sentiments reflecting Persian roots. Several new musical instruments appeared – the sitār, the tambūrā and the tablā, for example. Music was patronized in the courts and by the sultans.[39] The same was true of dance – a "new" dance form emerged known as ***kathak*** in which Persian motifs mingled with Hindu themes. Muslims and Hindus alike sang and danced the stories of Kṛṣṇa and Rādhā.

Architecture also combined Islamic (especially Persian) forms with Indian ones. A common style was the "tent motif" in which four pillars and a dome replicate the imagery of a tent in the desert. Tombs (thought inappropriate in orthoprax Islamic culture) were common in India. Geometric designs shared by both Muslim and Hindu traditions were found on these structures. Craftsmen were both Muslim and Hindu.

In the meanwhile, as we have noted, poetry proliferated in Hindī, Urdū, and various vernaculars. Not least important, translations had become a significant contribution to the literary landscape. These translations went both ways, from Persian into the vernacular and Sanskrit texts into Persian. The most intriguing example of the latter is the work attributed to Dārā Shikoh, a prince in Akbar's court. Portions of the *Mahābhārata* and *Rāmāyana* were translated into Persian in the sixteenth century, and in their Persian form became accessible to Europeans. Indeed, the first glimpses Europeans got of Sanskrit classics were offered through Muslim eyes in Persian.

The lifestyle, especially of North India, was impacted by the presence of Islamic "culture." The *purdah* (segregating women by the wearing of outer clothes) was adapted in some Hindu families. The pajama-style of dress for both men and women had extra-Indian origins. The use of wine and smoking of the *ḥuqqah* (pipe) became a shared part of North Indian culture, as did the preparation of various foods from biryānī to tandoori chicken.

It should not be a surprise then that religion was also accommodated to the ambiance of the period. Amongst "Hindu" *bhaktas* and saints, one finds an increased impatience with caste, iconography, brahmanic orthopraxy, and expressions of sectarian identity. Amongst Muslims, especially Sūfīs, one finds the incorporation of music, legends, and myths derived from "Hindu" sources. Pilgrimage sites came to share stories of Hindu deities and Muslim saints (*pīrs*). The building of tombs and visiting these sites (*dargahs*) on regular occasions was commonplace as was the conducting of *'urs* – the annual fair or festival performed on the anniversary of the saint's death. Many rites of passage performed by Muslims, from the naming of a child to marriage, shared many rituals and customs with those of Hindus who lived in the same region. There was even the rather loose development of a "caste" system within Islam based, in part, on a perceived distinction between the descendants of immigrants (known as ***as̱hrāf***) and those who were converted in India. Occupational distinctions also became part of the mix – virtual castes based on the work of the family into which one was born.

These accommodations were particularly striking in the case of Sūfīs who borrowed freely from their Hindu counterparts. Nowhere, perhaps, was this trend more dramatic than in the "theological" system developed by Dārā Shikoh. Dārā Shikoh adapted many traditional Hindu elements into his Sūfī vision: the *Vedas* and *Upaniṣads* were sources of revelation; Brahmā, Viṣṇu, Śiva were among the angels; Hindu thinkers could be counted among prophets. Allāh was *paramātman,* the highest form of the divine; Muḥammad the *avatār* of Allāh's word.

Conversion

There is little doubt that there were conversions during this period. Most of these were into various forms of Islam, most commonly into Sūfī strands. Rarely does one find evidence of conversion from Islam. Rather, "Muslims" may have moved away from orthopraxy and appropriated *bhakti* motifs without necessarily becoming "Hindu." Such was the case with many Sūfī sheikhs and laity whose religious life closely illustrated the patterns of accommodation sketched above. The conversion into Islam occurred for many reasons, any one of which seldom tells the whole story, and the story differs from region to region. Generally speaking, however, the conversions that occurred into Islam occurred on the fringes of the subcontinent (East Bengal, Kashmīr, Western Panjāb especially) where Buddhism had once been present only to become decimated and where various "Hindu" sects had failed to take root with the general populace. Occasionally, conversion occurred for material betterment, as when craftsmen sought better opportunities for employment or payment in a sultan's court. In some cases, those who converted had been alienated from the power structures or economic "brokers" of their region. Most commonly, however, it was the result of people's becoming increasingly comfortable with and attracted to those religious functionaries who were accessible and seemed to have the good of the common people at heart. Usually, these functionaries were Sūfīs. But the picture is more complex. It might be useful to look at one setting and explore some of the issues that led to massive conversions in that case. We examine the case of Kashmīr.[40]

In Kashmīr, Buddhism had been the religion of most of the population in the third century BCE. By the eighth century CE, brahmanism in its various forms was an important part of the landscape and many of Kashmīr's people had opted for worship of Śiva, Viṣṇu, or the Goddess. But poverty had become the common lot of people at the lower echelons of society. This was so for a variety of reasons, not least of them that kings from the eighth to the thirteenth centuries imposed very heavy taxes on their subjects. From

Jayapida (753–82) to **Unmattavant** (937–39) and again by **Suhadeva** (1301–20), kings are described as "oppressive" and "avaricious" by historians like Kalhana and Hangloo.[41] Meanwhile, brahmans had been given considerable lands by said kings in keeping with the pattern found in other regions where the "state" used brahmans as their advisers and rhetoricians. Neither brahmans nor others of the landed aristocracy were taxed as severely; as a result, by the fourteenth century the economy of Kashmīr was flowing upward into the hands of rulers and aristocracy.

Matters became worse when disunity set in amongst the dominant groups. Revolts by tantrins and other sects and hunger strikes by brahmans became frequent. There was a struggle for power by the tenth century which pitted rulers against brahmans. Kings hated what they perceived to be the dominance and greed of brahmans, which led a number of them from **Samkarvarman** (883–902) to **Harṣa** (1089–1101) to plunder temples. Meanwhile, Sarvāstivāda Buddhism, which had been the dominant form of Buddhism in Kashmīr, had fallen on hard times. It was accused of corruption and superstition by brahman and king alike. Buddhist *vihāras* by the thousands were destroyed by such kings as Nara and Mihirakula. No unified religious traditions were available to replace Buddhism, as inter-sectarian rivalries were rife.

To be sure, a significant tradition of Śaiva philosophy developed in Kashmīr thanks to the teachings of such as Abhinavagupta, but this was designed to encourage the pursuit of wisdom and spiritual discipline as a way to attain release, measures hardly accessible to the common people. Into this relative religious vacuum came Islam. For centuries, Muslim traders and craftsmen had been entering Kashmīr for purposes of doing business. A number of these began to settle by at least the thirteenth century. Among those who represented the character of Islam were Sūfī saints who spoke of the social equality espoused by Islam and the notion that human beings were the sacred creations of god. These Sūfīs lived amongst the poor, spoke their language, setting examples of piety and, for the most part, avoiding any attempt to convert people.

It was the fourteenth century before Islamic rule became a part of the Kashmīrī landscape. One **Shahmir** (1339–42) established cordial relations with brahman chiefs, even marrying his daughter to one of them. The first five sultans of this dynasty were relatively low key in their espousal of Islam. They patronized Sūfīs to teach and established institutions like the *madrasa* as a place for learning about Islam. It was **Sultan Sikander** (1389–1414) who took more drastic measures. Following a policy used by Hindu kings a century earlier he demolished temples and confiscated the wealth of brahman establishments. It is said that there were conversions, even by brahmans, to Islam in the wake of these actions. Indeed, Sikander's actions were abetted by his prime minister, **Subhabhata**, a brahman who later became a Muslim. Moreover Sultan Sikander offered patronage to Turks and Persians who came into Kashmīr in large numbers bringing with them technological skill and work for the lower echelons of society. The increased trade with Central Asia provided peasants the opportunity to learn new crafts. **Sultan Zayn-al-Abidin** (1420–70) made available opportunities to develop such crafts as bottle, shawl, and carpet making. People, in short, became more economically independent and had access to religious opportunities as well.

The readiness of the Kashmīrī people for change was facilitated by a woman *bhakta* named **Laleshwarī**. Her songs expressed indignation at the brahmanic "establishment," and oppression by the aristocrats, and expressed the need for a form of religion that went beyond the worship of icons and *pūjās* in temples. Similarly, one **Shaikh Nur al-Din** was concerned to establish a community where equality was possible. Other Sayyids and sheikhs followed into Kashmīr teaching the rudiments of their faith. Rather than countenance the destruction of temples, they sought to remove icons and convert temples into mosques and places of Islamic learning. In addition to teaching religious precepts these "missionaries" passed on various skills and knowledge of a variety of things to the local people. Converts came mostly from various artisan classes, craftsmen, village peasants, and menial laborers.

In sum, conversion to Islam in a region like Kashmīr was a complex process in which several elements were present. Among them were a sense of poverty and marginality on the part of society's lower echelons; corruption at the top; fragmentation and disunity on the part of power brokers, a religious "vacuum" amongst the poor, and the concomitant presence of religious functionaries who lived amongst the poor, taught them, and helped pass along a variety of skills.

Syncretism

Yet a different kind of response is what is here termed "syncretism." Syncretism, used here, means the creation of a new form or movement with explicit borrowing from one or more sources. Some of the *panths* (movements) emanating from Kabīr's life and thought may be termed syncretistic. Some would call the theology of Dārā Shikoh a form of syncretism.

The finest example of syncretism in this period was the emergence of Sikhism, a movement forged by gurus which has become a full-blown "religion."

Sikhism

The story of Sikhism starts, for all intents and purposes, with Gurū Nānak. There were a number of influences that informed the life and thought of Nānak. That background included a significant presence of Sūfīsm and *bhakti* in Panjāb (literally, "the five rivers"). As mentioned earlier, there was a series of gurus who preceded Nānak. They included Jayadeva, who emphasized recitation of the name of god in a way that is reminiscent of both the *vaidika* recitation of sound and the Islamic recitation of the Qu'rān. The sound itself was understood to represent the divine and the cosmos. Another saint, Rāmānanda, sought a religious orientation free of "legalism" and caste. "Legalism" was the unnecessary following of disciplines thought to be extraneous to "true" religion. Vegetarianism, for example, was thought to be a form of legalism. Rather, religion was a matter of internal reform. Something of this attitude was found in Kabīr (1440–1518), who was apparently raised by Muslims and influenced by Hindus. Kabīr rejected the use of icons and rituals that were not deemed central to attaining religious fulfillment. Scripture was useful only insofar as it was combined with the inner experience of "truth." He wrote in the vernacular in a way that made his monotheism attractive to a broad range of people.

Nānak (1469–1539) followed in the spirit of these antecedents. He was born Hindu but raised in contact with Muslims. A storekeeper, he decided he wanted to find some answers to the questions troubling him; he left his home and spent time as a wandering minstrel. The tradition insists he had a life-changing vision one day while bathing. In his vision, Nānak saw himself in paradise (as if in a temple) and heard the word of the one God (*ek ōmkār*); the metaphor of listening and hearing the name of the divine became central to his thought.[42] His life was reoriented, and he became a *gurū*, establishing the community of Sikhs.

Gurū Nānak's religious ideas were drawn from many sources. God was one (*ek*); he was unseen, sovereign, and transcendent (in a manner consistent with orthodox Islam). But God was also accessible in ways both Sūfī and *bhakti* poets had sung: God was to be celebrated and relished; He made himself manifest in a personal way. Human beings were made for submission to God. Yet *māyā*, like *avidyā*, hid the reality of God. One must move beyond appearances and book knowledge to wisdom and acting according to the truth. That truth could be discerned by reciting the names of the one God. The aim of life was to discover and serve God, the omnipotent and the immanent, He who infused the world. With the free will given to humans, one was to discern the flow of God's purpose in the cosmos.

Nānak established a system of *gurū* succession. The *gurū* was a perfected exemplar who teaches, passes on the tradition, and gives leadership to the community.

Nānak once wrote:

> The guru is the ladder, the dinghy, the raft by means of which one reaches god;
> The guru is the lake, the ocean, the boat, the sacred placed pilgrimage, the river.
> If it please thee I am cleansed by bathing in the lake of truth.[43]

Nānak's immediate successor was **Angad** (1539–52) who started collecting the scripture of the community, the *Adi Granth*, later known as the *Gurū Granth Sāhib*, based on the poems of the *gurūs*. He also established the ***langar*** (common kitchen), a symbolic representation of the idea that all persons were equal and could eat food prepared by any member of the group (an explicit critique of brahmanic culinary fastidiousness).[44]

Amar Dās (1552–74), successor to Angad, emphasized egalitarianism further, and expressed concern for the social well-being of the community. Ascetism was discouraged in favor of altruism and community life. A caste group known as *jāts* (farmers and warriors) was beginning to be attracted to the community; Amar Dās therefore instituted certain rituals intended to develop a sense of community and identity. Rituals for marriages and funerals, for example, though borrowed largely from Hinduism, were intended to provide a uniquely Sikh way of being in community. Not least important, this *gurū* identified Amritsar as the place where the Sikhs would be centered and which, with the construction of a temple, would become a Sikh pilgrimage center.[45]

It was left to his successor **Rām Dās** (1574–81) to raise funds for and start the building of the famed Golden Temple at Amritsar (the lake of *amṛt* [the nectar of immortality]). The fifth *gurū*, Arjun (1581–1606), completed construction of the Amritsar temple and made it a pilgrimage center with a distinct language and ritual tradition. Arjun also continued compiling the sacred scripture of the community, the *Gurū Granth Sāhib*.

By now tensions were growing between the Sikh community and the Mughals, largely because Jahāngīr, the son of Akbar, reversed Akbar's policy of tolerance to all faiths. In addition, Sikhs had supported Jahāngīr's son in revolt against his father, thereby initiating a perpetual tension with the Mughal court. Jahāngīr honored Islamic figures, ignoring Sikhs and other saintly figures. The Mughals perceived Sikhs, who were becoming more powerful in the valleys of Panjāb, as a threat. The result: Arjun was executed in 1606 and the Sikhs and Mughals were at odds with each other.[46]

Hargobind (1606–45) became *gurū* at the age of eleven. He was the first to assemble a military force and take up arms as a defense against the

Mughals as well as against Afghans and Marāthās, who coveted the fertile area of the five rivers. Controlling the Panjāb became a major concern of the Sikhs; hence, Hargobind spoke of two swords – one political and one religious. The increased number of *jāts* in the community and these political-geographical issues moved Sikhism increasingly into a defensive force.

The tenth and last *gurū* was **Gobind Singh**. He was ten years old when he assumed his responsibilities in 1666. His predecessor had been executed, this time by Aurangzeb. After Gobind Singh, the tradition of living *gurūs* was replaced by the scripture, the written legacy of the *gurūs*. The scripture (the *Gurū Granth Sāhib*) serves as the center of worship and of the community to the present. In fact, the Sikh place of worship even today is known as the gurdwārā (the doorway to the *gurū* as represented in the book). According to the tradition, Gurū Gobind Singh was responsible for making the movement even more militantly oriented and giving it a more visible identity: from now on, males were to take five vows, by which they would take the name of Singh (lion) as a surname. The five vows were: the wearing of under drawers (*kach*), indicating a readiness to move quickly; an iron ring on the right arm or bangle (*karā*), an insignia of strength; a small dagger (*kirpān*), a symbol of one's readiness to defend oneself; long hair (*keś*), representative of saintliness as well as strength; and a comb (*kanghā*) which holds in the hair and represents cleanliness and neatness (all men were to wear turbans to cover the hair). This new "brotherhood," known as the *khālsā*, is said to have been inaugurated in 1699, though some aspects of it may have been added later as the influence of the *jāt* community increased.[47]

After Gobind Singh, the Sikhs were rather loosely organized into *misls* (circles) while fighting for rights to the Panjāb continued. Afghans, Marāthās, and, eventually, the British sought hegemony over the "five waters." A low point in the life of the community was the infamous *gallūghārā* (devastation) of 1762. Afghans entered the Panjāb and slaughtered many Sikhs. The tragedy galvanized the community, which longed for greater centralization: **Ranjit Singh** managed to bring together the various *misls* and restored the Sikhs to a point where they were able to retain hegemony in the area until the British took over in 1849. Subsequently, it has been difficult to distinguish political concerns from religious ones.

In a number of ways the experience of the Sikhs in the twentieth century mirrored the experience of India at large. Sikhs were among the first Indians to migrate to North America, for example, first settling as farmers in Northwestern Canada then working their way down into the US. The Sikhs experienced considerable discrimination in British Columbia and Washington State in the first decade of the twentieth century.[48] But by the 1920s Sikhs were settling in California, marrying Mexican women and constructing the first Indo-American religious edifice, a gurdwārā, in Stockton,

California. During this same period, Sikhs had also migrated to the Malay Straits to work in security positions.

Meanwhile back in the Panjāb, the Akāli Dal ("army of the immortals") was formed in 1920–21 to oversee gurdwārās and maintain Sikh identity and rights.[49] A year earlier, a second "*gallūghāra*" had occurred, with the massacre by British troops of non-violent Sikhs protesting near Amritsar. After independence in 1947, when Panjāb was partitioned between India and Pakistan, Sikhs continued to struggle for their rights in the Panjāb. Though against the partition in 1947 and siding with Hindus at that time, they believed their rights were diminished thereafter. Indian Panjāb was split into two regions, in which Sikhs were the majority in the south but still believed themselves to be without power because: the state government was supposed to be secular, yet its Sikh administrators were perceived to be bending over backwards not to offend Hindus; and more and more Sikhs were learning Hindī and there was fear that increased "Hinduization" was occurring. Hindī and Panjābī were made the official languages in the state, yet in 1953 while no Sikhs were in positions of leadership, the central government decided there would be no Panjābī-speaking state, increasing Sikh frustration. By 1967 that decision was reversed, when the area was divided again, creating two new states, Haryana and Himachal Pradesh, leaving Panjāb to a majority of Panjābī-speaking peoples. Even then there was some disarray amongst the Sikh political leadership, leading by 1978 to the increased visibility of a separatist movement led by those who wanted the creation of an autonomous state, to be called "Khalistan," evoking a suggestion thought to have once been made by Gurū Gobind Singh. Among those agitating for autonomy was a Sikh fundamentalist named **Bhidranwalla**. Bhidranwalla was accused of an assassination and asked by the central government to lay down his arms. When he refused to do so he was labeled a terrorist and was sought by government forces. The "crisis" came to a head in 1984, when, while Bhidranwalla was "hiding" in Amritsar's Golden Temple, the Indian army, led, ironically, by a Sikh general, attacked the Golden Temple and the alleged terrorists within. While the government's view was that the raids were justified, the Sikhs saw this event as an act of genocide and became increasingly galvanized to action. At the least, "Operation Bluestar" managed to kill a number of pilgrims during a festival, and review committees which were not sympathetic with the Congress Party, studying the events *post facto,* agreed primarily with the Sikh position. Among the results of the tragedy was the assassination of Prime Minister **Indira Gandhi** by two of her own Sikh bodyguards. This was followed by Hindu–Sikh conflicts, riots, and reprisals which led to communal tensions for years. While some of the issues troubling the Sikhs were subsequently addressed, others are still pending. Nonetheless, outright hostilities have been kept to a minimum in recent years and the

Sikhs continue to play a significant role in Indian life, not least as progressive farmers in the fertile Panjāb valleys where 25 per cent of India's rice is raised, and as members of various security forces.

Recommended reading

Pre-modern history, literature, and arts

Bayly, Susan. *Saints, Goddesses, and Kings: Muslims and Christians in South Indian Society, 1700–1900.* Cambridge: Cambridge University Press, 1989.

Gordon, Stewart. *The Marathas: 1600–1818.* Cambridge: Cambridge University Press, 1993.

Hangloo, R. L. *The State in Medieval Kashmir.* Delhi: Manohar, 2000.

Metcalfe, Barbara and Thomas, R. *A Concise History of India.* New York: Cambridge University Press, 2002.

Spear, P. *India: A Modern History.* Volume two (reprint). London: Penguin Books, 1990.

Post-medieval *bhakti*

Clothey, F. W. *Quiescence and Passion: The Vision of Aruṇakiri, Tamil Mystic.* Bethesda, MA: Austin & Winfield, 1996.

Davis, R. H. *Ritual in an Oscillating Universe: Worshipping Śiva in Medieval India.* Princeton: Princeton University Press, 1991.

Flood, G. *Body and Cosmology in Kashmir Śaivism.* San Francisco: Mellon Research University Press, 1993.

Hawley, J. and Juergersmeyer, M. *Songs of the Saints of India.* New York: Oxford University Press, 1988.

Hedayetullah, M. *Kabir: The Apostle of Hindu-Muslim Unity.* Delhi: Matilal Banarsidass, 1978.

Lutgendorf, P. *The Life of a Text: Performing the Rāmacaritamanas.* Berkeley: University of California Press, 1991.

Ranade, R. D. *Mysticism in India: The Poet-Saints of Maharashtra.* Reprint. Albany: SUNY Press, 1982.

Young, K. and Sharma, A. *Images of the Feminine – Mythic Philosophic and Human in Buddhist, Hindu and Islamic Traditions: A Biography of Women in India.* Chico, CA: New Horizons Press, 1974.

On Sikhism

Grewal, J. S. *The Sikhs in the Panjab.* Cambridge: Cambridge University Press, 1990.

Macauliffe, M. A. *The Sikh Religion: Its Gurus, Sacred Writings, and Authors.* Six volumes. Reprint. Delhi: S. Chaud, 1963.

Mcleod, W. H. *Gurū Nānak and the Sikh Religion.* Oxford: Oxford University Press, 1968.

Singh, Khuswant. *A History of the Sikhs.* Two volumes. London/Princeton 1963, 1966. Reprint. Delhi and Oxford: Oxford University Press, 1977.
Singh, Khuswant. *et al. Selections from The Sacred Writings of the Sikhs.* New York: Weisner, 1973.

Timeline of Chapters 6 and 7

	Cultural/political events		Religious events
	7th–10th century: pockets of Muslim settlements in South and Northwest India		
1000	Mahmūd of Ghaznī (999–1030)		
	Al-Bīrūnī in India (b. 973)		
	c. 1050 Emergence of Rājput dynasties		
1100	Senas of Bengal (1118–99)		
	Muhammed of Ghor (1163–1203)		
		1198	First mosque built in Delhi
1200	"Slave king" sultanate in Delhi (1206–90)	1225	Qutb Minar built
		c. 1230	Konārak Sun Temple
			Jnāneśvara (Marāthī *bhakta*) (1271–96)
1300	Khaljī sultanate (1290–1316)		
	Three Mongol invasions (1300–1307)		
	Tughluq sultanate (1320–88)	1350	Increased patronage of Vaiṣṇavism and neo-classical Hindu culture under Vijayanagara kings
	Muḥammed bin Tughluq (1325–51)		
	Vijayanagara dynasty (1336–1565)		
	Bahmani (independent sultanate in Deccan) (1347–1482)		
1400	Lodī sultanate (1451–1526)		Rāmānanda ("reformer" in Panjāb c. 1400–70)
			Kabīr (1440–1518)
			Guru Nānak (1469–1539 – start of Sikhism)
			Caitanya (1485–1533)
1500	1506 Agra founded		
	1526 Bābur founds Mughal dynasty		
	Akbar (1556–1605)		
			Tulsīdās (1532–1623)
1600	Jahāngīr (1605–27)		Tukārām (1598–1650)
	Shāh Jahān (1628–58)		Compilation of Sikh scriptures, *Gurū Granth Sāhib* (1603–4)
	Aurangzeb (1658–1707) – in Deccan (1681–1707)		Building of Tāj Mahal (1631–53)
	Śivājī founds Marāthā state (1677–80)	1699	Gurū Gobind Singh forms Sikh brotherhood

Note: All dates are CE unless otherwise stated.

8

Streams from the "West" and their Aftermath

The Indian subcontinent, from its earliest millennia, has been something of a crossroads of cultures and religions. Ideas and peoples have migrated outward, influencing Southeast Asia, China, Japan, and, in the last two centuries especially, virtually every continent. That is a story we shall explore in the final chapter. It is also apparent that many peoples and ideas came into the subcontinent in various ways becoming part of the enormously diverse landscape. Prior to the coming of any European groups, for example, there were at least a score of influences with "foreign" origins. These included a number of dynasties in the late urban period, such as the Kuṣāṇas, Śakas, and Bactrian Greeks. It included merchants, warriors, and saints of Persian, Arabic, or Afghan origin.

In this chapter, we explore something of the "European" impact on India and the subcontinent's response to it.

In the classical period, there is considerable evidence of Roman and Greek contacts and/or influence. While the Phoenicians may have been the first to sail to ports of India in the tenth century BCE, it was after the discovery of the trade winds in the first century BCE that maritime contact increased. Greek and Roman coins of the period were left in the ports of South India where "foreign" merchants were called *yavaṉās*.[1] The Greek influences on the northern portions of the subcontinent were mediated through the Persian empire at first, and then through the eastern satrapies of the Greek empire. The Bactrian Greeks became one of the mediators of this influence. As observed earlier, among the results of this influence were the flourishing of new forms of anthropomorphized iconography, an increasingly sacralized notion of kingship, even a theology that helped shape the ideas of the Buddha in the Kuṣāṇas' court and perhaps of the brahmanical deities patronized in the subsequent "*vaidika*" courts.

Religious minorities

Among the early migrants into the subcontinent were three religious streams, which became a permanent if small part of the Indian "quilt." These were Jews, "Syrian Christians," and Zoroastrians or Pārsīs whose story is worth noting, even if in brief.

Jewish communities

There were at least three separate migrations of Jews into India – one group, known as the Cochin Jews, settled in the southwestern area now referred to as Kerala; another known as "Bene Israel" settled largely in what is now Mumbai; the third was a small nineteenth-century migration of entrepreneurs and their families known as Baghdadi Jews. Of the three, the first two groups are clearly the oldest and the most striking for what they reveal about continuities and accommodations.

"Cochin Jews"

The earliest settlements of Jews were in Cranganore on the Kerala coast. It is possible these folks came early in the Common Era as Roman traders are said to have referred to them. However, it is more likely most of them came and settled around the seventh century along with Arab merchants. These communities were primarily mercantile; indeed, their economic and political rights were affirmed in a copperplate inscription struck around the late eighth century by a local Hindu monarch. In this inscription, we learn that Jewish settlers were given economic property rights, apparently including land grants such as were commonly given to groups which a local monarch wanted to include under his hegemony. The inscription affirms the right of Jews to hold public festivals and declares that one Joseph Rabbani (who may have been an adviser in the royal court) was the leader of the community.[2]

The community came to be comprised of "white" Jews and "black" (literally, "copper") Jews. The "black" Jews were those who had been there from the earliest days and whose number had been increased by intermarriage or conversion. Extant synagogues, dating from the twelfth century CE were associated with these Jews. "White" Jews were apparently descended from Spanish Jews migrating around the thirteenth to fifteenth centuries; early generations of those immigrants spoke Spanish and were Sephardim in orientation.[3]

When Cranganore was razed in 1524 by Islamic marauders, the Jews scattered, most of them settling in Cochin. There, they were caught in the colonial battles between the Portuguese and the Dutch. The Dutch were generally supportive, and hence received Jewish cooperation; however, when the Portuguese captured Cochin, Jews were generally harassed. Cochin is the site of the oldest extant synagogue associated with the "white" Jews. It was built in 1666 with Dutch help and with products imported from many sources, including tiles of Chinese origin (these tiles had been imported by the local ruler, but were rejected for building purposes because they were said to have been made at the cost of bullocks' blood!).[4]

The customs retained by these Jews were a mix of local and traditional Jewish practice. The "black" Jews, for example, were said to dress like local Muslims – wearing a turban in the temple and skullcap outside; they dressed in multicolor tunics, a waistcoat, white trousers, and wooden sandals, spoke Malayalam (the local vernacular), and used Hebrew liturgically. Their adaptations of "Hindu" customs included the practice of tying a ***tāli*** (marriage cord) around the neck of the bride at the time of marriage and locating the synagogue at the center of streets populated by Jews, a practice emulating brahman tradition.

The communities practiced a number of Jewish rituals: circumcision on the eighth day; Sabbaths; Passover with its distribution of unleavened bread; the festivals of Pentecost, Trumpets, and Tabernacles (perhaps the most elaborate of all their festivals). Fasts were held on the day of atonement and the remembrance of the destruction of the temple. "White" Jews celebrated seven days for marriage, culminating on a Sunday; "black" Jews celebrated fifteen days of marriage, culminating after sundown on a Tuesday.

Bene Israel

Those Jews who call themselves the Bene Israel have an even more obscure past.[5] Their myth of origin claims their ancestors landed on the Indian coast in the first century CE as the result of a shipwreck. They claim that their ancestors maintained Jewish traditions consistent with the Israelite communities prior to the destruction of the first temple. These are said to include performance of circumcision by "cohens," the reciting of the "shema Israel" before or during all rites of passage, the celebration of Yom Kippur at home in silence, and use of a funeral shroud exactly as described in the Hebrew Bible. Certain festivals, dating after the destruction of the first temple (e.g., Hanukkah and Purim), were celebrated, though Rosh Hashanah, Passover, and Sabbath have also been celebrated.

Whatever their origins, members of the community trickled into Mumbai in the late 1740s, working largely as oil pressers, who, because they refused to work on the Sabbath, came to be known as the Sabbath oil pressers "caste." Three events brought about a renaissance in the community which theretofore had little conscious sense of their religious identity. The first of these events was the visit of **David Ezekiel Rahabi** from Cochin in the eighteenth century. Rahabi was said to be Arabic and a member of the Maimonides family. He imparted religious and biblical education to young and old alike, taught prayers in Hebrew, and trained cantors orally (a method of teaching common in the Indian tradition). A second event was the establishment of the first Bene Israel synagogue in 1796. The third event was the work of **John Wilson**, a Scottish Presbyterian missionary who founded a college and some twenty-five Marāthī-medium schools and published a Bible translated into the vernacular. In some of the schools and in the college (eventually known as Wilson College) Jewish religion and Hebrew were taught. Many Jews took advantage of these educational opportunities.

The "Bombay Jews" in the modern period have maintained some nine synagogues, three of these for the exclusive use of Baghdadi Jews (the oldest of these built in 1851). The size of the community at its largest was some 20,000 in 1951, but since then increasing numbers of them have emigrated to Israel so that only a handful of families remain in the Mumbai area. An interesting measure of the community's adaptations to the Indian landscape was the extent to which "Hinduization" has occurred in its ritual life. The tying of the *tāli*, for example, is used to mark a marriage, though a locket is tied to the *tāli* with the husband's name inscribed in Hebrew; similarly, the bride's hands are adorned with henna as in local tradition. Elders of the community speak of the "faith of Abraham" as consistent with the monism of Advaita.

While virtually all Indian Jews will have disappeared from India within the next generation, their presence on the subcontinent for well over a millennium is testimony to the hospitality of their neighbors and their capacity to adapt and respond in the Indian environment.

Syrian Christians

There is abundant evidence that Christians, generally called "Syrian Christians," were living along the coast of Kerala by at least the mid-fourth century. Legends claim this community was founded by the apostle Thomas who is said to have died in South India. Historical reality is much less clear. It is believed from references in Greek texts that Thomas did visit the court of Gondophernes, a Bactrian Greek "king" situated in the upper Indus Valley. What is also known is that one **Thomas Cana** of Edessa in Syria landed on the southwestern coast around 345 CE together with a group of followers apparently fleeing persecution by more "orthodox" Christians.[6]

These early communities of Christians were supplemented by other heterodox Christian groups. These included some Nestorians who were considered to have unorthodox views of the Christ figure and refused to accept the doctrine of Theotokos (Mary as "Mother of God"). Many Nestorians, however, moved further eastward into China. Another unorthodox group that migrated into the southwest were the Monophysites, a group founded by **Eutychus**, who claimed Christ had only a single, divine nature. Both of these movements provided clergy for the Kerala Christians. These early Christians came to be known as Jacobites, who maintained ties to the Syrian ecclesiastical hierarchy and followed Syrian ritual and creed.

Like the Jews of Kerala, these early Christians were granted certain rights and property by local rulers as evidenced in three separate copperplates struck in the late eighth century. These rights included space for a township or even "mini-kingdom" complete with church.[7] The Syrian Christians remained relatively prosperous and peaceful through the fourteenth century.

Circumstances changed for these Christians with the coming of the Portuguese in the sixteenth century and the Dominicans, Franciscans, and Jesuits patronized by the Portuguese colonialists. The low point in Catholic–Syrian Christian relations came in 1599, when a **Bishop Meneze** burned many of the books of Syrian Christians and ordered their conversion to Catholicism.[8] Many did so, but some defected and sought to resume their ties to Antioch. The result of these machinations was the emergence of three separate church bodies by the seventeenth century: the Romo-Syrians, who used a Syrian rite, maintained adherence to the pope and hence were Catholics of the Syrian rite; "Jacobite Syrians," who maintained their adherence to the Syrian hierarchy and not to the pope; and finally, Catholics who followed the Latin rite due largely to conversions by Portuguese-sponsored

Figure 7 Roman Catholic Church near Nāgārjunakonda, Andhra Pradesh, showing indigenous features. Photograph by Rob F. Phillips.

groups. A fourth branch emerged in the eighteenth century as an offshoot of the "Jacobite Syrians." This "new" group followed the leadership of a local bishop, one **Mar Thomas Athanasius**, and became an autonomous church known as the "Mar Thoma" Christians, whose headquarters are in Kerala itself.

The "Jacobite Syrians" tended to be more nearly "Catholic" in their orientation. For example, they affirmed that tradition was as important as the Bible in matters of interpretation; relics were venerated; communion was understood more as a sacrifice than as a commemoration; their clergy were not to marry. Further, they observed certain fasts and feasts, which were regarded as "superstition" by the more nearly "Protestant" Mar Thomans.

Most of these groups, nonetheless, have appropriated customs from their Indian or Hindu neighbors which were observed into the twentieth century: there has been some use of horoscopes, especially in the case of newborn babies; the *tāli* has been used to mark marriages; death pollution was observed for ten to fifteen days; and there have been anniversary ceremonies for the dead not unlike the Hindu *śrāddha* ritual. In addition, the rite of passage, known to Hindus as *annaprāśana* (the first feeding of solids to an infant of six months), was observed; intermarriage between sects remains rare as some claim their ancestors to have been converted brahmans or high-caste nayars (landowners). Indeed, in some settings, low-caste persons were not permitted into the church premises well into the twentieth century.

Zoroastrians or Pārsīs

Zoroastrianism started as a reform movement founded by an Iranian priest named **Zoroaster** (the Greek term for Zarathustra), who probably lived in the seventh century BCE. The religion was based on certain ancient Iranian practices, which were similar to those found in Vedic India. There had been a fire cult; the sacrifice of *hoama*, thought to have been the intoxicating sap of a plant; the sacrifice of animals; a cult of twins leading to notions of a cosmic dualism. In this ancient religion, certain forces of nature were considered sacred, especially the sun, moon, earth, fire, water, and wind. Varuṇa and Mithra personified water and fire respectively and Ahura Mazda came to be seen as ruler of the cosmos. *Ahuras* (good spirits) and *daevas* (bad spirits) peopled the cosmos.[9]

Zoroaster campaigned against the "excesses" of this ancient religion, especially its polytheism, animal sacrifice, and intoxication by the priests (magi) during *hoama* sacrifice. He established a form of monotheism which posited that Ahura Mazda, the primal one, fathered twin spirits, Spenta Mainyu, the demiurge or creator of all things good, and Angra Mainyu, the demiurge of evil. Zoroastrianism was apparently the first religious tradition to posit an eschatology (doctrine of end times) at which good would triumph over evil, a resurrection of the dead would occur, human beings would have the opportunity to become immortal, and a judgment bridge connecting the cosmic mountain at the center of the world to paradise would have to be crossed.

Zoroastrianism became the "state religion" of the Achaemenids (sixth century BCE), and the Sasanids (224–637 CE). During the first of these periods the scriptures emerged, including hymns used for the rituals (***yasnas***), and the *Gāthās*, poems ascribed to Zoroaster himself. These became known as the *Avesta* by the sixth century CE. By the time of the Sasanids, a greater degree of mythologization had developed – e.g., time was divided into mythological segments – and a ritual life had flourished. These rituals included the practice of six major festivals, the use of fire temples serving as microcosms in which the sacred fire could be maintained, and the use of ***dachmas*** ("towers of silence") in the disposal of the dead. Because earth, fire, and water were sacred, these could not be used for disposal of the dead; rather, the dead were to be exposed so that birds of prey could convey the deceased symbolically to the upper reaches of the cosmos.

When Islam spread into Persia in the seventh century, Zoroastrians began to migrate into India to the area now known as Gujarat. While some Zoroastrians remained in Iran, where even today there are some 140,000, most of them eventually settled in Gujarat, between 651 and 963 CE. A local king was hospitable to the migrants, and, in due course, the community adapted the language and dress of Gujarat. They lived amicably with their new neighbors while retaining many of the religious traditions brought from Iran, thanks to those priests who had settled with them.[10]

In 1469, the community moved to another part of Gujarat, but by the nineteenth century had, for the most part, migrated into Mumbai. There the Pārsīs (as they came to be called in India) experienced a renaissance as the result of several factors.[11] Not least important, Elphinstone College was founded by the British East India Company in 1827 to teach "the languages, literature, sciences, and moral philosophy of Europe." Many Pārsīs attended here and studied Zoroastrian scriptures and religion, often through the eyes of such seventeenth- and eighteenth-century European scholars as **Thomas Hyde** and **A. Duperron.** Meanwhile, the Scottish Presbyterian missionary John Wilson, on the basis of his reading of Zoroastrian scriptures, challenged a Pārsī leader in 1843 as being out of touch with the "scientific" study of his own tradition. Other Western scholars offered varying views on what was "authentic" Zoroastrianism. A German philologist, **Martin Haug**, for example, teaching Sanskrit in Poona in the 1860s, argued on the basis of the oldest scripture, the *Gāthās*, that the religion should be a form of pure monotheism, free of rituals. On the other hand, **E. W. Wiest**, an English engineer studying Pahlavī literature, and **Henry S. Olcutt**, a theosophist, both maintained, on the basis of the later texts, that dualism and the practice of ritual was indeed the appropriate form of the religion.

In the context of these discussions, a Zoroastrian priest/scholar named **Evachi** published a catechism in 1869 in which he sought to reassert what he thought were the essential teachings of Zoroastrianism. He published a Pahlavī dictionary and made available to the community teachings from manuscripts only available theretofore in Avestan, Pahlavī, Persian, and Arabic.

Most Pārsīs in Mumbai today share certain common beliefs based on Evachi's catechism. Ahura Mazda is now known as Ohrmazd; fire consists of sparks of Ohrmazd and embodies the sun and moonlight, healing warmth, creative power, purification, wisdom, and the force of righteousness (***asha***). Six festivals of creation are to be celebrated each year; appropriate litanies should be addressed to the sun three times daily, and to the moon thirteen times a month. In the fire sacrifices (*yasna*), elements representing "good creation" are offered and once consecrated, embody the good guardian spirits of the cosmos.

Ethics are an important part of the Zoroastrian lifestyle. Evil powers, led by Angra Mainyu, the spirit of evil, cause human beings to engage in evil acts such as causing pain, and polluting the earth. Good ethics lead to immortality in paradise. Such ethics consist of living the "good life"; being charitable and industrious; avoiding greed, arrogance, and vengeance; and seeking wisdom. Not least of all, it is important to engage in appropriate funeral rituals for the deceased over a three-day period, lest the earth be contaminated by a dead body.

Not all Pārsīs agree on everything, of course. For example, an "occult" group arose, which stressed reincarnation and multiple planes of being. Others venerate contemporary "gurus" in a manner emulative of Hindus. Yet another divisive element is the question of which "calendar" to follow: the "Gregorian" or "Western" calendar; the ancient Iranian (Qadīmī) calendar; or the calendar believed to be that of ancient Persian kings. Despite the lack of unanimity, Pārsīs have been a significant presence on the landscape of Mumbai. Their impact far exceeding their numbers, the community has spawned major industrialists and philanthropists (e.g., **Tata** and **Godrej**), constructed hospitals, colleges, and schools; and in various ways contributed to the social welfare of the city.

The "colonial impact"

Starting in the sixteenth century, the Indian subcontinent became the venue for an acting out of European nationalisms, especially the desire for economic windfalls and the extension of political hegemony perpetrated by "East India" trading companies, in collaboration with the crowns of several European nations. The Portuguese were the first on the scene, followed within a century by the Danish, Dutch, French, and British traders. These contacts brought about the era of colonialism, which led in turn to Indian responses and the dawning of modern India.

The Portuguese, British and other Europeans

After the visit of **Vasco da Gama** to Calicut in 1498, the west coast of India became a main focus of Portugal's worldwide naval hegemony. By 1508, **Albuquerque** and his men had defeated the local armies of the khan governing Goa and claimed the port as a Portuguese possession. He permitted his men to marry the widows of defeated soldiers and to settle along the coast. For generations, Portuguese culture permeated the west central coast of the subcontinent. Portuguese Indians farmed the soil and introduced a number of crops from other parts of the Portuguese empire: tobacco, pineapple, cashew nut, peanuts, sweet potatoes, even certain forms of red pepper. In addition, cash crops for export were developed: coconut, cotton, and such spices as pepper, ginger, and cinnamon. Because the Portuguese navy assumed hegemony of the Arabian Sea (theretofore controlled by the Arabs), the Portuguese language became the virtual "lingua franca" of the Indian ports of trade. The tight organization of the Portuguese militia was emulated by the Mughals and the Marāthās alike. Not least of all, Goa became an outpost for the copying of Portuguese art, architecture, and religion. The European-style printing press was introduced. Grammars and translations of indigenous languages were spawned and Roman Catholicism became a vigorous part of the Indian landscape.[12]

Religion was an important part of the Portuguese legacy. Catholic missionaries of various orders were sponsored – Dominicans, Franciscans, and especially Jesuits were a visible presence, as were seminaries in the training of new clergy. The work of three Jesuit missionaries, in particular, will illustrate the scope and nature of their work.

Enrique Enriquez, who was in India from 1546–1600, was instrumental in developing lexicons and grammars of Tamil, Marāthī, and Konkanī (the language of the coastal region). The purpose, of course, was to make the vernaculars accessible for the foundation of Christian ideology; yet one of

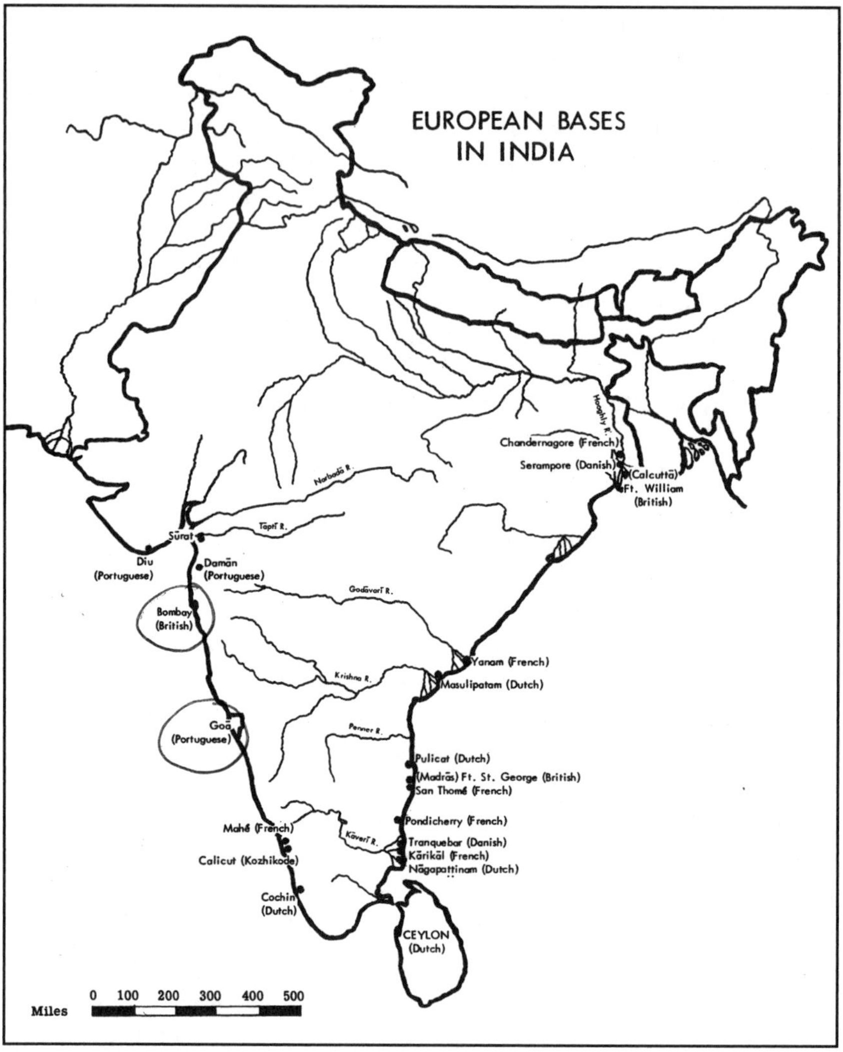

Map 5 European Bases in India

Reprinted with the permission of Professor Joe Elder, editor: "Lectures in Indian Civilization" (Dubuque, IA: Kendall/Hunt Publishers, 1970).

the ultimate results of this kind of language study was the stimulation of pride and renaissance amongst the speakers of such languages. Nonetheless, Enriquez started the process of developing an Indian Christian vocabulary in which Greek and Hebrew terms were expressed in Indian idiom.[13]

Robert de Nobili was noted for the experiments he started in the city of Maturai, Tamil Nadu, in 1605. He donned the robe of a *samnyāsi,* lived the lifestyle of an ascetic, engaged in conversations with brahmans, and sought to present the Bible as a "fifth Veda." A small mission was established in Maturai, primarily comprised of upper-class converts who were later joined by such foreigners as missionary scholar **Constantine Beschi** (1710–47), whose Tamil had native fluency.[14]

Francis Xavier spent several years in Goa before and after visiting China (1542–45 and 1948–49). Xavier's legacy is mixed. He promised Portuguese protection for fisher folk (paravars) along the Kerala coast in exchange for their being baptized. Accordingly, he lined up and baptized thousands of them though their education into Catholicism was minimal. It was also Xavier who wrote to **King Joao II** of Portugal to urge him to hold his representatives accountable for propagating Christianity and increasing conversions. In partial response, King Joao instructed his viceroy to "destroy all idols," penalize any who "dare to make an idol" or "shelter . . . a brahman" and to afford special favor to Christians in filling appointments and receiving material aid.[15] The inquisition had been imported to India and the converting or scattering of non-Christians in Goa had accelerated.

The Dutch East India Company's interest in India was not as intense as its commitment to the Indonesian islands, which were perceived to be richer in the spices and goods Europeans sought. Nonetheless, small Dutch outposts were established along the southern coast at Cochin, Nagapattinam, Pulicat, *et al.* As noted earlier, their greatest contribution to the subcontinent may have been their support of Jewish communities and their amelioration of Portuguese excesses. Otherwise, they had little religious impact.

The French were relative latecomers to the subcontinent. Founded in 1664, la Compagnie des Indes Orientales did establish seaport enclaves in Chandernagore (Bengal) and Pondicherry (Tamil Nadu). In fact, for two decades in the mid-1700s, under the leadership of the skilled administrator, **Joseph F. Dupleix**, the French had considerable hegemony in the south.[16] However, by the end of the century, they were defeated near what is now Kolkata (once Calcutta) by British and local troops led by **Robert Clive**. By then the British were better funded, not only by their annexations in India, but also by their China trade. Nevertheless, Pondicherry remained a pocket of French access to India until 1954 and even now includes a center for the study of Indian culture and religion by French scholars.

The Danish East India Company established enclaves in Serampore (Bengal) and Tranquebar (Tamil Nadu), which were to prove significant for development in the religious life of India. In the early years of the European trading companies supported by "Protestant" crowns, only chaplains were made available to work with the households of European nationals. The Danish crown was the first to make an exception. In 1709, the Danish crown sponsored the recruitment and support of **Bartholomaus**

Ziegenbalg, who with his colleague, **Plutschau**, became the first Protestant missionaries in India. Settling in Tranquebar, Ziegenbalg, a German seminary dropout, proved to be a resourceful addition to the landscape. He established elementary schools in both Portuguese and Tamil, contributed to the development of a Tamil lexicon, and, not least of all, wrote two manuscripts seeking to describe the religious life of South India. These manuscripts were deemed by his sponsors to be too supportive of Indian religion and were not published for over a century.[17]

Almost a century later, Serampore became the enclave in which the first English missionaries lived. **William Carey**, a Baptist cobbler, arrived in 1793, established an indigo factory and botanical gardens, set up a printing press, and began translating the Bible into several languages. Joined by **Joshua Marshman** and William Ward, the trio became active in the critique of Indian religion and culture. They lobbied the English East India Company to make changes in their "hands-off" policies, and were partially instrumental in the eventual decision to outlaw such practices as *satī* (widow burning) and infanticide. It was Ward's scathing book, purporting to be a study of Hinduism, that informed the mind-set of evangelical Christians in Britain and North America for generations.

The British East India Company, founded in 1600, first established a trading post in Surat (Gujarat) with the permission of the Mughal court and eventually in Kolkata, Mumbai, once known as Bombay (a gift to the British crown from the Portuguese), and Chennai (once Madras). The British company's presence can be divided into several stages.[18] The first stage, running until 1813, was one of primarily economic and military activity: siphon off as much wealth and raw material as quickly as possible for marketing back home; ward off the French and those local princes perceived to be a threat to company interests; establish puppet regimes through whom the company could attain surrogate power and increased wealth. By the 1770s, in fact, Bengal had been stripped of most of its surplus wealth.[19] When the company's coffers were depleted from waging wars with the Marāthās and in the Southern Deccan, its leaders, like **Warren Hastings**, did not hesitate to "extort large sums" from their Indian allies.[20] It is no wonder the British East India Company's men during this period were perceived as robber barons by the local population and not a few historians.

In 1813, the company became more "imperialistic." Its hegemony was extended through alliances and conquest of local leaders. Laws restricting *satī* and other practices were passed. Missionaries were supported. Development of an infrastructure intended to strengthen British hegemony began: British-style policies and legal systems were established, replacing indigenous ones. Transportation systems of trains and roads were developed to facilitate the export and import of goods; money was set aside for the construction of schools and colleges, intended to educate an Indian elite in British "ideas." By 1835, English was established as the medium of education and exchange, following the advice of economic utilitarians and evangelicals, but contrary to the advice of "orientalist" scholars. A greater priority was given to higher education and several English-medium colleges were founded (e.g., Elphinstone College in Mumbai and Fort Williams College in Calcutta).

These policies of development and education received a severe jolt in 1857, when Indian soldiers, trained by the British for service in the army, engaged in a rebellion, apparently supported by disaffected princes, peasants, and others. Known as the "Sepoy Mutiny," it was triggered when some soldiers refused to use ammunition believed to have been lubricated with animal fat. These soldiers were imprisoned and their colleagues set out to free them. Though the uprising was quelled within nine months, the company lost its governance in India to the British crown. India was made officially part of the British empire, its parliament the official policy maker for Indians, and Queen Victoria was the Empress of India. Once India became part of the British empire, it became Britain's "barracks" in Asian seas. By 1880, Britain had sold 20 percent of its goods in India and invested 20 percent of its overseas capital.[21] There was now greater ambivalence about the wisdom of increasing higher educational opportunities and more discussion on the need to build on India's past. In the face of Indian criticisms of British policies, a rationale for the British presence in India was now increasingly articulated: having trusteeship of India was the "white man's burden"; the British could assure protection of minorities and "backward classes" (and there is some evidence of a policy of divide and conquer); the British claimed they were the most efficient of administrators and without their presence India would fragment into many parts.

The Indian response

It is clear that these "streams" from the West and especially the coming of British colonialism and Christianity had a permanent impact on the Indian landscape. Ironically, in the sixteenth and seventeenth centuries, the civilizations flourishing in India exceeded those of Europe in most respects. Yet by the mid-eighteenth century, the industrial revolution came to Europe, whereas India was experiencing one of its least productive centuries. On the subcontinent, political patronage of the arts had dwindled; rural areas still suffered from famine and drought; and political fragmentation and infighting were common. In fact, the era of European colonialism in India was made possible in part by the decline of the Mughals and the concomitant political fragmentation of the subcontinent. At Aurangzeb's death, his own sons had battled for power at the center; within two decades Mughal wealth and power had been dissipated. Regional leaders who had chafed under the autocratic rule of Aurangzeb now sought hegemony over their various domains. Inter-regional fighting and civil war within regions were not uncommon. Various kingmakers (such as the Sayyid brothers in the Deccan) would establish a series of puppet "kings" over whom they could exercise control. Among those re-establishing claims to parts of the subcontinent were the Marāthās fighting into the Deccan and points south; Afghans invading the northwest; Sikhs trying to protect their claims to the Panjāb; even the Persians, whose army under **Nadin Shah** sacked Delhi in 1739. In the northeast, regional rulers in Oudh and Bengal sought to enlarge their domains. Meanwhile further south, the Nizam of Hyderabad who had left Delhi in 1723 re-established control in the Deccan, where, for several decades, inter-regional warfare ensued involving the Marāthās. Still later in the century, **Tipū Sultān**, headquartered near Mysore, enjoyed several decades of sub-regional hegemony.[22]

Once the British established control over some three-fifths of the subcontinent, a certain degree of stability did ensue. Yet the British presence brought a variety of results, many of them mixed. The infusion of Western technology brought the printing press, railways, and Western forms of science and medicine. The study of Indian languages and translations of its literature by "orientalists" spurred a renaissance of pride and appreciation for things indigenous. At the same time, the scathing critique of the evangelicals led to soul-searching and new defensiveness. English-style education, for better or worse, stimulated both renewal and critique amongst Indian intellectuals. Indeed, India in the nineteenth century could be described as one of the liveliest places in the world for experimentation in responding to "global" currents, envisioning a new society, and rethinking the nature and role of religion. Many of India's intellectuals were people living and thinking "on the boundaries" in ways that presage the challenge of many living in the twenty-first century around the world.

Stage one

One of the early responses was that of a radical critique, even toward secularization, by some young Anglicized Indians. **Henry de Rozio** (1809–31), an Anglo-Indian Bengālī, was a case in point. Writing poetry at the age of seventeen, and assistant to a headmaster at a Christian college, he called upon young Indians to join him in seeking radical change from unreflected traditions. De Rozio lived only briefly, but his work exemplified one approach in shaping a new era.[23]

Perhaps more common was the approach that sought reform. **Ram Mohun Roy** (1772–1833) became a leader in seeking change in the indigenous landscape while retaining what were thought to be the best principles of the Indian heritage.[24] Often called the "Father of Modern India," Roy retired at the age of forty-two to devote his life to his causes. He had studied Persian, Sanskrit, and English, had met Unitarians and Deists in England and in Calcutta, and interacted with the Baptist missionaries of Serampore. He favored the use of the English medium in public education and believed cooperation with the British would bring new opportunities to India. He was bitterly opposed, nonetheless, to both the doctrinaire trinitarianism of the Baptists and some of what he perceived to be the excesses of his own tradition, including the burning of widows, a practice that had become all too common in orthoprax families of his time (including his own). He was concerned with other social issues as well: the early marriage of children, the rights of women, the right to education. He found the ethics of Jesus to be a useful model to emulate, albeit selectively. Not least important, he founded the Brāhmo Samāj in 1828, a fellowship of like-minded Bengālī brahmans, who followed a form of monotheism or monism (espousal of a single divine principle), an ethic of reform, and selective appropriation of both Indian ideas and Western values.

The Samāj survived for several generations, for a while under the leadership of **Debindranath Tagore** (1817–84) who tended toward an internalization of religion, and **Keshub Chandra Sen** (1834–84) whose ideas, in fact, led to a split and eventual decline of the Samāj. Sen believed it important to practice fidelity to the throne of England and receive Western art and science in exchange for sharing with the world the wisdom of India's ancients. He spoke of an "Asiatic Christ" who was the quintessential human and the culmination of Asian wisdom. The "church" of the future would espouse a god who inspires both quiet meditation (Hinduism) and fervent service (Islam and Christianity). The religion would be universal, yet reflect the values of each culture.[25]

A far more conservative approach to the British presence was that of **Dayananda Sarasvati** (1824–1883). A Gujārati brahman brought up somewhat more removed from the British centers at Calcutta and Bombay, he nonetheless became disenchanted in his early years with certain popular forms of Hinduism such as the use of iconography, and determined to become an ascetic and seek the truth. His understanding of Hinduism and its need for change was that it ought not to be indebted to Western models, but to the *Vedas.* He claimed that Vedism was the only true Hinduism (though of course, it was his interpretations of the *Vedas* that became definitive for him). He was against caste, brahmanic excesses, and iconography on the grounds that these were not consistent with Vedic principles. At the same time, he sought to restate "Vedic" ideas in contemporary dress: for example, that God was one, but took on many forms and had many names. He coined the term *sanātana dharma* to speak of the eternality of the *dharma*, one reason why Hinduism was deemed superior to Islam and Christianity. Not least important, he founded the Ārya Samāj in 1875 to become the instrument for the purifying and homogenizing of Hinduism and for making it the national norm. As such, he (and especially his followers) wanted to reconvert Muslims and Christians, establish a Hindu state, and outlaw the killing of cows, a symbolic expression of Hindu piety.[26] The Ārya Samāj became the model for later, even more militant, religious-political groups that sought to Hinduize the Indian body politic: the Jan Sangh, the Rashtriya Swayamsevak Sangh (RSS), and the Vishwa Hindu Pariṣad (VHP).

Stage two

From the mid- to the late nineteenth century, a number of developments marked the Indian landscape. One of these was the strengthening of a sense of Indian nationalism. Ironically, fueled in part by the nationalisms of Europe, it took at least two forms. The first was a moderate effort to nudge the British to more responsive policies and Indians to various forms of self-reform. **Nairoji** (1825–1917), for example, a Pārsī graduate of Elphinstone College, moved to England in 1855 where he was eventually elected to the British parliament (1892) to represent a section of London. He continually sought to urge the crown to redress the financial exploitation of India and to provide her more political representation.[27]

Similarly, two Maharashtrian brahmans were active in this form of moderate nationalism. **Ranade** (1842–1901) worked toward certain social reforms – the elimination of child marriage and the increase of women's rights among others. In speeches, he argued for the need for change in certain Indian attitudes – no longer should Indians perceive differences between people based on heredity, which led to fragmentation of society and the propensity to ignore people outside of one's inner circle. One should learn to accept responsibility for oneself and follow the dictates of conscience and not of other men.[28]

Ranade's friend and follower **Gohhale** (1866–1915) similarly fought for certain causes: famine relief, Hindu–Muslim unity, and elevation of the "lower classes" among them. At the same time, he attacked the British policy of taxation that did not yield economic benefit for Indians. He became active in the Indian National Congress, which in 1883 became the official organ through which Indians would work toward independence.[29]

In some cases, the nationalism was more militant. Another Maharashtrian brahman, B. G. Tilak (1856–1920) illustrated that pattern well. Tilak was a judge who succeeded in politicizing religion and linking it to the common people. He evoked the *Bhagavadgītā*; the role of Śivājī, the Marāthī warrior, and Rāma to legitimate violence in the name of political freedom.[30] Two of Tilak's enterprises illustrate his approach. The first was in the form of a play performed for the first time in 1907, in which he recast a story of the *Mahābhārata* as an anti-British drama. Draupadī was India seized by Kīchaka (Britain). Yudiṣṭhara (the "moderate") counseled caution. Bhīma (the "extremist") insisted Kīchaka must be slain. In due course Bhīma, in the form of Bhairava, Śiva's terrible manifestation, descended to strangle Kīchaka and free Draupadī.

The second of Tilak's ploys was the way in which he popularized and politicized the Ganeṣa Chāthurthi festival. The festival had been observed largely within homes until Tilak had it performed publicly in 1894. The celebration of Ganeṣa's birthday became a venue for the performance of Hindu myths in public, for processions that often passed through Muslim sections of town, and for the denunciation of "*mlecchas*" (i.e., "barbarians" or "foreigners") – especially British as well as Muslims.[31] In 1895, some Muslims who found the procession and its songs to be offensive as it passed a mosque rushed out and engaged in a scuffle resulting in at least one death. Consequently, the government requested that the form of the festival be moderated. The festival remains one of Maharashtra's most popular events today: entire cities come to a virtual standstill as large clay icons of Ganeṣa are immersed in the waters at the festival's end.

Yet another form of religio-political nationalism was that found in the writings of the Bengālī brahman, poet, and dramatist, **B. C. Chatterjee** (1838–94). Just as Tilak had written in his vernacular, Marāthī, so Chatterjee used the Bengālī language and religious idiom to rally the public to a sense of regional and national pride. Kālī, the mother goddess of Bengal was equated to Bengal itself. The motherland was the place where pristine Hinduism would be restored and the British and Muslims alike would be ousted.[32]

Neo-*bhakti*

Quite apart from the explicitly nationalistic revival of religion, one finds by the end of the nineteenth century, a resurgence of religious piety or neo-*bhakti*. One form this took was the emergence of gurus and mystics offering an internalized form of religion. The popular and controversial Bengālī **Rāmakrishna** (1834–86) represented this model. A devotee of Kālī, he was endowed with a capacity for trance perceived as a form of "god-intoxication" and a charismatic personality which attracted disciples who were more formally educated than he. He was perceived to be the epitome of sainthood and the model of religion at its most positive.[33] One of his best-known disciples was Vivekananda (1863–1902), who combined his Western education with piety. He became one of the first "missionaries" to North America, establishing Vedānta centers in several cities in the eastern United States.[34] He was also responsible for reforming and "classicizing" temples around India. Near Srinagar, Kashmīr, for example, he was said to be instrumental in transforming a shrine to a tantric, even demonic, deity into a vegetarian goddess who came to be known as Kīr Bhāvanī (Lady of the Place of Sweet Milk).[35]

Other such reformers/pietists dotted the Indian landscape. Upgrading or establishing centers for meditation and worship, many sought to apply Western technology (e.g., print media) in reinterpreting various religious movements. **Bhaktivinoda Thakur**, for example, sought to recover and enliven the Gaudiā Vaiṣṇava movement in Bengal (the sect associated with Caitanya) and make it more attractive and accessible to an emerging middle class of urbanized Bengālīs. His work included the creation of a pilgrimage site, of centers for meditation and scholarly work, and literature articulating a "modern" expression of Caitanya's message.[36]

The last quarter of the nineteenth century witnessed the resurgence of religion in various forms. Renovations were made to temples, pilgrimages were encouraged, and the festival and ritual life associated with such centers increased. Often associated with these renovations was the recovery and publishing of classical literatures in the vernacular languages and the increased popularity of deities with strong regional ties – such as Kālī in Bengal; Ganeṣa and Viṭhobā in Maharashtra; and Murukaṉ in Tamil Nadu. In addition, the religions of folk communities became increasingly visible as transportation and communication improved. "Folk deities," such as Māriammaṉ, the goddess of smallpox in Tamil Nadu, were often ascribed an anti-British mythology. (For example, when a British surveyor came to a particular village to plan for the construction of a railroad through it, Māriammaṉ is said to have knocked him from his horse and made him change his plans.[37]) Increasingly, such temples as those of Māriammaṉ were assigned brahman priests and the "folk" goddess was linked to the classical tradition. Yet, at the same time, there was, in some quarters (as in Tamil Nadu), increased anti-brahman sentiment to the point that non-brahman communities sought to develop a cultic life that could emulate brahmanical religion without benefit of a brahman priest. By the 1920s, India's cultic life had mushroomed geometrically as roads and railroads made pilgrimage centers more accessible to more common folk. By then, India's fourth major surge of *bhakti* had taken hold; like its three predecessors, this movement combined several elements at once: responding to but selectively appropriating from alternative options; selectively appropriating indigenous and vernacular forms of mythology, theology, and cultus; and using the idiom and technology of the times to restate a sense of heritage and identity. A new India, religiously and politically, was dawning.

Muslim responses to coloniality

In the context of British hegemony, Muslims were faced with a triple dilemma: political, economic, and religious. No longer having access to patronage in the courts of the Mughals, many Muslims were unsure where to turn to find a political haven where Islamic principles could be applied, and where economic opportunity could be found. In the face of political and economic decline, what did it mean to be Muslim? Surely Allāh did not let his people down. Where does one turn for renewal of a sense of one's heritage?

Even before the British came to power these questions were arising in the mind of **Shāh Walī-Allāh** (1703–62). He was aware of increasing Hindu revivalism, but also the movement associated with **al-Wahhāb** in Saudi Arabia. Working with the Saudi royal house, al-Wahhāb had purged the Arabian peninsula of elements considered inappropriate to Islam and installed a puritanical form of the religion. Walī-Allāh's response in India was to seek greater harmony amongst Muslims and attempt a moral and religious "reform" based on the Qu'rān. He helped translate the Qu'rān into Urdū, calling upon Muslims in India to return to the pristine form of their religion. He was not opposed to using military action against other militants, and attempted to get Afghanī help against the Marāthās.[38]

Within two generations, Walī-Allāh's influence had led to the establishment of a *mujāhidīn* (an Islamic militia), especially in Afghanistan wherein *jihād* became an article of faith. Under **Sayyid Ahmed Barelwi**, Islamic courts were established and Muslims were encouraged to eschew "Hindu" practices. Especially in Bengal, several conservative movements were spawned which sought to distinguish Muslim from Hindu and confronted Hindu landlords and the British administration. **Saiyid Ahmed Khan** (1786–1831), similarly, set a goal of returning to the "pristine Islam" of the past and declared India to be a "land of warfare" (***dār al-ḥarb***) as opposed to a land of peace (***dār al-islām***). *Jihād* could appropriately be invoked (as by Afghans on the Sikhs in the Panjāb). Indeed, it was some of Saiyid Khan's followers who were involved in the "Sepoy Mutiny."[39]

After the rebellion, there was some change in strategy. Urdū was flourishing in such places as Lucknow and had become the language of culture and of some colleges. Especially instrumental in setting this new tone was a different **Syed Ahmad Khān** (1817–98). Khān was impressed by the reforms undertaken in earlier eras of Islam – especially those of **al-Mālmūn**, the fifth 'Abbāsid caliph. By the mid-eighth century, al-Mālmūn had made Baghdad a center of philosophy, science, the arts, and a place where the Qu'rān and philosophy were apparently reconciled under Ḥanafī scholarship. Ahmad Khān also saw Egypt and Turkey as nations where modernization was successfully occurring in his own time. Accordingly, Khān argued that Muslims needed the British and vice versa. Education in the arts and sciences would help Muslims compete; further, he argued, Islam was not incompatible with other forms of knowledge insofar as Allāh is the source of all truth and nature is the work of Allāh. Muslims and Hindus should be able to get along, as both were the products of migration centuries before, though now both groups were indigenous to the subcontinent. India was like a beautiful bride, with two eyes, one Hindu, one Muslim.[40]

Khān's attempts at reconciliation led to the founding of Alīgarh College where both the "Western" sciences and Islam were taught and where the Alīgarh movement was spawned. The movement did inspire a number of Muslims to take advantage of Western forms of education, and led to the founding of colleges in various parts of India where Muslims could study the sciences. Yet Ahmad Khān's "modernism" either spawned other reactions, or developed alongside some that were more conservative.

One of these developments was the founding of Deoband Madrasa (Seminary) in 1867, which sought to re-establish contact between the Muslim middle classes and classical Islam. Its theological positions were decidedly orthodox; indeed, the school received some visibility in recent years as a major source of Islamic education for the advisers to militants in Pakistan and Afghanistan's Talibans. Other conservative reactions included the work of **Sayyid Amin** (1840–1928) who developed an apologetic on behalf of Islam, and **Nawwab Saddiq** and **Hassan Khan**, who, while writing in Urdū, led a movement known as *ahli-ḥadīth* wherein innovation was condemned as being contrary to the *sunna*.[41]

In the meanwhile, there were also other responses: **Nu'mani**, for example, founded a school in Lucknow in 1894, which contributed to Indo-Islamic studies and published more "liberal" scholarship. Pietism was yet another response. **Hali** (1837–1914), for example, a Sūfī poet and saint, continued the tradition of Sūfī mystical poetry expressed in the Urdū *g͟hazal* wherein religion is internalized. There was, in addition, even the creation of a new Islamic sect. It was founded by one **Mirza Ghulani Ahmad** of Qadiyan (1839–1908), who proclaimed himself both the Messiah and the Mahdī (who was the expected "redeemer" at the end of history). He was presented as an incarnation of both Kṛṣṇa and Christ. His followers came to be known as the Ahmadiyah movement, which sought to defend Islam against the polemics of the Ārya Samāj and Christian missionaries while co-opting elements from both religious traditions. They maintained, for example, that Jesus had come to India and was buried in Kashmīr.[42]

Inter-religious relations: conciliation and confrontation

As evident from the preceding discussions, relationships between religious communities were often fragile in the mid- and late nineteenth century. Without doubt, these relationships were at times confrontational. On the Muslim side, for one, there were occasional outbreaks of hostility. In the 1850s, for example, in what were apparently the first Hindu–Muslim skirmishes in Ayodhyā, the Sunnīs (some one third of the city's population at the time) led battles against entrenched Hindu warring ascetics on the grounds that a Muslim pilgrimage site had been taken over by Hindus. Some militant Hindus, for their part, were known to "bait" Muslims: in 1893, a Cow Protection Movement was launched (the first of several) trying to prevent Muslims from slaughtering cows; and in the mid-1890s, the Ārya Samāj launched its attempt to reconvert Muslims. The situation was exacerbated by certain British policies wherein caste and religious distinctions were highlighted: identity cards were issued which indicated a person's caste and religion; a quota system was used to assign places in the civil service; and certain communities were granted permission to follow their own laws, not least important, Muslims who were permitted the right to follow the *sharī'a*. This last policy led to protests by some Hindus in 1907 and thereafter. These policies, in general, tended to lead to the creation of power blocs based on caste or religion and to the phenomenon known in India as communalism[43] – the propensity to make the values of one's "community" more important than those of any other community, including those of the nation-state itself.

One response on the part of Muslim leaders was that of calling for a separate electorate for Muslims. Even the moderate Ahmad Khān had worried that because Muslims were only 20 percent of the subcontinent's population, they would be unable to find appropriate representation in the face of the majority. In 1906, the Muslim League was founded to press for demands that Muslims be elected from separate Muslim electorates and that the percentage of these be higher than the percentage of the population.[44] In light of these developments, the contribution of **Muhammed Alī** and **Muhammad Iqbal** are apropos.

Muhammed Alī (1878–1931) was born of a conservative Muslim family, studied at Alīgarh College and at Oxford. In England, he observed the results of British hegemony over other Islamic areas and the decline of the Ottoman empire. This increased his resistance to the British, especially during the First World War for which he was incarcerated. Mahatma Gandhi sought his release; subsequently, he became an admirer and ally of Gandhi, working for a united and independent India. He believed cooperation between Hindu and Muslim was essential and that non-violence was the way to self-rule. Hindus, he argued, needed to understand that Muslims were trying to catch up economically and politically, and that Muslims were a people of two identities, one fully Indian and, like Hindus, waiting to be free, the other "supernational" shaped by the principles of Islam.[45]

Muhammad Iqbal (1873–1938), a native of Panjāb, was trained in law, continental philosophy, and Islamics. Less the activist than the poet and thinker, Iqbal argued that Islam's contribution to the world was its belief in the unity of humankind, its abhorrence of injustice, and its insistence that the self be developed to its fullest extent. At the same time, Islam needed to embrace the modern world and rethink its fundamental message in light of contemporary thought. One such rethinking lay in how Islamic principles could be applied in a democratic state: the classical Sunnī principle of *ijmā'* (consensus of the '*ulamā'*) could be the basis for parliamentary government – that is, consensus by an elected body. His poetry, in both Urdū and Persian, was rich in expressing his beliefs – that love, for example, was the basis, not for quiescence, but for "righteous action" for the betterment of humankind; that the self was the gift of God and deserved to be free and conscious of the fullness of life's values.[46]

Relationships between Christians and Hindus were also fragile at times, though they seldom took on violent form into the early twentieth century. More often, the confrontations were intellectual. Two illustrations will suffice.

John Wilson was a Scottish Presbyterian missionary in Bombay from 1829–75. He helped establish a college and schools in English and Marāthī, and, together with his wife, the first school for girls in Bombay in 1832. Wilson was also a scholar who became comfortable in Marāthī, Gujārati, Hindūstānī, Hebrew, Portuguese, Persian, Sanskrit, and Arabic. His style, nonetheless, was confrontational, as he would write pamphlets and offer lectures, challenging intellectuals of Pārsī, Hindu, and Muslim communities to rethink the essential nature of religion. When two Pārsīs were converted in 1839, and a brahman in 1843, responses were generated especially amongst the brahmans of Bombay. The more conservative group, led by a man named **Prabhu**, came to oppose attendance at mission schools and re-entry into caste after such attendance. By the late 1840s, they published journals in Marāthī and Gujārati, defending Hinduism, resisting change, and calling for a return to orthoprax ritual activities. A more "progressive" group led by **Sāstrī** took a different tack: they believed re-entry into caste was possible after contact; they espoused social reform, and the rethinking of Hindu "essentials." Some studied Hindu classics more deeply in order to defend it more adequately, and to reject those practices not deemed consistent with "*vaidika*" tradition.[47]

The other illustration follows from the writings of **John Muir** (1810–82), a Scottish administrator in the East India Company and maverick lay theologian. His writings in "church Sanskrit" reflected a "theology" of conciliation, in which he sought to present Christianity as an expression of "truth" through rational discourse. He sought to convey a "benign humanism" which entailed empathy and scholarly knowledge of his intended audience, in this case Hindus. In his writings, he presented the idea of "God" and "true religion" in ways consistent with a Christian perspective.

Responses to Muir's work were of several kinds: a moderate Maharashtrian brahman (**Somanatha**), for example, concurred that *mokṣa* (enlightenment) is possible in non-Hindu religions so long as one follows the scripture of that religion. A more virulent response, that of a Calcutta brahman (**Haracandra**), was to castigate Muir as a prejudiced and blind infidel, and critiqued Christianity for its newness, its sectarianism, and imperiousness, as well as its naivete (for accepting such "legends" as those of the virgin birth as "true").[48]

Out of the responses emerged a Hindu apologetic shaped in contradistinction to Christianity. The principles of this defense included the following ideas: 1) *Sanātana dharma* was more ancient than Christianity, hence more true. 2) The fundamental human problem was epistemological (that is not knowing the truth) rather than moral. Indeed, the concept of "original sin" was deemed illogical and unjust. 3) Hinduism was a religion with a variously adaptable deity (rather than one confined to a single revelatory moment) and its various viewpoints (*darśana*) afforded flexibility for different types of people. 4) The Hindu goal of *mokṣa* was superior to any idea of a literal heaven. 5) Vedic authority was beyond question and brahmanhood was authentic inasmuch as it was rooted in *karma*.[49]

Despite such confrontations, there were also accommodations and borrowings between the communities. On the Christian side, there was adaptation of Sanskrit and vernacular terminology to express Christian ideas; the appropriation of such institutions as the ashram for meditation and study; and the appropriation of local accretions in the celebration of festivals and rituals, especially within Catholic circles. Not least important, there was some reinterpretation of basic Christian ideas. Hence, one would find some Christian thinkers expressing the nature of the Christ figure in terms that reflected the Indian landscape: as the "bringer of a new created order" (**Chenchiah**); the paradigmatic *guru* and true *avatāra* of the divine (**Chakkarai**); and the "eternal ***oṃ***" and personality who embodies *ahiṃsa* (**S. Jesudason**).[50] In addition, there were those upper-class Christians who sought to retain caste identities after conversion (despite missionary protests), and some who became partners with other Indians to fight for freedom and human dignity. Some Hindus, for their part, borrowed from Christianity. There was emulation of aspects of Christian ethics that were, nonetheless, simultaneously rediscovered in their own ancient sources:

for example, a spirit of egalitarianism, and self-giving service. Institutions of social activism were formed. Strategies of communication (e.g., street preaching and printing pamphlets) were often borrowed from Christian propagandists.[51] Not least important, there was a co-opting of Christian ideas and making these consistent with Hindu traditions. Thus, Hindus could speak of Christ as "true guru" (**Subba Rao**), the "perfect god-man" (**Brahmandero**), and exemplary renunciant, oriental *avatāra*, and embodiment of "true religion" (Vivekananda), or the yogin par excellence (**Swami Akhilananda**).[52]

Pre-independence India

As intimated above, many of the issues which fueled discussion of India's nineteenth century informed discourse in the first half of the twentieth century as well: the concern for envisioning a new India which took its place in a global network; the role of history in shaping the present; the concern for a people free of colonial control; and the place of religion in a modern setting; all these continued to be part of the agendas of India's elites. The thought and contribution of several significant figures can illustrate the trends in pre-independence India.

Mohandas Gandhi (1869–1948) was certainly one of the significant figures on the Indian scene from the 1920s until independence. Born in Gujarat of an industrious father and deeply religious mother, and influenced early in life by Jain neighbors, Gandhi studied law in London. There, he rediscovered the *Bhagavadgītā* and his Hindu identity through the eyes of Western seekers. Unable to find work in India, he went to South Africa for two decades where he became active in helping Indians resist the racist laws of the white administration; it was in South Africa that his religio-political strategy of *satyagraha* (the force of truth) developed. This principle affirmed that truth was the very nature of the universe (*satya* [truth] equals *brahman* [cosmic essence]); that all peoples shared a common essence; that the force of that truth could be enacted in non-violent action that would embarrass and force an oppressor to change laws. The strategy was designed to unite all persons, irrespective of educational, religious, or economic status into boycotts, marches, and protests that would put economic and international political pressure to bear on repressive regimes. It was also in South Africa, where Gandhi stayed for a while in the home of Plymouth Brethren missionaries, that he came to appreciate aspects of Christian social ethics while disdaining doctrinaire Christian theology.

When Gandhi returned to India at the age of forty-five, he became actively engaged in the Indian National Congress. By now he had adapted a simple lifestyle as he experimented with approaches that would combine indigenous health practices with religious orientations forged by the influences of Jain non-violence, Christian ethics, and a reinterpretation of the *Bhagavadgītā* as the story of an internal battle wherein each one was obliged to "wage war" with the passions and temptations within. These elements were combined with a political strategy that sought to unite all Indians, including Hindus and Muslims, upper castes and "outcastes" (whom Gandhi called "harijans" or "children of God") for the purpose of attaining political and financial independence of India from British rule. Through fasts and marches, identifying with highly placed and low alike, many joined Gandhi in protesting British policy. Nonetheless, when independence finally came in 1947, Gandhi was deeply disappointed that the country was divided into two nations – India and Pakistan – and that his call for village-based economics and simple lifestyle went largely unheeded.[53]

Another significant figure during this period was **Rabindranath Tagore** (1861–1941). The fourteenth child of Debindranath Tagore, Rabindranath did not need to earn his own livelihood, so had time as a youth to experiment with writing. By 1912 he had published *Gītāñjalī* (song offerings) for which he won the Nobel Prize for literature. He founded a school at Shantiniketan, which became a retreat and a center for the cultivation of the creative arts. Here too a university was established in 1921 for the promotion of "world brotherhood and cultural interchange."[54]

Tagore was soon a world traveler and global figure. He was impatient with Indian nationalism, whether of the Gandhian or the Bengālī variety. Tagore's was a "religion of man" (the title of one of his books), characterized by a fundamental faith in humanity and its divine source and in the notion that humankind's hopes lay in the reaffirmation of the fundamental spiritual values to be found in all religions. India's role was not only to be reawakened to its own spiritual roots, but also open to more of the world at large. Throughout his life, he celebrated the variety and beauty of life, was prolific in the production of poetry, drama, and song and sought to infuse India with a sense of its kinship and place in the world at large. One brief poem captures Tagore's spirit:

> Where the mind is without fear and the head is held high;
> Where knowledge is free;
> Where the world has not been broken up into fragments by narrow
>   domestic walls;
> Where words come out from the depth of truth;
> Where tireless striving stretches its arms towards perfection;
> Where the clear stream of reason has not lost its way into the dreary
>   desert sand of dead habit;

Where the mind is led forward by thee into everwidening thought and action –
Into that heaven of freedom, my Father, let my country awake.[55]

Aurobindo Ghose (1872–1950), a Bengālī schooled in England, returned to India in 1893 intending to serve in the civil service. Soon he was seeking to rediscover his Indian heritage. He studied Sanskrit and read the works of Rāmakrishna, Vivekananda, and B. C. Chatterjee, the Bengālī nationalist. He soon found himself embroiled in the "extremist politics" of Bengal. His speeches and writings made him a "*persona non grata*" with the British and he was jailed for "sedition."

While in prison he had a series of religious experiences, which led him eventually to abandon politics and Bengal. He withdrew to the French protectorate, Pondicherry, to practice his yogic discipline and to let his religious thought mature. While he had once idealized Indian nationalism and Hinduism, in his later years his thought became more eclectic, and he sought to wed notions of the Indian spiritual tradition with Western science and philosophy. His religious orientation turned inward as he sought to live and express union with the divine. What he called "Integral Yoga" was the "rendering in personal experience of the truth which universal nature had hidden in herself and which she travails to discover. It is the conversion of the human soul into the divine soul and of natural life into divine life."[56] For Aurobindo, the hope for the future lay not in nationalistic politics or even the establishment of a universal religious creed, but rather in the realization that all persons share an inner spirit and could evolve through appropriate discipline to their true nature. To assist followers in that quest, Aurobindo, and a French woman of similar bent, established an ashram in Pondicherry. Another less successful product of Aurobindo's vision was the establishment of a universal village known as Auroville, intended to be a commune where work, resources, and faith could be shared by all, irrespective of background.

A final figure illustrating in a very different way the kind of sentiment stirring in the first half of the twentieth century is **V. D. Savarkar** (1883–1966). A Maharashtrian brahman, Savarkar was influenced by the politics of B. G. Tilak and by several incidents in his youth, including the hanging of two Maharashtrian "terrorists." Savarkar became a firebrand in the cause of Hindu nationalism.

As a youth he learned the art of bomb making from a Russian revolutionary and organized groups to protest British policies, from the throwing of stones, the building of bonfires, and the advocacy of violence, to the writing of a pamphlet glorifying the "Sepoy Mutiny" as the "First Indian War of Independence." For his activities, he was imprisoned for years and restricted from political activity. Yet he served as president of the Hindu Mahasabha for seven years, one of the most militant and "communalistic" of the Hindu organizations.

Savarkar advocated the reconversion of Muslims and Christians to Hinduism and the incorporation of the untouchables into Hindu institutions. He coined the term "Hindutva," which represented his vision for Hinduizing the Indian polity and making Hinduism more militant. Hindutva incorporated the idea that all of India shared a common geography and culture that was infused with sacrality. That sacrality was the heritage of the *Vedas* and the Epics which should become the basis for India's political order. Hinduism was to be more homogenized, its central "unity" transcending sectarianism. Converted Muslims and Christians would be part of the vision only insofar as they reaffirmed their Hindu roots.[57]

Savarkar's legacy has continued to be part of India's religious landscape. One of his disciples assassinated Gandhi for the latter's alleged softness toward India's Muslims. Some of the organizations which have become the exponents of Hindu nationalism today draw inspiration from Savarkar's agenda: these include the Rashtriya Swayamsevak Sangh (RSS – the National Assembly of Volunteers), and the Jan Sangh (People's League).

The religious landscape of nineteenth- and early twentieth-century India was marked by a wide range of activity. There was reawakening and rediscovery of some elements from a perceived past; accommodation, confrontation, and negotiation between communities in a pluralistic landscape; the rearticulation of Hindu and/or Muslim identities; the resurgence of vernacular sensibilities at the same time as there was increased national and global consciousness; the use of religion for political purpose; the increased visibility of folk practice and its intermingling with neo-classical developments; and a resurgence of pietism and popular religion. It was, in short, a century of transition that set the stage for the contemporary period and, in the process, illustrated the religious options available to a globe facing similar dynamics in the twenty-first century.

Recommended reading

On religious minorities in India

Beyrenther, E. *Bartholomaeus Ziegenbalg.* Trs. S. G. Lang and H. W. Gensichen. Madras: Christian Literature Society, Diocesan Press, 1955.

Boyce, M. B. *Zoroastrians: Their Religious Beliefs and Practices.* Third revision. London: Routledge & Kegan Paul, 1988.

Brown, L. W. *The Indian Christians of St. Thomas.* Cambridge: Cambridge University Press, 1956.

Clarke, Sathianathan. *Dalits and Christianity: Subaltern Religion and Liberation Theology in India.* Delhi: Oxford University Press, 1998.
Cronin, V. *A Pearl to India: The Life of Robert de Nobili.* New York: E. P. Dutton, 1959.
Drewery, Mary. *William Carey: A Biography.* Grand Rapids, MI: Zondervan Publishing House, 1979.
Fischel, W. J. *The Jews in India.* Jerusalem: Ben Zvi Institute, Hebrew University, 1960.
Forrester, D. B. *Caste and Christianity: Attitudes and Policies on Caste of Anglo-Saxon Protestant Missions in India.* London: Curzon Press, 1980.
Ingham, Kenneth. *Reformers in India, 1793–1833.* Cambridge: Cambridge University Press, 1956.
Insler, S. *The Gāthās of Zaruthustra.* Actan Iranica Volume one. Leiden: Mouton, 1975.
Katz, N. *Who are the Jews of India?* Berkeley: University of California Press, 2000.
Kotwal, F. W. and Boyd, J. W. eds. *A Guide to the Zoroastrian Religion.* Chico, CA: Scholars Press, 1982.
Kulke, E. *The Parsees in India: A Minority as Agents of Social Change.* Munich: Weltforum Verlag, 1974.
Lehman, E. Arno. *It Began at Tranquebar.* Madras: Christian Literature Society, 1956.
Luke, P. Y. and Carman, J. B. *Village Christians and Hindu Culture.* London: Lutterworth Press, 1968.
Neill, S. *A History of Christianity in India: the Beginning to 1707.* Cambridge: Cambridge University Press, 1984.
Neill, S. *A History of Christianity in India: 1707–1858.* Cambridge: Cambridge University Press, 1985.
Parasurama, T. V. *India's Jewish Heritage.* New Delhi: Sagar Publications, nd.
Richter, J. *A History of Missions in India.* New York: Fleming H. Revell, 1908.
Samartha, S. J. *The Hindu Response to the Unbound Christ.* Madras: Christian Literature Society, 1974.
Strizower, S. *The Children of Israel: the Bene-Israel of Bombay.* Oxford: Oxford University Press, 1971.
Thomas, P. *Christian and Christianity in India and Pakistan.* London: G. Allen & Unwin, 1956.
Thurston, F. *Castes and Tribes of South India.* Seven volumes. Reprint. Delhi: Asian Educational Services, 1993.
Tiliander, Bror. *Christian and Hindu Terminology, A Study of their Mutual Relations with Special Reference to the Tamil Area.* Uppsala: Almquist and Wiksell Tryckeri, 1974.
Timberg, T. Alex. *Jews in India.* New York: Advent Books, 1986.
Tisserant, E. C. *Eastern Christianity in India: A History of the Syro-Malabar Church from the Earliest Time to the Present Day.* Westminster, MD: Newman Press, 1957.
Webster, J. C. B. *The Dalit Christians: A History.* Delhi: ISPCK, 1992.

The colonial period

Bayly, C. A. *Indian Society and the Making of British India.* Cambridge: Cambridge University Press, 1988.
Boxer, C. R. *Race Relations in the Portuguese Colonial Empire, 1415–1825.* Oxford: Oxford University Press, 1963.
Boxer, C. R. *Portuguese Society in the Tropics.* Madison, WI: University of Wisconsin Press, 1965.
Copland, Ian. *India 1857–1947: The Unmaking of an Empire.* London: Longman, 2001.

Dirks, Nicholas. ed. *Colonialism and its Forms of Knowledge.* Princeton: Princeton University Press, 1996.
Fisher, Michael. *Indirect Rule in India.* Oxford and Delhi: Oxford University Press, 1993.
Gopal, S. *British Policy in India, 1858–1905.* Cambridge: Cambridge University Press, 1965.
Lewis, M. D. ed. *The British in India: Imperialism or Trusteeship?* Boston: Beacon Press, 1962.
Metcalf, Thomas R. *Ideologies of the Raj.* Cambridge: Cambridge University Press, 1994.
Parry, B. *Delusions and Discoveries: Studies on India in the British Imagination, 1880–1930.* Berkeley: University of California Press, 1972.
Philips, C. H. *The East India Company. 1784–1834.* Second edition. Manchester: Manchester University Press, 1961.
Stokes, Eric. *The English Utilitarians and India.* Oxford: Clarendon Press, 1959.
Trautmann, Thomas. *Aryans and British India.* Berkeley: University of California Press, 1997.

The Indian experience (pre-independence)

Ambedkar, B. R. *The Buddha and the Dhamma.* Third edition. Bombay: Siddarth Publications, 1984.
Baljon, J. M. S. *The Reforms and Religious Ideas of Sir Sayyid Ahmad Khan.* Leiden: Mouton & Co., 1949.
Brown, D. Mackenzie. *The Nationalist Movement: Indian Political Thought from Ranade to Bhave.* Berkeley: University of California Press, 1961.
Chakravarty, Amiya. ed. *A Tagore Reader.* Boston: Beacon Press, 1961.
Crawford, S. C. *Ram Mohan Roy: Social, Political and Religious Reform in Nineteenth Century India.* New York: Paragon House, 1987.
Fischer, L. *The Life of Mahatma Gandhi.* Bombay: Bharata Vidya Bhavan, 1959.
Gandhi, M. K. *An Autobiography. The Story of my Experiments with Truth.* Harmondsworth: Penguin, 1982.
Ghose, Aurobindo. *A Synthesis of Yoga.* Pondicherry: Sri Aurobindo Ashram, 1971.
Guha, Ranajit. *Elementary Aspects of Peasant Insurgency in Colonial India.* Oxford and Delhi: Oxford University Press, 1984.
Harischandra, Vasudha Dalmia. *The Nationalization of Hindu Traditions.* Oxford and Delhi: Oxford University Press, 1997.
Hawley, J. S. ed. *Satī, the Blessing and the Curse: The Burning of Widows in India.* New York: Oxford University Press, 1994.
Hay, S. ed. *Sources of Indian Tradition.* New York: Columbia University Press, 1988.
Heimsath, C. H. *Indian Nationalism and Hindu Social Reform.* Princeton: Princeton University Press, 1964.
Jones, Kenneth. *Arya Dharm: Hindu Consciousness in Nineteenth Century Punjab.* Berkeley: University of California Press, 1976.
Jones, Kenneth W. ed. *Religious Controversy in British India.* Albany: SUNY Press, 1992.
Keer, Dhananjay. *Dr. Ambedkar Life and Mission.* Bombay: Popular Prakashan, 1990.
Kopf, D. *British Orientalism and the Bengal Renaissance: The Dynamics of Indian Modernization, 1773–1834.* Berkeley: University of California Press, 1969.
Kopf, D. *The Brahmo Samāj and the Shaping of the Modern Indian Mind.* Princeton: Princeton University Press, 1979.

Lavan, Spencer. *The Ahmadiyah Movement: A History and Perspective.* New Delhi: Manohar, 1974.

Lelyveld, D. *Aligarh's First Generation: Muslim Solidarity in British India.* Princeton: Princeton University Press, 1978.

McLane, J. R. *Indian Nationalism and the Early Congress.* Princeton: Princeton University Press, 1977.

Metcalf, Barbara D. *Islamic Revival in British India: Deoband, 1860–1900.* Princeton: Princeton University Press, 1982.

Metcalf, Thomas R. *The Aftermath of Revolt: India, 1857–1870.* Princeton: Princeton University Press, 1964.

Oddie, G. A. ed. *Religion in South Asia: Religious Conversion and Revival Movements in South Asia in Medieval and Modern Times.* London: Curzon Press, 1977.

Robinson, F. *Separatism Among Indian Muslims: The Politics of the United Provinces: Muslims, 1860–1923.* Cambridge: Cambridge University Press, 1974.

Whitehead, H. *The Village Gods of South India.* Second edition. New Delhi: Asian Educational Services, 1988.

Wolpert, Stanley A. *Tilak and Gokhale: Revolution and Reform in the Making of Modern India.* Berkeley: University of California Press, 1962.

Young, Richard Fox. *Resistant Hinduism.* Vienna: E. J. Brill, 1981.

9

Religion in Contemporary India

The context

At midnight on August 15, 1947, India attained its independence from Britain. For many on the subcontinent it proved to be a bittersweet moment, for it resulted in the partition of India and Pakistan. Pakistan, a nation primarily intended for Muslims, was divided into two parts: West Pakistan, comprised of northern Panjāb and the provinces of Sind, Baluchistan, and the Northeast Frontier, and East Pakistan, comprised of East Bengal. East

Pakistan would become Bangladesh in 1971. At the time of the partition, many families, Hindu, Muslim, and Sikh, voluntarily or involuntarily, left behind the lands of their foreparents, afraid they would be living in a nation unsympathetic to their faith. Some 10 million persons are said to have moved from their ancestral homes in 1947, of whom at least a million are estimated to have died in the violence that ensued. Many Hindus from Sind or East Bengal, for example, were cut off from their family roots, as were Sikhs who had lived for generations in northern Panjāb. While many Muslim families also moved, millions of others opted to stay in the new nation-state of India, preferring to keep their businesses and lands.

From its inception, Pakistan was engaged in debates as to what it meant to be an "Islamic state." Its more liberal leadership, including **Muhammad Ali Jinnah**, who had fought for the creation of the state, and **Liaquat Ali Khan**, its first prime minister, wanted to assure a democratic republic which offered opportunity for all. The more conservative '*ulamā*', as voiced by **Syed Abu'l-ala Maududi**, wanted to be sure the country was in every respect run on the principles of the Islamic *sharī'a.* After the death of Jinnah in 1948 and, especially, after the assassination of Ali Khan, in 1951, considerable turbulence ensued, leading, in 1958, **General Ayub Khan** to seize control as a military governor. Since then, the military has assumed political dominance in Pakistan, with the '*ulamā*' and more liberal Muslim intellectuals variously seeking to exercise power.[1]

Fortunately for India, those in power led it to become a rapidly developing democracy. Within two decades of independence and especially in the years when **Jawarhalal Nehru** was India's first prime minister (1947–64), the young country had made rapid strides toward an industrialized democracy. States which had remained autonomous under the British were incorporated into the new nation (whether by accession or force). By January 26, 1950, the country had a constitution, thanks to a drafting committee chaired by Dr. B. R. Ambedkar, which enfranchised all its citizens, including those once known as "untouchables." A series of five-year economic plans initiated in the first fifteen years, led to attempts to develop village economies, and increased production of food and industry. Indeed, by 1966, India was the seventh most industrially advanced nation in the world and by 1989, thanks to the so-called Green Revolution, food production had increased several fold.

The legal status of women was elevated significantly through a series of laws: one removing inter-caste barriers to marriage (1949); another giving Hindu women the right to divorce and raising the minimum age for marriage for males to eighteen and females to fifteen (1955); yet another gave female children equal rights as males to inherit property (1956). By 1957 some 40 percent of the 92 million women qualified to vote cast ballots, helping to elect twenty-seven women to the national lower house (Lak Sabha) and 105 women to state assemblies.[2]

Similarly, the third five-year plan targeted the need for enhancing educational possibilities by increasing the number of schools and teachers available for youngsters. By 1960, as a result, some 50 million Indian students were attending almost half a million schools and the literacy rate had risen to 23.7 percent, though only 12.8 percent of India's women were literate by that time.[3]

For the rest of the century, India continued its development on many fronts. The literacy rate has grown with the creation of more schools. Virtually every village has been electrified and provided with modern communication facilities; the founding of highly competitive national Institutes of Technology has helped create a community of scientists, now among the three largest in the world. The economy, once based on a socialist pattern with many nationalized industries, was opened to foreign investment in 1991, thereby stimulating more competition amongst its business elites.

Of course, problems have persisted: a large portion of the population – perhaps more than half a billion – continues to live in relative poverty. Cities cannot keep up with the flow of immigrants, who now live on the sidewalks and in slum pockets. The population explosion, especially among the poor, continues almost unabated. There is jostling for space in crowded cities; a quest for power amongst those once disenfranchised; frustration that prosperity and literacy have not reached many at the lower echelons of society; and corruption and cynical exploitation on the part of some politicians, national and local. India, in short, is a microcosm of the modern world, lunging forward toward still unattained possibilities while selectively trying to retain elements of its storied past.

As for religion, it is alive and very visible in India today. Despite predictions by social scientists that forces of modernization, globalization, secularization, and economic development would consign religion to India's trash bin, in fact the reverse has been true: not only is religion alive, it has been resurgent in many corners of the subcontinent. In fact, it may be not so much *despite* these kinds of currents, but because of them that religion is resurgent.

To be sure, many Indians have become "secularized" and are interested in attaining "material" prosperity even while the number of technologically and scientifically trained people on the subcontinent has mushroomed. Yet scholars and even casual observers have noted that prosperous people are not necessarily irreligious and that scientists are often engaged in the building of temples and the rethinking of religion, especially in the Indian diaspora.

Of course, globalization has come to India's cities bringing satellite television, e-mail, cyber cafes, Internet, and most of the wizardry of global communication. The outcome of this process, on the one hand, obviously, is that some people experience what might be called a global consciousness. But globalization can be measured in different ways: it is accessible to different degrees – more accessible in urban areas and to elites – that is, to the educationally and economically privileged and less accessible in rural areas and to the half billion persons who remain poor in India. Further, a "global consciousness" is appropriated selectively. Some pick and choose those parts of the "global culture" of which they will take advantage. These appropriations may be more external than internal. That suggests, further, that a global mind-set may be internalized by relatively few: just because one uses Colombian coffee, for example, doesn't mean one thinks Colombian. Not only that, one may be "global" and Indian, global and ethnic at the same time, or "global" in one context and "ethnic" in another. Furthermore, "globalization" has spawned resistance and renewed interest in local and national values. We noted in the last chapter how patterns that might be called "global," or at least originating outside India, nonetheless, led to a rebirth of Indian self-consciousness, including a resurgence of religion.

Similarly, "modernization" is not the opposite of "tradition" as if "tradition" stood for some monolithic past that was unchanging in contrast to some dynamic "modern era." In fact, we have noticed how India's past has been constantly changing. Each new moment obviously reflects its own time and place; yet the "past" is perceived and celebrated selectively. People tend to reclaim a past, reinterpret it, perceiving it in terms that suit their own moment. This is the nature of "tradition": people constantly reconstruct it based on their perceptions of what must have been. Hence, in India today, new religious movements are said to be consistent with the Vedic past or with āgamic practice. Such claims have the character of myth: the present is read into the past. Such perceptions of the past, often glorified, provide a sense of rootedness and identity. Over a century ago, Nietzsche noted that "modern man" was given to groping in his past for a sense of lineage and roots – that is, for "myth";[4] in a similar way, over a quarter of a century ago, sociologist Robert Bellah commented that modernization was marked by rapid social change, but also by a kind of romanticism that found in language, ethnicity, and religion a sense of continuity and identity.[5]

True, many families have discontinued the details of rites of passage so elaborately described in classical texts. Of course, Vedic fire rituals are done much less commonly than might have been the case in ancient India (but, in fact, there have been attempts to recover and re-enact some of these in recent years). Hence, while religion may have changed, it is by no means dead in India. In fact, religion may be as visible in India today as it ever has been – in pilgrimages and festivals, in renovated temples, in the private *pūjā* rooms of affluent families. It is worth attempting to capture something of the flavor of this dynamic religious landscape.

The practice of religion

The most visible and common way in which religion is expressed on the subcontinent is in its practice, especially in the form of diverse and colorful rituals. There are many reasons why ritual is so popular in India today. For one thing, from the beginning of Indian civilization, ritual has served to express one's fundamental place in the social and cosmic order. Ritual acts out one's relationship to family and kin, expresses one's obligations consistent with *dharma*, and enacts "tradition" in such a way as to make that "tradition" accessible to the senses. One can see, hear, taste, even smell the "tradition"; one can experience "tradition" somatically. One expresses one's identity as a member of a particular family or village/city or of a regional or linguistic matrix. Ritual also serves a pragmatic purpose in contemporary life as many see in it a strategy for changing the circumstances of their lives – the quest for better jobs, educational opportunities, etc. are often expressed ritually. In a ritual one can negotiate or reflect the various passages and boundaries that modernity imposes – between global and sub-ethnic identities; between the past and the contemporary moment; between generations; between "us" and "them."

Pilgrimages and festivals

More people have been making religious pilgrimages in India today than has been true at any other point in history. While classical texts identify any number of places where a pilgrim may attain special grace, the building of roads and railway connections, vigorous advertising, and increased wealth all have made pilgrimage an enormously popular enterprise today throughout the subcontinent. Sacred places abound: riverbanks and junctures, hill tops, geographically suggestive landscapes – many have been mythologically enhanced. One or another deity is said to have set up residence or to have performed a certain act in a specific place. Śiva, Viṣṇu, or a goddess are said to have sacralized at least 108 places each throughout India. The subcontinent itself is said to be sacred land centered as it is by Kailaśa, the mountain at the center of the world. A given state can be rendered mythologically sacred as when Tamil Nadu is said to have six *cakras* or sacred places – sacred, that is, to the Tamil's favorite god Murukaṉ. Tamil Nadu, as a whole, is thereby rendered congruent to the body of a yogin and to the cosmos and each holy stead of Murukaṉ becomes a point of access to heaven itself. Geographer S. N. Bhardwaj has noted that there are several levels of pilgrimage in the Indian context ranging from the national to the local.[6] There are the national or even international sites, such as Vārānasī, Tirupati,

Hardiwar, or Rameshwaram because of their geographical and mythological significance nationwide. Pilgrims to these centers are often more affluent or classically oriented than those who attend more local shrines. But there are also regional centers which usually serve pilgrims with distinctive ethnic or regional ties while local centers often celebrate 'folk' deities or sacred figures with strong local attachments. Some pilgrimage centers have roots a couple of millennia old – such as Vārāṇasī, while others are the products of dynastic patronage in the late medieval period – such as Tirupati, the famed pilgrimage site of the Vijayanagara kings. Still others have mushroomed into popularity within the last century, despite claims to antiquity. Such is the case, for example, with Sabaramala, Kerala.

The reasons for going on pilgrimage are manifold: because one has a vow to keep if a certain wish has been granted; to seek improvement in the very mundane aspects of life; to seek grace, immortality, or healing at the hands of the deity; to educate oneself or one's family as to the story of the particular deity of the place; and many others. Serious religious activity is mixed with recreation and play. It should be worthwhile to look more closely at one or two pilgrimage locales.

Vārāṇasī

Vārāṇasī – or Kāśī or Banāras, as it is also called – is one of the oldest pilgrimage centers in the world. It is a place where Buddhist and Jain sages visited in the sixth century BCE and today it attracts millions of pilgrims in any given year. The sacrality of Vārāṇasī is based on several factors in addition to its historical importance.[7] For one thing, the Ganges river itself is said to be sacred, flowing, as it is believed, from the abode of the gods. But at Banāras the river takes a special turn: it assumes the form of a crescent and flows momentarily from south to north. It is here Śiva is said to have caught the Gaṅga in his hair as it was plunging out of heaven; this is why his iconography often depicts him with a crescent in his hair. Moreover, the ideology of the ***tīrtha*** or crossing place is focused on Vārāṇasī. A *tīrtha* is a place where one can "cross over," where one can experience the expiation of sins. Here, saints and gods are said to have bathed so as to be purified preparatory to attaining enlightenment. There are over 300 propitious places or *tīrthas* in Banāras alone and the riverbanks are jammed with bathers each morning at dawn. Vārāṇasī, further, is a major cult center for Śiva, known here as Viśvanātha (Lord of all Directions). Virtually all visitors to Banāras will visit the temple to Viśvanātha in hopes of attaining *mokṣa* or ultimate liberation. Finally, Vārāṇasī is a place propitious for dying and performing the rituals associated with death. Hospices dot the landscape and funeral pyres can be seen along the river's banks. To die here is to go straight to the land of the ancestors. The orthoprax come to Vārāṇasī to perform *śraddha* or memorial rituals for their deceased ancestors.

Quite apart from the golden temple of Viśvanātha, there are numerous other shrines, for example, to the goddesses Annapurna and Lakṣmi, believed able to bring wealth; to various manifestations of Viṣṇu; and to any number of local folk deities, where priests are non-brahmans. At many of these shrines the local deities are thought able to address specific problems, for example, removing of obstacles (Sankatamochan or Sankata Mai) or warding off evil spirits (Kal-bhaira or Pishamochan). Almost three-quarters of the shrines of Vārāṇasī are of local significance, looked after by local inhabitants; another 5 percent or so of the shrines are maintained by particular ethnic groups – these include, for example, shrines to Amba and Gopal, attractive to Gujāratis, and Visalakṣi, popular with Tamilians.[8] Nonetheless, it is the classicized and pan-Hindu temples (about 6 percent of the total) that attract pilgrims from afar.

Prof. L. P. Vidyarthi and his colleagues studied the makeup of the pilgrim population to Banāras in a recent year. They found that over 50 percent of all pilgrims came with their families (about 39 percent came alone); a third of Vārāṇasī's pilgrims were brahmans and 76 percent held a college or graduate degree (only 6 percent were illiterate); some 30 percent of these traveling pilgrims had come more than six times; about a half of the pilgrims did come from the nearest states – Bihar, Bengal, and Uttar Pradesh. Many would stay in facilities run by those who spoke their own language, or were members of their own sect.[9] While in Vārāṇasī, in addition to visiting the temple to Viśvanātha and bathing in the Gaṅga, pilgrims would perform ***ārati*** (the waving of lamps) and receive *darśan* (vision) of the deities of their choice and perform vows (***vratas***). Some pilgrims will perform the last rites of cremation and memorial (*antyeṣṭi pūjā*).

While pilgrims will go to Vārāṇasī at virtually any time of the year, certain occasions are deemed especially important. These days of national significance include Śivarātri (the night of Śiva), falling on the fourteenth day of the dark fortnight of February to March; this is said to be the day of Śiva's marriage to Pārvatī. Another such occasion is the full moon of Kārtikkai (November to December) when the gods are said to descend to earth. In addition, there will be special days associated with specific deities and local shrines. Ambitious pilgrims will also perform the *pañcakosi parikrāma* – the pilgrimage to the "five halting places." These five centers are said to represent the entire cosmos as they are thought to represent all the major pilgrimage centers of India (e.g., Mathurā, Hardiwar, Kāñcīpuram, etc.). Vaiṣṇavas who make this mini-pilgrimage believe the circumambulation to be in the form of a conch, Viṣṇu's special insignia.

Pa<u>l</u>ani, Tamil Nadu

Yet another pilgrimage center (of the many that could be described) is Paḻani in the state of Tamil Nadu. Now one of the wealthiest temple complexes in the south, Paḻani has been truly popular only in recent times. It is true that Tamil texts dating back to the sixth century refer to a site which this temple claims as its own, and the temple's *tālapurāṇa* (story) claims that medieval kings came to worship here.[10] The site was also associated with medicinal ascetics in the medieval period. Further, certain festivals (for example, the Tai Pūcam in January–February) were known to have been held here in the seventeenth century. But it is only after the building of roads and railroads that the site, tucked into the shadow of the Paḻani Hills, became truly accessible. The favored deity at Paḻani is Murukaṉ, Tamil Nadu's favorite god. He is ensconced atop the local hill in the guise of an ascetic, where he is said to have come when angered by his parents, Śiva and Pārvatī, who had offered a fruit symbolic of their favor to Murukaṉ's elder brother Ganeṣa. It is only after Śiva came and told Murukaṉ that he *was* the fruit (*Paḷam nī*), that is, the true embodiment of his father's authority and attributes, that the young god was assuaged.

Since the 1950s as temple authorities aggressively advertised the virtues of worshiping at Paḻani, pilgrims have poured into the town, specially for four festival months – one each in October–November, January–February, March–April, and May–June. The pilgrims are primarily Tamil; they often walk from their home villages, bearing water for the deity. They are encouraged to participate in various kinds of ritual activities at various subsidiary shrines. They may carry colorful *kāvaṭis* on their shoulders (these are shoulder arches decorated with peacock feathers), and the pilgrims' dance is said to emulate the dance of the peacock, Murukaṉ's mount. At the shrine of Karuppucāmi (the black servant god), pilgrims may enter into trance or watch the non-brahman priest smear the icon with boiling oil ladled from his bare palm. In short, while classical āgamic ritual procedures are conducted in the main temple by brahman priests, various forms of folk worship are encouraged at subsidiary shrines, where non-brahman priests preside. Devotees have their heads shaved and bring gifts representing various economic strata. A poor man may give a live rooster; a millionaire or a corporation donates a silver or gold chariot. Different families and communities take turns sponsoring various ritual events. All the trappings of "modernity" are used by the temple authorities – from web pages to electronically enhanced chanting, even while attempts are made to evoke images of the past, which are thought to legitimate the proceedings. Most of the temple's festivals, however, are not more than a few hundred years old; indeed, many of the activities and amenities are accretions of the twentieth century. The temple complex, as a result, is an amalgam of classical and folk, pan-Hindu and regional, relatively ancient and distinctly modern, national and local expressions – all in juxtaposition with one another. Pilgrims express many of their multiple identities at once when they come to Paḻani.

Festivals

Just as there are many types of pilgrimage centers, there are many kinds of festivals that are popular in India today. Each classical temple, for example, generally celebrates a series of *brahmotsavams* or celebrations of the local deity's exploits. Generally, these festivals come to their climax on the day of the month when full moon and lunar constellation (*nakṣatra*) coincide; thus, there may be as many as twelve major festivals in a classical temple, though more commonly there will be anywhere from two to six. The festival calendar in such temples or pilgrimage centers will generally follow the career of the presiding deity – his or her "birth," marriage, conquests, etc. – in a manner that is juxtaposed into the seasonal calendar. Many temple festivals, for example, fall between the winter and summer solstices – in the "light" half of the year and occur during the waxing half of a lunar cycle.

Festival activity, even of the classical kind, often combines ritual sequences with forms of entertainment and play. Crowds mill in bazaars and attend puppet shows, lectures, or concerts sponsored by the temple authorities. Yet, for most who attend there is a serious purpose – to celebrate the exploits of a deity and internalize his or her power, to fulfill vows and bring offerings that express gratitude for favors granted and ask the deity's blessing for a variety of needs.

In addition to those festivals that are centered on temple premises, festivals can be celebrated in a home with local displays, home *pūjā* (worship), the visitation of guests, and the exchange of gifts. Moreover, fairs often spill over into the streets of a village or town and are characterized by street entertainment, shopping in open bazaars, and processions. Here again, for illustrative purposes we focus on two distinct festivals.

Makara Vilakku, Sabaramala, Kerala

Around mid-January every year, hundreds of thousands of men, dressed in black shirts and shouting "Ayyappa, Ayyappa" ascend to a small temple in the forests of Kerala.[11] It is the culmination of a festival known as Makara Vilakku. For forty days, groups of men from a variety of cities, especially in South India (but increasingly in the north as well), have been gathering daily under the tutelage of a "guru." They have sworn to refrain from sexual activity and the consumption of meat and alcohol. They wear black shirts and call each other by the name of their deity Ayyappaṉ. They have formed these groups which transcend normal barriers of caste and socio-economic lines. They have become part of this annual event for a variety of reasons. The longing for community attracts some who have lost a sense of belonging to normal kinship systems. Most have heard that the deity is unusually powerful and can correct any of a host of problems. Some find the rigor and adventure of the experience challenging. As with most classical festival events, menstruating women are not permitted to participate, in this case, on the grounds that the "deity is a bachelor" and might be distracted. At the appropriate time, pilgrims set out for Sabaramala by car or train then walk the last few kilometers. They carry small bifurcated bags bearing their rations as the deity is said to have done in his days as a human. On the climax of the trek, pilgrims stand at one of eighteen steps leading to the temple, the step determined by the number of times one has made the pilgrimage. That night, as all pilgrims watch, the sky is lighted mysteriously as if to indicate the deity's pleasure with those who have undergone this discipline.

While a century or two ago, a handful of tribal people and others made their way to this remote shrine, by the mid-1950s increasing numbers of Keralites, Tamilians, and others made their way to Sabaramala. Plays and poems had been written extolling the powers of the god. The deity's devotees spread the word that Ayyappaṉ transcended caste and social boundaries – that in this pilgrimage genuine community could be experienced and virtually any problem resolved. The light that flooded the skies (though artificially created by the resident *tantris* or priests) symbolized the start of the light half of the year and the beginning of new possibilities. Those who have made the trip believe it to have been one of the most compelling experiences of their lives and want to return. Shrines to Ayyappaṉ have subsequently spread especially throughout South India and overseas where Keralites have gone.

Bonalu, Hyderabad, Andhra Pradesh

A very different phenomenon is the festival known in Andhra Pradesh as Bonalu (literally, "feeding [of the goddess"). Occurring in the months of June–July, the festival honors goddesses of neighborhoods and families and invokes their power for the days and months ahead.[12] The roots of the festival lie in rural settings where goddesses are represented by trees or rocks smeared with red and yellow (vermilion and turmeric) stripes. The goddesses were protectors of a village or portion of land and were believed able to ward off diseases and other evils. Accordingly, the goddesses were offered sacrificed goats and rice boiled and processed in clay pots. When in 1869 a pestilence of the plague infected the Hyderabad area, the feeding of goddesses took on greater import.

As village people trickled into the city, they brought their local goddesses with them – Ellamma, Maiasamma, Peddamma, and others. They were established at small shrines near a tree or a smeared stone. Come June or July, at the first new moon after the summer solstice, the goddesses would be fed at each local shrine; women carried on their heads pots of rice smeared with vermilion and turmeric, and topped with a small fire (these are known as "gathams") and bring their gifts to the shrine of the goddess. Often the goddess is thought to reside in the gatham itself. Accompanying the goddess will be men smeared in ash and carrying whips, calling themselves Pōtharāju, attendant, brother (and by some mythical accounts, husband) of the goddess. At the shrines where the folk goddess still presides goats are slaughtered and consumed in family picnics. Often women carrying the pots will go into a trance and are believed to become possessed by the goddess. At times a transvestite is employed by a particular family to represent the goddess and tell fortunes, once "possessed."

In time some goddess shrines have become "classicized." Goat sacrifices are replaced by the cutting of pumpkins or other vegetarian fare. She is given the name of the "high goddess" Kālī or an entirely new name. This occurs as former villagers become more affluent in the city or rub shoulders with more affluent neighbors, and they seek to upgrade their shrines and even install a brahman priest.

Figure 8 Bonalu Festival, Hyderabad, Andhra Pradesh: roadside shrine to "folk" goddess Maiasamma. Photograph by Rob F. Phillips.

Figure 9 Bonalu Festival, Hyderabad, Andhra Pradesh: worshipers bearing gifts (gatham) for the goddess atop Golkonda Hill. Photograph by Rob F. Phillips.

Bonalu is like a garland of individual celebrations continuing over the space of several weeks. Families and neighborhoods come to be linked together in the festival. Non-Telugu speakers, villagers, and tribal peoples may be integrated into the city through their participation in the festival, even while they maintain their specific 'identities' through their worship of a particular goddess and maintenance of a particular shrine. The goddess is invoked, not so much any longer to assure good crops or a successful monsoon, so much as to assure prosperity in the time of any adversity and to provide a sense of safety in the face of external threat.

At another level the festival has also been used by such agencies as the Ārya Samāj to attempt to homogenize the practice of Hinduism and to integrate "folk" and tribal people into the Hindu fold. In fact, processions of Bonalu have been used as rituals of confrontation as, in the mid-1980s, paraders made their way through Muslim neighborhoods, thereby instigating resentment, even skirmishes. The festival has now become, along with Ganeṣa Chāthurthi, one of the most popular festivals of Hyderabad; planning committees have come to work with participants at specific shrines to co-ordinate the whole enterprise and provide a semblance of structure. Yet spontaneity persists as individuals and families participate and interpret their experience in their own terms.

Festivals in other religious communities

Muslims, Christians, Jains, and other religious communities similarly participate in festival life across the subcontinent. Muslims, for their part, observe at least two feast days (*'īd*). One, known as *'īd al fitr,* is the feast that ends the fasting month of Ramaḍān. During Ramaḍān Muslims observe the fast (*ṣaum*) and abstinence (*imsak*) from dawn to dusk each day. When the new month begins, families gather, sometimes in larger community settings, to celebrate in the sharing of foods that represent their cultural and ethnic heritage.

The other feast, *'īd al aḍḥā,* is the feast of sacrifice. This occurs on the tenth day of the month of pilgrimage or *ḥajj*: after the event known as ***jamrat*** (stoning of pillars) that occurs in the pilgrimage, pilgrims, and many Muslims in solidarity with them, commemorate Ibrahim's act of sacrificing a ram rather than his son Ishmael. On this occasion, an unblemished sheep or goat is sacrificed *ḥalāl* (with its face toward the *Ka'ba* and with the incantation "in the name of Allāh"). This becomes an opportunity to remember the goodness and mercy of Allāh and human dominion over animals. The flesh of the sacrificed animal is distributed to the poor as well as to friends.

In addition, Muḥarram is observed by Shīites who mourn the assassination of Husain, son of 'Ali. On this occasion, in some parts of Bombay, young men can be seen slashing themselves with knives as if to re-enact the tragedy Muḥarram commemorates. Various other feast days will be observed, especially by Shīites: these include the birthday of Muḥammad and of other saints or *pīrs.* Some Muslims will cluster at the tombs (*dargah*) of such saints and make pilgrimages to shrines deemed sacred. In many rural settings, especially, there will be the celebration (***'urs***) of a saint's birth, in which both Muslims and Hindus will participate. Occasionally, Hindus and Muslims will share a common pilgrimage center inasmuch as a Muslim saint is associated with that spot. Such is the case with Sabaramala, Kerala, where a shrine to Vavar, said to be a Muslim "friend" of Ayyappaṉ, is honored. In recent years, however, militants of both camps have contested these shared spaces.

The festivals of Christians, especially of Catholics, have sometimes taken on the accretions of the Indian landscape. The days devoted to commemorating the lives of saints, for example, are often marked by the procession of palanquins bearing the icons of the honored saints. Further, some Christian shrines have become enormously popular for pilgrims of all communities. This is specially so, for example, with the shrine of Lady Vēḷaṅkaṇṇi, the Virgin who is enshrined along the seashore of Tamil Nadu. Thousands of pilgrims, Christian or Hindu, pour into the small pilgrimage town on September 9 to seek healing or other favors at the shrine. For ten days prior to the ninth, starting with a flag raising, various rituals and novenas are performed in honor of the Virgin who was believed to have appeared at this spot.

Within Jainism, laypersons of all the sects will participate in certain annual holy days. These include a commemoration of the "first" giving of alms to a mendicant (one named Ṛṣabha) in the month of May–June. This celebration honors the special relationship that exists between laity and the ascetic order. Also commonly observed are the anniversaries of Mahāvīra's birth (April–May) and death (October–November). Yet the single most massive celebration for Jains is the ***mastābhiṣekam*** (head anointing) offered every twelve years at the gigantic image of Bāhabuli in Karnataka. Bāhabuli is considered an exemplary figure – one who renounced power and possessions to attain instant liberation (***kevalajñāna***). For several weeks during this celebration the fifty-seven-foot image of Bāhabuli is offered various libations from above, from water to sandalwood paste.[13]

The shrine or temple as the focus of religious expression

Millions of shrines of great diversity dot the Indian landscape. Many of these are very simply marked – a sacred tree, a snake hill, a smeared stone, a picture of a favored deity. A worshiper may stop at such a place, circumambulate, prostrate, or in other ways do obeisance to the sacred presence. If the shrine is that of a goddess, the worshiper, usually a woman, may shower vermilion or turmeric over the sacred object and themselves. In many cases such shrines will have a local non-brahman priest, male or female, usually representing the particular family or community for whom the shrine is important. On special occasions, at such non-brahmanized shrines, a goat or chicken may be sacrificed and family picnics are enjoyed.

For a variety of reasons, some of these "folk" shrines become classicized. Some of the patrons of a particular shrine may become more affluent; other neighboring groups may begin to use the shrine and increase its income; there may be an impetus to "brahmanize" the shrine for purposes of demonstrating increased status; other groups may even co-opt the shrine and use it for their own purposes. Classicization of such shrines usually entails hiring a brahman priest to do at least some rituals that are more nearly "āgamic" and constructing a brick or stone shed over the shrine. An icon may be installed in a manner that reflects classical style. The name of the deity may even be changed to reflect how he or she is integrated into the mainstream Hindu pantheon. Occasionally such shrines are upgraded without benefit of brahman input inasmuch as the community wants to retain complete autonomy over the shrines.

A fully classical temple is rich with symbolism and ritual life. The inner sanctum (*garbhagṛha* – literally, "womb house") is below the central tower of

Figure 10 "Folk" religion is classicized: a shrine to goddess Mutalayamma, near Hyderabad, Andhra Pradesh. To the left: old stone icon. Center: new more classical icon with Śiva's trident. To the right: artist's depiction of the "great" goddess, Durgā. Photograph by Rob F. Phillips.

Figure 11 "Folk" religion is classicized: artist upgrades a shrine to the goddess Renuka near Hyderabad, AP, by linking her to Kālī as well as folk hero Potturāja. Photograph by Rob F. Phillips.

the temple. The tower is known as a *vimāṉa* in the south or *śikhara* in the north. The tower represents Mt. Meru, the center of the universe; the *hiraṇyagarbha* (golden reed) from which the universe is said to have arisen; and a human torso. The inner sanctum is the womb in which the icon of the deity is implanted like an embryo. Inasmuch as temple-based worship and iconography were stimulated during the era of kingship, the representation of the deity is treated like a king. It is believed the essence of the cosmos (*brahman*) permeates the entire cosmos and can become manifest at any point in the created order, and, once the rituals of enlivening the icon (***prāṇapratiṣṭhā***) are done, it is believed the icon is an authentic embodiment of the divine. Temple priests thus become servants of the god-sovereign, awakening him or her in the morning and putting him or her to rest at night. In theory, there are twelve sacred hours during the day appropriate for ritual, each congruent to a commensurate period of the solar year. Most of the ritual occurs before dawn, between dawn and noon, and after dusk. There are certain basic rituals, which will be done in most classical temples – these include the ritual libations (*abhiṣeka*) when the deity is bathed and libated with various offerings such as milk, curds, sandalwood paste, fruits, and honey. This ritual is generally done at least once a week, but during festivals or in large temples as often as once a day. The libation is followed by the dressing and adorning of the deity (*vastra*) when clothing and jewelry, once donned, represent the deity's readiness to "hold court." At this stage worshipers may watch the showing of lights in honor of the deity (*ārati*), experience viewing (*darśan*) of the deity, and receive foodstuffs, which have been offered to and blessed by the deity (*prasāda*). Some devotees may patronize the recitation of 108 or 1,008 names of the deity and thereby invoke the deity's blessings. Some devotees, especially couples, will ask that the deity be ritually married to the consort(s) as if to enhance their own marriage.

Worshipers will most commonly visit such temples with their families or friends and/or stop in briefly for *darśan* before going to work or after working hours. Seldom is such worship congregational, though devotees may gather in the sanctuary to sing devotional songs (*bhajaṉs*) and share a sense of community.

It is quite possible to be "religious" in the Hindu world without visiting a temple at all. It is not uncommon for families to have *pūjā* (worship) rooms in their homes. These are rooms set aside to display the icons representing the family's favored deities. In the houses of the affluent, these rooms can be very elaborate indeed. More commonly, the *pūjā* room is a modest space set aside for family worship. Usually the eldest woman resident in the house will maintain the room and conduct the *pūjā*. In many families this will occur early in the morning after bathing and before the other chores of the day have started.

Ritual in other religious communities

Some Jains, especially the Murti Pujak Jains (of the Śvetāmbara sect), have an active ritual life not unlike that of their Hindu counterparts. Whether in *pūjā* rooms at home, or in the often elaborate temples to which lay Jains contribute generously, any number of symbolic representatives can be found – icons of *tīrthaṇkaras*, representatives of living saints as well as of certain Hindu deities. Lay Jains will perform *pūjā* at any or all of the representations. *Pūjā* will usually start with libations of water, milk, and/or other substances; the icons may be dabbed with sandalwood paste and offered flowers. Prayers will be recited. Offerings, for example, of rice, fruit, or coins may be placed before the icon. *Ārati* (the waving of an oil lamp before the icon) will occur; the ritual usually concludes with a period of prayer and meditation.

The performance of *pūjās* in Jainism differs from that in Hinduism in several respects. The Jain worshiper does not expect the worshiped figures to help her – each Jain is obliged to work out her own liberation and think of the object of her devotion as a means of meditation, representative of a state of being worthy to be emulated. Further, each Jain layperson will perform the *pūjā* on his/her own at one's own speed and depend on temple "servants" (known as ***pūjāris***) merely for support or instruction, whereas, in Hindu worship, the *pūjāri* (priest) performs the rituals on behalf of the devotee who often expects the deity to respond to his requests.[14]

Devout Muslims also maintain an active ritual life. The high point of the week is Friday noon, when the faithful gather at a mosque for midday prayers. Prayers (***namāz***) will also be led by the elder at the local mosque five times a day as prescribed by the Qu'rān. Women are not permitted into many mosques, but many engage in the *namāz* at home, often together with neighboring women. Unlike the Hindu temple, the mosque is barren of any representations of Allāh, though quotations from the Qu'rān are often inscribed on the inner and outer walls. The mosque is generally oriented in such a way that prayers can be done facing Mecca, the birthplace of Islam and the seat of the sacred *Ka'ba* stone.

Thus far we have noted a number of ways by which people express their religious orientations through ritual and performance. Ritual does many things at once. With their bodies and through their senses, people act out in ritual something of who they understand themselves to be. Sometimes the ritual is orthoprax, attempting to reconstruct a sense of rootedness and antiquity. Sometimes the ritual is a hybridization – mingling of folk and classical and of various regional and family "traditions." Ritual selectively reappropriates and re-presents perceptions of the past even as it embodies elements of the present. Local spaces and shrines may be linked to pan-Hindu or classical ones. Festivals and pilgrimages often have a way of bringing together a diverse assortment of people, sometimes acting out distinct social identities, sometimes transcending them. Attempts to homogenize rituals within both Hinduism and Islam suggest how certain agencies such as the Ārya Samāj want to "purify" practice so that it will conform to perceptions of a pristine past. Such groups seek to free the rituals of "folk" accretions and even want to use certain rituals such as processions as forms of confrontation with "outsiders." Many of the conflicting dynamics of religion in contemporary India, in short, are expressed in its ritual life: selective appropriation from a perceived past, classicalization, and brahmanization; hybridizations and homogenizations; conciliations and confrontations between diverse groups. This performative landscape serves as a kaleidoscope of the nature of religion in the world today.

Religious innovation, hybridization, and reinterpretation

Religion continues to change in the Indian setting even as it reinterprets past expressions. People who were once disenfranchised have increasingly become part of the political, cultural, and religious mix and bring their orientations to the practice of religion. People of differing linguistic and religious background interact in cities and the result is sometimes an eclectic form of religion. Temples, for example, and their iconography embody the reciprocities of changing (and often upwardly mobile) neighborhoods. The "past" is selectively appropriated, not least of all those forms of brahmanic religion once inaccessible to the lower echelons of society.

These currents are expressed in a variety of ways. There is the quest for gurus and swamis who are thought to be worthy of emulation. There is the resurgence of old deities, the emergence of relatively new ones, even the hybridization of the attributes of deities and their cultic life. There is the emergence of "new" religio-intellectual movements forged of syncretisms and the restatement of neo-Hindu ideas. Disenchantment with the "establishment" has also led to conversions to new forms of Hinduism or Buddhism and to various sects of Islam or Christianity. Not least of all, there is the use of religion for political ends and the concomitant attempt to construct governmental polities that support one's religious ideology often at the expense of others. To some of these developments we now turn.

The changing faces of deities

Hindu deities have always been rich symbolic expressions, reflecting many aspects of the human condition. As we have noted in earlier chapters, the imaging of deities often reflects their cultural history – hunting gods reflecting hunting motifs, etc. It is not surprising, then, in the dynamic cultural interactions of India today, deities are perceived in varying terms. The intermingling of ethnic groups from various parts of India in a single city; the work of popular artists who paint pictures of deities in ways that combine features from several sources; the classicizing of folk deities – all these factors have led to deities becoming more eclectic and even to the emergence of "new" deities who combine features of old deities. Here again a few illustrations of this process will suffice from the world of goddesses.

The favored deity of orthodox Tamil *smārta* brahmins living in Mumbai is a goddess named Rājārājeśwarī (literally, "the sovereign of sovereigns"). This is a deity/name suggested to the group by a swami visiting from Madras. The goddess has roots in Tamil country – for example, as Śiva's consort in the Cōḻa court – yet she is considered "new" enough to be ascribed all the attributes of all previous goddesses. Hence, on the one hand, she is said to have been the favored deity of the famed philosopher Śaṅkara, and the one to whom ancient mantras were addressed; yet, at the same time, her very newness is indication that she is the epitome of goddesses. All *śakti* (power) is vested in her. To enthrone her within oneself is to internalize the supreme power of the universe.[15]

Quite a different story is associated with Śrī Jagadamba (Goddess of the universe), the name given to the goddess of a shrine at Golkonda Hill outside Hyderabad. She was once known as Ellamma, the goddess of the Madigas, or shepherds, a "scheduled caste" also known as "dalits" (literally, the "broken ones") historically outside the pale of Hindu society. Ellamma's story, however, suggests how the shepherds perceive her true nature and their own: once Ellamma was the primary goddess of the universe. Desiring a sexual companion, she created first Brahmā, then Viṣṇu, both of whom refused to have sex with their own mother. For this they were punished. Ellamma then created Śiva who agreed to comply with her request. But Śiva tricked Ellamma, saying she should give him her third eye, her trident, and other paraphernalia. Now empowered, Śiva reduced Ellamma to a weakened role. She wandered about for some time, found work within a duplicitous king's palace only to lose favor and escape. She hid amongst the buckets of pelt on which the Madigas were working. The Madigas "adopted" her and she has protected them to this day.[16]

Now the Ellamma shrine on Golkonda Hill has been taken over by an inter-caste committee representing various constituencies in the Golkonda area, which has sought to "upgrade" the shrine. While the priest of the shepherds continues to function at the shrine, a brahman priest has been installed. Rituals performed at the shrine are more nearly "āgamic" – goat sacrifices must be performed elsewhere on the hill; not least of all the goddess has been given the name Śrī Jagadamba. Those Madigas who support such a change would claim that, if now the goddess has been elevated to a more "noble" state, it is only her just due, as from the beginning she was the supreme being!

The social elevation of other communities has been reflected in the way by which their goddesses have been linked to brahmanical mythology. Such goddesses as Māriammaṉ, Renuka, and Peddamma, for example, share variations of a common myth. Māriammaṉ and Peddamma have very recently been the deities of "folk," agrarian communities, while Renuka has been classicized for a much longer period. Their shared myth may be summarized as follows: once the goddess was a very chaste woman married to a sage. Everyday her chastity permitted her to bring water home on the top of her head (by some accounts, without benefit of a pot!). One day, when bringing water home she was momentarily diverted by a heavenly male figure and the water splashed all over her and she arrived late. When her husband saw what had happened, he was furious and ordered his sons to slay their mother. Only one of them, Parāśurāma, the cosmic "hatchet man," was willing to do the job, beheading his mother and her laundry maid with one stroke. The father was so pleased at the completion of the job, he offered Parāśurāma a favor. The latter asked that his mother be restored to life; the boon was granted. In his haste, Parāśurāma switched heads in restoring life – one was the head of a brahman woman, the other the head of the low-caste cleaning woman.[17] In restoring life, the distinctions between caste were collapsed. The one had become brahman, the other retained a brahmanic body. These goddesses are often depicted in portraits at their shrine only by a head. Increasingly, their shrines (especially in the case of Renuka and Māriammaṉ) have brahman priests as the goddess of the "folk" has become "classicized." This newly brahmanized goddess is also linked at times to the tantric goddess Chinnamasta, who is known to sever her own head in order to nourish her attendants.

Conversions of another kind

On June 30, 2001, *The Hindu*, a prominent Indian newspaper, reported that some 1,000 people from some 225 low-caste families living in villages near Coimbatore, Tamil Nadu, had "embraced" Christianity. The people alleged, through their spokesperson, that they had not been allowed to worship in a particular temple, and, in fact, had been "humiliated" at a festival event on June 6 of that year. Despite several attempts to present their grievance to authorities, they claimed such authorities did not respond. Hence, their "mass" conversion to Christianity.[18]

While this incident is increasingly uncommon there have been cases of people, especially from the lower echelons of society, converting to minority religions in quest of greater economic, social, and, at times, religious satisfaction. From the Paravars along the Kerala coast who were baptized by Francis Xavier in the sixteenth century to such tribals as the Nagas and Mizos of the Northeastern Himalayan foothills, who became Baptists and Presbyterians in the twentieth century, disenfranchised groups have turned to Christianity, Islam, or Buddhism when given the opportunity. In parts of Tamil Nadu, and Andhra Pradesh, in particular, groups have come forward as family or caste units in particular villages to espouse an alternative religion. This was the case in Meenakshipuram, Tamil Nadu in the 1980s when a significant portion of outcaste persons "became" Muslim in quest of greater dignity. This was the case in the late 1800s when a number of *shānāṇs* (toddy tappers) in Tirunelveli District, Tamil Nadu, unable to get into temples of caste groups above them, converted to Christianity. These *shānāṇs* assumed the caste name *nāṭars* (lord of the land); their women insisted on wearing blouses to cover their breasts (prior to that time, many low-caste women were obliged to remain unclothed above the waist). The Christian converts changed the name of their towns to Nazareth and Bethlehem, *et al.*[19]

Perhaps the single most dramatic act of conversion is that which occurred in Maharashtra subsequent to 1956. The Mahars, constituting nearly 10 percent of the population of Maharashtra, had been suffering the fate of most "untouchables" or dalits: they were unable to use public wells in their own villages or let their shadow fall on caste persons. One of their number, B. R. Ambedkar (1891–1956), had suffered similar indignities as a youth. But he went on to receive a doctorate and law degree and helped to write the Indian constitution. He also fought for the rights of his fellow Mahars even clashing with Mahatma Gandhi, as to whether to make the rights of untouchables a central aspect of the freedom campaign. For much of his adult life, Ambedkar had been studying Buddhism and eventually came to believe that in Buddhism there was a sense of the equality of all persons, a spirit of compassion, and an opportunity for all persons to fulfill their own possibilities. Accordingly, in 1956, a few months before his death, he renounced Hinduism and adopted Buddhism (as he reinterpreted the Buddhist *dhamma*) as his religion.[20] Many of his fellow Mahars and other dalits joined him, and until today Buddhism (or neo-Buddhism, as it is sometimes called) is the fastest growing religion in Maharashtra. In Mumbai, the third most popular religious community now (after Hindus and Muslims) is the Buddhists, occupying the place held by Roman Catholics prior to the 1980 census.

Some "conversions" have been less dramatic. There are Muslims, for example, who, after working in the Persian Gulf for a few years where they witnessed a more puritan form of Islam, especially in Saudi Arabia, return to India seeking to purge Islamic practice of "non-Islamic" accretions. Other Muslims may join sectarian Islamic movements that are perceived to be more "global" or more "pristine." Hindus may become followers of certain gurus or sectarian movements that offer specific interpretations of the Hindu way. These include followers of such "god-men" as Satya Sai Baba or such movements as the Brahmākumarīs. Other movements attracting a sizable following, especially of upper-class Hindus, are the Ārya Samāj or the Rashtriya Swayamsevak Sangh; these latter movements are especially committed to making India a polity in which core Hindu values will dominate. We turn to the story of some of these movements.

Gurus and their movements

A practice that goes back at least to the days of the *Upaniṣads* is that of seekers associating themselves with particular teachers or gurus. It is a practice one finds in contemporary India as well as in the Indian diaspora. As people seek to rediscover the essence of their faith, and, in the process, their own identities, they attach themselves to the exponent of a particular school of thought or practice, whether from a distance through the guru's books, or in ashrams or *maṭhas* to meditate in the presence of the teacher. Such teachers are selected for any number of reasons: a friend recommends someone with whom he or she has been in contact; one is impressed, by word of mouth, with a guru's style or "miracles"; the guru speaks one's own vernacular; or, if one is an Anglicized urbanite, one may be impressed by the guru who is also Anglicized and a globe-trotter. So, if one is a Tamil *smārta* brahman, for example, living in Mumbai, away from one's home, one may look to the Śaṅkarācāryā (the exponent of Śaṅkara's Vedānta) for guidance – usually the Śaṅkarācāryā of Kāñcīpuram if one is from eastern Tamil Nadu and the Śaṅkarācāryā of Sringeri, if one is from the southwest. "Gurus" are abundant in the Indian landscape; there is little quality control save as devotees become impressed with the charisma or "wisdom" of the teacher. At times each guru starts movements distinctive to his or her own particular perceptions of the "truth."

The Brahmākumarīs

Take, for example, the Brahmākumarī movement. While the Brahmākumarīs (Daughters of Brahmā) are not a numerically large group by Indian standards (perhaps 100,000 devoted members over all), it illustrates one of the ways in which the Hindu tradition is reinterpreted in the modern period.[21] It was founded by a Sindhī businessman, **Dada Lekhraj**, who died in 1969. It was founded, in part, from a sense of disenchantment with the world that Sindhīs were experiencing in middle-class households. Sindhī businessmen were away from home for extended periods while the women were expected to engage in traditional wifely duties back home. This sense of disaffection with the world was exacerbated with the dispersal of Hindu Sindhīs during the partition at the time of independence. In any case, Lekhraj was given to visions by means of which he reconfigured Hindu notions about the nature of history and of the self. Succinctly put, the world would come to an end soon and people should prepare for it by purifying themselves accordingly. While its official headquarters are in Mt. Abu in Rajasthan, the movement, nonetheless, has some 800 local centers especially in such northern cities as New Delhi, and, increasingly, overseas. The Brahmākumarīs encourage the practice of yoga, vegetarianism, abstinence from tobacco and alcohol, and, most controversially, of celibacy. The group proselytizes vigorously, especially through exhibits, advertisements, and lectures.

Based on Lekhraj's visions and teachings, the Brahmākumarīs believe the real self to be the immaterial self or *ātman* within one. The self's true home is *paramātman* (the supreme Self), in which Śiva or Shiv Baba presides at the top of the universe. The self's intention is to eschew material attachments and become one with its true nature at the end of history. History, for the Brahmākumarīs, is an accelerated form of the Hindu *yuga* system; rather than being comprised of ageless cycles of time, however, history is a matter of four finite cycles becoming increasingly degenerate. We live near the end of the final cycle, the ***kaliyuga***, where torpor and ignorance (*tamagun*) prevail. This age will come to an end very soon, but, thanks to the grace of Shiv Baba, through Dada Lekhraj, people can learn how to make the transition into the world to come.

To prepare for the new world, as in traditional Indian concerns for cosmology, one must understand the nature of the universe as perceived in the Brahmākumarī system. Not only must one *know* the truth, however, one must *perform* it. Lifestyle should be completely transformed, often requiring living in the established centers: eating proper food, keeping company with the faithful, practicing *rāja yoga* (as reinterpreted by the group), and practicing celibacy are among the requisites of preparation. The practice of celibacy alone can be considered controversial, especially for women, who were traditionally considered auspicious insofar as they gave birth to sons. Nonetheless, not only do widows, widowers, and couples whose children have grown join the group; the core of the movement and, especially of its local centers, are women (known as sisters) who propagate the faith and serve the needs of seekers.

While many of these ideas are clearly derived from classical Indian speculations (the importance of cosmology, the need for proper practice, etc.), the nuances given by the group are often seen as controversial, especially the emphasis on millenarianism and the notion that women should be celibate. Yet even these notions have resonances of earlier images: an end of history was intimated in the mythology of Kalkī, the incarnation of Viṣṇu who would come to rescue the world in the end; and female celibacy was countenanced by those women who turned to the monastic life in the early days of Buddhism and in the experience of those medieval poetesses – devotees who sought only to live in the presence of their Lord. Be that as it may, the Brahmākumarīs are highly disciplined and their impact on the Indian landscape exceeds their numbers, especially in the cities of North India.

The Satya Sai Baba movement

Yet another movement that has gained great popularity in India's current milieu is that of **Satya Sai Baba**. While he has his detractors who speak of him as a charlatan and an exponent of "easy" religion, not a few middle- and upper-class urbanites, many of whom have lost touch or confidence in more "traditional" forms of religion, find him to be a charismatic and attractive figure. "Satya Sai Baba" was born in 1926 in a village now in Andhra Pradesh.[22] His boyhood is said to have been filled with a variety of miraculous occurrences, including a "disclosure" at the age of thirteen when he declared himself to be an incarnation of **Sai Baba**, the Muslim-Hindu guru who died in 1918. In a later "revelation" (in 1963) he declared himself to be the embodiment of Śiva and Śakti (literally the divine totality), in the flesh. In the meanwhile, he had begun to attract considerable attention through his "miracles," his travels throughout the south, and the establishment of his ashram in Puttaparthi, the village of his birth. He predicted he would live until the age of ninety-six and that the latter half of his life would be devoted to teaching, the performing of miracles, and, eventually, offering intensive teachings to selected groups.

Even though he is thought to be the incarnation of all the deities and is called Bhagavan ("God") by his devotees, Satya Sai Baba is especially associated with Śiva and is depicted most commonly in the company of Śiva's *liṅga* (an aniconic representation). In addition, he is most noted to his followers for his ability to make sacred ash (*vibhuti*, commonly used in Śaiva worship) appear at will and in massive amounts.

The movement which Satya Sai Baba has established has mushroomed into a major pan-Indian phenomenon. Its funds are kept in a trust fund. The Central Shri Satya Sai Trust supports ashrams, engages in philanthropic activities, publishes a magazine, and endows at least four colleges.

The demands on devotees are considerably less rigorous than for such a movement as the Brahmākumarīs. These activities range from moderate vegetarianism to daily meditation and participation in social activities and devotional singing. Clearly the center of the movement is Satya Sai Baba himself – he is the object of worship and the *raison d'etre* of the movement. Worship of Satya Sai Baba, in other words, is primarily a form of pietism – of *bhakti* – whereby, it is thought, one is directing one's thanksgiving and one's personal requests to God himself. It is clear that many of these *bhaktas*, sometimes referred to as "urban alienates," are economically well-placed. Though many have never seen Satya Sai Baba in person, they have come to believe in his persona, and in his claims for himself and even attest to miracles wrought in their own lives. No profound theological claims need be affirmed; no rigorous discipline needed. One need only worship at the "altar." Little wonder millions find this attractive, while others dismiss it as "pop religion."

The resurgent right

Among the movements that mark the contemporary landscape of India are those which represent the Hindu right wing; at least six such movements should be mentioned. The oldest is the Ārya Samāj, founded by **Dayananda Saraswati** in 1875. From its founding its intention has been to return Hinduism to its "Vedic" roots (as these "Vedic" roots were interpreted by Dayananda). It has sought to homogenize Hindu practice, rid it of its "folk" elements, including the elimination of the slaughter of animals and other "non-Vedic" practices. It espoused the doctrine of *sanātana dharma*, the "eternal truth," that was thought to characterize the Hindu experience.[23] By the 1890s it was also involved in political agitation which was implicitly or explicitly directed against Muslims: there was the Cow Protection Movement of 1893; the crusade, started in 1895, to reconvert those believed to have been forcibly converted to Islam or Christianity; protests launched in 1907 against the perceived pro-Muslim bias of British authorities; and others.[24] Today the presence of the Ārya Samāj continues on many fronts; one illustration is the attempt to change the character of the Bonalu festival, mentioned earlier, so that animals are no longer sacrificed, in favor of vegetarian rituals. That is, the movement is involved in trying to include the previously disenfranchised subaltern groups within mainstream Hinduism and standardize Hindu practice by all groups.

The Rashtriya Swayamsevak Sangh (RSS) was founded in September 1925 by a Maharashtrian brahman and physician named **Hegewar** (1889–1940).[25] It was launched at a time when Hindu–Muslim skirmishes were breaking out all over India during the Dasara festival in October to November, which celebrates Rāma's victory over Rāvaṇa. Indeed, the corps' favored deity is Rāma, who is particularly popular amongst Hindī-speakers especially since the time of the Hindī *bhakta*, Tulsīdās (1532–1623), and in Maharashtra where Rāma became a sacred symbol of Marāthī autonomy since the time of Śivājī and Rāmdās. The RSS is comprised of a cadre of dedicated "missionaries" ("pracharahs"), many of them celibate males. Many of them were trained as young men in the political and martial arts in gymnasia. In addition to Rāma, most are dedicated to Hanuman, the monkey general of Rāma's army, known in Maharashtra as Maruti. The movement is committed to fostering a national consciousness and cohesion amongst Hindus and working toward making India a Hindu polity rather than a "secular" country. RSS "sevaks" (volunteers) have been active in trying to construct Hindu temples on the sites where mosques have stood and were largely responsible for the destruction of the famed Babri Mosque in Ayodhyā in 1992. At the time of the Ayodhyā incident the RSS included some 35,000 local units and about 2.5 million active members.[26]

The Jan Sangh was founded as the political arm of the RSS in 1951 with the assistance of the politically conservative **B. Modhak** (born 1920).[27] The Jan Sangh has led demonstrations to Hinduize the Indian government. For example, it was active in leading a demonstration march in 1967 seeking a national law banning the slaughter of cows and has worked with other groups subsequently to implement the vision of "Hindutva" – a nation representing Hindu values.

The Vishwa Hindu Pariṣad (VHP – Hindu World Federation) was founded in 1969 and is specially active amongst overseas Indians. The VHP believes Sanskrit to be the oldest of languages and *sanātana dharma* the oldest of humankind's religions. Many of its members believe Sanskrit should be compulsory in all India's schools; and that the slaughter of cows should be forbidden by law. They assume all mosques and churches were originally Hindu shrines and should be restored to their "original" state. It is similarly assumed that Jains, Buddhists, and Sikhs are really Hindus (despite the insistence of these communities to the contrary).[28]

The Shiv Sena was spawned in Maharashtra as a movement to advance Marāthī interests over those of other ethnic groups. It was named after Śivājī, the presumed Marāthī hero and founder of the Marāthā empire. The Shiv Sena early in the twentieth century was resisting migrations into Mumbai of ethnic groups from the south who were presumably taking jobs away from the locals. Under the leadership of **Bal Thackeray**, a former journalist, the Shiv Sena became an increasingly militant movement often baiting Muslims and other minorities and seeking to bring about a more nearly homogeneous Marāthī–Hindu culture. The group has been known to threaten non-Hindu shopkeepers and instigate riots in various parts of Mumbai.

Many of these groups support the Bharata Janata Party (BJP – the party for the victory of India), which was founded in 1980 as a successor to the Jan Sangh, as the Hindu alternative to an increasingly ineffective Congress Party, and as a way of installing Hindu values on the national government. Hindu–Muslim tension had been exacerbated in the 1980s by several factors: the conversion of low and outcasted people to Islam in the village of Meenakshipuram, Tamil Nadu, in the early 1980s; response to the strident reaction of Muslims to the killing by tribals of over 1,000 Muslim migrants from Bangladesh into Assam; and the ruling of the Supreme Court in a case known as the Shah Bano case. Simply put, in this case a Muslim woman sought redress from a divorce ruling favoring her husband. The court's decision was perceived by some Muslims as a threat of "secular" law to the Islamic *Sharī'a* and conversely, because the Congress Party sought to pass a law permitting Muslims to abide by the *Sharī'a,* the decision was perceived by many Hindus as the Congress Party's politicization of ethnicity, that is, as a favoring of Muslims who were permitted to follow Islamic law, while Hindus were obliged to follow secular law.

Studies indicate that, like most of these right-wing Hindu movements, the BJP's activities are most commonly supported by brahmans, non-brahman upper castes, especially those who are traders and small businessmen, white-collar workers, and those over forty-five years of age – that is, amongst those who seek to retain a certain way of life. Students and laborers are least likely to support the BJP, though there are those upwardly mobile lower-caste men who see in such groups as the RSS a way to improve their circumstances.

These groups combined to engage in a whole range of activities and processions in the 1980s and 1990s. Marches or *yatras* were held in 1983 and after, seeking "national integration." In these processions a political-religious agenda was obvious. Large trucks carried brass vessels filled with Gaṅga water and a picture of "Mother India." Water would be distributed to Hindu temples along the route. By 1984–86 the processions were designed to reclaim certain mosques for Hindu use, especially that at Ayodhyā. The marches asked for sacrifice to liberate the "place of Rāma's birth" (Ayodhyā) and while the response in Ayodhyā itself was modest, a number of Hindus along the way were energized. In 1990 yet another *yatra* was performed, this time launched by the BJP in seeking votes. Hindu symbols were used for political ends: the national journey (to Ayodhyā) was a pilgrimage; the vehicle carrying the leader of the BJP, at the time **Advani**, was the "chariot of Rāma." Indeed, the symbol of the BJP is the lotus revered as a sacred symbol of "new creation" throughout the subcontinent and frequently held iconographically by a goddess. Advani exhorted the faithful to be devoted to Rām and exercise people's power.

While the 1990 procession ended in Advani's arrest by the government of Uttar Pradesh, yet another procession in 1992 led to destruction of the mosque in Ayodhyā. By then the UP government was controlled by the BJP, and the central government by Congress, which thought it had reached a compromise with the pilgrims to permit them to worship at the Ayodhyā site, then move on. However, some zealous "sevaks" (volunteers) climbed the mosque and within the day had demolished it with handheld tools. The event led to a series of riots and reprisals that particularly affected crowded parts of cities like Mumbai.

These movements continue to put pressure on the BJP party to Hinduize the national polity. They seek to homogenize the practice of Hinduism through education and socialization; they try to upgrade and include into the Hindu mainstream dalits and scheduled castes who had for years felt disenfranchised by power brokers. They increasingly have sought to become the voice of the "Hindu establishment" which determines the way festivals should be organized and Hindu dharma should be expressed. And while these organizations receive considerable resistance from academics, dalit power blocs, minority communities, and others, they remain very much a part of the contemporary religious landscape of the subcontinent.

The people of India are living at a particularly crucial juncture of history. In many respects, the subcontinent is a microcosm of the world itself, and, in a real sense, that world looks to India to see whether and how it may be possible for people of great diversity to share the same space. On the one hand, the Indian nation-state has made strides since independence which have been remarkable: discriminations based on caste or religion have been constitutionally outlawed; a democratic and unified nation has been maintained despite its great variety (something Europe has yet to do); the opportunity for education has been provided for all its people; resources for medical care have increased; there has been the creation of a large middle class that cuts often through caste, ethnic, and religious boundaries; one of the world's largest communities of scientists has been created – this is to name but a few of the achievements of the past half century.

Yet "fault lines" persist not so far beneath the surface, which threaten the body politic. Religion has certainly been a part of the rich heritage of India, but religion can also be one of the "fault lines," used as an excuse to legitimate hatred, suspicion, and violence, as it has been in other parts of the world and in India itself. Seldom is religion the sole (or even the main) cause of these eruptions – rather, economic and political marginalizations; the cynical exploitation by politicians of cultural divisions; the fundamental ignorance of members of one community about the history, character, and values of other communities all contribute to the frustrations that sometimes lead to acts of hostility.

Yet, India has had a remarkable history of hosting an enormous spectrum of religious expressions. The present moment has become yet another test of the Indian people's resilience of spirit. As brahman rubs elbow with dalit, and Muslim or Christian with Hindu, and "folk" forms of religion interact with the "classical," this is a good time to evoke the sense of humility implied in the tradition which understands every perception of the truth to be a *darśan* – a viewpoint – each one a strand in the multicolored fabric of humanity's religious life.

Recommended reading

On Contemporary Indian Society

Beteille, A. *Inequality and Social Change.* New Delhi: Oxford University Press, 1972.

Biardeau, M. *Hinduism: The Anthropology of a Civilization.* New Delhi: Oxford University Press, 1989.

Blackburn, S. and Ramanujan, A. K. eds. *Another Harmony: New Essays on the Folklore of India.* New Delhi: Oxford University Press, 1986.

Brass, Paul. *The Politics of India since Independence.* Cambridge: Cambridge University Press, 1990.

Chandra, B. *Essays on Contemporary India.* New Delhi: Haranand Publications, 1993.

Chatterjee, Partha. ed. *Wages of Freedom: Fifty Years of the Indian Nation-State.* New Delhi: Oxford University Press, 1998.

Daniel, E. V. *Fluid Signs: Being a Person the Tamil Way.* Berkeley: University of California Press, 1984.

Das, Veena. *Structure and Cognition: Aspects of Hindu Caste and Ritual.* Second edition. New Delhi: Oxford University Press, 1982.

Das, Veena. *Critical Events: An Anthropological Perspective on Contemporary India.* Oxford: Oxford University Press, 1999.

Dumont, L. *Homo Hierarchus: An Essay on the Caste System.* Tr. M. Sainsbury. Chicago: University of Chicago Press, 1970.

Dumont, L. *Religion, Politics and History in India.* Paris: Mouton, 1970.

Fuller, C. J. *Caste Today.* New Delhi: Oxford University Press, 1998.

Guha, R. ed. Subaltern Studies I. *Writings on South Asian History and Society.* New Delhi: Oxford University Press, 1982.

Gupta, Dipankar. ed. *Social Stratification.* New Delhi: Oxford University Press, 2000.

Hasan, Mushiru. ed. *India's Partition: Process, Strategy, Mobilization.* Oxford and Delhi: Oxford University Press, 1993.

Jaffrelat, Christine J. *The Hindu Nationalist Movement in Indian Politics.* New York: Columbia University Press, 1996.

Menon, Rita and Bhasin, Kamla. *Borders and Boundaries: Women in India's Partition.* New Delhi: Kali for Women, 1998.

Mills, Margaret A., Claus, Peter J., and Diamond, Sarah. eds. *South Asian Folklore: An Encyclopedia.* New York and London: Routledge, 2003.

Nehru, J. *The Discovery of India.* New York: John Day.

Shils, E. A. *The Intellectual Between Tradition and Modernity: The Indian Situation.* The Hague: Mouton, 1961.
Singer, M. ed. *Traditional India: Structure and Change.* Philadelphia: American Folklore Society, 1959.
Singer, M. *When a Great Tradition Modernizes.* New York: Praeger Publishers, 1972.
Srinivasan, M. N. *Social Change in Modern India.* Hyderabad: Orient Longman, 1972.

Religion in contemporary India

Anderson, W. K. and Dhamle, S. D. *The Brotherhood in Saffron: The Rashtriya Swayamsevak Sangh and Hindu Revivalism.* Boulder, CA: Westview, 1987.
Ashby, P. H. *Modern Trends in Hinduism.* New York: Columbia University Press, 1974.
Babb, L. A. *The Divine Hierarchy: Popular Hinduism in Central India.* New York: Columbia University Press, 1975.
Babb, L. A. *Redemptive Encounters: Three Modern Styles in the Hindu Tradition.* New York: Columbia University Press, 1975.
Baird, R. D. ed. *Religion in Modern India.* New Delhi: Manohar, 1981.
Basu, T. *et al. Khaki Shorts and Saffron Flags.* New Delhi: Orient Longman, 1993.
Clothey, F. W. ed. *Images of Man: Religion and Historical Process in South Asia.* Madras: New Era, 1982.
Clothey, F. W. *Rhythm and Intent: Ritual Studies from South India.* Madras: Blackie and Son, 1982.
Diehl, C. G. *Instrument and Purpose: Studies on Rites and Rituals in South India.* Lund: Gleerup, 1956.
Duvvury, V. K. *Play, Symbolism and Ritual: A Study of Tamil Brahman Women's Rites of Passage.* New York: Peter Lang, 1991.
Erndl, K. M. *Victory to the Mother.* Oxford: Oxford University Press, 1993.
Fuller, C. J. *Servants of the Goddess: The Priests of a South Indian Temple.* Cambridge: Cambridge University Press, 1984.
Fuller, C. J. *The Camphor Flame: Popular Hinduism and Society in India.* Berkeley: University of California Press, 1988.
Gold, A. G. *Fruitful Journeys: The Way of Rajasthani Pilgrims.* Berkeley: University of California Press, 1988.
Haberman, D. *Journey Through the Twelve Forests.* Oxford: Oxford University Press, 1994.
Hanchett, S. *Coloured Rice: Symbolic Structure in Hindu Family Festivals.* New Delhi: Hindustan Publishing Corporation, 1988.
Larson, Gerald. *India's Agony over Religion.* Albany: SUNY Press, 1995.
Leslie, J. ed. *Roles and Rituals for Hindu Women.* London: Pinter Publishers, 1991.
Minor, R. ed. *Modern Indian Interpretations of the Bhagavadgītā.* Albany: SUNY Press, 1986.
Morinis, E. A. *Pilgrimage in the Hindu Tradition: A Case Study of West Bengal.* New Delhi: Oxford University Press, 1984.
Öster, A. *The Play of the Gods, Locality, Ideology, Structure and Time in the Festivals of a Bengali Town.* Chicago: University of Chicago Press, 1980.
Preston, J. J. *Cult of the Goddess: Social and Religious Change in a Hindu Temple.* Second edition. Prospect Heights, IL: Waveland Press, 1985.
Ruhela, S. P. and Robinson, D. eds. *Sai Baba and His Message.* New Delhi: Vikas, 1976.

Sax, W. S. *Mountain Goddess: Gender and Politics in a Himalayan Pilgrimage.* New York: Oxford University Press, 1991.
Shrivistava, S. *The Disputed Mosque: A Historical Inquiry.* New Delhi: Vistar Publications, 1991.
Underhill, M. M. *The Hindu Religious Year.* Calcutta: Association Press, 1921.
Van der Veer, Peter. *Religious Nationalism.* Berkeley: University of California Press, 1994.
Vidyarth, L. P., Jha, M. and Saraswathi, B. N. *The Sacred Complex of Kashi.* Delhi: Concept Publishing Co., 1979.
Wadley, S. *Shakti: Power in the Conceptual Structure of Karimpur Religion.* Chicago: University of Chicago Press, 1975.
Wangu, M. *A Goddess is Born: the Emergence of Khir Bhavanī in Kashmir.* Wexford, PA: Stark Publishers, 2002.

10

India's Global Reach

Greater India in Asia
The westward impetus
Early contacts
The colonial period
The modern era
The emigration of South Asians
Recommended reading

We have had occasion to observe frequently in previous chapters how the Indian subcontinent and its religion have been influenced by migrations and cultural infusions from various parts of the world. In this final chapter we reverse directions and explore briefly the ways in which India, its culture, people, and ideas have influenced the religious and cultural life of the rest of the globe. That influence is nearly as old as Indian civilization itself and today extends into every continent.

Greater India in Asia

We start with the outflow of these influences to the north, east, and south into the rest of Asia. That impact was primarily Buddhist, but also included Hindu and Islamic stages, especially in Southeast Asia. By at least the time of the Kuṣāṇas (first century CE) and, no doubt earlier, Buddhist monks and traders were making their way through the Khyber Pass and the Silk Route, establishing centers of Buddhist culture in Afghanistan and much of Central Asia. By late in the first century of the Common Era, Buddhism had reached Western China as monasteries and Buddhist art were to be found in centers near Loyang, the eventual capital of the Northern Wei dynasty. This Buddhism was primarily of the Mahāsāṅghika variety, though later migrations brought elements of the Yogācāra, Mādhyamika, and Vajrayāna sects.[1] Buddhism came relatively late into Tibet, around the eighth century, when forms of Vajrayāna (tantric) Buddhism were grafted onto the indigenous Bon religion, spawning in Tibet a school peculiar to that region.[2] Buddhas were grafted onto the numerous spirits of Bon which populated the universe. Indigenous shamanism came to inform the stages of Tibetan Buddhist meditation and of death. The convictions of the Indian personalists (*pudgalas*) provided the seeds for the belief in reincarnation found in Tibet, but also in later schools of China.

The Buddhism that spread into Sri Lanka and eventually into Southeast Asia was Theravādin. Once King Tissa of Ceylon was converted by Aśoka's emissary, the island became a Buddhist stronghold. Thereafter monks migrated there, and stored, wrote, and copied Theravādin texts. From Sri Lanka in turn, Theravāda Buddhism spread into Burma, the Indonesian Islands, Cambodia, and Thailand. In addition one of the Indian centers that influenced Buddhist art and thought in Southeast Asia was the Buddhist monastic community of Amarāvatī now in Andhra Pradesh.

Hindu influences in Southeast Asia in the medieval period were significant, if largely temporary and focused on royalty. These influences were of several kinds. On the one hand, there were Indian travelers who married indigenous women and occasionally assumed the role of king or advisers to the kings. This was the case with such dynasties as Funan in Vietnam in the early centuries CE; certain of the Śrīvijayas of Sumatra; and apparently, the early Khmers of Cambodia as well.[3] In addition, there were Hindu merchants who settled and occasionally constructed temples to Viṣṇu or Sīva – for example, a Viṣṇu temple was built near Pagan, Myanmar, by the eleventh century.[4] Then there were those Buddhist kings – for example, of Pagan – who used brahman advisers to help in the development of a royal cult and the construction of their cities, temples, and palaces. The model for these royal centers – from Polonnaravu, Sri Lanka, to Pagan; Angkor, Cambodia; and Ayuthia, Thailand – was significantly Hindu, mingled with Buddhist and indigenous motifs. Thanks to the influence of the Guptas prior to the fifth century, and, later, of the Palas of Bengal, and the Pallavas and Cōḻas of Tamil Nadu, much of the art and architecture of the city, palace, and temple reflected Indian cosmology and Śaiva or Vaiṣṇava forms. The temples built at Angkor, for example, often mirrored the architecture of the Pallavas,[5] while Śaiva expressions, generally incorporating the canons of the *Śaivāgamas*, carried orally by Śaivite advisers could be detected in the architecture of Pagan and Ayuthia.[6] The model of the king was that of the Hindu *devaputra* (son of the divine) coupled with the Buddhist notion of the *cakravartin*. Palace and city were microcosms, embodying the multilayered cosmology of India, wherein Mt. Meru stood at the center of the world and the numerology of five, thirty-three, etc. reflected Indian cosmography.[7] In time, forms of dance and shadow-puppet theater made their way into Southeast Asia as well where to this day one can see renditions of the *Rāmāyaṇa* in Islamic Indonesia and Buddhist Thailand, modified, to be sure, to reflect indigenous sensitivities.

The Islam that made its way into Southeast Asia was also heavily influenced by Indian sources (as well as Persian ones). Muslim merchants from Gujarat, Bengal, and Tamil Nadu were trading and settling by at least the thirteenth century in the coastal towns of Indonesia and Malaysia. Sūfīs filtered into these communities by invitation of settled merchants and local rulers. As sultanates developed, along the Malay Straits, the Mughal court became the model for kingship and Sūfīs often became ministers in the courts by the sixteenth and seventeenth centuries.

The more recent influx of Indians into "Greater India" is a story in itself. When the British empire ruled in 1835 that slavery would no longer be legal, plantation owners, British and French, sought cheap labor to replace their slaves. Within a few years, boatloads of lower-caste and outcaste workers were recruited, especially from Bengal and Tamil Nadu, but also from Bihar and the northwest. While the Bengālī traffic in human cargo slowed, it increased out of the Tamil ports of Madras and Nagapattinam. Plantation owners appointed two kinds of assistants – one "assistant," drawn from the castes of workers recruited, would attend festivals and villages of Tamil Nadu (or other areas), recruiting young workers for "three-year" stretches. The other type of assistant was of a higher class and knew both English and the vernacular (e.g., Tamil) and could serve as clerks, accountants, and liaison between the British and the laborers.[8] Into various parts of the British empire (and to a certain extent the French empire), indentured South Asians were sent: to Trinidad and Tobago in the Caribbean, East Africa, Sri Lanka, the Malay Straits, and the French-controlled islands of Mauritius and Reunion. By the end of the nineteenth century, thanks to unemployment and underemployment exacerbated by floods and droughts, the number of workers leaving Tamil Nadu alone was in the tens of thousands a year.[9] Many of these never returned to India.

On the tea plantations of Sri Lanka and the rubber and the palm plantations of Malaysia (where most of the laborers were Tamil), these workers were offered limited amenities – known in Malaysia pejoratively as the "three t's". Toddy shops became one of the few forms of entertainment; elementary schools in the Tamil medium, usually led by under-trained teachers, succeeded in providing minimal literacy in Tamil, but none in either English or Malay, thereby inhibiting the mobility and assimilability of the workers. Finally, temples began to dot the landscape of the plantations, usually in small plots of land made available to the foreman or clerk (that higher-caste figure). Makeshift icons of protector deities such as Maturai Vīraṉ or Maṉmath were implanted. Also common were shrines to Māriammaṉ, the goddess of smallpox, rain, and fertility. Those workers who were not farmers – those who worked in husbandry, construction, clearing of land, etc. – preferred shrines to Kālīyammaṉ, the goddess who protected and presided over the work of hewing and shepherding (and who had been part of the Tamil pantheon since the thirteenth century).

These laborers and their bosses were joined by the start of the twentieth century by Indians who came voluntarily seeking better work opportunities – Sikhs often working in security positions, Sindhīs or Gujāratis usually in business, Ceylon Tamils who worked in civil service and the professions, Tamil Chettiars who were the bankers and money lenders. Many of these Indians or their descendants stayed, so that in Singapore today some 6 percent of the population is Indian (primarily Tamil) and in Malaysia some 10 percent is Indian (roughly 90 percent of them Tamil). Similarly, this combination of indentured and voluntary migration of South Asians has meant that a significant percentage of the population in several countries around the world today is of South Asian descent, especially those of Mauritius, Trinidad, Guyana, Myanmar, Fiji, and South Africa. The voluntary eastern migration of Indians throughout the twentieth century has led to pockets of Indian settlers in areas where they believed they could make a better life for themselves – Australia, Hong Kong, Indonesia, as well as Malaysia, and Singapore. Nonetheless, in Malaysia especially, the vast majority of the Indian population is descended from the indentured servants brought originally to the plantations. Indeed, Indians in Malaysia own slightly more than 1 percent of Malaysia's wealth, and 90 percent of that is in the hands of the top 10 percent of the Indian Malaysian population. The other 90 percent live at a level below a hypothetical poverty line.[10]

The religious life of these communities is as diverse as their cultural roots. Generally speaking, however, many of them have found religion to be one of the ways to express their ethnic identity. They are engaged in various forms of reinterpretation of their own heritage – following gurus who are perceived to represent their values; meeting together for study, orations, or song fests; and sharing family traditions with one another. Not least important, they are engaged in building or upgrading temples, gurdwārās, or mosques which become social-cultural spaces where they can present to their children and themselves a sense of their heritage. These shrines help provide a sense of place and permanence to those who have migrated into new societies quite removed from their homeland. And, as with their counterparts who remain in India, ritual forms a significant dimension of their religious expression insofar as ritual enacts and embodies the sense of one's lineage. Many of the temples will host festivals, some modest, some quite elaborate indeed.

One of the most colorful of these festivals of Southeast Asia is Tai Pūcam held in January–February. While it occurs at a number of Hindu shrines throughout Malaysia and Singapore, nowhere is it more popular or dramatic than in the Kuala Lumpur area. The festival appears to have been brought to Malaysia by the Chettiars who were worshipers of the Tamil god Murukaṉ as he is enshrined at Paḻani, where the Chettiars traded in the seventeenth century and were given a special role in the festival. However, for at least the last century, other Indian groups have participated in the festival to the point that it has become virtually the "national" festival of Malaysian Indians.

On Tai Pūcam day, the icons of Murukaṉ and his consorts, which had been paraded from Kuala Lumpur some 12 km away, have been set up near a limestone bluff known as Batu Caves; within the cave itself, ***svayambhu*** (self-manifest) representations of Murukaṉ are the center of devotion this day. People come bringing gifts of various kinds – pots of milk, *kāvaṭis* (shoulder poles bearing peacock feathers or other paraphernalia), and other offerings. Most have taken a vow that they will come to Batu Caves in exchange for a favor the deity has granted. All will climb over 300 steps to the shrine in the cave on the side of the bluff.

The most dramatic of the pilgrims (some several hundred in any given year) are those who go into a trance and subject their bodies to various forms of "sacred wounding," especially piercing the cheeks or tongue with a lance (the symbol of the deity) or placing hooks throughout the body. It is believed by such pilgrims that they are receiving the grace (*aruḷ*) of the divine while fulfilling a vow. Many other Hindus, especially those who are Anglicized and upper class, tend to view such activity as an aberration of Hinduism and seek to reduce or eliminate the practice. Yet Batu Caves attracts several hundred thousand pilgrims on Tai Pūcam day acting out their sense of what it means to be Indian Malaysian, Tamil, and/or Hindu – through pilgrimage, taking of vows, *darśan* (viewing the deity), and, occasionally, undergoing more extreme forms of devotion.[11]

The westward impetus

Early contacts

Contacts between India and the Mediterranean world were numerous in ancient times. Since 975 BCE when the Phoenicians traded with Western India, contacts increased between the two arenas. The Persian empire served as a mediating agency once **Darius** initiated contact with India around 510 BCE.[12] There are hints that some Indian influences were known in the Greek world by the fifth or sixth century BCE. **Herodotus** (born in 484 BCE), for example, knew something of India though he was given to some overstatement: India had enormous wealth, was given to extreme forms of religion, etc. These perceptions may have been learned from one of his "neighbors" – one **Scylax of Caryanda**, who had been sent to India by Darius.[13] It appears that Indian soldiers had participated in the Greek invasion of Persia in 480 BCE and Greek officials were appointed to serve throughout the empire, including India. There are some hints that Indian ideas were known in the classical Greek world. **Pythagoras** (born in 580 BCE), for example, who lived in cosmopolitan Samos, shared ideas of reincarnation also found on the subcontinent. **Plato** and **Empedocles** similarly entertained notions of metempsychosis. Were these results of contacts or coincidence? It is hard to say; however, one Greek writer, **Eusebius**, claimed that certain learned Indians, presumably Buddhist or Jain, had visited Athens and conversed with **Socrates**.[14]

After **Alexander**, contacts increased. Not only did influences come into the subcontinent, during the time of the Mauryas, Kuṣāṇas, and Bactrians; they went out as well. Aśoka sent emissaries into cities in the Greek world and subsequently one finds small settlements of Indians in such cosmopolitan cities as Alexandria, Antioch, and Palmyrah. By the end of the first century CE, Alexandria was a major port where one-half of the world's ships were said to dock, and there is relatively frequent reference to Indians living in the city, more than likely Buddhist or Jain as orthodox brahmans may have been reluctant to cross oceans into unknown (and from the standpoint of brahmanic cosmography, profane) spaces. Similarly, Antioch and Palmyrah – a city in the desert near the Red Sea, which was an important trading center from 130–273 CE – would have hosted merchants and/or teachers from India. Indeed H. A. Rawlinson argued that specific Middle Eastern figures may have had Indian teachers: **Appollonius of Tyana** (about 50 CE) is said to have gone to Taxila to study under brahmans. **Bardesanes**, a Babylonian gnostic, is said to have learned from an Indian embassy official during the years 218–22 CE. **Plotinus**, the founder of Neo-Platonism, is thought to have accompanied an expedition into Persia in 212 CE apparently hoping to meet Indian teachers. **Clement of Alexandria** mentions Buddha in his writings and **Basilides**, an early second-century gnostic teacher and Hellenized Egyptian, is thought to have been influenced by Indian thought.[15] While many of these specific contacts remain speculative, it is at least plausible that some forms of Middle Eastern gnosticism were influenced by Buddhism.

By 762 Baghdad had replaced Alexandria as a major cultural center. Under the fourth and fifth 'Abbāsid caliphates, scholars were brought to the city from all over the world. The sciences brought from India included aspects of astronomy, medicine, and math (the "cipher" and "Arabic" numerals are said to have their origins in India). Literature and folk stories informed Arabic and eventually European cultures. The *Pañcatantra,* for example, that anthology of Indian folk tales, was translated into Pahlavī in the sixth century and thence into Arabic (*c.* 750), then into Persian, Syriac, Hebrew, and Spanish. A German version (1481) was one of the first printed books in German, and translations into Italian and English followed. Among the themes in "European" stories that may have had Indian origins are talking beasts; Sinbad the Sailor (found in the *Arabian Nights* with many Indian references); the princess and the pea; and many others. One intriguing story that appeared by the fifth century in Greek is that of Josaphat, a young Christian prince who renounces the world to become an ascetic. Translated into several European languages by the sixteenth century, it appears to be based on the story of the Buddha as found in the *Lalita Vistara,* albeit now the prince is in Christian guise.[16]

The colonial period

The coming of the Portuguese and other European colonial powers to India, in addition to the impact it had on the subcontinent, also spawned considerable interest in Europe about India.[17] Travel reports and literature stimulated and perpetuated this intrigue, obviously filtered through European lenses. Goa, for example, became a center for European visitors and one of the earliest reports was that of **Camoens** (1525–80), who romantically described Vasco da Gama's landing *post facto.* **Thomas Stephens**, an English Jesuit living in Goa as of 1575, wrote a grammar in Konkanī; a poem *Kristana Purāṇa* (the Purāṇa of Christ) was written by an admirer of the Marāthī language. **Van Linschoten**, a guest of the archbishop in Goa from 1583–89, wrote a rather sensitive report, entitled "Itineratio," which was published in 1595.[18]

The Mughal court had a variety of European visitors. One of the earliest, an Englishman named **Fitch**, returned to England with such glowing reports it prompted the East India Company to request permission to set up a factory in Surat in 1608. Two East India chaplains (**Lord**, 1630 and **Ovington**, 1689) reported on Surat. That and other travel literature influenced the poetry of **John Milton**. There were resplendent descriptions of the Mughals by **Dryden** (1675), **Tavernier** and **Bernier** (1684), and others.[19] Perhaps the most important development during the Mughal period were the translations of Dārā Shikoh into Persian. The translations of fifty-two *Upaniṣads* were completed in 1657, then translated into French by Duperron in 1801.[20] Imperfect as these translations were and being presented through Islamic, then European, eyes, they became the stimulus for generations of study of Indian languages and thought and a resource for a number of philosophers and writers. One cannot trace all these strands, but it may be worth noting the study of Sanskrit and Sanskrit texts was partially influenced by the European Enlightenment and the concomitant study of Christian scriptures. For generations it was thought (with a very Protestant assumption) that the quintessence of Indian religion lay in its texts. Accordingly, the first rendering of a Sanskrit work in English was **Charles Wilkins**' translation of the *Bhagavadgītā* in 1785. **William Jones** (1746–94) followed with translations of Kālīdāsa's play *Śakuntalā* and the *Laws of Manu.*

It is believed the study of Sanskrit was actually introduced into Europe by **Alexander Hamilton**, an official in the East India Company detained in Paris during the Napoleonic wars.[21] One of his students was **van Schlegel**, who published in German, "On the Language and Wisdom of the Indians," a text which in turn helped fuel German romanticism and, at least indirectly, the thinking of **Schopenhauer**, **Kant**, **Schiller**, **Goethe**, **Herder**, and **Schleiermacher**. The race, one might say, was on.

Interestingly, the first novel in English about India was a relatively sensitive one. *Hartley House, Calcutta*, published in 1789, was written by an anonymous woman in the form of a series of letters back home.[22] The novel describes the life of the powerful in Calcutta and proved to be relatively sympathetic to Hinduism.

The explosion of Europeans' interest in India in the nineteenth century is too extensive to recount in this context: it proved to be a wide spectrum in both discipline and attitude. Some of the early pioneers in Buddhist studies, for example, included **Barnouf**, **Lassen**, the **Rhys Davids**, **Stcherbasky**, and **Trenchner**, among others. Invariably these scholars read into Buddhism and its notion of *nirvāṇa* their own prejudices and value systems.[23] Archaeologists included **Cunningham** (whose interpretations of the Ayodhyā shrines are believed to have helped sour Hindu–Muslim relations) and, somewhat later, the work of **Marshall** and **Wheeler** in the Indus Valley. French intellectuals who showed a fascination for India included **Lamartine**, **Hugo**, and **de Vigny**. Writers on India include **Hesse** whose novel *Siddhārtha* was a Westernized and romanticized story of Buddha. **Leo Tolstoy** (1828–1910) was influenced by the doctrine of *ahiṃsa* and, in turn, influenced Gandhi's interpretation of the same. **Romain Rolland** (1866–1944) romanticized India's nineteenth-century reformers. **E. M. Forster**'s *Passage to India* took the British colonial system and its attitudes toward Indians to task, while **Rudyard Kipling**'s novels, based on a boyhood spent as part of the British Raj in India, glorified the very life Forster critiqued.

America's fascination with India, while not as long as Europe's, nonetheless goes back at least a couple of centuries to the time of the

Transcendentalists. **Ralph Waldo Emerson** read translations of Sanskrit, Pāli, and Persian literature which informed his Unitarian vision, while **David Henry Thoreau** found Indian ideas spiraling through his own reflections. By the mid-nineteenth century, the United States' interest in India had reached a peak of sorts. Well over half of the ships in Calcutta harbor were from the US. The completion of the railroad across the US was hailed by Walt Whitman as a "passage" to India. Whitman gave further voice to this romanticism in his *Leaves of Grass* where he describes India as the source of "primeval thought," "reason's early paradise," the "birthplace of wisdom," and the home of "innocent institutions" and "fair creation."[24]

The modern era

The impact of Indian religion on the "West" in the modern period might be divided into three stages. The first was the period before the First World War. Following on the heels of the fascination with India of European romantics and German philosophers, there was a flood of translations making accessible in English various texts of classical Indian thought. **Max Muller**'s translations of the *Sacred Books of the East* were an enormous undertaking, and along with other texts, such as G. Buhler's translations of the *Laws of Manu*, and J. H. Woods' translation of Patañjali's *Yogasūtras* made classical India available for study and reflection.

But religious interest in India was also piqued by the visits of Swami Vivekananda to the US. After lecturing at the Parliament of Religions in Chicago in 1893, he was invited to lecture to a variety of groups in cities along the eastern seaboard. He established "Vedānta societies" in many of the cities. Those Vedānta centers were a highly protestantized form of Neo-Hinduism which affirmed a simplified monism, the universality of truth, and the divinity of man. Their chapels hosted worship on Sunday mornings; their walls were lined with pictures of Christ along with those of Rāmakrishna, Vivekananda's mentor, and other Hindu and Buddhist figures. These Vedānta groups, still extant in North America, provided a mixture of meditation, devotion, work, and thought. Another group through which Indian ideas were filtered into Western idiom was the Theosophical Society. While it claimed to be rooted in ancient Egyptian and Celtic mythology, it had selectively borrowed from a Hindu vocabulary and both **Madame Blavatsky**, its founder, and **Annie Besant** were enamored of Indian thought. Indeed, Annie Besant was so committed to India that she moved to Adyar, just outside of Madras, to set up the international headquarters of the movement and enter into the social and cultural life of her adopted country.

In addition to these two major sources of Indian ideas in North America, there was a variety of other less well-known influences which left an impact on some of America's religious "free thinkers." There was a trickle of "gurus," both Euro-Americans and Indian-born, who planted small groups in American cities or left a literature reflecting Indian sentiments. **Baba Premanand Bharati**, for example, came to the US in 1902 from Bengal and started his "Krishna Samaj," a form of Caitanya's Krishna Consciousness movement, in New York City and Los Angeles.[25] A somewhat more ambiguous character was American-born **William Walker Atkinson**, who combined elements of "New Thought" (the generic term used for such alternative religious ideas as Mesmerism, Pantheism, Perennial Philosophy, etc.) with more explicitly Hindu notions expressed in his persona as "Yogi Ramacharaka."[26] The result of these various strands was an openness on the part of some Americans of European descent to ideas and rituals that had their origins in India.

The second significant wave of Indian influence occurred between the World Wars. During this period, an increasing number of yogins and gurus made their way to North America to establish ashrams for meditation and "self-realization." These meditation centers and techniques, while based on Indian tradition, were usually eclectic. They were presented as being "attachable" to Christianity or any other religion. Such was the case with the Self-Realization Fellowship, founded in California in 1920 (see below). Worship in the center of that movement included hymns and scriptures of various traditions. Among the gurus who came to offer lectures and enlightenment or whose movements impacted North America were **Sri Deva Ram Sukul**, an Indian living in Chicago, who founded the Hindu Yoga Society in Chicago and California in the 1920s; **Srimath Swami Omkar**, a Tamil, who established a branch of the Sri Mariya Ashram in Philadelphia in 1923; and **Rishi Krishnamanda**, who founded his "Para-Vidya Center" in Los Angeles in the 1930s; and others.[27]

We might look a little more carefully at two of the persons who figure prominently in the developments of this period. One is **Swami Paramahansa Yogananda**. Born in Bengal in 1893, he decided in his youth to follow a religious life. From his family's guru, **Lahiri Mahasaya**, he learned a technique known as "kriya yoga," which became his "special message" to the world. At the age of seventeen, he became a disciple of **Sri Yukteswar**, a disciple of Mahasaya, who led him through an experience of "cosmic consciousness" and encouraged him to receive a college degree. After a period of apprenticeship in India, Paramahansa was sent to the US in 1920, where he crisscrossed the country for the next three decades, lecturing and gathering devotees, first in Boston and eventually Los Angeles, where he established the headquarters of the Self-Realization Fellowship. Yogananda was a charismatic speaker and skillful marketer. He taught yoga and wrote, most notably, the book *Autobiography of a Yoga*, which was published eventually in 1946. Yet the signature feature of his work was the technique he marketed known as "kriya yoga." "Kriya yoga" selectively appropriated aspects of the traditional yoga system, but he simplified it for adaptation for any modern person. He claimed the technique had been used by ancient sages, including St. Paul and Christ and that it could be used irrespective of one's religious orientation. At the same time, he used a quasi-scientific vocabulary to give the technique a modern rationale.[28]

Yogananda developed a significant following partially because of his ability to appropriate a Western and liberal Protestant vocabulary, partially because of his charismatic personality and partially because his promise of a "ritual that worked" appealed to an audience that sought just that.

If Yogananda's appeal lay largely in the offering of a ritual technique, that of **Jiddu Krishnamurti** claimed to be of a different sort. Krishnamurti was born into an orthodox brahman family in South India in 1895.[29] By 1909 he had begun to work at the headquarters of the Theosophical Society, by then located in Adyar near Madras city. Members of the society saw spiritual leanings in the young man; indeed, before long he was understood to be an incarnation of the "Maitreya," the future "world teacher" and as such was worshiped by devotees. Nonetheless, by the time he was twenty-six, Krishnamurti became increasingly disenchanted with the Theosophical Society – its ideas, its constraints, and the way it was using him. Before long he was undergoing his own spiritual experiences and developing his own ideological system. While he continued to work within the system until 1928, he eventually set out to lecture on his own, giving his first public lecture (one not intended exclusively for Theosophical Society members) in May 1928. For several decades, he lectured in the US, India, and Europe. His message insisted that the truth was not to be found in any particular religion. Rather, while he claimed a special status as a universal teacher who had a sense of the truth, he sought not for men to follow him but to be "free." While he tended to eschew all rituals, he nonetheless, claimed that "mindless awareness" was a form of meditation – much like zen practice – which could make persons free.

As ideas such as these made their way into North America several indigenous movements were spawned that at least purported to have an Indian flavor. The I Am movement, for example, was founded in the 1930s by one **Guy Ballard** (1878–1939). Ballard's movement Americanized aspects of Theosophy and certain occult practices. Mt. Shasta, California, for example, became the group's mythological center and they believed themselves able to see auras around people's heads. Scientology, founded by **Ron Hubbard** in 1911, adapted Buddhist terms to describe the religious experience and declared its leader to be a shaman and "magus" (wise spiritual leader). Science fiction terms were adopted to describe the relationship between microcosm and macrocosm as perceived by the founder.[30] The emphasis during this period seemed to be experimentation and openness to rituals that were thought to create community and/or self-realization and to ideas that were considered universal. Clearly, charismatic leaders were able to attract those who sought some embodiment of authentic humanhood and spiritual insight. Nonetheless, it must be made clear that such movements were far removed from classical forms of Indian religion. Indeed, orthoprax Hindus insist such hybridizations as these were inauthentic, even bastardized forms of Hinduism or Buddhism.

Meanwhile, some of the first immigrants were trickling into North America in the twentieth century. The first South Asians to appear and settle were primarily Sikhs, who were arriving in British Columbia by 1899 and by 1906 had made their way into the Western US. By 1907, these migrants were the target of various forms of discrimination – from "anti-Hindu" riots to editorials favoring their deportation in various newspapers in both British Columbia and Washington State.[31] Undaunted, the Sikhs, virtually all of them bachelors and sojourners, made their way southward into California, where eventually they generally married Mexican women and set up the first Indian religious establishment in the US, a makeshift gurdwārā, in Stockton, California, in 1906, followed by a more permanent structure in 1929.[32] But, while Indians had been migrating voluntarily into such places as the Malay Straits and East Africa for over a generation, the flow into Europe and North America was modest indeed. As late as 1950, there were fewer than 1,000 Indian women living in the US. The trickle was to become a significant stream, however, within decades.

The third period of this modern influence is that which followed the Second World War and especially since the 1960s. For one thing, things Indian had influenced American popular culture and subsequently global culture. There were several factors contributing to this phenomenon. There was, on the one hand, a certain alienation by 1965 especially on the part of the young with "Western" values of consumerism and international hegemony. There was a perceived loss of respect for authority figures exacerbated by the Vietnam War and the Nixon years. There was an increased sense of mobility and depersonalization, a perceived need for community and roots. One of the results of this relative malaise was a willingness to accommodate "newer" or more eclectic forms of religion. Some have estimated that perhaps as many as 1,000 "alternative" religious movements have been spawned in North America alone since the Second World War. Among these alternatives was the International Society for Krishna Consciousness, a movement shaped in the Gaudiā Vaiṣṇava tradition founded by Caitanya and brought to the West by **Swami Prabhupada**. While the movement has remained relatively small in the US and Europe, many "outsiders" became familiar with the rigorous discipline of the movement, its characteristic garb, and public chanting of "Hare Rāmā, Hare Kṛiṣṇa." Yet another movement was forged by **Swami Maharishi Mahesh Yogi** and his technique of meditating for "transcendental consciousness" ("TM"), packaged and sold as twenty minutes a day of meditation designed to focus the mind and clear it of unnecessary debris. Other gurus have come and gone – **Rajneesh** of Oregon fame is but one of hundreds who have made their way through North America and Europe. Scores of other "alternative religions" have also been engendered, some for brief periods before returning to relative oblivion. Anand Marg and Eckankar are but two such. The latter, founded by one **Paul Twitchell**, takes its name from the Panjābī term for God (*Ek* – the One) and purports to enable the devotee to free the soul to travel through the multiple planes of the cosmos only to return totally enlightened.

These impeti, especially those of the TM and the International Society for Krishna Consciousness groups, were given popular currency by the Beatles, whose songs resonated with Indian idioms and whose donations supported such movements. Not least important in this process of popularization has been the way yoga has been made available throughout the West – as a form of exercise, virtually stripped of its cosmological and soteriological context. Such South Asian terms as "karma" and "nirvana" have become part of the English language, obviously nuanced with their new cultural trappings. While the fascination with India cooled in the 1980s and 1990s, it was piqued further as the emigration of South Asians increased.

The emigration of South Asians

It was also subsequent to the 1960s that South Asians began to arrive in significant numbers in Great Britain, Europe, and the United States. In Britain, the mass migrations started shortly after the peoples from the Caribbean had arrived. Many went at first as refugees. First there were the Panjābīs; then peoples from East and West Pakistan (especially after the war of 1971); from East Africa (especially Gujāratis and others fleeing Idi Amin's "eviction notice" from Uganda); from Bangladesh; and Tamils fleeing the war in Sri Lanka. These were joined by those who came for professional and economic reasons. They settled in cities away from London at first – Birmingham, Leeds, Leicester; they tended to keep to themselves, followed parental discipline, and worked hard to save money. They were generally lumped into a generic category known as "Asian." Yet in recent decades, as their numbers increased, as British society came to value "multiculturalism" more than "integration," as democratic politics tended to encourage power blocs, as migrants learned more about the politics of their home countries and states – for all these reasons, these migrants came to see themselves more as Kashmīrīs, Bengālīs, and Gujāratis, as Hindus, Muslims, and Sikhs. Increasingly, the communalism found in the Indian subcontinent has fueled (and, occasionally, been fueled by) communalism in Great Britain.[33]

By the late 1960s, South Asian sojourners to the United Kingdom were becoming settled and women and children were joining the men who had come to seek work. The first Hindu temple was constructed in Coventry in 1967. Since the end of mass immigration in 1973, temples and places of worship have proliferated – estimates are that by 1982 there were some 100 Hindu temples in the UK and that these had increased to over 300 in the early 1990s. By the mid-1990s there were over 1.25 million South Asians in Great Britain, of whom some 440,000 were Hindus.[34]

Other European countries have witnessed migration on a more modest scale. In the Netherlands, for example, most of the Hindus are of Surinamese background. Some 100,000 such Hindus have brought their particular form of Caribbean Hinduism, divided into factions associated with the Ārya Samāj and Sanātana Dharma and maintaining some twenty temples all told. In addition, some 4,000 Tamil Hindus and 3,000 Hindus from Uganda have settled in the Netherlands. Furthermore, scholars have estimated that some twenty-seven Hindu-related groups are to be found in the country. There is considerable rethinking of the nature of Hinduism among these settlers as they look to India and well-established centers in London for guidance in this process of reinterpretation.[35]

Germany, in the meantime, has received refugees, especially from Afghanistan and Sri Lanka. About 75 percent of the 60,000 refugees from Sri Lanka are Hindus; while most of the 40,000 Afghan refugees are Muslim.[36] Other countries of Western Europe have even less visible South Asian populations. In Portugal, for example, it is estimated there are some 20,000 persons of Goan Catholic descent and another 5,000 or so Hindus who are refugees from Mozambique.[37] In France, some 60,000 Hindu Tamil refugees from Sri Lanka have found asylum, while some 10,000 Gujārati Hindus, most of them from Uganda, have settled. In Switzerland, most of the South Asian settlers are Tamils, about 24,000 of them, who have established fifteen places of worship in the country's major cities since the mid-1980s. In Scandinavia, there are said to be a total of 10,000 Hindus, about half of these Sri Lankan Tamils while most of the others are Gujāratis from Uganda.[38]

The year 1965 witnessed a change in US immigration laws. These changes were such that professionals and their families could enter much more easily and a steady stream of Indians have made their way into the US ever since. According to one study, some 85 percent of this early wave of immigrants in a particular city held graduate degrees and were professionally employed,[39] though in the 1980s and 1990s, more than half of these immigrants were joining families already here. Apparently unlike the early migrants into Britain, these immigrants were quite conscious of their ethnicity, religion, and caste. The same study cited above, for example, found that 40 percent of the pre-1980 immigrants claimed to be brahmans and most of the respondents were more likely to identify themselves by their linguistic/ "ethnic" nature (e.g., Tamil, Gujārati) than by any other designation.[40] At first these immigrants understood themselves to be temporary residents in the US and practiced their religious expressions within their homes. But as they stayed on and their children grew to the age of accountability, many sought more permanent ways of expressing their Indian–American passage. Makeshift "cultural centers" became temples, especially for the South Indians for whom a temple made a town "home." Moreover, as family and "ethnic" networks succeeded in bringing more kin into specific cities, the tendency for these communities to associate by language and/or caste affiliations increased. The higher the caste and the larger number of members of that caste in a given city, the more likely was the tendency to express those caste and "ethnic" associations. The same study cited above indicated that Indian immigrants in the US into the 1980s were likely to draw their best friends from their own language groups.[41] Hence, while Indians in the US have succeeded remarkably well in the professions and have forged Indo-American alliances and entered increasingly into the discourse of American public life, in their private relationships they remain, in significant measure, Tamil brahmans or Gujārati patels.

One of the most visible ways in which these Indian settlers have expressed their religious sentiments in the US is in the building of temples which represent the lineage and taste of its builders. Within these temples, not only are rituals conducted with various degrees of orthopraxy, but festivals and holidays representing the appropriate region "back home" are also conducted. Classes in classical dance and/or music are offered to girls in the effort to train them into representations of Indian or sub-Indian culture. Languages are taught sporadically, summer camps are held, oratorical contests are conducted – all to increase visibility of the "home" culture to a second generation. The temple, in short, has increasingly replaced the home as the sphere where "tradition" is enacted, complete with the compromises that life in a new society requires.

The story of one community settling into a small American city can illustrate certain of the patterns to be found in a number of North American and European cities. Pittsburgh, Pennsylvania, had attracted many East European workers into steel mills and other industries in the late 1800s. They had built churches in which their cultural and ethnic values were enshrined. By the late 1960s Pittsburgh was losing its steel base and beginning to go

Figure 12 Śrī Veṅkaṭeśvara Temple, Malibu, California. Photograph by Rob F. Phillips.

"high-tech." Indian professionals were finding study opportunities in its universities and jobs in its hospitals and technological industries. By the early 1970s their children were coming of age and a certain nostalgia was setting in. Accordingly, an apartment in one part of town was set aside as a cultural center and *pūjā* room. A desire for a ***pucca*** (authentic) temple increased, especially on the part of the South Indians. These same southerners established connections with the famed pilgrimage center at Tirupati, whose officials promised help in the form of advice and provision of services. An old Baptist church was purchased in a Pittsburgh suburb and served for a while as a cultural center for all South Asians. At the same time, preparations were made for building a temple dedicated to Śrī Veṅkaṭeśwara, the manifestation of Viṣṇu to be found in Tirupati. The North Indians, however, were not comfortable with what they perceived to be a regional and narrowly focused temple and wanted something more "catholic." Accordingly, the community split – South Indians purchased land in another suburb and constructed the Śrī Veṅkaṭeśvara Temple in Penn Hills. Its groundbreaking, dedicatory ceremonies, and ongoing ritual practices were orthoprax, following as closely as possible the Pāñcarātra Vaiṣṇava tradition. Its priests were traditionally trained and represented the southern states of the temple's builders.[42] This temple has continued to offer classes in Bharata Nāṭyam and Kuchipudi dance, styles which are part of the South Indian tradition. A summer 'academy' in Carnatic (Southern) music is offered, as are occasional classes in Tamil, Telugu, Kannada, and Sanskrit.

The "SV Temple" has sponsored elaborate ritual events, some for the first time in the US. Because it was one of the first and claims to be the most "authentic" of the South Indian temples to be built it has become a major pilgrimage center for Indian-Americans on the eastern seaboard. Families come there for rites of passage (e.g., marriages, ear-borings). Indeed by the time of its twenty-fifth anniversary in 2001–2002 it had become one of the two or three most prosperous Hindu temples outside of India. It is viewed by South Indians throughout North America as the prototypical temple to be emulated as new temples are built throughout the continent.

In the meanwhile, North Indian Hindus and Jains were collaborating in building the Hindu-Jain Temple on the property originally purchased in Monroeville. Upon its completion, Jain *tīrthaṅkaras* and a variety of Hindu deities were enshrined and represented by the kind of white marble icons favored in North India. The temple sponsors language study and cultural events for its various clientele – Bengālīs, Gujāratis, etc. The people of this temple have continued to express their North Indian roots within the structure. They sponsor such holiday events as Dīvali, and provide Indian dance entertainment for the city's annual folk festivals.

The cooperation of the Jains in the construction of this temple is itself of historic significance. Not only is it one of the few structures in which Hindus and Jains worship under the same roof (a few Hindu temples in North America may include a Jain *pūjā* room, but seldom does one find shared space). More than that, thanks to the vision of a local Jain physician, Digambaras and Śvetāmbaras worship in the same building, contrary to tradition and all known advice back home. It was the Birla family, known for the building of temples in a number of Indian cities, who helped with the construction of the building and the provision of icons. In addition to the ongoing ritual life at the temple, in which lay Jains offer rice and *ārati* to the *tīrthaṅkaras*, Jains gather from miles around for two special occasions during the year. One of these is Mahāvīra Nirvāna, the *samādhi* (death) of Mahāvīra, which occurs at the new moon of October–November (the same new moon which marks Dīvali, and the New Year in Northwest India). The other is Mahāvīra Jayanthi (the birthday of Mahāvīra) in March–April. Traditionally, the former celebration is of special interest to Digambara Jains, and the latter to Śvetāmbara Jains; but here all Jains commemorate both events.

By 1984 the Sikhs had built their own gurdwārā. The construction was done entirely with "local help" by copying pictures of favored gurdwārās in India. The structure serves some 75–100 families in southwestern Pennsylvania who are proud of their Sikh identity, careful to distinguish themselves from both Hindus and Muslims. Weekly rituals will include a reading of a portion of the *Gurū Granth Sāhib* and the community meal (*laṅgar*). Among the festivals taken most seriously by the community is the birthday of Gurū Nānak (celebrated at the Dīvali New Moon of October–November) which includes a reading of the *Gurū Granth Sāhib* over a period of two days; and the anniversary of the formation of the Sikh brotherhood (*khālsa*) by Gurū Gobind Singh (observed in December–January). The gurdwārā also sponsors a regional conference in September for Sikh youth living in the eastern United States.

In a similar fashion, Muslims of South Asian descent have built their own *masjid* and maintain their own traditions within it. In the 1970s South Asian Muslim immigrants were meeting in the simple cultural center in the university district (Oakland) shared by all the Muslims in the city. Yet as their numbers grew and with it the perception that the Oakland "mosque" was being run by students and other short-term visitors from the Middle East, the "South Asian" families determined to have their own center closer to where they lived and more representative of their own more "liberal" points of view. Accordingly, a house was purchased in an eastern suburb (Monroeville, where most of the other religious edifices serving South Asian settlers are to be found). This house served as a cultural center until the early 1990s when construction was started on an authentic *masjid.* A social hall was completed first and on May 13, 1995 the completed mosque was dedicated.

It is here that families gather for most social, cultural, and religious events. On Sundays, classes are offered in Arabic and in the interpretation of the Qu'rān run by lay participants. Open discussions are held on various issues arising in the community: should American Muslims be free to eat meat prepared by Jews and Christians even though these may not be strictly *ḥalāl* (the consensus was yes)? Which religious days should be observed? (Most of the participants are of Sunnī background, so Shīa observances are generally ignored). Other elements of the Sunday agenda are a time for public prayers (*namāz*) and a common meal. The *masjid* is also open for prayer daily for the handful who can attend and on Friday noon when all those of the community who can will participate.

The *masjid* was established primarily for South Asian emigrés and at least three-quarters of its constituency of some 150 families are South Asian, whether Indian, Pakistani, or Bangladeshi. They have been joined by persons of other national origins – Indonesian, Malaysian, Egyptian, even Euro-Americans who have married into the community. The South Asians share a common language, Urdū, but insist their primary identities are "American Muslim." Yet at mealtime, in patterns of dress, and in accent, such sub-identities as Panjābī, Hyderabadī, or Bengālī became apparent.

Figure 13 Śrī Veṅkaṭeśvara Temple, Pittsburgh, PA. Photograph by Ann Clothey.

Figure 14 The Hindu-Jain Temple, Pittsburgh, PA. Photograph by Rebecca Clothey.

Figure 15 The Sikh Gurdwāra, Pittsburgh, PA. Photograph by Rebecca Clothey.

Figure 16 Masjid, founded primarily by South Asian Muslims, Pittsburgh, PA. Photograph by Rebecca Clothey.

The major annual celebration is Ramaḍān. The '*īd* closing the Ramaḍān fast is usually marked by prayers held in a large auditorium with all the other Muslims of the city. But socialization thereafter reverts to the "home mosque" and to "family gatherings" where ethnic, sub-ethnic, and family traditions may be maintained. The other major annual event is the '*īd* that marks the "day of sacrifice" during the *ḥajj*. This is usually observed in the "home mosque" and at home.

These South Asian settlers of the Pittsburgh area share much in common with their compatriots of whatever religious commitment. The men are almost invariably professional and well-placed in the community. Most of the women are similarly professionally engaged – and the majority of those working in the home are at least college graduates. The laity of the groups are active in the governance of the religious institutions; leadership is elected and rotates regularly. The women have an active role in the institutions' lives – an extension, as more than one put it, of their domestic agendas. They assume roles, not only as cooks for public meals, but also as teachers, officers, and interpreters of the tradition. For each community, the religious structure serves not only as religious space, but also as a cultural and social space for the socialization of their children and for sharing of common concerns relative to living in a society where they remain a religious minority.

The story of the global dispersion of Indian ideas, culture, and people, only sketched here, suggests a number of implications. It is clear, for example, that religion is now transnational. No longer is "east east" and "west west." Hindus, Muslims, Sikhs, and Buddhists have become the neighbors of Christians and Jews. Muslims, for example, are the second largest religious population in France and are as abundant in the US as are Jews. Hinduism is not confined to India and to Indians; Buddhism, with its active publishing agencies in the US and the concomitant construction of *stūpas* and meditation centers is stronger in the US than it was in its first century in China, where it became the "state religion" within centuries.

This leads us back to the conclusion with which we started this study. It is not possible to ignore these religious traditions in our study of history, of religion, or of the human experience, for to do so would be to ignore something of the world's history and of the changing face of the West's religious landscape. In fact, the presence of these alternative religions and of South Asian immigrants in most countries of the world is an invitation for persons raised in any single religious tradition or in no religion at all, to rethink the ways in which fundamental human issues are answered in light of the questions raised by these transnational migrations. After learning what we can from the people of South Asia, their questions, their interactions, their responses to the exigencies of history and the modern world – we should not be able to remain the same as we were before we started this study.

In many ways, Indians who have sought to revivify or reinterpret their religious orientations since the nineteenth century have been a people living "on the boundaries." They have been renegotiating identities in response to multiple cultures and religions. They have reacted – even over-reacted – to the effects of colonialism and have been tempted by the lure of nationalism, orthopraxy, and ethnicity. They have sought to maintain anchorage in the face of increased mobility, and the loss of a sense of rootedness and community. Their experience has become, in many respects, a mirror of the experience of most persons living in the twenty-first century. Many persons today live "on the boundaries," familiar with more than one culture or religion through travel, education, or life experience. Many persons look for authentic humans worth emulating, experiment with "rituals that work," and long for a sense of community. Not infrequently, people "on the boundaries" have turned to orthopraxy – the practice of a "tradition" thought to affirm certainty and heritage. Others experiment with alternative ideas and construct collages of religion. In any case, the Indian experience demonstrates that we have come to an exciting and important moment in the history of religions, one in which new religious landscapes continually emerge like the images of a kaleidoscope and where people will have to learn whether it is possible to share the same planet. In effect, the search for a new world order – to say nothing of more satisfying religious orientations – has just begun.

Recommended reading

On the global dispersal of South Asian culture and people

Agarwal, P. *Passage From India: Post 1965 Indian Immigrants and Their Children.* Palos Verdes, CA: Yuvati Publications, 1991.

Ballard, R. ed. *Desh Pardesh, the South Asian Presence in Britain.* London: Hurst, 1994.

Buchignani, N. *et al. Continuous Journey: A Social History of South Asians in Canada.* Toronto: McClelland and Stewart, 1985.

Coedès, G. *The Indianized States of Southeast Asia.* Honolulu: East-West Center Press, 1968.

Daniels, R. *History of Indian Immigration to the United States.* New York: The Asia Society, 1989.

Desai, S. *Indian Immigrants in Britain.* London: Oxford University Press, 1963.

Jain, Ravindra K. *South Indians on the Plantation Frontier in Malaya.* Kuala Lumpur: University of Malaya Press, 1970.

Jensen, J. M. *Passage From India: Asian Indian Immigrants in North America.* New Haven, CT: Yale University Press, 1988.

Kamath, M. V. *The United States and India.* Washington: The Embassy of India, 1976.
Rawlinson, H. G. *Intercourse Between India and the Western World.* Cambridge: Cambridge University Press, 1916.
Riepe, D. *The Philosophy of India and its Impact on American Thought.* Springfield, IL: Charles C. Thomas, 1970.
Rukumani, T. S. ed. *Hindu Diaspora: Global Perspectives.* Montreal: Concordia University, 1999.
Saran, P. *The Asian Indian Experience in the United States.* New York: Praeger Publishers, 1980.
Saran, P. and Eams, E. eds. *The New Ethnics: Asian Indians in the United States.* New York: Praeger Publishers, 1980.
Singh, J. *et al. South Asians in North America.* Berkeley: University of California Press, 1988.
Singh, J. and Bahadur, J. ed. *The Other India: the Overseas Indians and their Relationship with India.* New Delhi: Arnold Heinemann, 1979.
Tinker, H. *The Banyan Tree: Overseas Emigrants from India, Pakistan and Bangladesh.* Oxford: Oxford University Press, 1977.
Vikram, R. *Ayahs, Lascars, and Princes: Indians in Britain, 1700–1947.* London: Pluto Press, 1986.
Wales, H. G. Q. *The Malay Peninsula in Hindu Times.* London: Bernard Quaritch, Ltd., 1976.
West, M. L. *Early Greek Philosophy and the Orient.* Oxford: Clarendon Press, 1971.

Religion and the Indian diaspora

Barrier, N. G. and Dusenberg, V. A. eds. *The Sikh Diaspora.* Columbia, MO: South Asia Books, 1989.
Bhachu, P. *Twice Migrants: East African Sikh Settlers in Britain.* London: Tavistock, 1985.
Boucher, S. *Turning the Wheel: American Women Creating the New Buddhism.* Boston: Beacon Press, 1993.
Burghart, R. ed. *Hinduism in Great Britain: the Perpetuation of Religion in an Alien Cultural Milieu.* London: Tavistock, 1987.
Coward, H., Hinnels, J. R. and Williams, R. eds. *The South Asian Religious Diaspora in Britain, Canada, and the United States.* Albany: SUNY Press, 2000.
Ellwood, R. S. *Alternative Altars: Unconventional and Eastern Spirituality in America.* Chicago: University of Chicago Press, 1979.
Ellwood, R. S. and Partin, H. *Religious and Spiritual Groups in Modern America.* Second edition. Englewood Cliffs, NJ: Prentice Hall, 1988.
Fenton, J. Y. *Transplanting Religious Traditions: Asian Indians in America.* New York: Praeger, 1988.
Fenton, J. Y. *South Asian Religions in the Americas: An Annotated Bibliography of Immigrant Religious Traditions.* Westport, CT: Greenwood, 1995.
Haddad, Y. Y. *The Muslims of America.* New York: Oxford University Press, 1991.
Helweg, A. *Sikhs in England.* Delhi: Oxford University Press, 1985.
Hinnels, J. R. *Zoroastrians in Britain.* Oxford: Clarendon Press, 1995.
Jackson, C. T. *The Oriental Religions and American Thought: Nineteenth Century Explorations.* Westport, CT: Greenwood Press, 1981.
Jackson, C. T. *Vedanta for the West: the Ramakrishna Movement in the United States.* Bloomington: Indiana University Press, 1994.

Jackson, R. and Nesbitt, E. *Hindu Children in Britain*. Stoke-on-Trent: Trentham Books, 1993.

James, A. *Sikh Children in Britain*. London: Oxford University Press, 1974.

Kalsi, S. S. *The Evolution of a Sikh Community in Britain*. Leeds: Leeds University, 1992.

Kanitkar, H. and Jackson, R. *Hindus in Britain*. London: University of London Press, 1992.

Knott, K. *Hinduism in Leeds*. Leeds: Gmmumth Related Projects, 1986.

La Brack, B. *The Sikhs of Northern California, 1904–1975*. New York: AMS Press, 1988.

Manikka, Eleanor. *Time, Space, and Kingship*. Manoa: University of Hawaii Press, 1996.

Miller, T. ed. *America's Alternative Religions*. Albany: SUNY Press, 1995.

O'Connell, J. T. *et al.* eds. *Sikh History and Religion in the Twentieth Century*. Toronto: University of Toronto, 1988.

Rayaprol, A. *Negotiating Identities: Women in the Indian Diaspora*. Delhi: Oxford University Press, 1997.

Raza, M. *Islam in Britain: Past, Present and Future*. London: Volcano Press, 1991.

Richardson, E. A. *Islamic Cultures in North America: Patterns, Belief and Devotion of Muslims from Asian Countries in the United States and Canada*. New York: The Pilgrim Press, 1981.

Richardson, E. A. *East Comes West: Asian Religions and Cultures in North America*. New York: Pilgrim Press, 1985.

Sharma, J. C. *Hindu Temples in Vietnam*. New Delhi: Sankalp Publications, 1997.

Singh, N. *Canadian Sikhs: History, Religion, and Culture of Sikhs in North America*. Ottawa: Canadian Sikhs Study Association, 1994.

Tatla, D. S. *Sikhs in America: An Annotated Bibliography*. New York: Greenwood Press, 1991.

Trout, P. *Eastern Seeds, Western Soil: Three Gurus in America*. Mountain View, CA: Mayfield Publishing, 2001.

Tweed, T. and Prothero, S. *Asian Religions in America*. Oxford: Oxford University Press, 1999.

Williams, R. *Religions of Immigrants from India and Pakistan*. Cambridge: Cambridge University Press, 1988.

Williams, R. B. ed. *A Sacred Thread: Modern Transmission of Hindu Traditions in India and Abroad*. Chambersburg, PA: Anima, 1992.

Glossary

All terms are Sanskrit in origin unless otherwise noted by (U) Urdū, (T) Tamil, (AV) Avestan, or (A) Arabic.

abhinaya **(abhi-naya)** performance of a mood (*rasa*) in dance or drama (see also: *rasa, rāga, tālā, mudrā*).

abhiṣeka **(abhi-sheka)** "anointing," refers to the act of pouring of water upon temple icons; other liquids may also be used, e.g., ghee or honey; this is usually the first ritual performed on an icon each day. It may also refer to the inauguration of a king.

ācāryā **(ā-charya)** teacher, usually in the sense of a *guru.*

adhvaryu priest associated with the *Yajur Veda,* the prose *Veda* which gives detailed explanations of Vedic rituals.

advaita **(a-dvaita)** "non-dualism"; concept often associated with forms of Vedānta philosophy (see also: *dvaita*).

āgama **(ā-gama)** ritual manual; different *āgamas* are used by various sects (e.g., *Śaivāgamas, Pāñcarātrāgamas, Vaikānasāgamas*).

ahiṃsa **(a-himsa)** Jain concept of non-violence or harmlessness; abstention from injury to living things.

ajīva **(a-jīva)** "non-life entity"; important concept in Jainism (see also: *jīva*).

ājīvika **(ā-jīvika)** materialist; name of a heterodox philosophical movement.

akam (T) poetic term from *caṅkam* poetry of Tamil Nadu; refers to the world of home, and is characterized by love (see also: *puṟam*).

alaṃkāra "ornamentation" or embellishment, particularly used in language as a literary technique, e.g., metaphors, plays on words, similes, puns.

ālaya-vijñāna **(ā-laya-vi-janāna)** "storehouse consciousness"; Mahāyāna Buddhist term, especially associated with the Yogācāra school of Buddhism.

anātman **(an-ātman)** "no-self"; opposite or negation of *ātman*; a fundamental concept in early Buddhism.

anattā "no-self"; Pāli spelling of *anātman.*

āṇava (T) ego.

aṇḍa egg.

anitya impermanence; used especially in Four Noble Truths of Buddhism to describe the nature of reality; implies that there is no logic to the succession inherent in *karma.*

annaprāśana Hindu ceremony involving the first feeding of solids to an infant of six months.

aṉpu (T) love of god toward a human being.

anumāna **(anu-māna)** perception by analogy (taught by Śaṅkara).

aparigraha **(a-parigraha)** "non-possession," one of the five Jain vows.

ārati worship involving the waving of lamps before a deity.

arcana **(arch-ana)** ritual offering or gift-giving.

arhat "perfected person," refers to the ideal person in Theravāda Buddhist sects. (Pāli: *arhant.*)

artha statecraft; aim/goal of life; wealth; one of the four *puruṣārthas* or goals of humankind (see also: *kāma, dharma,* and *mokṣa*).

arthavāda **(artha-vāda)** "explanation of the purpose; praise," expositions of the acts of rituals, e.g., *Brāhmaṇas.*

aruḷ (T) grace or mercy; occurs when a deity possesses an individual as a sign of the deity's favor.

āsana "seat"; refers to yogic postures.

asha (AV) in Zoroastrianism, the force or path of righteousness, with emphasis on good thoughts, words, and deeds.

aṣẖrāf (A) an individual who claims to be and is accepted as a descendant of Muḥammad through his daughter, Fatima.

āśrama **(ashram)** stage of life; monastery; stage in a brahman's life.

asteya non-stealing; one of the precepts of Jainism.

āstika believing or pious (see also: *nāstika*).

asura demon, particularly in Vedic mythology.

aśvamedha **(ashva-medha)** horse sacrifice.

ātman "self"; literally, "breath" or "life" (see also: *anātman*).

avaidika anyone who is not a follower of the *Vedas,* e.g., "heterodox" groups like the Buddhists, Jains, and Ājīvikas (see also: *vaidika*).

avatāra incarnation of a deity; literally, "one who crosses down," that is, one who comes to earth.

avidyā ignorance.

bandha that which binds together; in Jainism, the process which binds together *jīvas* and *ājīvas.*

bhakta one who is devoted to a deity or *guru*; hence, a devotee.

bhakti devotion to and "participation" in or with a deity.

bheda to divide; in statecraft, becoming an ally of one's enemies' enemy; division, separation, splitting.

bodhisattva enlightened person in Mahāyāna Buddhism who vows not to attain final enlightenment until all sentient beings have become enlightened; thus, a bodhisattva is viewed as exceedingly compassionate (see also: *arhat*).

brahmacarya religious study or the religious studentship of a brahman youth, passed in celibacy, being the first stage in the religious life of a brahman.

brahmadeya abode of brahmans.

brahman supreme essence of the universe in Hindu cosmology.

brāhmaṇa (also **brahman**) priestly class; highest of the four classes (see also: *kṣatriya, vaiśya, śūdra*).

buddhi intellect, wisdom, insight.

caitya **(chaitya)** uppermost feature of a Buddhist *stūpa*, symbolizing the Buddha's having transcended the cosmos.

cakra **(chakra)** literally, "wheel" (see also: *cakravartin*); a physio-psychical center, of which there are seven in classical yoga.

cakravartin **(chakra-vartin)** "turner of the wheel"; in Buddhism, one who sets in motion the wheel of *dharma*.

caṅkam (T) **(sangam)** from Sanskrit *sangha*, meaning "assembly"; poems that are arranged into two main categories, the interior or *akam*, relating to love and family life, and the exterior or *puṟam*, relating to war and kings.

cit **(chit)** intellect, senses, mind.

civam (T) **(sivam)** formless or aniconic reality (see *liṅga*); term used in Śaiva Siddhānta.

civaṉ (T) **(sivan)** formed or active deity; term used in Śaiva Siddhānta.

dachma (AV) in Zoroastrianism, a tower-like structure on which dead bodies are exposed, also known as the "tower of silence."

daeva (AV) in Zoroastrianism, a demon.

dāna gift, giving; "bribing" as a means of statecraft (*artha*).

daṇḍa "club," as in a weapon; refers to the policy whereby one defeats one's enemy through battle.

dār al-ḥarb (A) "world of hostility"; in Islam refers to lands not under the guidance of God's law.

dār al-islām (A) "world of peace"; in Islam refers to lands under the guidance of God's law (see *sharī'a*).

darśana **(darshana)** sight, vision; act of seeing and being seen by a deity, usually through an encounter with an iconic representation of the deity, particularly when the icon is filled with "power"; also means "viewpoint," as in philosophical viewpoint. (Hindi: *darśan*.)

deva deity (see also: *devī*).

devanāgarī script used in writing Sanskrit; literally, "city [writing] of the gods."

devapūjā act of giving honor to a deity (*deva*); often performed to an icon through the giving of flowers, incense, fruit, etc. (see also: *pūjā*).

devaputra son of god or the gods; a title given to kings.

devī goddess (see also: *deva*).

dhamma Pāli word for *dharma.*

dhāraṇa focus or concentration; associated with yogic or meditative practice.

dharma that which upholds the universe; righteousness; law; proper way of acting; order as opposed to chaos; probably the term that most closely resembles the Western notion of "religion" (see also: *ṛta*).

d̲h̲immī (A) "protected" persons; according to Islamic teaching, *d̲h̲immī* are the non-Muslim members of an Islamic society who must pay tax (*jizyah*); in return, they are protected.

dhyāna concentration; meditation without objects.

digambara literally, "sky-clad"; refers to Jain ascetics.

dīkṣā **(diksha)** initiation.

duḥkha misfortune, suffering, unhappiness; the first of the Four Noble Truths of Buddhism is that life is characterized by *duḥkha.*

dvaita dualism (see also: *advaita*).

garbhagṛha **(garbha-griha)** womb-house; the area of the temple in which the icon resides.

g̲h̲azal (U) a Persian lyric poem; rarely of more than a dozen couplets and in the same meter.

gopura large entryways to South Indian temples, especially seen in temples built from the eleventh–twelfth centuries onward. (Tamil: *kōpuram.*)

gṛhastya **(griha-sta)** householder stage of life (see also: *brahmacārya, vānaprastha, samṇyāsi*).

gṛhya **(grih-ya)** "household"; type of ritual performed in one's home, often by a brahman priest.

guṇa quality; Sāṁkhya teaches that three strands (*sattva, rajas, tamas*) are the fundamental elements of which the universe is composed.

guru teacher; also *gurū* in Sikh context.

ḥadīth (A) commentaries on things said or deeds undertaken by the Prophet Muḥammad.

ḥajj (A) pilgrimage to Mecca; one of the Five Pillars of Islam is pilgrimage to Mecca, which should be done at least once during one's lifetime (also *ḥadj̲j̲*).

hiraṇyagarbha golden seed/womb; refers to the creation myth in which the sun appears to be rising out of the water as it reflects off the water at dawn, as if the water were a golden seed/womb.

hoama (AV) also *homa*; name of a plant with medicinal and spiritual properties; also refers to the name of the spiritual being presiding over the *hoama* plant.

hotṛ **(hotri)** Vedic priest who pours libations into the sacrificial fire and chants hymns from the *Ṛg Veda*; literally, "one who offers sacrifice."

huzūr (P) "sacral presence" of Allāh in the courts of the Islamic sultanates.

'īd (A) "festival" or "day."

'īd al aḍḥā (A) "festival of the sacrifice"; commemorates the day on which the Prophet Ibrahim tried to fulfill Allāh's command to sacrifice his son Ishmael, but was prevented from doing so by an angel.

'īd al fiṭr (A) "festival of the breaking of the fast." It is a time of celebration and rejoicing for it officially brings the observance of fasting during Ramaḍān to a close.

ijmā' **(A)** consensus of legal scholars regarding a particular moral or ethical issue, it is one of the four sources of Sunnī Muslim jurisprudence (also *īdjmā'*).

imām (A) individual interpreter of the Qur'an, especially in Shīite Islam; often the imām is both a religious and political figure.

īśvara **(ishvara)** lord; a personal deity found in some forms of *yoga*.

itihāsa history; literally, "thus it was"; the *Mahābhārata* is referred to as *itihāsa* literature.

jamrat (A) the three stone pillars which symbolically represent the locations where the devil attempted to tempt the Prophet Ibrahim away from the path of Allāh; pilgrims symbolically stone these pillars.

jihād (A) "striving" to carry out the will of Allāh.

jīva life-entities, associated with Jainism (see also: *ajīva*).

jizyah (A) the tax paid by non-Muslims (*ḏhimmīs*) in exchange for protection.

jñāna knowledge, wisdom; one of the principal means of ascertaining how one ought to live in order to live in accordance with *dharma*; a means of attaining *mokṣa* (see also: *dharma, mokṣa*).

ka'ba (A) sacred stone that is in the center of the Grand Mosque of Mecca, toward which Muslims face in prayer and to which they make pilgrimage.

kaliyuga the last of the four cyclical time periods in Hindu cosmology.

kāma aesthetics; life of culture, e.g., literature, arts; love (i.e., *Kamasūtra*); one of the four goals/aims of humankind (*puruṣārthas*).

karma action; especially important in Buddhism, Jainism, and other ethical, action-oriented systems.

kathak North Indian style of classical dance, characterized by rhythmic footwork.

kevalajñāna in Jainism, knowledge isolated from karmic obstruction; infinite knowledge; omniscience; knowledge involving awareness of every existent thing in all its qualities and modes.

kṣatriya warrior class, previously known as *rajanyas*; second of four-fold class scheme (see also: *brahman, vaiśya, śūdra*).

lakṣārcana praising by 1,000 names; a type of ritual performed to temple icons.

langar communal kitchen in Sikhism.

laya yoga ethical *yoga.*

līlā literally, "play"; the view espoused by *Nāṭyaśāstra,* a text which elaborates upon aesthetics, that is, drama, music, art; associated generally with Kṛṣṇa, particularly in his childhood, and his playful mischievousness; the world is seen as a "play" that one enters into joyfully.

liṅga aniconic representation of the deity Śiva; literally, "mark" or "auspicious mark."

mahākāvya type of poetry; literally, "great poem."

mahārāja great king.

manas mind; in its widest sense, mind as the seat of intellectual operations and of emotions.

maṇḍala circle, cycle; in literature, refers to cycles or chapters of a particular work; also, used in meditation practice as a visual aid.

maṇḍapa part of the Hindu temple; pavilion. (Tamil: *maṇṭapam.*)

mantra syllable, word, or group of words which have some special significance, often sacred in nature; used in meditation, chanting, and temple ritual.

mārga path; a particular means or way by which one lives a "religious" life, or a path leading to release or liberation (*mokṣa*); for Buddhists, the Eightfold Path that leads to the cessation (*nirodha*) of suffering (*duḥkha*).

mastābhiṣekam **(mast-abhi-shekam)** head anointing ceremony (see *abhiṣeka*).

maṭha monastery or solitary hut of an ascetic or student. (Tamil: *maṭam.*)

mātsya nyāya literally, the "law of the fishes"; since big fish swallow smaller fish, powerful rulers will "swallow" weak rulers.

māyā the measured world; illusion.

mleccha **(mlekkh-a)** foreigner or barbarian.

mokṣa "liberation" or "release" from the vicissitudes of dharmic existence, for example; the goal of a religious path; one of the four *puruṣārthas* or "goals" of the human (see also: *kāma, artha, dharma*).

mudrā specific hand pose, each with a different meaning; used in art, dance, and iconography.

mūlamantra "primal insight"; usually given to a disciple by a *guru.*

muzuri (A) an Islamic emperor who is perceived to be a representative of Allāh.

nakṣatra constellation; twenty-seven through which the moon passes each month.

nāma name; *nāma* and *rūpa,* together, designate an entity that has "name and form," as opposed to merely an abstract or conceptual existence.

namāz (U) Urdū for *ṣalāt,* the Islamic canonical prayer. The means given by Allāh for mankind to make contact with him. It is a worship of the whole person; heart, mind, tongue, and body. It is the second of the Five Pillars of Islam.

nāstika atheist, or non-believer (see also: *āstika*).

nirguṇa without qualities or form; deities tend to be worshiped either as having qualities (see also: *saguṇa*) or not having qualities, i.e., spirit.

nirodha cessation (of *duḥkha*), which is the third of the Four Noble Truths; also, according to Yoga philosophy, the "cessation/suppression of the transformations of awareness" is *yoga.*

nirvāṇa literally, the "blowing out" of the "flame" of existence, as in a candle; the goal of early forms of Buddhism; the cessation of thirst; a change in consciousness, not a place. (Pāli: *nibbāna.*)

niyama "commission"; appropriate actions, according to ethical yoga (*laya*); (see also *yama*).

oṃ Sanskrit sacred syllable which becomes, among other things, equated with the totality of the universe.

pāca (T) The "bonds" of existence, according to Śaiva Siddhānta thought (see also: *āṇava, māyā, karma, and pacu*).

pacu (T) "soul" or "cow"; takes the form to which it adheres; Śaiva Siddhānta term (see also: *pāca*).

pakśa **(paksha)** fifteen days.

Pāli language of early Buddhist canon; actually, the designation of the corpus of early Buddhist literature, which later became the name of the language in which that corpus was written.

panthā "path" (see also: *mārga*).

paramātman the "One"; supreme *ātman*, emphasized by Śaṅkara.

pati lord; also, husband.

pīr folk hero in some sects of Shīite Islam; *pīrs* are worshiped at cemeteries after death.

pitṛloka **(pitri loka)** heaven; literally, "world of the fathers" in *Vedas.*

prajñā **(prajana)** "wisdom" or "perfection"; especially important in Mahāyāna schools of Buddhism; in Yogacāra philosophy, the ten perfections become personified.

prakāra "world"; concrete manifestation of *brahman.*

prakṛti **(prakriti)** original, natural form or condition; matter, female (see also: *puruṣa*).

prāṇapratiṣṭhā consecration of an icon; literally, breathing life into an icon.

prāṇayama breath control; literally "suspension of breath."

prapatti surrender (as to a deity).

prasāda favor or grace; symbolized by the offering of camphor, food, etc. to devotees after such items have been "blessed" by the deity.

pratītya-samutpāda chain of dependent causation or co-arising in early Buddhism.

pratyāhāra control of the senses; sense perceptions of the world, which tend to cause illusory images of reality.

pucca literally, ripe or complete.

pudgala person; notion posed by the Vātsiputrīya Buddhists as being similar to, but not the same as, *skandhas.*

pūjā honor, respect, or hospitality given to a deity, *guru,* king, or icon; the ritual activity of offering honor.

pūjāri priest; in Jainism, temple "servant."

puṟam (T) Tamil poetic orientation that refers to city life and the social order (see also: *akam*).

purāṇa literary form, primarily mythological texts retelling the activities or lives of the gods.

purdah (A) veiling or covering of Islamic women in public; a symbol of "purity."

puruṣa man, male, spirit (see also: *prakṛti*).

rāga "tune"; color; redness; passion, vehement desire, love, affection.

rājanya "kings" who later became *kṣatriyas.*

rājarāja "king of kings."

rajas one of three strands/qualities of which the universe is comprised (see also: *sattva, tamas*).

rājasūya ritual coronation of a king.

rāja yoga the "king" of yogas, it is concerned directly with the mind.

rasa flavor, taste, or essence; become "moods" through which the body can become congruent with the cosmos, i.e., through the arts.

ṛta **(rita)** "cosmic order"; in the *Vedas,* it is the god Varuṇa who maintains *ṛta;* (see also: *dharma*).

rūpa form or beauty.

śabda **(shabda)** sound, word, voice, or noise; also a philosophical means of knowing through inner-understanding taught by Śaṅkara.

saguṇa with qualities/form/attributes.

śakta **(shakta)** follower of *śakti* cult.

śakti **(shakti)** power, ability; female active energy of a deity.

samādhi trance; highest level of concentration in yoga; in Jainism, "release" which occurs when the *jīvas* predominate over *ajīvas.*

sāman "conciliation" or "appeasement"; strategy of *artha.*

Sāṁkhya number or enumeration by categories; a way of wisdom, according to the *Gītā;* name of a philosophical school of yoga.

samṇyāsi **(sam-nyasi)** ascetic; final stage of the Four Stages of Life (*āśramas*).

samsāra eternal cyclicality of life processes; "flow" or "flux" of life; transmigration, perpetual succession of births, cycle of existence with all its sorrows.

saṁskāra "rite of passage" marked by ritual activity.

saṁskṛta **(sanskrit)** sacred language used by learned classes; language of sacred texts.

samudaya arising (of *duḥkha*), which is the second of the Four Noble Truths.

sanātana dharma "eternal dharma"; modern, indigenous term used for the Western concept of "religion."

sangat "brotherhood" in Sikhism; refers to the notion of equality.

sankīrtaṇa singing or chanting the name of the divine.

śāstra **(shastra)** texts which explain or elaborate upon particular topics.

sat-chit-ānanda being/truth-knowledge/intellect-bliss; the ultimate goal, i.e., knowing/being the truth brings about bliss; term often associated with Vedānta philosophies.

satī ideal woman/wife; later, the practice of widow burning on a funeral pyre.

sattva one of three strands/qualities (*guṇa*) of which the universe is comprised (see also: *rajas, tamas*).

satya truth.

savikalpa knowing the One, according to Śaṅkara.

sharī'a (A) the "law" of Islam in accord with the Qu'rān, *qiyās, sunna,* and *ijmā'.*

śikhara **(shikara)** part of Hindu temple architecture; literally, "pointed, peak, or pinnacle."

śilpa **(shilpa)** art of appearance; *Śilpaśāstras* are manuals describing just how to create, for example, iconography and temple architecture.

śivarātri literally, "the great night of Śiva," celebrated on the moonless night of the month of Phalguna (the fourteenth day in the dark half).

skandha "aggregates" or "bundles" of senses which constituted the person in early Buddhism.

śloka **(shloka)** verse; type of Sanskrit meter that is prevalent in epic literature, consisting of two lines of text, sixteen syllables each.

soma fire ritual of early Āryans; "intoxicating" drink that gives power; probably the sap of a plant.

śrāddha Hindu funeral ritual.

śrama **(shrama)** weariness, exercise, religious, or studious effort.

śramana **(shramana)** ascetic, renouncer; name usually applied only to non-Vedic ascetics, e.g., Buddhists and Jains.

śrauta **(shrauta)** public ritual.

śruti **(shruti)** "that which is heard"; refers to *Vedas,* as opposed to *smṛti* literature which is "remembered" and, therefore, not necessarily "revealed/heard."

sthāla purāṇa history of a temple or place, usually written from an insider's perspective. (Tamil: *tālapurāṇa*).

stūpa dome-like mound which is an aniconic representation of the Buddha.

śūdra member of the fourth or servile class.

sunna normative traditions regarding the words and actions of Muḥammad (see also *ḥadīth*).

śūnyatā **(shunyata)** emptiness, voidness; Mahāyāna Buddhist term, especially important in Nāgārjuna's philosophy.

sūtra compilation of aphorisms and/or couplets, often in poetic language; literally, "thread" or "string."

svabhāva having being or existence on one's own.

svarūpa having its own form.

svayambhu self-existent, independent, as an icon which appears of its own accord.

śvetāmbara **(shvet-ambara)** "white-clad" Jain ascetics (see also: *digambara*).

tālā meter or beat of music.

tālapurāna stories/myths about specific temples or places; especially developed during the twelfth to fifteenth centuries in South India.

tāli a saffron-dyed string placed around the neck as part of the wedding ritual.

tamas one of the three strands/qualities (*guṇas*) of which the universe is comprised (see also: *sattva, rajas*).

tantra name given to oral, then written, texts in which the human body is homologized to the cosmos; used for personal *bhakti.*

tantri an adherent of *tantra.*

tapas heat generated through ascetic practices; homologized to heat of the Vedic sacrificial fire and its messenger (Agni) to the gods.

taṭalai (T) "head and foot"; the activity in which a devotee places his/her head to the foot of a *guru*/deity.

tathāgata the "thus-gone-one" (namely, the Buddha).

tathāgatagarbha "the womb of the thus-gone-one"; Buddhist teaching that the essence of the Buddha lives on in all human beings.

tat tvam asi "that thou art"; saying in *Chāndogya Upaniṣad* that refers to the realization of one's *ātman* as being of the same essence as the cosmic *brahman.*

tejas majesty, glory, prestige.

tīkā argument/apologetic in which one viewpoint (*darśana*) is defended over and against another view.

tīrtha crossing place; sacred place.

tīrthaṅkara in Jainism, "one who has crossed the ford"; that is, one of twenty-four in a line of "heroes/leaders" who have "crossed over" from this world to one characterized by pure "jīvic" existence (see also: *jīva* and *ajīva*).

tithi lunar day.

tratāra "he who presides over all kings."

tṛṣṇā **(trishna)** "thirst" (for things which are actually impermanent, according to early Buddhism); fundamental human problem. (Pāli: *taṇhā.*)

turiya the perception of non-duality; the highest stage of consciousness, according to Śaṅkara's Vedānta.

udgatṛ name for priests and priestesses who sang/chanted hymns of the *Sāma Veda*

'ulamā' ***(A)*** scholars and/or clergy who are qualified to offer moral guidance to individuals and at times to Islamic society at large.

'urs (A) wedding or a joyous occasion signifying the meeting of two beings; in Sūfīsm, the passing of a saint, seen as the ultimate unification with God the Beloved; also, the anniversary of same.

vāc speech; also, name of a goddess.

vaidika orthodox; one who traces one's lineage to the Vedic period; of, or relating to, the *Vedas.*

vaiśya maintainers of the social order; third of four-fold class structure.

vānaprastha "seeker"; literally, "forest" or "going forth to the forest"; third of the Four Stages of Life (*āśramas*).

varṇa color or class, as in the four-fold class structure of *brahman, kṣatriya, vaiśya,* and *śūdra.*

varṇaśrama dharma system formulated by brahmans that describes one's "position" in society according to one's class (*varṇa*), life-stage (*āśrama*), and proper mode of acting (*dharma*).

vastra ritual dressing of an icon.

vāstupuruṣamaṇḍala a geometric design combining space and the human body, which is then placed horizontally onto the temple floor; symbolic of the homologization between the human body and the cosmos.

vidhi rules for ritual.

vihāra Buddhist monastery.

vimāṇa the "tower" in South Indian Hindu temple architecture.

vinaya rules; one of the "baskets" of the Buddhist *Tripiṭika* ("three baskets"), or Theravāda Buddhist canon, that elaborates rules for monastic life.

vīrya heroism; strength.

vrata penance in consequence of a vow.

vyavahāra the manifold, phenomenal world (emphasized by Rāmānujan).

yakṣa **(yaksha)** *yakṣī* attendant of the Buddha; dwarf-like figures found on entries to *stūpa* grounds.

yama restraint (e.g., non-stealing, celibacy); associated with ethical *yoga* (*laya*).

yantra a ritual map that is geographically expressed; a diagram for ritual/meditation.

yasna (AV) the Zoroastrian ritual invocation of fire; corresponds to the Hindu ritual of *yagna.*

yoga discipline; also, specific "schools of yoga" (e.g., *rājā, laya, haṭha, karma, sāṃkhya,* and classical).

yogin one who practices the discipline of *yoga.*

yuga a cycle of time; presently we are in the *kaliyuga,* the cycle of decline before the next cycle of creativity.

Notes

1 On Wearing Good Lenses

1 William Ward, *View of History, Literature, and Mythology of the Hindoos* (5th edn rev. 3, Madras: J. Higginbotham, 1863), p. xxix.
2 Cited by Milton Singer, *When a Great Tradition Modernizes* (New York: Praeger, 1972), p. 17.
3 Ibid.: 18.
4 cf. J. W. McCrindle, *Ancient India as Described in Classical Literature* (Westminster: Archibald Constable, 1901).
5 Walt Whitman, "A Passage to India" in Emory Holloway, ed., *Walt Whitman: Complete Poetry and Selected Prose and Letters* (London: The None-Such Press, 1938), pp. 372–81.
6 Cited by Singer, *op. cit.*, p. 26.
7 *The Laws of Manu*, Tr. Wendy Doniger and Brian K. Smith (New York: Penguin, 1991), pp. xx–xx1.
8 Cited by Singer, *op. cit.*, p. 28.
9 Edward Conze, *Buddhism: Its Essence and Development* (London: Oxford University Press, 1951), pp. 20–22, 40, *et al.*; p. 53; pp. 23, 24, *et al.*
10 *Al-Bīrūnī's India: An Account of the Religion, Philosophy, Literature, Geography, Chronology, Astronomy, Customs, Laws and Astrology of India about AD 1030*, Tr. Edward Sachau (London: K. Paul, Trench, Trubner & Co., 1910), pp. 24, 28.
11 Ibid.: 110.
12 J. N. Farquhar, *The Crown of Hinduism* (London: Oxford University Press, 1913); Raimundo Panikkar, *The Unknown Christ of Hinduism* (Mary Knoll, NY: Orbis Books, 1981).
13 H. Oldenberg, *Das Mahābhārata* (Göttingen: Vandenhoeck and Ruprecht, 1922).
14 Mircen Eliade, *Cosmos and History* (Princeton: Princeton University Press, 1971 [1954]).
15 Frits Staal, "The Meaninglessness of Ritual" in Ronald Grimes, ed., *Readings in Ritual Studies* (Upper Saddle River, NJ: Prentice Hall, 1996), pp. 483–94.
16 Caroline Humphrey and James Laidlaw, *The Archetypal Actions of Ritual* (Oxford: Clarendon Press, 1994), Chapter 4.
17 Arjun Appadurai, "Kings, Sects and Temples in South India, 1350–1700 AD" in Burton Stein, ed., *South Indian Temples* (Delhi: Vikas Publishing House, 1978), pp. 47–74.

18 Max Weber, *Religion in India* (Glencoe, IL: Free Press, 1958).
19 Peter Berger, *The Sacred Canopy* (Garden City, NJ: Anchor Books, 1969).
20 Rudolph Otto, *The Idea of the Holy*, Tr. J. W. Harvey (New York: Oxford University Press, 1958).
21 Clifford Geertz, "Religion as a Cultural System" in W. A. Lessa and E. Z. Vogt, eds, *Reader in Comparative Religion* (4th edn, New York: Harper and Row, 1979).
22 Otto, *op. cit.*, p. 42f.

2 Sources of Indian Religion

1 M. L. K. Murty, "The God Narasimha in the Folk Religion of Andhra Pradesh, South India" in *Journal of the Society for South Asian Studies.* Vol. 13 (1987), pp. 179–88.
2 See, for example, H. D. Sankalia, *Prehistory and Protohistory of India and Pakistan* (Bombay: University of Bombay Press, 1962), pp. 152–53.
3 F. R. Allchin, *Neolithic Cattlekeepers of South India* (Cambridge: Cambridge University Press, 1963).
4 Katheryn Linduff in conversation.
5 N. R. Banerjee, *The Iron Age in India* (Delhi: Munshiram Manoharlal, 1965), pp. 55ff.
6 Kenneth A. R. Kennedy, "A Reassessment of the Theories of Racial Origins of the People of the Indus Valley Civilization from Recent Anthropological Data" in K. A. R. Kennedy and G. L. Possehl, eds, *Studies in the Archeology and Paleoanthropology of South Asia* (New Delhi: American Institute of Indian Studies, 1984), pp. 99–107 and Katheryn Linduff in conversation.
7 Katheryn Linduff in conversation.
8 This interpretation of Indus Valley religion is summarized in A. Hiltebeitel and T. Hopkins, "Indus Valley Religion" in M. Eliade, ed., *Encyclopedia of Religion* (New York: Macmillan, 1986), Vol. VII, pp. 215–23.
9 See Irene Winter, "Idols of the King: Royal Images as Recipients of Ritual Action in Ancient Mesopotamia" in *Journal of Ritual Studies.* Vol. 6, No. 1 (Winter, 1992), pp. 13–42.
10 D. P. Agrawal, "The Harappan Legacy: Break and Continuity" in Kennedy and Possehl, 1984, p. 443.
11 See, for example, Ann Feldhaus, *Water and Womanhood* (New York: Oxford University Press, 1995) and David Shulman, *Tamil Temple Myths* (Princeton: Princeton University Press, 1980).
12 A. L. Basham, *The Origins and Development of Classical Hinduism* (New York: Oxford University Press, 1991), pp. 43–44.
13 Georges Dumezil, *The Destiny of a Warrior*, Tr. Alf Hiltebeitel (Chicago: University of Chicago Press, 1970).
14 These positions are summarized in full in Edwin Bryant, *The Quest for the Origins of Vedic Culture: The Indo-Aryan Migration Debate* (Oxford and New York: Oxford University Press, 2001).
15 S. Jamison, *Sacrificed Wife, Sacrificer's Wife: Women, Ritual and Hospitality in Ancient India* (Oxford: Oxford University Press, 1996), pp. 30–31.
16 Brian K. Smith, *Classifying the Universe* (Oxford: Oxford University Press, 1994), pp. 14 and 26ff.

17 Ibid.: 15.
18 Ibid.: 26ff.
19 These rituals are described at length in the scholarly literature. See, especially, J. C. Heesterman, *The Ancient Indian Royal Consecration* (The Hague: Mouton, 1987) for discussion of the *rājasūya* and S. Jamison, *op. cit.*, pp. 65–88 for description of the horse sacrifice.
20 See David Knipe, *In the Image of Fire* (Delhi: Motilal Banarsidass, 1975).
21 P. Olivelle, Tr., *The Upaniṣads* (Oxford: Oxford University Press, 1996), p. xlvi.
22 D. Knipe, "*Sapiṇḍikarana*: The Hindu Rite of Entry into Heaven" in Reynolds and Waugh, eds, *Religious Encounters with Death: Insights from the History and Anthropology of Religion* (University Park, PA: Penn State University Press, 1976), pp. 111–24.
23 *Ṛg Veda* 10.90 as cited by Ainslee Embree, ed., *Sources of Indian Tradition* (New York: Columbia University Press, 1988), pp. 89–90.
24 For the dating of these texts, I follow the suggestions of R. S. Sharma, *History of Pancala* (New Delhi: Munshiram Manoharlal, 1983) pp. 3–4; Romila Thapar, *Ancient Indian Social History: Some Interpretations* (New Delhi: Orient Longman, 1978), pp. 42–55; and Aloka Parasher Sen, *Mlecchas in Early India. A Study in Attitudes towards Outsiders up to AD 600* (New Delhi: Munshiram Manoharlal, 1991), p. 287.
25 Basham, *op. cit.*, p. 28.

3 The Early Urban Period

1 P. Olivelle, Tr., *Saṃnāyasa Upaniṣads* (Oxford: Oxford University Press, 1992), pp. 29–32, citing A. Ghosh, *The City in Early Historical India* (Simla: Indian Institute of Advanced Study, 1973) and R. Gombrich, *Theravāda Buddhism* (London: Routledge & Kegan Paul, 1988).
2 Cited by R. S. Sharma, *Material Culture and Social Formations in Ancient India* (Delhi: Macmillan, 1983), p. 76.
3 That the term *bandhu*, "connections" or secret doctrine, is the core meaning of the term *Upaniṣad* is the conclusion of Patrick Olivelle, following Renou (Louis Renou, "Connexion et Védique, 'cause' en Bouddhique" in Dr. C. Kunhan Raja, *Presentation Volume* (Madras: Adyar Library, 1946), Falk (H. Falk, "Vedisch Upaniṣad" in *Zeitschrift der Deutschen Morganländischen Gesselschaft*. Vol. 136 (1986), pp. 80–97), Jaroslav Vacek, and others. This connotation has come to replace an earlier notion posited by Deutsch and others that *Upaniṣad* had to do with "sitting at the feet of perfection" (P. Olivelle, Tr., *The Upaniṣads* (Oxford: Oxford University Press, 1996), p. liii.
4 Olivelle, 1996, pp. xxxix, 41.
5 Ibid.: 1.
6 Ibid.: xxix.
7 Patrick Olivelle, 1998. *The Upaniṣads* (Oxford World's Classics reissue of 1996 edn), translating *Chāndogya Upaniṣad* VI. 14. 11–13, pp. 154–55. Reprinted by permission of Oxford University Press.
8 Ibid.: 274, Olivelle translating *Muṇḍaka Upaniṣad*, 3.1. 1, 2. Reprinted by permission of Oxford University Press.

9 Ibid.: 155, Olivelle translating *Chāndogya Upaniṣad,* VI.14. 14. Reprinted by permission of Oxford University Press.
10 Richard J. Cohen in conversation.
11 Padmanabha Jaini, *The Jaina Path of Purification* (Berkeley: University of California Press, 1979), p. 37. Prof. Jaini suggests the numbers offered in the Jaini texts are gross exaggerations; namely, 14,000 monks; 36,000 nuns; 159,000 laymen, and 318,000 laywomen.
12 Richard J. Cohen in conversation. Cohen suggests the contemporary term "*sheth,*" generally referring to bankers and sometimes associated with lay Jains may have derived from this early designation of the "perfect one" (*śreṣṭin*).
13 Padmanabha Jaini in conversation.
14 This summation is found in Ainslie Embree, ed., *Sources of Indian Tradition,* Vol. I (New York: Columbia University Press, 1988), pp. 76–78.
15 Romila Thapar, *Ancient Indian Social History. Some Interpretations* (New Delhi: Orient Longman, 1978), p. 64.
16 C. A. F. Rhys Davids and K. R. Norman, Trs., eds, *Poems of Early Buddhist Nuns* (Oxford: Pali Text Society, 1989), pp. 88–91.
17 Ainslie Embree, *op. cit.*, p. 108, citing V. Trenckner, ed., *Milindapañha* (London: Williams and Norgate, 1880), p. 715.
18 The previous discussion is condensed from that in R. H. Robinson and W. Y. Johnson, *The Buddhist Religion* (Belmont, CA: Wadsworth, 1996), pp. 58ff.
19 Romila Thapar, *A History of India* (Baltimore: Penguin, 1966), p. 66.
20 T. O. Ling, *A Dictionary of Buddhism* (New York: Charles Scribners, 1972), p. 213 citing the report of a Chinese pilgrim, Hsuan Tsang, in the seventh century CE.

4 The Urban Period

1 N. Q. Pankal, *State and Religion in Ancient India* (Allahabad: Chugh Publications, 1983), p. 103.
2 Romila Thapar, *A History of India.* I (London: Penguin Books, 1966), pp. 59 *et al.*
3 A. L. Basham, *The Wonder that was India* (New York: Grove Press, 1959), p. 60. Basham's book remains a classic for its discussion of this period.
4 Ibid.: 87.
5 Fred W. Clothey, *The Many Faces of Murukan* (The Hague: Mouton, 1978), pp. 57ff.
6 Doris Srinivasan, "Vaiṣṇava Art and Iconography at Mathurā" in D. M. Srinivasan, ed., *Mathurā: The Cultural Heritage* (Delhi: American Institute of Indian Studies, 1989), pp. 388ff., *et al.*
7 Alf Hiltebeitel, "Kṛṣṇa at Mathurā" in Srinivasan, ed., *op. cit.*, p. 98. See also Hiltebeitel's "Kṛṣṇa in the *Mahābhārata.* A Bibliographical Study" in *Annals of the Bhandarkar Oriental Research Institute.* Vol. LXI (1979), pp. 65–107.
8 Clothey, 1978, pp. 160ff.
9 Arthur Anthony Macdonnell, *A Practical Sanskrit Dictionary* (London: Oxford University Press, 1969).
10 Percy Brown, *Indian Architecture (Buddhist and Hindu Periods)* (Bombay: D. B. Taraporevala Sms & Co., 1965), plate XII.
11 Ibid.: plate XVIII.

12 For fuller discussion of these rites of passage, see R. Pandey, *Hindu Saṁskāras* (Delhi: Motilal Banarsidass, 1969).
13 See the discussion, for example, by Vasudha Narayanan in "The Hindu Tradition" in W. Oxtoby, ed., *World Religions: Eastern Religions* (New York: Oxford University Press, 2002), pp. 94–104.
14 Ibid.: 98.
15 Ibid.
16 Basham, *op. cit.*, p. 166.
17 Ibid.: 167.
18 Ibid.: 168.
19 Clothey, *op. cit.*, p. 35.
20 Thapar, *op. cit.*, p. 152.
21 George Kliger, ed., "Bharata Nāṭyam: History, Cultural Heritage and Current Practice" in G. Kliger, ed., *Bharata Nāṭyam in Cultural Perspective* (New Delhi: Manohar, 1993), p. 5.
22 David Kopf, "Dancing 'Virgin,' Sexual Slave, Divine Courtesan in Celestial Dances: In Search of the Historic Devadāsī" in Kliger, ed., 1993, p. 172.
23 Ibid.: 172.
24 Kliger, *op. cit.*, p. 5.
25 Kopf, *op. cit.*, p. 172.
26 *Śatapatha Brāhmaṇa* 6.6.3.11, as cited and translated in W. Doniger and B. Smith, Trs. *The Laws of Manu* (London: Penguin Books, 1991), p. xxvi.
27 Narayanan, 2001, pp. 84ff.
28 For more extended discussion of yoga, see M. Eliade, *Yoga: Immortality and Freedom* (Princeton: Princeton University Press, 1973).
29 See Robert Goldman, general ed., *The Rāmāyaṇa of Valmiki: An Epic of Ancient India* (Princeton: Princeton University Press, 1984) for an introduction and translation of the epic.
30 A. K. Ramanujan, "Three Hundred *Rāmāyaṇas*" (paper delivered at a conference in February, 1987), pp. 14ff. This paper was eventually published in Paula Richman, ed., *Many Rāmāyaṇas: The Diversity of a Narrative Tradition South Asia* (Delhi: Oxford University Press, 1991).
31 Ramanujan, 1987, p. 19.
32 Basham, *op. cit.*, p. 417.
33 Cited by Thomas Coburn, *Encountering the Goddess* (Albany: State University of New York Press, 1991), p. 17.
34 Adya Rangacarya, Tr., *Nāṭyasāstra* (Bangalore: Ibh Prakashara, nd.), chapter VII.
35 Basham, *op. cit.*, p. 417.
36 Ibid.
37 Ibid.: 385.
38 Ibid. 383.
39 Rangacarya, *op. cit.*, p. xi.
40 P. V. Kane, *History of the Dharmaśāstras.* Vol. V. (Poona: Bhandarkar Oriental Research Institute, 1930–62), p. 186. Kane speculated that this practice had started by at least the fourth century CE.
41 Basham, *op. cit.*, p. 336; Kane, *op. cit.*, p. 165.
42 Derek O. Codrick, "Buffalo" in Margaret A. Mills, Peter Claus, and Sarah Diamond, eds, *South Asian Folklore: An Encyclopedia* (New York and London: Routledge, 2003), p. 85.
43 Vasudha Narayanan, "*Navarātri*" in Mills *et al.*, *op. cit.*, p. 443.

44 Kane, *op. cit.*, pp. 164–65, citing the *Kālikapurāṇa*'s references to these practices.
45 Basham, *op. cit.*, p. 316.
46 Clothey, *op. cit.*, p. 34.
47 Basham, *op. cit.*, p. 319.
48 Ibid.
49 Clothey, *op. cit.*, p. 52.
50 See descriptions in the early Tamil literature as cited by Clothey, *op. cit.*, pp. 26f.
51 John D. Smith, "*Mahābhārata*" in Mills, *et al.*, *op. cit.*, p. 366.
52 Alf Hiltebeitel, "Draupadī" in Mills *et al.*, p. 166.
53 Basham, *op. cit.*, p. 264.
54 R. Robinson and W. Johnson, *The Buddhist Religion* (Belmont, CA: Dickenson Publishing Co., 1977), p. 83.
55 Ibid.: 95.
56 These are the dates suggested by Aloka Parasher Sen, pp. 289–90.

5 The Post-classical Period

1 For fuller description of the period, see A. K. Ramanujan, *The Interior Landscape* (Bloomington, Indiana: Indiana University Press, 1969).
2 Ibid.: "Afterword".
3 Burton Stein, *Peasant State and Society in Medieval South India* (Delhi: Oxford University Press, 1980), pp. 83ff.
4 A. K. Ramanujan, *Hymns for the Drowning* (New York: Penguin Books, 1993), p. 108, translating Nammāḻvār 7.4.1. Ramanujan offers a useful discussion of the *bhakti* experience.
5 Ramanujan, 1993, p. 117.
6 Ramanujan, 1993, p. 169, translating Nammāḻvār 7.9.1.
7 Ramanujan, 1993, pp. 118–19, translating *Tiruvācakam* IV. 59–70.
8 Arjun Appadurai, "Kings, Sects and Temples in South India, 1350–1700 AD" in B. Stein, ed., *South Indian Temples* (New Delhi: Vikas Publishing House, 1978), pp. 52ff.
9 Paul Younger, *The Home of Dancing Śivan* (New York: Oxford University Press, 1995), p. 74.
10 Ibid.: 181.
11 For further discussion of these *tālapurāṇas*, see David Shulman, *Tamil Temple Myths: Sacrifice and Divine Marriage in the South Indian Śaiva Tradition* (Princeton: Princeton University Press, 1980).
12 R. Nagaraj of the Folk Studies Center of the University of Hyderabad in conversation.
13 Shulman, 1980, pp. 158ff.
14 A. K. Ramanujan, *Speaking of Śiva* (Harmondsworth: Penguin Books, 1973).
15 A. L. Basham, *The Wonder that was India* (New York: Grove Press), p. 314.
16 Based on conversations with several scholars of Kerala's history.
17 For fuller discussion of the history of Śāstā, see F. W. Clothey, "Śāstā-Aiyaṉār-Aiyyappaṉ" in Clothey, ed., *Images of Man* (Madras: New Era Publications, 1982), pp. 34–71.
18 For further discussion, see V. A. Devasenapati, *Of Human Bondage and Divine Grace* (Annamalai: Annamalai University Press, 1963).

19 For a succinct summation of Advaitin thought, see Karl Potter, *Encyclopedia of Indian Philosophies*. Vol. III. *Advaita Vedānta up to Śaṃkara and His Pupils* (New Delhi: Motilal Banarsidass, 1981), pp. 6–7.
20 Ibid.: 103.
21 Rāmānuja's thought is explored more deeply in J. Carman, *The Theology of Rāmānujan* (New Haven, CT: Yale University Press, 1974).
22 Basham, *op. cit.*, pp. 162–63.
23 Romila Thapar, *A History of India*. I (Baltimore: Penguin Books, 1966), p. 142.
24 Ibid.: 253ff.
25 Herman Kulke, *Kings and Cults: State Formations and Legitimation in India and Southeast Asia* (Delhi: Manohar, 1993), pp. 93ff.
26 Wayne Begley, "Hindu Temple" in Joe Elder, ed., *Lectures in Indian Civilization* (Dubuque, IA: Kendall Hunt Publishing, 1970), p. 120.
27 Aloka Parasher Sen in conversation.
28 Klaus Klostermaier, in *A Survey of Hinduism* (Albany: SUNY Press, 1994), pp. 285–86, summarizes this complex system.
29 Romila Thapar, *Ancient Indian Social History: Some Interpretations* (New Delhi: Orient Longman, 1978), p. 77.
30 This is the suggestion of David Kinsley in *The Sword and the Flute: Kālī and Kṛṣṇa: Dark Visions of the Terrible and Sublime in Hindu Mythology* (Berkeley: University of California Press, 1975).
31 See Thomas Coburn, *Devīmahātmya: The Crystallization of the Goddess Tradition* (Delhi: Motilal Banarsidass, 1984).
32 These are Norvin Hein's speculations in "Comments: Rādhā and Erotic Community" in J. Hawley and D. Wulff, eds, *The Divine Consort: Rādhā and the Goddesses of India* (Boston: Beacon Press, 1986), p. 121.
33 For fuller discussion of the Rādhā story see Hawley and Wulff, *op. cit.*
34 There is an extended literature on Kālī as well as Durgā. The reader may want to refer first to David Kinsley, *Hindu Goddesses: Visions of the Feminine in the Hindu Tradition* (Berkeley: University of California Press, 1986).
35 Padmanabha Jaini, "The Disappearance of Buddhism and the Survival of Jainism in India: A Contrast" in A. K. Narain, ed., *Studies in the History of Buddhism* (Delhi: B.R. Pub. Corp, 1980) p. 87, citing M. Govinda Pai "*Dharmasthalada Śiva-lingakke Mañjunātha emba lesara nege bantu?*" in *Samarpaṇe*, Felicitation Volume in Honour of Shri Manjayya Heggade (Mangalore, 1950), pp. 65–77.
36 Jaini, *op. cit.*, p. 86.
37 Ibid.: 84.
38 Ibid.: 85.
39 Ibid.: 90, n. 20.

6 The Coming of Islam

1 For a thorough discussion of the origins and development of Islam, see John L. Esposito, *Islam: The Straight Path* (New York: Oxford University Press, 1991); and Frederick M. Denny, *An Introduction to Islam* (New York: Macmillan, 1994).
2 Esposito, *op. cit.*, p. 109.

3 See Romila Thapar, *A History of India*. I (Baltimore: Penguin Books, 1966), pp. 229–34 for description of Mahmūd's campaigns.
4 Juan Campo in conversation.
5 Cited by Sheldon Pollock "Rāmāyana and Political Imagination in India" in *The Journal of Asian Studies*. Vol. 52 No.2 (May, 1993), p. 286.
6 Thapar, *op. cit.*, p. 238.
7 Ibid.: 274.
8 R. L. Hangloo in conversation.
9 Thapar, *op. cit.*, p. 282.
10 Robert E. Frykenberg, "Administrative System in Muslim India" in Joe Elder, ed., *Lectures in Indian Civilization* (Dubuque, IA: Kendall/Hunt Publishing Co., 1970), p. 138.
11 For a description of the Mughal period, see, for example, Stanley Wolpert, *A New History of India* (New York: Oxford University Press, 2000), chapters 9–12.
12 Frykenberg, *op. cit.*, p. 138.
13 Esposito, *op. cit.*, pp. 73–74.
14 Ibid.: 46.
15 For discussion of the Ahmadiyah movement, see Spencer Lavan, *The Ahmadiyah Movement: A History and Perspectives* (Delhi: Manohar, 1974).
16 John A. Williams, "Islamic Doctrine, Thought, Law" in Elder, *op. cit.*, p. 132.
17 Esposito, *op. cit.*, pp. 47–48.
18 Saiyid Athar Abbas Rizvi, *A History of Sufism in India* (New Delhi: Munshiram Manoharlal Publishers, 1986). Rizvi's two-volume work is an excellent treatment of Sūfīsm in India.
19 Ibid.: 32ff.
20 See, for example, R. L. Hangloo, "Sufism in Medieval Deccan: Politics and Worship." Presidential address for Andhra Pradesh History Congress (January, 2000).
21 R. L. Hangloo in conversation.
22 R. L. Hangloo, lecture (August, 1999).
23 Rizvi, *op. cit.*, pp. 322ff.

7 Developments in the Late Medieval Period

1 Sheldon Pollock, "Rāmāyana and Political Imagination in India" *The Journal of Asian Studies*. Vol. 52 No. 2 (May 1993), p. 286.
2 See Burton Stein, *Peasant State and Society in Medieval South India* (Delhi: Oxford University Press, 1980), pp. 266ff. for fuller discussion of the Vijayanagara dynasty.
3 A. K. Warder, "Classical Literature" in A. L. Basham, ed., *The Cultural History of India* (Oxford: Clarendon Press, 1975), p. 194.
4 Stein, *op. cit.*, pp. 366ff.
5 For fuller discussion of the Marāthās, see Stanley Wolpert, *A New History of India* (New York: Oxford University Press, 2000), pp. 170ff.
6 Yeshi Sel, "Problems in Recapturing Mīrābaī." Unpublished M.Phil. thesis. University of Hyderabad, History Department, 1996, p. 43.
7 Robert E. Frykenberg, "Administrative System in Muslim India" in Joe Elder,

ed., *Lectures in Indian Civilization* (Dubuque, IA: Kendall/Flint Publishing Co., 1970), p. 138.
8 Pollock, *op. cit.*, pp. 276–77.
9 Sanjay Subrahmanyam, "Before the Leviathan: Sectarian Violence and the State in Pre-Colonial India" in K. Basa and Subrahmanyam, *Unravelling the Nation: Sectarian Conflict and India's Secular Identity* (Baltimore: Penguin Books, 1996), pp. 52–53.
10 Ibid.: 62–64.
11 R. L. Hangloo, "Accepting Islam and Abandoning Hinduism: A Study of Proselytization Process in Medieval Kashmir" in *Islamic Culture.* Vol. LXXXI No. 1 (January, 1997), pp. 94–95.
12 Subrahmanyan, *op. cit.*, p. 51.
13 R. L. Hangloo, "Islam and the Cult of Bhakti" in Yusuf Husain, ed., *Glimpses of Medieval Indian Culture* (Bombay: Asia Publishing House, nd.), pp. 1–27.
14 J. T. F. Jordens, "Medieval Hindu Devotionalism" in A. L. Basham, 1975, p.26.
15 Ibid.: 265.
16 This was the observation of an anonymous reviewer of an earlier draft of this manuscript; however, Jordens, *op. cit.*, p. 368, suggested Jnāneśvara was the one who used the "form meant for *kīrtan* chanting."
17 Jordens, *op. cit.*, p. 269.
18 See Eleanor Zelliott "Medieval Encounters between Hindu and Muslim: Eknath's Drama-Poem *Hindu-Turk Saṃvād*" in F. W. Clothey, ed., *Images of Man: Religion and Historical Process in South Asia* (Madras: New Era Publications, 1982), pp. 171–95.
19 Jordens, *op. cit.*, p. 270.
20 I am indebted to Jeff Brackett in conversation for this interpretation of Rāmdās.
21 J. Brackett in conversation.
22 See C. Mackenzie Brown, "The Theology of Rādhā in the *Purānas*" in J. Hawley and D. Wulff, *The Divine Consort* (Boston: Beacon Press, 1986), pp. 57ff.
23 Jordens, *op. cit.*, p. 271.
24 Ibid.: 272.
25 Ibid.: 272–73.
26 Krishna Kripalani, "Medieval Indian Literature" in A. L. Basham, 1975, p. 306. These "Hindī" poet-saints are treated more extensively in J. Hawley and M. Juergensmeyer, *Songs of the Saints of India* (New York: Oxford University Press, 1988).
27 Jordens, *op. cit.*, p. 274.
28 Hawley and Juergensmeyer, translating *Kabingranthavali,* 174 and 191. *Songs of the Saints of India* (New York: Oxford University Press, 1988).
29 Jordens, *op. cit.*, p. 275.
30 Hawley and Juergensmeyer, *op. cit.*, translating *Surdāsji Ka,* 368.
31 Hawley and Juergensmeyer, *op. cit.*, pp. 16f.
32 Jordens, *op. cit.*, pp. 276f.
33 Hawley and Juergensmeyer, *op. cit.*, pp. 120ff.
34 See Fred W. Clothey, *Quiescence and Passion: the Vision of Aruṇakiri, Tamil Mystic* (Bethesda, MD: Austin and Winfield, 1996).
35 Kripalani, *op. cit.*, p. 306.
36 Ibid.
37 Ibid.: 307.

38 Frykenberg, *op. cit.*, p. 138.
39 See N. Jairazbhoy, "Music" in A.L. Basham, 1975, pp. 221–22.
40 I am indebted to Prof. R. L. Hangloo, Dept. of History of the University of Hyderabad and especially to his article, cited above (1997), pp. 91–111, for this discussion. A version of this article was eventually published as chapter two in his volume *The State in Medieval Kashmir* (New Delhi: Manohar, 2000).
41 Hangloo, 1997, p. 50.
42 Hawley and Juergensmeyer, *op. cit.*, pp. 70ff.
43 As translated by McLeod and cited by Ainslee T. Embree, *Sources of Indian Tradition.* Vol. 1. (New York: Columbia University Press, 1988), p. 505.
44 For extended discussion of the history of Sikhism, see Kushwant Singh, *A History of the Sikhs.* Two volumes (Delhi: Oxford University Press, 1977).
45 Ibid.: 54.
46 Ibid.: 60.
47 Ibid.: 83ff.
48 Ibid.: 168ff.
49 Ibid.: 49.

8 Streams from the "West" and their Aftermath

1 Romila Thapar, *A History of India.* I (Baltimore: Penguin Books, 1966), pp. 102ff.
2 This and subsequent discussion of "Cochin Jews" is derived in large measure from that of F. Thurston, *Castes and Tribes of Southern India.* Vol. II (Delhi: Asian Educational Services, 1993), pp. 460–88.
3 Adam Shear in conversation.
4 Thurston, *op. cit.*, p. 484.
5 These observations are the result of conversations with the author by members of the Bene Israel community.
6 This and subsequent discussion of Syrian Christians is derived from Julius Richter, *A History of Missions in India* (New York: Fleming H. Revell, 1908), pp. 33ff. and from Thurston, *op. cit.*, VI, pp. 408ff.
7 Thurston, *op. cit.*, pp. 415ff.
8 Ibid.: 427.
9 Mary Boyce, *Zoroastrians, their Religious Beliefs and Practices* (London: Routledge & Kegan Paul, 1979), p. 11. I am indebted to Boyce's book for much of this discussion on Zoroastrianism.
10 Ibid.: 166.
11 Much of this discussion on Pārsīs in Mumbai is derived from *A Guide to the Zoroastrian Religion: A Nineteenth Century Catechism with Modern Commentary.* Eds and Trs. by F. M. Katwal and J. W. Boyd (Chico, CA: Scholars Press, 1982), pp. xi–xiv.
12 On the Portuguese in India, see, for example, J. B. Harrison, "The Portuguese" in A. L. Basham, ed., *A Cultural History of India* (Oxford: Clarendon Press, 1975), pp. 337–47.
13 See Bror Tiliander, *Christian and Hindu Terminology: A Study of their Mutual Relations with Special Reference to the Tamil Area* (Uppsala: Almquist and Wiksell Tryckeri, 1974).

14 See V. A. Cronin, *A Pearl to India: the Life of Robert de Nobili* (London: Darton, Longman and Todd, 1966).
15 Richter, *op. cit.*, pp. 52–54.
16 Stanley Wolpert, *A New History of India* (New York: Oxford University Press, 2000), pp. 175f.
17 See E. Arno Lehman, *It Began at Tranquebar*, Tr. S. G. Lang and H. W. Gensicher (Madras: Christian Literature Society, 1956).
18 For fuller discussion of the British period in India, see Percival Spear, *A History of India*. II (London: Penguin Books, 1990) or Stanley Wolpert, *op. cit.*, pp. 187–249.
19 Wolpert, *op. cit.*, p. 188.
20 Ibid.: 193.
21 Anil Seal, "Europe's Changing View of India" in Joseph Elder, ed., *Lectures in Indian Civilization* (Dubuque, IA: Kendall/Hunt Publishing Co., 1970), p. 154.
22 This is summarized from Wolpert, *op. cit.*, pp. 168ff.
23 W. Theodore Dubary *et al.*, eds, *Sources of Indian Tradition* (New York: Columbia University Press, 1966), pp. 565f.
24 For extended discussion of the Indian intellectual climate in the nineteenth and twentieth centuries, see Stephen N. Hay, *Sources of Indian Tradition*. Vol. II (New York: Columbia University Press, 1988).
25 Hay, 1988, pp. 44–51.
26 Hay, 1988, pp. 52–61.
27 Hay, 1988, pp. 87–96.
28 Hay, 1988, pp. 102–12.
29 Hay, 1988, pp. 113–19.
30 Hay, 1988, p. 140.
31 Wolpert, *op. cit.*, p. 260.
32 Hay, 1988, pp. 130–39.
33 Hay, 1988, pp. 62–71.
34 Hay, 1988, pp. 72–83.
35 Madhu Wangu, *A Goddess is Born: the Emergence of Khır Bhavani in Kashmir* (Wexford, PA: Stark Publishers, 2002), p. 208.
36 Jason Fuller in conversation.
37 From a story told the author by an anonymous villager.
38 See Stephen N. Hay, "Muslim Intelligentsia in the 18th and 19th Centuries" in Joseph W. Elder, *op. cit.*, pp. 206–07.
39 Hay, 1970, p. 206.
40 Hay, 1988, pp. 180–94.
41 Hay, 1970, pp. 206–07.
42 Spencer Lavan, *The Ahmadiyah Movement: A History and Perspectives* (Delhi: Manohar, 1974), pp. 35ff.
43 This discussion is derived from Jan Platvoet, "Ritual as Confrontation: The Ayodhya Conflict" in Jan Platvoet and Karel van der Toork, eds, *Pluralism and Identity: Studies in Ritual Behavior* (Leider: E. J. Brill, 1995), pp. 196–200.
44 Hay, 1988, p. 175.
45 Ibid.: 195–200.
46 Ibid.: 205–21.
47 This discussion is derived largely from Vijaya Gupchup, *Bombay, Social Change 1793–1857* (Bombay: Manmohan Bhatkal, 1993), pp. 122ff.

48 Richard Fox Young, *Resistant Hinduism* (Vienna: E. J. Brill, 1981), pp. 25ff.
49 Ibid.: 49ff.
50 S. J. Samartha, *The Hindu Response to the Unbound Christ* (Madras: Christian Literature Society, 1974), pp. 128ff.
51 Geoff Oddie, "Anti-Missionary Feeling and Hindu Revivalism in Madras. The Hindu Preaching and Tract Societies, c. 1886–1891" in F. W. Clothey, ed., *Images of Man: Religion and Historical Process in South Asia* (Madras: New Era Publications, 1982), pp. 217ff.
52 Samartha, *op. cit.*, pp. 49ff.
53 There are many books on Gandhi, but a concise summary of his life and work can be found in Hay, 1988, pp. 248–74.
54 These are Hay's terms, 1988, p. 227.
55 Hay, 1988, p. 227, citing Tagore's *Gitāñjalī*, translation in A. Chakravarty, *A Tagore Reader* (Boston: Beacon Press, 1961), p. 300.
56 Hay, 1988, p. 155, citing Aurobindo, *Letters on Yoga*, in *Sri Aurobindo Birth Centenary Library*. Vol. 24, p. 57.
57 Once again, Hay, 1988, pp. 288–95, provides a succinct discussion of Savarkar's life and works. I am indebted to Hay's reader for these brief encapsulations.

9 Religion in Contemporary India

1 Stephen N. Hay, ed., *Sources of Indian Tradition*. Vol. 2 (New York: Columbia University Press, 1988), pp. 380ff.
2 These statistics are drawn from Stanley Wolpert, *A New History of India* (New York: Oxford University Press, 2000), pp. 351ff., as is much of this discussion on independent India's early years.
3 Ibid.: 368.
4 F. Nietzsche, *The Birth of Tragedy* (New York: Gordon Press, 1974).
5 R. Bellah, *Beyond Belief* (New York: Harper & Row, 1970), pp. 64ff.
6 S. N. Bhardwaj, *Hindu Places of Pilgrimage in India* (Berkeley: University of California Press, 1983), pp. 97ff.
7 For much of this discussion, I am indebted to L. P. Vidyarthi (with M. Jha and B. N. Saraswati) *The Sacred Complex of Kashi* (Delhi: Concept Publishing Co., 1979). See also D. Eck, *Banares: City of Light* (New York: Columbia University Press, 1998).
8 Ibid.: 39.
9 Ibid.: 319.
10 This discussion is based on the author's own research. See especially Clothey, *Rhythm and Intent* (Madras: Blackie and Son, 1982), pp. 20ff.
11 This discussion is based on the author's own research. For added details see especially Clothey, "Śāstā-Aiyaṉar-Ayyapaṉ: The God as Prism of Social History" in Clothey, ed., *Images of Man: Religion and Historical Process in South Asia* (Madras: New Era Publications, 1982), pp. 34ff.
12 This discussion is based on the author's own research and from conversations with R. Nagarajan and A. Anand of the Centre for Folk Culture Studies at the University of Hyderabad.
13 Padmanabha Jaini, *The Jaina Path of Purification* (Berkeley: University of California Press, 1979), pp. 193–94, 203ff.

14 C. Humphrey, and J. Laidlaw, *The Archetypal Actions of Ritual* (Oxford: Clarendon Press, 1994), p. 43.
15 This summary is based on conversations held in Mumbai in the summer of 1990.
16 This is a condensation of a myth with many variations found amongst folk communities of Andhra Pradesh.
17 Again, there are many variations to this myth. Its intention, nonetheless, includes the idea that a non-brahman "goddess" has been given a "brahman" head.
18 *The Hindu* (June 30, 2001), p. 3.
19 Edgar Thurston, *Castes and Tribes of Southern India.* Vol. VI (New Delhi: Asian Educational Service, 1993), pp. 363ff.
20 The story of the Mahars and of Ambedkar can be found in many sources. Stephen Hay, 1988, pp. 324ff. offers a brief synopsis of Ambedkar's life and thought. Ambedkar's *The Buddha and His Dhamma* (Bombay: Siddharth Publication, 1984) is a useful introduction to Ambedkar's thought.
21 This brief summary is derived from Alan Babb's excellent discussion in Babb, *Redemptive Encounters* (Delhi: Oxford University Press, 1987), pp. 93–155.
22 Again, this summary of Satya Sai Baba's life and movement is drawn from Babb *op. cit.*, pp. 158–201.
23 Hay, 1988, p. 53.
24 J. Platvoet, "Ritual as Confrontation: The Ayodhya Conflict" in J. Platvoet and Karel van der Toork, *Pluralism and Identity: Studies in Ritual Behaviour* (Leiden: E. J. Brill, 1995), p. 197. Much of this and subsequent discussion is derived from Platvoet's excellent and scholarly summation of Hindu–Muslim conflicts over the last century. A number of other studies have addressed these issues, perhaps, most importantly, P. van der Veer, *Gods on Earth: The Management of Religious Experience and Identity in a North Indian Pilgrimage Center* (London: The Athlone Press, 1988), and other essays.
25 Platvoet, *op. cit.*, p. 188, fn. 9.
26 Ibid.: 188.
27 Hay, 1988, pp. 359ff.
28 Platvoet, *op. cit.*, p. 202.

10 India's Global Reach

1 For fuller discussions of Buddhism in China, see Robinson and Johnson, *The Buddhist Religion* (Belmont, CA: Wadsworth, 1996); and Ch'en, *Buddhism in China* (Princeton: Princeton University Press, 1972).
2 For discussion of Buddhism in Tibet see Robinson and Johnson, *op. cit.*; and Stephen V. Beyer, *The Cult of Tara* (Berkeley: University of California Press, 1973).
3 For discussion of Indian influences in Southeast Asia see Robinson and Johnson, *op. cit.*; A. L. Basham, ed., *The Cultural History of India* (Oxford: Clarendon Press, 1975), pp. 442–54; Clothey and Long, eds, *Experiencing 'Śiva'* (Delhi: Manohar, 1982), pp. 81–86, 189–202; George Coedès, *The Indianized States of Southeast Asia* (Honolulu: East–West Center Press, 1968); and Eleanor Mannikka, *Angkor Wat, Time, Space, and Kingship* (Honolulu: University of Hawaii Press, 1996).

4 Michael Aung-Thwin, *Pagan: The Origins of Modern Burma* (Honolulu: University of Hawaii Press, 1985), p. 34.
5 Mannikka, *op. cit.*, pp. 24–25.
6 Jean Filliozat, "The Role of the Śaivāgamas in the Saiva Ritual System" in F. W. Clothey and J. B. Long, eds, *Experiencing Śiva* (Delhi: Manohar Books, 1983), pp. 81–86.
7 Paul Wheatley, *The City as Symbol* (London: H. K. Lewis, 1969), p. 32, fn. 34.
8 Frank Heidemann, *Kanganies in Sri Lanka and Malaysia* (München: Anacon, 1992), pp. 110ff.
9 Colin Clarke, Ceri Peach, and Steven Vertovec, "Introduction: Themes in the Study of the Indian Diaspora" in Clarke, Peach, Vertovec, eds, *South Asians Overseas: Migration and Ethnicity* (Cambridge: Cambridge University Press, 1990), p. 8.
10 *Sucked Oranges: The Indian Poor in Malaysia* (Kuala Lumpur: Iusan, 1989), pp. 2–20.
11 This description is based on the author's own research and on studies by E. F. Collins, *Pierced by Murukaṉ's Lance* (DeKalb, IL: Northern Illinois University Press, 1997).
12 Much of the following discussion of contacts in classical times is derived from H. A. Rawlinson, "Early Contacts Between India and Europe" in A. L. Basham, ed., *The Cultural History of India* (Oxford: Clarendon Press, 1975), pp. 425–43.
13 Ibid.: 426.
14 Ibid.: 429.
15 Ibid.: 435–36.
16 Ibid.: 436.
17 Much of the following is condensed from F. Wilhelm and H. G. Rawlinson, "India and the Modern West" in Basham, 1975, pp. 470–86.
18 Ibid.: 470.
19 Ibid.: 471–72.
20 Ibid.: 473.
21 Ibid.: 474.
22 Ibid.: 473.
23 Guy Welbon, *The Buddhist Nirvana and its Western Interpreters* (Chicago: University of Chicago Press, 1968).
24 Milton Singer, *When a Great Tradition Modernizes* (New York: Praeger Publishers, 1972), pp. 23–24.
25 P. Trout, *Eastern Seeds, Western Soil: Three Gurus in America* (Mountain View, CA: Mayfield, 2001), pp. 62–63.
26 Ibid.: 64.
27 Ibid.: 62–63.
28 This discussion is derived from Trout, *op. cit.*, pp. 109–46.
29 This discussion is derived from Trout, *op. cit.*, pp. 147–76.
30 See Robert Ellwood's *Religious and Spiritual Groups in Modern America* (Englewood Cliffs, NJ: Prentice Hall, 1973 and 1988).
31 For further discussion of the experience of these early migrants in the northwest, see Roger Daniels, *Indian Immigration to the United States* (New York: The Asia Society, 1989), pp. 7–25.
32 Raymond Williams, *Religions of Immigrants from India and Pakistan* (Cambridge: Cambridge University Press, 1988), pp. 71–72.

33 Sunil Khilkani, "Who are you calling Asian?" *The Sunday Times*, London, April 29, 2001 and *The Hindu*, July 1, 2001.
34 M. Baumann, "The Hindu Diasporas in Europe and an Analysis of Key Diasporic Patterns" in T. S. Rukmani, ed., *Hindu Diaspora: Global Perspectives* (Montreal: Concordia University, 1999), p. 62, citing K. Knott, *Hinduism in Leeds: A Study of Religious Practices in the Indian Hindu Communities and in Hindu-Related Groups* (Leeds: Community Related Projects, 1986).
35 Baumann, *op. cit.*, p. 63.
36 Ibid.: 64.
37 Ibid.: 65.
38 Ibid.: 66.
39 From a study conducted by the author in 1978 and funded by the Pennsylvania Council for the Humanities.
40 See Clothey, *Rhythm and Intent* (Madras: Blackie and Son, 1982), pp. 175–76.
41 Ibid.: 175.
42 For a fuller discussion of the development of this temple, see Clothey, 1982, pp. 164–200.

Index